56871

Students and External Readers		Staff & Research Students
DATE DUE FOR RETURN		**DATE OF ISSUE**
		15. JUL 1980
- 2 JUL 2012		
		N.B. All books must be returned for the Annual Inspection in June

JOHN SCOTT RUSSELL

John Scott Russell

A GREAT VICTORIAN ENGINEER
AND NAVAL ARCHITECT

George S. Emmerson

JOHN MURRAY · LONDON

Printed in Great Britain by
Butler & Tanner Ltd, Frome and London
0 7195 3393 7

Contents

10

Illustrations

ILLUSTRATION SOURCES

3 Crown copyright, the Victoria and Albert Museum London. 4 National Maritime Museum Greenwich. 5, 6, 7, 8 Eastman International Museum New York. 9 Illustrated London News. 10 from Scott Russell's *Modern System of Naval Architecture*. 11 The Science Museum London. 12, 14, 15 Illustrated London News. 16 The Science Museum

Illustrations

London. 17 Eastman International Museum New York. 18 National Maritime Museum Greenwich. 19 The Science Museum London. 21 Historisches Museum der Stadt Wien.

LINE DRAWINGS IN THE TEXT

LINE DRAWING SOURCES

1 Redrawn from: C. E. Lee, 'Centenary of the London Motor Omnibus', *Trans. Newcomen Socy.*, Vol. XIII, 1932–33. 2 J.S.R., *Modern System of Naval Architecture*, 1865. 3 David R. MacGregor, *Fast Sailing Ships*, 1975. 4 J.S.R., op. cit. 5 John W. Griffiths, *A Treatise on Marine and Naval Architecture*, 1857. 6 J.S.R., op. cit. 7 Ibid. 8 Ewan Corlett, *The Iron Ship*, 1975. 9 J.S.R., op. cit. 10 J.S.R., op. cit. 11 Redrawn from sketch by A. L. Holley, *Engineering*. 12 J.S.R., op. cit. 13. Ibid. 14 *Engineering*, 1873. 15 Dixon Kemp, *Yacht Architecture*, London, 1897.

Acknowledgements

It is regrettably necessary to confine my acknowledgements to but a select few of the many to whom I owe a debt of gratitude for contributions which have helped to make this biography possible. If help were always accorded without stint it might not command special notice, but it is not and therefore does.

I feel particularly indebted to John Hollingworth, F.I.C.E., C.Eng., who not only granted me access to his Brunel collection but who encouraged me, by word and deed, in my pursuit of Russell over the years. I also thank George Mabon, a pioneer in Russell studies, for his generosity in placing some of his data at my disposal. In my search for Russell's descendants I was greatly assisted by his great-great-granddaughter Susanna Knyphausen and by Dr W. Amsler of Schaffhausen who was a family friend of Russell's daughter, Alice. Also, in this connection, I am much obliged to Mrs Frank Phillips of London, Una Addison of Florida, Mrs W. Goodall and Frank Robertson of Errol, Mrs A. H. Rausch of Locarno, and Dorothy Wentworth Chapple and Mr Garton of London.

The enlightened and constructive policies of the libraries of the University of Western Ontario and the University of Strathclyde have been indispensable to my research. I have enjoyed much help and forbearance from both and the genial interest of their officers. I must also thank the libraries of Bristol University, the Victoria and Albert Museum, the Institution of Civil Engineers, the Royal Society of Arts, the Royal Institution of Naval Architects, the British Museum, and Columbia University; the British Transport Archives, the State Library of the Commonwealth of Massachusetts, and the Pierpont Morgan Library. I am most grateful to Reginald Allen for granting me access to his collection at the latter and for his stimulating enthusiasm. Nor must I overlook the liberality of the Institution of Civil Engineers in enabling me to transcribe relevant minutes of Council and correspondence; nor the contributions of George Maby, archivist at Bristol University; Dr W. Maurmann of the Eisen Bibliothek, Schaffhausen; Dr B. Glaus of the Eidgenossisch Technische Hochschule, Zurich; and Dr E. V. Telfer, past president of the R.I.N.A.

In reproducing many of the line diagrams and illustrations I am much

ix

Acknowledgements

obliged to the University of Strathclyde and to the Technical Services Department of the University of Western Ontario.

My researches were greatly advanced by two travel grants from the Canada Council and sabbatical leave from the University of Western Ontario for which I am very grateful.

The book has been published with the help of a grant from the Humanities Research Council of Canada, using funds provided by the Canada Council. It is most appropriate and satisfying that it should be published by the publisher of Samuel Smiles.

I have been especially fortunate in having the able and generous practical help of Elizabeth Milliken, secretary and typist par excellence. I thank Jack Craig for his professional assessment of the accounts of the E.S.N. Co. and Rosemarie McNamara for looking into the Osbornes of Tipperary on my behalf. For further miscellaneous but significant help I thank my cousin Anne Macleod and my daughter Rosslyn.

I apologize to my wife for making John Scott Russell so long a part of our life and thank her for treating him and me so well in the circumstances, with so much understanding and interest.

GEORGE S. EMMERSON

Faculty of Engineering Science
University of Western Ontario
London, Ontario, Canada

CHAPTER ONE

There was a Lad

*What tho' on hamely fare we dine
Wear hodden gray an' a' that?
Gie fule's their silks and knaves their wine
We daur be puir for a' that!*

BURNS

One of the most striking of the early photographs, exuding the strength and self-assurance of the men who built nineteenth-century industrial Britain, shows the great engineer Isambard Kingdom Brunel with three companions observing the preparations for the launch of the *Great Eastern*. This historic ship was so gigantic that she completely dwarfed all existing ships and was not to be equalled in size for nearly fifty years. The photograph was taken by Robert Howlett, one of the first artists in the medium, probably on the first day of the great ship's launch, November 3, 1857. In it we see Brunel standing in characteristic pose, his legs astride in the manner of Holbein's Henry VIII, thumbs in waistcoat pockets and inevitable cigar projecting defiantly from the side of his mouth. On his left, with becoming deference stands Thomas Treadwell,[1] the contractor of the launching ways, and on his right, with a roll of drawings in hand, the gangling figure of one of Brunel's assistants on haulage gear, Henry Wakefield, the latter's only claim to historical notice. Farther over to Brunel's right, with a suggestion of independence from the trio just named, stands the remaining figure, handsome, of medium height, well built and with a proprietary air. This latter person is John Scott Russell, Brunel's engineering partner in the project, the naval architect and contractor of the Great Ship.

Now at the age of forty-nine, his name was known wherever ships were built and navies assembled—France, Germany, Russia and America—and the most influential period of his life lay ahead. Time was to reveal him as a zealous educator, an idealistic social reformer and even a would-be peacemaker between nations, as well as the undisputed and respected leader of his profession. Yet there fell a shadow on his expectations and deserts, a strange antipathy of fortune hinted at by his division from the others in that historic photograph. This division was exploited

1

by L. T. C. Rolt, in his much acclaimed biography of Brunel. On the meagre evidence available to him, he styled Russell as a 'strange character', a 'megalomaniac', and an 'evil genius' who was Brunel's 'jealous enemy'. Readers of this fervent and plausible destruction of Russell's character are left with the idea that Russell caused Brunel's premature death, tried to damage the *Great Eastern* by causing an explosion on her trial trip and committed some dire offence associated with gun-running in the American Civil War which led to his expulsion from the Institution of Civil Engineers,[2] all of which is untrue. Yet, because the details and facts of Russell's fascinating life have never been investigated, this unjust calumny has since been trustingly repeated and even expanded by innumerable journalists and writers on nineteenth-century engineering.

Had it not been for the testimony to his undoubted brilliance provided by Russell's published work and some agreeable memories of him which persisted, no perturbed eyebrows might have been raised at the one-sided assault.

There have been great difficulties in the way of writing a biography of John Scott Russell or it would have been accomplished before now. It is believed that Samuel Smiles, author of *Self-Help* and *Lives of the Engineers*, was preparing to embark on the task just prior to his incapacity. Others have since considered the project, including the late J. Foster Petrie, editor of *Engineering*, but have been deterred by the paucity of primary sources and the perplexing erasures of time.

If, as some might have it, Russell had more than his share of vanity, then it must be said that his vanity did not extend to care for his place in posterity. Brunel, in contrast, preserved his lengthy memoranda and letters and documented each act and decision, while his family has rightly seen to it that it has all been put to its intended purpose. Not so Scott Russell. The result has been a dramatic illustration of the harmful propensities of silence, exacerbated, in this case, by the perversities of Russell's fate.

It was with much apprehension, therefore, that I began, and for a time I feared that I might become another casualty of the malign fate which dogged my subject and his memory, but, with persistence, a remarkable and unexpected story unfolded. There is much satisfaction in revealing the unknown but even more in righting a great wrong.

John Scott Russell's life resembled the landscape into which he was born on May 9, 1808, in the eighteenth-century weavers' village of Parkhead, in the environs of Glasgow, a landscape of rocky knowes of broom and brambles, but, in season, joyful and beautiful enough, and diffusing a natural genius of colour despite the sun's reluctance. He was the first-born of David Russell, the third son of John Russell, a local farmer. David was then about twenty-four, a matriculant of the University of Glasgow, earning a living as a parish school teacher. His colleague, John Kingham, recorded as the first teacher of Tollcross parish school nearby,[3] was a witness at John's baptism in the Barony Church of Glasgow. John's mother, Agnes Clark Scott, was related to the Arbuthnot family of Aberdeenshire, and through her John later came into possession of a silver teapot from which tea had been poured for Samuel Johnson in the course of his celebrated Highland jaunt in 1773.[4]

It would be a very humble white Scots stone cottage in which John was born, not unlikely one of a row of weavers' cottages, small-windowed and thick-walled with butts for rainwater at the gables. He would not remember his mother, for she died not long after his birth. When he was about three his father procured a ministerial appointment with the Colinsburgh Relief Church in Kirkcaldy,[5] one of the oldest congregations of that persuasion of seceders from the established Church of Scotland which began with the founding of the 'Presbytery of Relief' in 1761. The original Relief congregations were dissatisfied with what they regarded as a persistent disregard of liberty and right, of over-strictness on the one hand and laxity on the other, in the conduct of the established church. Their objections were rooted in liberal democratic principles—the equality of all men before civil and ecclesiastical law, no discrimination against any man because of his religious or political convictions, no taxation without representation, freedom of the pulpit and of the right of the people to choose their own ministers 'without let or hindrance'. These were the first precepts of the rights of man impressed upon the consciousness of the young John Russell and they laid the basis of that tolerance and social concern which characterized his life.

David Russell completed only one year with his first charge then accepted a call, at £120 per annum, from a more numerous congregation at the new Allars Kirk in Hawick, on the Borders,[6] and married again. His new wife was a Miss Ann Titterton, and their first child, David, was born in the following year, 1813. John's education had probably already begun, but he left no account of his early life. Educational facilities in Hawick at that time were almost non-existent. What was called the 'Grammar School' was a casual meeting of pupils in whatever barn or wright's shop happened to be available. John probably had private tuition supervised by his father; but however his education was acquired it was peculiarly thorough, and he was obviously an able student. With such promise, there would be no doubt in his father's mind that John was destined for the calling of a man o' learnin'. There was no calling higher in the esteem of Scottish families—he would be a minister, or a schoolmaster, or a medical doctor. Sunday after Sunday, too, he would take his place in the family pew with his stepmother or the housekeeper, his black hair well brushed and his face soaped, to be regaled with his father's sermons, one hour long and extemporaneous, in the custom of the Kirk. We can imagine him, like many another boy in like circumstances, scrutinizing the markings on the bench in front of him during the 'long' and 'short' prayers, then, with much relief, following the lead of the precentor in the singing of the much-loved metrical psalms and paraphrases which, unaccompanied, magisterial and fervent, formed their only devotional music at that time. Young John could not fail to be imbued with the dominant theme of such an upbringing—man's chief end was not to enjoy himself but to glorify God and do his duty! John inherited his father's handsome features and deportment, and also, one suspects, his expository gifts. It has come down to us that it was a source of some concern to the father that his gifted son should devote so much time to tinkering in the blacksmith's shop near the manse; the boy too clearly displayed the aptitudes and interests of a mechanic.

Another son, George, was added to the family in 1817 and perhaps this finally persuaded the busy minister to attend to his economic welfare. The fact was that the congregation had been unable to meet the terms under which 'in an over-sanguine mood', they had engaged him, and he therefore decided to help both himself and his congregation by 'dissolving this connection' and seeking a more reliable appointment elsewhere. In the interim he officiated in Edinburgh and, after about a year, accepted a call from the Relief congregation at Errol and a stipend of £85 per annum, with free house and fuel allowance.[7] The village of Errol is situated close to the River Tay about eight miles on the road to Dundee from Perth and, in Russell's time, it was a busy place with hand-loom weaving and agriculture its staple industries. Small freighters loaded and unloaded at Port Allen, within sight of the attic rooms of the manse, some, trading with the Low Countries, may have been the first sea-going vessels John was able to study at close hand, for although he may have spent some of his childhood with his relatives in Glasgow, there were then nothing but barges and wherries to be seen in that great port of the future. Russell left us few details of his early life, but he does mention spending many an hour with 'other urchins' watching the great Newcomen pumping engines at the Carntyne mines near his birthplace. These, in fact, were the very first steam engines to be operated in the locality of Glasgow, being installed in 1768, at the very time James Watt was inventing the new engine which would revolutionize the world. Russell recalled the Carntyne engines with affection:

> Out of a round arch, in the end of an ugly brick tower, there used to project a gigantic, deformed elephant's head, black and clumsy, it used first to stoop its head very slowly, gradually down, reaching with its long trunk as far as it could stretch into the well of the mine; once down it took a long rest, and then, with a painful, slow, creaking, complaining, jerky motion, gradually and fitfully got its head up again to its original position, bringing with it the pump-rods and the water of the mine; how we used to watch it a long time, standing at the top of its stroke, wondering to ourselves if ever it could or would recover strength to make one effort more, and how at last it began to show symptoms of life, and creak, and jerk, and groan its way down again to take once more its long rest and recover strength for a new effort ... when the engine once more got to the bottom and rested there was a huge roar from the safety-valve of the adjacent boiler, which had held its breath so long and so hard in the previous effort, that it seemed to puff it out breathless from sheer exhaustion, but it was not the boiler which was exhausted, but the engine; the steam had to roar off until the engine could get once more ready to take in steam, then the expansion-cylinder once more swallowed the steam and prepared for another huge effort.[8]

The family was not long in Errol when John entered upon studies at St Andrews with a view to following in his father's footsteps, then, in the following year, matriculated to Glasgow University. He was only thirteen, but in those days this was not unusual among Scottish students sufficiently grounded in Latin. His selection of Glasgow University was probably influenced by the presence of relatives in Glasgow with whom he could board—no small consideration for so young a boy of limited means—and perhaps also by a desire to study practical science. He took this bold step into the world with his mother's name added to his own— John *Scott* Russell—it was not thus in the record of his birth.

The old college on the High Street still bore the impress of Cullen, Black, Adam Smith and Hope, who had all moved to Edinburgh in time, and, of course, it cherished the association with its former mechanic James

Watt. The period of Thomson and Rankine had yet to come. In the environs of the college, manufactories and steam engine works were becoming numerous and the hand-loom weavers in the small white cottages of the surrounding country, so familiar to Russell's family, were making a vain last stand against an overwhelming and cruel tide of change. It is difficult to conceive of Glasgow as it was then, served by a single post office with a complement of five employees. In a small shop in a side street near the college, Robert Napier and his brother James practised their craft of blacksmith and mechanic. Another twenty years would see Robert established as one of the greatest marine engineers and shipbuilders of his time. Was Russell as a teenage university student familiar with Napier's shop? Not unlikely, but he left no record of it, nor of embarking on one of the new steamboats which did duty on the river, a river which still provided the town with salmon and which Russell was to study in much detail in the near future. David Napier, Robert's older brother, was there, already leading the world in the design and construction of steamships, some of which plied the Irish Channel and at least one of which was already in service on the Thames. Russell was to enjoy familiar relations with the Napiers in the future and he would undoubtedly know what and who they were at this time in Glasgow, but he was still a mere boy. One of his obituarists alludes to his taking work in mechanics' shops in Glasgow during the university recesses, but we know no more and can be sure none of these shops was Napier's or we would have heard of it.

If young John Russell did voyage on a steamship down the Clyde at this time, and it would be remarkable if he did not, a knowledge of him would lead one to expect him to pay more attention to the operation of the vessel and its engines and to the action of the wash on the river banks than to the striking sylvan vistas extending each side, with their associations of Scotland's story. The works of his mother's great namesake, Walter Scott, were taking Europe by storm, but unlike so many of his distinguished countrymen of the period, such as Thomas Telford or Thomas Carlyle, John Scott Russell evidently was never touched by the romantic call of his native land. Science seems to have dominated his imagination. He may not have read poetry or novels but he did read works of philosophical erudition and certainly then, or shortly after, Brewster's *The Mechanical Philosophy of Dr. Robinson*, Young's *Theory of Elasticity* and Laplace's and Euler's works on mechanics. 'I took their mind entirely out of their books into my own' he wrote forty years or so later—'I drew in their spirit from their books, into which, it seemed to me, they had breathed their souls. If I now know anything, it is because I see with their eyes, and search into it with their way of asking, and put it into their way of thinking.'[9]

He graduated M.A. from Glasgow in 1825, a mere seventeen years of age, and moved to Edinburgh where, as a mathematics teacher, he participated in the founding of a new university preparatory school called South Academy and, indeed, one who knew him personally tells us that this was a joint venture of himself and one of his friends.[10] It must have provided a very meagre livelihood, but from 1829 to 1831 he supplemented this by teaching at the new Leith Mechanics Institute,[11] and, in 1830, he had the honour of being engaged to offer annual courses of lectures on the mathematical sciences and natural philosophy for medical students, under the regulations of the Royal College of Surgeons. The exceptional clarity and power of expression which Russell could command and which were soon to be known to a wider world, made his lectures the most popular of their kind, having the highest attendance of any in the city—136 regular students and from 130 to 150 independent students. Such was Russell's achievement that the Town Council and University Senate entrusted him with the duties of Dr Leslie, Professor of Natural Philosophy, on the latter's death in 1832.

By this time Russell had installed himself in the new town, at 8 Stafford Street, a stone's throw from the residence of the illustrious Henry Cockburn whose 'memorials' of his time vividly recall the period of Edinburgh's recent intellectual grandeur, a grandeur which had not entirely disappeared. Walter Scott, John Wilson, J. G. Lockhart, Francis Jeffrey, Henry Cockburn and Thomas Chalmers were very much to the fore and Thomas and Jane Carlyle were in town starting out on a historic partnership. Easily within living memory were the great celebrities of science and letters who made Edinburgh the modern Athens. Russell attended some classes at the University, we have no details of them, but whatever thoughts he may have had about entering divinity studies were finally set aside, he was now primarily embarked on the task of making a living as a teacher. This was the most obvious and accessible means of subsistence available to him. But he had a mechanical bent which now manifested itself in the study of steam engines and boilers. It was a tradition in Errol that there, in his father's house, incorporating an old kettle for a boiler, he constructed a model of his steam coach which was later to prove remarkably successful.[12] It is likely that he did conduct some of his experiments at Errol in intervals from his duties in Edinburgh, especially if he had access to a blacksmith's shop, but it is doubtful that there was much scope for him to conduct mechanical work at the manse, for, although it was a commodious house with about five bedrooms in its two storeys and attic, the family had increased to about five boys and one girl.[13] We do know that he exerted much effort in the period 1825–34 towards developing an improved land boiler.[14] He replaced the usual cylindrical fire box or furnace tube, which tended to buckle under external pressure, with one of rectangular form. The flat surfaces of this were stayed in a manner which was widely emulated but he did not profit economically from these ideas.

Any thought which Russell may have had to apply for the vacant chair which he temporarily occupied at the University was set aside when it became known that the eminent Dr Brewster was a candidate. When, however, an equally young Scottish scientist, J. D. Forbes, seemed likely to be preferred, some of Russell's friends urged him to offer himself. Brewster's disadvantage was his marked deficiency in those expository powers which, along with political complexion, were important adjuncts to scholarship in recommendations for academic appointments at this time. Forbes was not only a better speaker but a member of a prominent Tory family congenial to the Edinburgh Town Council of the day.[15] Russell was right in judging that he had little chance and he did not compete. Forbes was appointed and he proved to be worthy of the post.

In any case, Russell now had other things on his mind, his steam coach was reaching fruition. Many of the early mechanical engineers turned their minds to the steam road carriage with indifferent success. James Nasmyth, who was an exact contemporary of Russell's, was one of these, and it is perplexing that there is no record of Russell's having seen Nasmyth's steam carriage tested over a period of three months on a five mile stretch of the Queensferry Road in 1827, nor any record of these two men with so many interests in common ever meeting at that time. Nasmyth's vehicle was only a simple truck carrying a load of eight passengers and the Society of Arts of Edinburgh, sponsors of the experiment, seem to have seen no future in it. Nasmyth sold the engines and boilers to finance his education and training with Maudslay in London. By 1831, Gurney's steam carriages were leading the field with speeds of twenty miles per hour on good roads and maintaining an omnibus service between Cheltenham and Gloucester. Then, in 1833, the Hancock brothers in London started a sixteen–passenger steam omnibus service between the Bank and Paddington, and a fourteen-passenger between the Bank and King's Cross with progressive extension to other routes.

These carriages were not well sprung and gave a very rough ride, which did not make them easy to drive. They were also very noisy and the passengers were imperfectly protected from the heat and dirt of the boiler. Russell solved these problems to a great extent, with the possible exception of the noise which, in his case, was largely concentrated in the exhaust steam puffing up the chimney in the manner of the railway locomotive.

A group of Edinburgh businessmen were sufficiently impressed by the possibilities of Russell's carriage to form the Scottish Steam Carriage Company and provide capital for the production of a prototype which performed extremely well. A fortune seemed within their grasp if they could but overcome the antipathies of the road trustees. Somewhat ironically, at this stage Russell was offered a contract by the Union Canal Company to investigate the feasibility of more rapid steamboat transit on canals. The Company was already running a daily service of three $7\frac{1}{2}$-hour passages each way between Edinburgh and Port Dundas, Glasgow, in co-operation with the Forth and Clyde Canal Company, which had earlier engaged William Fairbairn to report on the subject. The great Telford himself was currently carrying out experiments on models to the same end at the Adelaide Gallery in London. Through this random opportunity, Russell was to find his most important life's work. It was an odd twist of fate.

The Scottish Steam Carriage Co. proposed a steam omnibus service between Edinburgh and Glasgow and enlisted James Jardine, a respected Edinburgh civil engineer, to reassure the various road trustees of the harmlessness of the vehicle. But it was to no avail, the trustees established prohibitive tolls and the Company turned instead to the much shorter run, between Glasgow and Paisley, which legal loopholes made available to them. Six vehicles were constructed by the Grove House Engine Works, Edinburgh, and in March 1834, the service was inaugurated without much fanfare. The Glasgow Herald commented on the success of the venture on April 18:

> On Tuesday last a single carriage belonging to the Steam Carriage Company of Scotland performed the most successful runs that have ever been accomplished on common roads, having gone six successive trips with passengers between Glasgow & Paisley, and in an average of forty-three minutes, the first trip having been done in forty minutes, the second in forty-three

and so on, being a distance in all of forty-six miles in $4\frac{1}{2}$ hours—at a rate of more than 10 miles an hour. On the previous day the same carriage had run the distance four times at a similar rate, and on Wednesday it was done again within forty minutes. The other carriages continue running daily, and the communication between Glasgow & Paisley by means of these carriages may now be considered as fully and permanently established.

Soon the company was adhering to an hourly service maintained by running at an average speed of 14 miles per hour. The carriages were mechanical versions of a large family horse carriage. The main frame carried the boiler, engine and passenger cabin, and was supported on springs, while the cabin itself was suspended from supplementary grass-hopper springs. This made for a very comfortable motion. Steam was supplied from a stayed rectangular copper smoke-tube boiler to a two-cylinder engine mounted directly over the rear axle. The engine cylinders

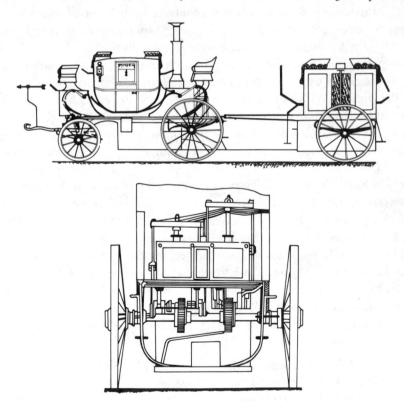

Scott Russell's steam carriage and tender with a view of the cylinders and drive arrangements

were vertical and of twelve inches bore, the piston rods with cross-trees or yokes attached to their extremities, extended upwards. A connecting rod ran from the end of each yoke down to the crankshaft, and spur gears on the crankshaft engaged mates on the rear axle with a ratio of 2 : 1. The gears were kept engaged, despite the movement of the axle as the wheels bumped over the road, by straps holding the two shafts together, in the manner of sun-and-planet gears. In addition, the rear springs were so mounted as to constrain the axle to move in an arc about the crankshaft. This was a very original arrangement. In turning corners, however, one of the driving wheels had to skid. Fuel and water were conveyed in a tender, or trailer, on which were mounted some extra seats for passengers. There was a crew of three: the engineman, who sat on the rear perch above the engine and boiler; the fireman, who stood on a step underneath the engineman; and the driver or steersman, who sat on the front perch. All were dressed in green livery with brass buttons inscribed with the Company's insignia. A total of 26 passengers could be seated.

The road trustees were, as nearly everywhere, hostile to the new vehicle and, being unable to stop its intrusion by legal means, went so far as to deposit heaps and thick layers of road metal on a particular stretch of the road. Their desire was achieved on the afternoon of July 29, 1834, when on starting after a fuelling stop at 'three mile house', the right rear wheel of one of the carriages collapsed. The rear of the carriage first tipped over on the unsupported hub, then dropped onto the road, crushing the furnace and part of the boiler with a great effusion of steam and cinders. All twelve passengers were more or less injured, chiefly by falling or leaping from the vehicle, and four of them succumbed to these injuries some hours or days after, thus establishing this vexatious mishap as probably the first fatal automobile accident.

It was commonly assumed that the accident was yet another case of a boiler explosion, the most widely feared hazard of steam locomotion, and so the Press tended to depict it. In vain the company protested that there had been no explosion, and the Scottish Court of Session interdicted the further operation of the vehicles. This was Russell's first experience of calamity; it was, alas, not to be his last. An action for damages brought by the company against the road trustees was settled out of court.

The lawyer of the Scottish Steam Carriage Company was William Dauney of Edinburgh whose book on early Scottish music gives him a lasting claim to fame. He travelled to London in November 1834 with one of the carriages, probably by sea, accompanied by the necessary

11

mechanics and operators. He had arranged to exhibit the vehicle to the Holyhead Road Company for use on the Greenwich Road. No amount of reassurance on the part of Dauney and his colleagues sufficed to overcome the fears of the prospective purchaser.[16]

The last record of Scott Russell's coaches appears in a newspaper advertisement of February 1835, which announced that George Robbins had been instructed to sell by auction, without reservation, at his rooms in Covent Garden on February 27, two splendid carriages which had just been completed after a long course of trials and were protected by the patents of John Scott Russell of Edinburgh. Demonstration runs between Hyde Park Corner and Hammersmith were offered and the coaches were suggested as being suitable for a London–Windsor service.[17] One authority described Russell's carriages as amongst the most successful ever designed.[18]

As this door closed on Russell, the British Association held its annual meeting in Edinburgh for the first time. The Association was then a mere three years old but it was already well established as the national forum for the discussion of all classes of scientific investigation. It was patronized by the most eminent British scientists and engineers and sought to organize important investigations in the national interest. Russell was a regular attender at the meetings of the Royal Society of Edinburgh and of the Society of Arts of the same city, but he had yet to offer a contribution to their proceedings. Now he took the opportunity to describe the progress of his experiments on the hydrodynamics of waves and floating bodies to the most august scientific assembly of the land. The manner of his presentation no less than the importance of the subject excited great interest and ensured him even greater audiences for his papers in subsequent years. After his presentation of his paper, 'On the Solid of Least Resistance', at the Dublin meeting in 1835, the Association commissioned him, as one of a committee of two with Sir John Robison, to continue his researches under their auspices. Sir John was the son of the celebrated Professor Robison of Edinburgh University and was then secretary of the Royal Society of Edinburgh.

By this time Russell had designed his first ships, three small iron vessels for experimental purposes which the Union Canal Co. paid for. The first of these, the *Wave*, of about sixty feet length, by six or seven feet beam, was shaped to hollow lines suggested by his initial studies, what he called the 'Wave Line'. He noticed, however, that since he had used very thin plates for lightness and had framed the ship in the conventional transverse manner, she exhibited some longitudinal weakness. This he rectified in the next vessel, a much larger boat, the *Storm*, a 120-foot shallow-draft steamer, and in the remaining ships of the series, by dispensing with transverse frames and stiffening the hull with a few transverse bulkheads and with T-bars reinforcing each longitudinal lap joint, as well as, in one case, a central longitudinal bulkhead. This was the prototype of the combination of bulkhead construction and longitudinal framing of which Russell was a pioneer and eloquent advocate. It was a system of iron ship construction which produced a very strong hull with a minimum of weight.

The lines of the *Storm* were not as hollow as those of the *Wave*, and the lines of the third ship of the series, the *Skiff*, were different from both. In 1836 a further experimental iron wave-line vessel was added, 120 feet × 12 feet, 30 horsepower with numerous transverse bulkheads and longitudinal stringers but no frames, which he named the *Scott Russell*, perhaps an excusable caprice of vanity in a youth of twenty-seven. These hulls were built by Robert Duncan in Greenock and engined, where necessary, by Caird and Co. In this way began Russell's association with the latter firm, and also his incentive to study the whole subject of hydrodynamics and naval architecture in depth; a task he undertook with characteristic energy. As a result, he must undoubtedly have become the most scientifically educated naval architect in Britain at this time. In searching for existing knowledge he found only one significant treatise available on the subject, the eighteenth-century Swedish work by Chapman which is better known to naval historians today than it was to British merchant shipbuilders at the time Russell first consulted it. He found that no one could tell how much power was required for a given speed nor how fast a given power would drive a given ship. Even sister ships built in the same yard, from the same lines, were turned out with the most opposite qualities. It was common, he declared, to see steam ship after steam ship turned out with the utter inability to stand upright. He found it accepted doctrine in Royal dockyards that 'shape of bow and shape of stern' had nothing to do with speed, and in other quarters that sharpness of bottom was everything and sharpness of ends nothing. He even found those who believed that buoyancy had to do with shape rather than bulk.[19]

He learned much about the practical arts of wooden shipbuilding from the brothers John and Charles Wood of Port Glasgow, adjacent to

Greenock, to whom he gave, at an early meeting of the Institution of Naval Architects in 1860, a most fulsome acknowledgement and appraisal: 'Whilst Charles Wood was a remarkable man,' he declared,

> and a man of genius, John was a diligent, accomplished, and scientific constructor ... a remarkable man for the great refinement of his taste ... a consummate artist in shipbuilding ... every line was as studied and beautiful as fine art could make it ... His ideas were not my ideas, but I must say I never conversed with John Wood without going away instructed. I must say this also, that a great deal of the love of my profession I owe to an early intercourse with John Wood, ...[20]

The Woods were the builders of Henry Bell's *Comet*; of the *Tug*—which gave its name to a 'useful class of steam vessels', and of the *Acadia*, the prototype of the early Cunard steamers. The latter were engined by Robert Napier, who, Russell remarked, was a rival to him in their profession, but 'a man whose moral and professional character we are proud to set before us as a pattern'.[21]

In addition to the experiments he conducted on the vessels we have noted, there was a host of others on models ranging from 3 to 25 feet in length at various degrees of immersion, and drawn at various velocities under controlled conditions along a channel varying from 30 to 2000 yards in length, and some on existing ships up to 1000 tons burden. The co-operation of various Clyde shipbuilders and designers in providing data and sharing in the experimental programme was readily obtained through the persuasive influence of Sir John Robison and Mr Smith of Jordanhill, a prominent shipowner.

Four 25-foot vessels of equal depth, breadth, weight, capacity and midship section, were built to different lines including the wave line, and their velocities compared when they were propelled with equal force, and propelling force compared for equal velocities. The wave form emerged superior from these tests.

In beginning his investigations, Russell formed the conception, in his own inimitable phrases,

> that the form of least resistance should be such as to remove the particles of water out of the way of the ship just sufficiently far to let the largest section pass, and not a jot farther, ... that the ship, finding the particles in her way at rest, should leave them at rest in the new place to which they are moved, ... that the time in which this movement has to be accomplished being given, the force to accomplish that should be a constant force and the least possible.[22]

These requirements initially suggested to him hollow bow lines of parabolic form which he soon afterwards refined to a sinusoidal form. The behaviour of the water as the several shapes of bow cleaved through it at various speeds was made more visible by floating oranges, the oranges, he theorized, being of a density close to that of the water. The ship, he reasoned, excavated a channel in the water as wide and deep as its widest and deepest section. What, he asked, became of this water? It would contribute much towards an answer, he thought, if he could discover what became of a heap of water added to water at rest. To study this he constructed a small trough of about one foot square in cross-section and of great length, and filled it with water to a depth of six inches. What he did next is best told in his own words, for the telling of it was one of Russell's greatest charms:

I made a little reservoir of water at the end of the trough, and filled this with a little heap of water, raised above the surface of the fluid in the trough. The reservoir was fitted with a movable side or partition; on removing which, the water within the reservoir was released. It will be supposed by some that on the removal of the partition the little heap of water settled itself down in some way in the end of the trough beneath it, and that this end of the trough became fuller than the other, thereby producing an inclination of the water's surface, which gradually subsided till the whole got level again. No such thing. The little released heap of water acquired life, and commenced a performance of its own, presenting one of the most beautiful phenomena that I ever saw. The heap of water took a beautiful shape of its own; and instead of stopping, ran along the whole length of the channel to the other end, leaving the channel as quiet and as much at rest as it had been before. If the end of the channel had just been so low that it could have jumped over, it would have leaped out, disappeared from the trough, and left the whole canal at rest just as it was before.

This is a most beautiful and extraordinary phenomenon; the first day I saw it was the happiest day of my life. Nobody had ever had the good fortune to see it before, or, at all events, to know what it meant. It is now known as the solitary wave of translation. No one before had fancied a solitary wave to be a possible thing. When I described this to Sir John Herschel, he said, 'It is merely half of a common wave that has been cut off.' But it is not so, because the common waves go partly above and partly below the surface-level; and not only that, but its shape is different. Instead of being half a wave, it is clearly a whole wave, with this difference, that the whole wave is not above and below the surface alternately, but always above it. So much for what a heap of water does: it will not stay where it is, but travels to a distance.

15

The second fact which I ascertained in reference to this solitary wave is a curious one, viz.: it will carry the water to a distance almost incredible. I have followed such a wave, on horseback and by other means, for miles; and I have met such a wave, of moderate size, after it has gone five or six miles. But, it is important to observe, these waves diminish themselves somewhat as they travel. They leave a little of themselves along the whole surface over which they pass. It is, however, very little of themselves that they leave.

The next important fact that I discovered is this: that whenever you force the bow of a ship through the water, you produce such a wave as I have described; and this wave is the travelling or carrier wave, which gets rid of all the water out of the canal that has to be dug. The bow of the ship raises a little heap of water before it, and that heap, once raised, runs away. The ship feels no more of it; it moves away, spreading the water that is displaced in a thin film all along the surface of the water ahead of the vessel,—not behind her, nor on either side, but in the direction in which she is moving, and with a far greater velocity than that of the vessel itself. This seems incredible, and must seem so to any one who will not take the trouble to make the little trough, and try the experiment for himself.

After having made these experiments on a small scale, I took vessels on a large scale, and had them dragged by horses, and in other ways, through the water; and I ascertained, by positive measurement and observation, what became of all the water displaced by the bow of the boat. I had the traffic of a very large canal, some thirty miles long, placed at my disposal; and I will tell you a phenomenon which I produced again and again: I drew so large a number of boats one way on one day along that canal, that the successive waves carried a great part of the water of the canal entirely from one end of it to the other; and we found in the evening the canal at the far end eighteen inches deeper, and at the other end eighteen inches shallower, than its normal depth. We thus proved that the water excavated out of the canal by each of the boats had been sent to the other end of the canal . . . the simple fact is this: that water can be got through with marvellously little resistance, simply from the fact that the water itself runs out of the way the moment you have produced an accumulation in front of the bow.

The velocity of the carrier wave does not depend upon the velocity of the vessel; whether that is going at five, ten, or fifteen miles an hour does not matter. The wave will clear the water away at the same velocity whatever the velocity of the boat is. What the velocity of the wave does depend on, and depends on entirely, is the depth of the water.

To his great satisfaction he discovered that the *solitary wave of translation* followed the curve of versed sines, the very curve to which he had already been led by reasoning and experiment for the bow lines of least resistance. He found that the speed of this wave varied with the depth of the water—the deeper the water the greater the speed. If a vessel attempted to increase its speed beyond that of the wave of translation corresponding to the depth of the water, it in effect had to climb up that wave, with its bow raised and its stern in the hollow, and thereby experience very much increased resistance. Russell also noted that the length of the wave of translation (measured from level to level) corresponded to its speed; the greater the length the greater the speed. This, reasoned

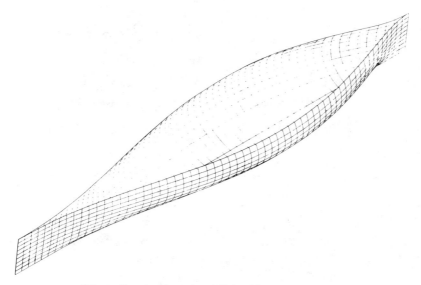

Wave line hull—'the solid of least resistance'

Russell, established the length of entrance for a ship of a given maximum cruising speed. The greater the speed desired, with minimum resistance, the greater the requisite length of entrance, the length being equal to that of the wave of the desired speed.

Although Russell talked loosely of the water being excavated by the ship, he also observed and understood that the particles of water comprising a wave described circular paths and were not actually transported by the wave.

Similar reasoning and experiments led Russell to advocate that the lines of the stern run should follow the curve of what he called the *wave of replacement*; this he identified as a curve of cycloidal form. Thus Russell

17

recommended after lines of cycloidal form, vertically and horizontally. His theory also established that the length of entrance should be to the length of stern-run in the ratio of three to two, and that the entrance and run could be united by a middle section of any length. It followed from all this that the greater the desired speed of a deep sea vessel, the longer it had to be.

These and some other minor criteria constituted the first scientific guide accorded shipbuilders in their pursuit of speed. They comprised a great and impressive contribution to the theory of naval architecture.

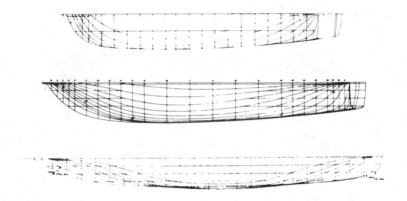

From 'cod's head and mackerel tail' to 'wave line': (*from the top*) *Venus*, 1807, an English example of cod's head and mackerel tail; *Malek-Adhel*, a modified Baltimore clipper, -1840; *Lightning*, extreme clipper wave line, 1854

Russell, of course, had noted that pirates, slavers, smugglers and the like, who had a vested interest in speed, had long favoured vessels with hollow lines, therefore he did not claim to be the discoverer of their virtue in this respect. What he did justly claim was to have established in scientific form the exact shape which the lines ought to follow, as well as the ratio of entrance to run which had to be satisfied, to permit a hull to be moved through water at a given maximum speed with minimum propulsive force.

It has to be realized too, as Russell often had to explain in later years, that the most favoured shapes for the hulls of ships at this period were the cod's head or duck's breast for the bow and a 'mackerel tail' for the after-body. Shipbuilders adhered to their own prejudices in these matters and, indeed, the unlettered boat-builder, Russell tells us, generally beat the trained one because he 'let the planks have their own way' and that 'way', he adds, was that

> if you take a couple of long planks to form the keel strakes of your boat, and, uniting them on each side of the stem, spread them out amidships to form a floor, and then look at the water line of the bow, you will find, that the pair have of themselves made for you a long, fine, hollow, wave water-line; take the two next strakes, and they will do the same, and a third pair will continue the line. So strong is this tendency, that it often leads to the opposite extreme of an entrance, too hollow, too fine, too long, which won't displace, and won't carry, as much as you want.[23]

The progress of these researches can be traced through the reports of Russell's annual papers to the B.A. from 1834 to 1844. His first papers produced from researches conducted under the auspices of the B.A. were: 'The Ratio of the Resistance of Fluids to the Velocity of Waves' and 'The Navigation of Shallow Rivers', presented to an august assembly at the Association's Bristol meeting in 1836. The acting President on that occasion, the Marquis of Northumberland, congratulated Russell and declared that he was due the gratitude of the nation for his experiments. The subject of steam navigation was very much to the fore at that meeting, much interest being attracted to Lardner's lengthy papers on the feasibility of extended voyages under steam, presented later in the week. Lardner was the most prestigious critic of the feasibility of viable transatlantic steamship travel, and, to add spice to the matter, two steamships were currently under construction with the intention of proving him wrong—the *British Queen* and the *Great Western*. The former was being built on the Thames for the American–British company of Junius Smith—the first of a proposed fleet of four 1000 ton paddle steamers, and the latter at Bristol for the Great Western Steamship Co. The *Great Western*, although of smaller displacement, was longer, the longest keel, indeed, yet laid down for a ship (205 feet). She was reinforced for longitudinal strength with cross ties of iron and wood. The design was Brunel's and the construction, in Patterson's yard, was under the direction of a 'Building Committee' comprising Thomas Guppy, the financial mainspring of the Great Western Railway and an inventive mechanical engineer, the ubiquitous Captain Claxton and Brunel himself. She was engined by Maudslay Sons and Field.

19

Lardner had recently gone so far as to declare that the direct voyage under steam from New York to Liverpool was chimerical and as unlikely as a voyage to the moon![24] It is the habit of writers on engineering history to represent him as a kind of Comic Cuts figure, following the lead of Thackeray who satirized him as a quack advertising one of his several cyclopaedias at dinner parties.[25] But this is a little less than just. He had good reasons for questioning the viability of transatlantic steamships when he based his calculations on data from the performance of existing steamships of greatest cruising range. He demonstrated that the transatlantic steamship would have to carry so much coal that there would be too little capacity left for a pay load. He seems to have given little attention to the fact that the larger the ship the smaller the proportion of space required for its power plant for a given duty, and hence the greater cruising range and pay load.[26] L. T. C. Rolt attributed the discovery of this fact to Brunel,[27] but Brunel himself wrote at the time that it was 'well known', and certainly there is ample evidence of its being common knowledge at least among some shipbuilders, to say nothing of the report of Guppy, Patterson and Claxton on their fact-finding tour of the great ports of the U.K. in the winter of 1835, which described at great length the advantages of large over small ships.[28] Russell, himself, in the course of his presentations at the same conference stated that he was convinced that by adopting a 'considerable' velocity the Atlantic might easily be crossed with steam vessels,[29] and it was emerging from his studies that for these considerable velocities, the longer and larger the ship the better. The expectant audience of distinguished engineers and scientists which packed the auditorium to hear Lardner's papers included I. K. Brunel, Joshua Field and Scott Russell. Lardner reiterated his reservations but was more cautious about his conclusions. He gave the impression that he thought it just possible that the steamships proposed for the Atlantic could make the whole voyage under steam provided the boilers could be fired with care and the heating surfaces kept free of salt incrustations, but he had his doubts. He sat down amid 'loud cheers'.

When the acclaim subsided, Russell was the first to speak. He 'confessed he had listened with the greatest delight to the lucid and logical observations they had just heard. He would merely add one word—let them try this experiment with a view only to the enterprise itself, but on no account to try any new boilers or other experiments, but to have a combination of the most approved plans that had been yet adopted.'

Brunel then rose to point out what he alleged were erroneous assumptions in Lardner's calculations. He was convinced nine or even ten miles an hour might be accomplished, and Dr Lardner had formed his conclusions upon old vessels, and not from one in which everything was done upon the most approved principles yet known, and thus reduced possibility to certainty. According to *The Times* correspondent, these statements of both Scott Russell and Brunel were received with 'cheers'.[30]

The marine engineering world had not long to wait for the calculations, estimates and prognostications to be put to the test. The *British Queen* was in the water by the following June, a few months ahead of the *Great Western*, but the original engine builder went bankrupt and the resulting delay found the *Great Western* ready for her maiden voyage in 1838, well ahead of her rival. In a desperate attempt to forestall this, the owners of the *British Queen* chartered the largest and newest of the ships running between Cork and London, the *Sirius*, and sent her off to New York full of coal and a few passengers. The story has often been told: the *Sirius* arrived in New York twelve hours ahead of the *Great Western* but, of course, had taken three days longer from Cork than her rival did from Bristol and had run out of fuel. The *Great Western* was clearly a model for the future and had things very much her own way until the *British Queen*, engined by Robert Napier, headed for New York over a year later, July 1839, but the *Queen* was withdrawn before long on the loss of her sister ship, the *President*, and the failure of the owners. Thus was the *Great Western* left for a time to rule the Atlantic. She proved to be an excellent vessel.

The Bristol meeting of the Association ended with the ceremonial laying of the foundation stone of Brunel's splendid suspension bridge over the gorge of the Avon, the Clifton Bridge. An impressive procession was fussily generalled by Captain Claxton, preceded by a grand assembly of flags and a band. The Marquis of Northumberland followed in a carriage with six greys. Then came on foot the lonely, stocky, determined figure of Brunel bearing the ceremonial trowel, mallet and inscribed plate, with the officials, dignitaries and general public bringing up the rear, Russell doubtless among them. What were Russell's thoughts? Here was Brunel, at the age of thirty, only two years Russell's senior, already responsible for works representing a capital investment of over five million pounds[31]—the Great Western Railway, sundry docks and bridges and a ship. Here, too, was fame.

21

If anything took Russell's mind off the experiences and events of that exciting week it would most likely be the personal matter which culminated in his marriage in St Thomas' Church, Dublin, on December 27, to Harriette, second daughter of Lieutenant Colonel and Lady Harriette Osborne. The colonel became Sir Daniel Toler Osborne, 12th baronet, of Tipperary, on succeeding to the title in the following year; his wife, Lady Harriette, was a daughter of the 1st Earl of Clancarty. How Russell met his cultivated and clever Irish wife is another of the many stories denied us. Perhaps it was on the occasion of the British Association's meeting in Dublin in the previous year, 1835, when Sir Daniel's daughter, Harriette, would be about twenty-three years of age. The newly-weds installed themselves at 11 Coates Crescent, Edinburgh, then later moved to No. 21.

There is a suggestion that around this time Russell was employed as a manager of the Greenock shipyard of which Messrs Caird and Co. later became the owners,[32] that is, of Thomson and Spiers. But this seems too early, for Russell did not move permanently to Greenock until 1838, although he certainly had been supervising the construction of the *Wave*, the *Storm* and the *Skiff*, the three small iron vessels which he designed to differing lines for study. Later in 1837, he was awarded the gold medal of the Royal Society of Edinburgh, then a very important body, for a paper on the results of his studies: 'On the Laws of Resistance of Floating Bodies'. This was published in the transactions of the Society (1838) and gave a full account of the 'wave' principle, including the criterion that the greatest section should be abaft the middle, with drawings of lines and details of the experiments. He was promptly elected a Fellow of the Society and a Member of Council. Then, at the Society's New Year's Day meeting, 1838, he presented another important paper, 'On the Terrestrial Mechanism of the Tides', followed, at the February meeting, by a minor one, 'On the Remarkable Properties of a certain Rectangular Parallelogram'. He was also appointed a Vice President of the Royal Scottish Society of Arts, to whom he demonstrated the universality of his studies in a paper on the 'curve of equal hearing' or 'isocoustic' curve, governing the elevation of successive rows of a seated audience for the optimum hearing of a sound projected from the front of the room. By a process of fundamental and original reasoning, he propounded theories of the propagation of sound which enabled him to explain whispering galleries, reverberation, acoustic horns, etc., and from which he deduced a series of important rules for the acoustic design of buildings. These

22

rules were later put to practical use by Cousins, a young Edinburgh architect, in the design of some large public rooms in 1842, whereupon Russell presented another paper on the subject to the British Association.[33]

Unfortunately for Russell—although he had no thought of this—he could not patent a principle and therefore, unlike the machinery or gun designer, could not turn his theories to pecuniary advantage.

His credentials were now such, however, that he was able to make a strong bid for the vacant Chair of Mathematics at Edinburgh University resulting from the retirement of Professor Wallace. This was not as appropriate an appointment for him as that in Natural Philosophy for which he had earlier declined to compete, but an academic career held strong attractions for him. In support of his candidacy he mustered an impressive array of generous testimonials from distinguished contemporary scientists, former pupils and prominent citizens.

Sir David Brewster commented on Russell's 'peculiar facility of expressing and explaining his ideas, and the fluency and eloquence with which he communicated an account of his hydrodynamical researches to the British Association which excited the admiration of a numerous and distinguished audience.'

Similar remarks were made by others. The Astronomer Royal of Ireland, Sir William R. Hamilton, described Russell as 'a person of active and inventive genius' and John Stevelly, Professor of Natural Philosophy at the Royal College of Belfast described Russell's manner as 'energetic and impressive', his voice 'clear and good', his elocution 'very distinct' and the arrangement of his material 'most lucid and methodical', and opined that Russell's 'kindness of manner and modest and gentlemanlike deportment' would ensure his harmonious intercourse with his brother professors. J. P. Nicol, Professor of Astronomy at Glasgow had 'no hesitation' in expressing his belief 'that the industry, tact and judgement' of Russell entitled him to rank among the few cultivators of science from whom important additions to philosophy could 'justly and confidently be expected'. And Lardner alluded to Russell's 'energy of mind, quickness of comprehension, and taste for the exact in science'.[34]

This differs little from the picture of Russell which we would compile from the evidence of his life and it is interesting to note that his peculiar talents and personal characteristics were well and truly established—as indeed we should expect them to be—by the time he was thirty.

When this bid failed, Russell was lost to the academic career for which he was so eminently suited and thus he was lost to Scottish university life too. Another life of practical affairs caught him up and carried him midstream through treacherous waters that allowed no refuge.

The year 1838 was notable for another important event in Russell's life; in September he gave his first really full exposition of his wave-line theory to the British Association. The closing of the door at Edinburgh University helped him to concentrate on the opportunities in shipbuilding which were opening up for him at Greenock where Messrs Caird now employed him. He and his wife moved to that town and took up residence in a substantial house at the head of Virginia Street.[35] He was immediately engaged on the design of his first wave-line ship for open waters, the steamship *Flambeau*, built by Robert Duncan and engined by Caird for service on the Irish Sea. Caird, like Robert Napier, was a marine engineer and sub-contracted the hulls of his ships.[36] Napier, indeed, at that very time contracted for a wave-line hull from Messrs Woods of Port Glasgow for a steam yacht named *Fire King* (700 tons, 230 horsepower) ordered by Assheton Smith, a wealthy sporting squire who had purchased two previous steam yachts from Napier and who had entertained the belief that hollow lines would be worth trying for them. Napier and other builders, however, had dissuaded Smith from this; but when a précis of Russell's report to the B.A. in 1838 was published in *The Athenaeum*, Smith prevailed on Napier to have his next yacht given hollow lines and, with the support of Napier, claimed precedence over Russell as the advocate of these.[37]

When Sir J. Eardley-Wilmot was preparing his biography of Smith in 1859, he invited Sir Roderick Murchison to pass judgement on the matter. Sir Roderick stated that Mr. Smith informed him in 1844 that he was led to consider the wave form when he was a boy at Eton, it having been pointed out in the course of a lecture that a flat stone when sinking in water described a gentle curve; and assuming it took the line of least resistance, he inferred that the entrance of a ship in the water should be in the form of a similar curve. Sir Roderick's conclusion was the obvious one, that Smith had certainly entertained the belief that hollow lines would induce less resistance but that Russell had established this and had affirmed the exact criteria by experiment and induction.[38] Russell's own comment was that

> As to the matter of priority of invention, no man can tell whose thought was the first. His (Smith's) own words to me, when we first met, were—'that I was the only person, but himself, who had had the same thought; and that when he saw my lines in the *Athenaeum* journal, he took courage,

and built his yachts of a form, against which, before that, all builders had dissuaded him.' Let no syllable of mine tend to deprive him of the claim to have worked out for himself the same thought another way.[39]

The *Flambeau* and the *Fire King* entered the water in 1839–40 and proved to be fast and excellent heavy-weather ships. Russell was aboard the *Fire King* on its trial trip on the Gareloch.

When Russell was asked what style of ship he thought should follow the *Great Western*, he suggested slightly enlarging the hull and giving it wave lines.[40] It was characteristic of Brunel, however, to seek maximum engineering innovation even if commercial exigencies demanded expedition and certainty. He was easily seduced by the thought of a much larger ship, which, because of its length, had to be constructed of iron: the *Great Britain*. The keel for this was laid in 1840 but it was not ready to assist the *Great Western* on the Atlantic until 1845. Meantime Samuel Cunard, under the sagacious guidance of Robert Napier and the brothers Wood, had contracted with Napier for four wooden steamships of about the size recommended by Russell, to maintain a regular transatlantic service with the Royal Mail contract. These ships made no speculative departures from proven technology and being managed by experienced operators of steamship lines they laid the foundations of one of the greatest commercial shipping successes of the century. Stimulated by the example of Cunard, the Royal Mail line in March, 1840, obtained a contract to carry the mails to the West Indies in at least fourteen 'good substantial and efficient steam vessels'. Russell was engaged as consultant naval architect to prepare designs and as shipyard manager, he also supervised the construction of four of them, the *Teviot*, *Tay*, *Clyde* and *Tweed*, which were built at Greenock by Thomson and Spiers, and engined by Caird. Russell decided to take the *Great Western* as his type and follow the recommendation he had given in vain to the Great Western Steamship Co.[41] He also designed the boilers of these vessels and took the opportunity to study the effect of very slight differences in their bow lines. This was how Russell thought progress should be made.

Russell's managerial responsibilities at Greenock did not prevent his continuing his research programme for the B.A. Sir John Robison who had opened many doors for him died in 1838, but the work was by then well advanced. He also devoted much effort to the solution of a multitude of problems associated with wave motion, tidal phenomena and the design of sea walls and embankments. In 1839, his commission was extended to report on tidal effects on the River Clyde. Then, in the course of some experiments on ship hulls (probably those in which, in the manner of Chapman's experiments, he hauled the hulls along a canal by means of weights applied to ropes passed over pulleys) he had occasion to build a tall metal frame. The behaviour of this frame led him to consider wind induced vibrations in slender structures. The failure of a suspension bridge at Brighton pier from this cause led him to publish his analysis of this phenomenon and to offer his recommendation for the manner in which suspension bridges should be stiffened through anchoring cables.[42] This was the first published analytical treatment of this serious problem. During the same period, Russell also completed his valuable articles on the Steam Engine and Steam Navigation for the 7th edition of the *Encyclopaedia Britannica* (1841) which appeared simultaneously in book form, and which were republished in 1846.[43] In 1843, he submitted his final 'Report of the B.A. Committee on the Form of Ships' containing the synopsis of a large number of experiments and about 20,000 observations made on more than 100 vessels of different forms ranging in length from 30 inches to 200 feet and above 1000 tons burden. The lines of each of these vessels were set out on large-scale drawings, and the whole body of text, tables, and illustrations formed a very large volume. This report does not appear to have been published, but was at one time held in the library of the Institution of Naval Architects. In the following year his corresponding final report on waves was presented, a most exhaustive study comprising eighty pages of letter-press and numerous illustrations, of which only one or two copies survive.[44] This work established Russell in the forefront of his profession.

Among the other contributions which he made at this time were some incidental inventions such as a pitot tube for measuring ship speed,[45] and a salinometer,[46] both of which saw much practical use, the latter earning him the silver medal of the Royal Scottish Society of Arts in 1842.

Among the many leading scientists, shipbuilders and engineers with whom Russell became acquainted during this incredibly busy and fertile period, was the French naval architect, Dupuy de Lôme, who was to remain a lifelong friend. De Lôme was one of a group of French naval constructors sent, in 1842, by the French Government to study iron ship-building in Britain. He was deeply interested in Russell's researches and spent many days at Greenock.

By 1844 the Scott Russell family comprised two children—a daughter, Louise, born in 1840, and a son, Norman, born probably around 1842 (there is no record of his birth in Greenock or Edinburgh).

The wave-line theory was well established and its author now widely recognized for his authority and brilliance. The first substantial wave-line ships were in the water and showing their paces. For one bent on a career of commercial shipbuilding, and particularly iron shipbuilding, the Clyde offered every promise of scope and opportunity. Messrs Caird now purchased the adjacent shipyard of Thomson and Spiers to enter upon iron shipbuilding, and Napier, and Tod and MacGregor, were their only competitors on the Clyde so far. Denny, Elder and Thomson had not yet entered the field—all, incidentally, products of the Napier organization.

There is no hint that he was unhappy with Caird. Still, Caird's son was slightly younger than Russell and was following him in the business; Russell was but an employee. One can only assume that Russell did not see his future lying there at his doorstep. It would appear that he believed that only in the great metropolis of the South would he find that wider stage on which his peculiar blend of talents could be exercised to greatest advantage, for he now wound up his affairs in Greenock and embarked on the steam packet for Liverpool, thence by rail to London where a new post awaited him—not in a shipyard or engine works, not in the University, not at the Admiralty, but at the editorial desk of a new weekly journal, *The Railway Chronicle.* C. W. Dilke, the noted editor of the *Athenaeum*, had seen the need for such a paper and had perceived in Russell an ideal recruit for his purpose. The railway boom was at its height and fortunes were being made, not only by speculators and promoters, but by the engineers who planned and built the railways and the engines, as witness Brunel and the Stephensons. It was a great time for a journal devoted to railway matters—there would never be a better. People of all walks of life were caught up in a fever of speculation in railway stocks, inflamed by the easy fortunes made overnight on the new railways which now revolutionized transportation in the British countryside. Powerful railway barons had risen from nothing—summer kings, of whom Hudson was about the most omnipotent, who reigned while the economic sun shone. The collapse, when it came, was sudden and catastrophic. 'King' Hudson himself fell among the debris; but in 1844 even the most outrageous railway proposal could find a multitude of supporters.

Greenock at this time was a busy seafaring town, its wharfs a forest of masts, smelling of pitch, hemp, fish, and the presence of the sea. Much Gaelic interlaced the braid Scots of its habitués, and although there was a strong core of learning and intellect as became Scottish burgh life, there was a sense of being remote from the mainstream of action and discourse.

27

This may have been less than congenial to a woman of the culture and talent of Mrs Russell, no less than to her husband, in spite of the compensations of the blue and purple glory of the Clyde estuary fringed by Ben Lomond, Ben More and the Cobbler herding lesser peaks to the clouds.

CHAPTER TWO

The Flower of Cities All

London, thou art of townes A per se
Soveraign of cities, semeliest in sight,
Of high renoun, riches and royaltie;
Of lordis, barons, and many a goodly knyght;
WILL DUNBAR on his embassy to London 1506

In London, the Russells first lived in Westminster, in a small two-room flat which they so filled with books that there was scarcely room to sit down. In later years, Mrs Russell told her daughters that she did not then venture outdoors until after dark because she felt her clothes were too shabby, but that she regarded this straitened time as one of the happiest of her life.[1]

Russell entered into his new work with Dilke on the *Railway Chronicle* with his customary enthusiasm and, after a few months, was able to move his family to a house in the suburban village of Sydenham, on the London–Brighton railway line. With the backing of his wife's superior social credentials and commensurate personal attributes, he set forth to move with confidence in the unfamiliar milieu. As a fellow of the Royal Scottish Society of Arts, he was welcomed into the older and sister society in London only to find it on the brink of dissolution, despite the fact that Prince Albert was its honorary president. Thomas Webster, a leading member, who was mounting a campaign to save the Society, immediately perceived in Russell a splendid recruit. The Society's purpose was the promotion of art and artifice in the teeming products of British industry, and while, as an obvious way of accomplishing its purpose, small exhibitions had been attempted, it was only now that, at the instance of the secretary, Francis Whishaw, W. Fothergill Cooke proposed that the Society organize an exhibition on a national scale. When apprised of the idea in June 1845, Prince Albert simply asked that he be kept informed. An exhibition committee was appointed, which included Russell, W. F. Cooke, Thomas Webster, Francis Fuller, Thomas Winkworth and Francis Whishaw.[2] Webster persuaded Russell to accept the secretaryship in July (1845) and together they set about re-vitalizing the Society.

The Secretary was provided with a town house adjacent to the Society's rooms in the Adelphi near Somerset House on the Strand, part of a fine Adam terrace still surviving. It was an arrangement which must have offered Russell many conveniences in his work for the *Railway Chronicle* no less than for the Society which, under his influence, was speedily restored. 'The steady improvement in the character of the papers brought before the evening meetings,' writes one of the Society's historians, 'was certainly to a large extent due to him.'[3] Russell was very enthusiastic about the idea of a national exhibition and, in view of the Society's poverty, suggested that each committee member subscribe £25 or more to cover initial expenses. On hearing about this, Robert Stephenson, the celebrated engineer, offered £1000. Then, at a meeting of the Council on December 6, Russell offered £50 to open a fund for prizes for improved designs of 'useful objects calculated to improve general taste'. He paid for additional clerical help out of his own pocket, declaring that his object was 'rather to serve the interests of the Society than to obtain emoluments for himself',[4] and indeed, as the Society's historian wrote, 'He seemed ever ready to place at the disposal of the Society not only his abilities, but what he had in much less abundance, the contents of his purse; for he frequently took upon himself the provision of expenses which assuredly he was not called upon to meet and which indeed he could not properly afford.'[5]

In the late summer of that year, Russell and Dilke were shown examples of illustrated charts for the guidance of travellers on the various railways leading out of London. These were produced by an industrious and ambitious Government archivist named Henry Cole. Cole's hobby was 'the collecting of information of public buildings having an archaeological and picturesque character',[6] and this ephemera provided the material for his descriptive notes on places of interest along the railway routes. He recruited some artist friends, notably Mulready, Horsley and Redgrave, to help him illustrate the charts, and he entered into a contract with Dilke and Russell to have them published as supplements to the *Chronicle* from time to time, before being placed on sale.

Cole, a stocky, round-faced little man, had already addressed himself, with much success, to such concerns as the preservation of the ancient records of England, the introduction of a penny post—it was he who proposed the use of adhesive stamps and designed the first Christmas card—and the more efficient conduct of railway operations. His life was to be one of zealous bureaucracy on behalf of the arts and crafts of nineteenth-

century England, each day being endorsed by his characteristic motto—
'whatsoever thy hand findeth to do, do it with thy might'. Russell was
to become very involved with him; he liked him, he trusted him and he
helped him, yet they were products of very disparate traditions and educational backgrounds. The ink had scarcely dried on Cole's contract when
Russell entertained him over the weekend of October 4 1845 at his home
in Sydenham. There the indefatigable and erudite civil servant met Mrs
Russell, whom he described as 'an Irish well informed Lady', and the
three children (Louise, Norman and baby Rachel).[7] On the Sunday, the
two men walked to Hayes Common and West Wickham Church, engaged
in 'very agreeable and chatty' conversation, and thus was begun a few
years of social intercourse between the Cole and Russell families.

It is evident from Cole's diary that he enjoyed the company of no
one more than Mrs Russell; she completely captivated him and, after
all, unlike her husband, whose nobility was only in his gifts, she was of
that class of society for which he had an instinctive respect. Russell immediately enticed Cole on to the *Chronicle* staff and obtained his agreement
to 'do the gossip, the accidents and progress of Works weekly at £2. 2.'[8]
'Never make a personal enemy except for a great object,' Russell advised
him. 'If you attack any one do it as if you were in his presence.'[9] Cole
does not tell us what he thought of this excellent advice, but certainly
attacks and great objects were to figure prominently in his glorious career.
Meantime he applied himself to his new journalistic experience with such
effect that he was able to relieve Russell on occasion and, on March 6,
1846, recorded with evident satisfaction: 'The whole of the compilation
of the R.Ch. this week done by myself without help.'[10]

Meantime, after some negotiations, Russell agreed to serve as Railway
Editor on Charles Dickens' new morning newspaper, the *Daily News*,
while retaining his position with the *Railway Chronicle*. The first issue,
featuring a long introductory dissertation by Dickens, appeared on
January 21, 1846, and immediately drew the hostility of *The Times* and
the Tory press generally. Dilke was not pleased that the publishers had
approached Russell over his head as he had been 'the cause of their knowing him'.[11] But 'complaints should only be made once a year',[12] he
remarked to Cole, an injunction to which he was unable to adhere, for
he was soon again confiding some of his irritations, notably to the effect
that Russell 'meddled with everything'. Russell, however, was ever mind-
ful of his new friend and persuaded the *Daily News* to employ Cole at
a salary of £750 a year, a tidy sum. At the same time Cole accepted a

31

commission from the Northern railway interests to conduct a press campaign for uniformity of railway gauge and the construction of docks to be served by rail at Grimsby. By 'uniformity of gauge' was meant uniformly *narrow* gauge in opposition to I. K. Brunel's broad gauge lines running south and west from London. Russell was persuaded to authorize Cole to spend £150 on the campaign in the columns of the *Railway Chronicle*, but the *Railway Record* also carried columns by Cole on this subject and a spate of propaganda pamphlets poured from his pen in the course of the next two years. One of these, entitled 'Inconsistencies of Men of Genius ...,' directed a vigorous attack on I. K. Brunel's pronouncements on the broad gauge.

Russell was quick to realize that Cole had much to offer on the subject of industrial design and promptly recruited his help in compiling ideas for the competitions he was planning on behalf of the Society of Arts. One of the items which Cole suggested was a tea service for common use, to which, indeed, Cole turned his own hand in co-operation with a Stoke pottery firm. A small exhibition of the entries to the competition was held in the Society's rooms and Cole's tea service, entered under the pseudonym of Felix Summerly, was awarded a prize. Cole asked Russell to write to Prince Albert about the tea service,[13] and as a result they were invited to call at the Palace to present it.[14] In this way was Henry Cole first introduced to the Prince. The Prince especially admired the milk jug[15] and Cole's tea service became a firm favourite with the public over many years, the first of a whole series of household artifacts bearing the name of 'Summerly's Art Manufactures', in which Cole and several of the best English artists and manufacturers became involved.

In December of that year, 1846, Russell had occasion to go to Scotland and Cole noted in his diary that it was 'to be kept a secret profound'. This coincides with a crisis in Russell's father's affairs. His church in Errol was in difficulties, his stipend had fallen about £115 in arrears, the church debt had risen to £90, and he had been stricken with a mental debility. One suspects that these facts embraced both cause and effect. After a slight recovery, David Russell suffered a relapse from which he never recovered and his congregation placed itself, at least for a time, under the ministry of the established Church of Scotland. The old minister survived in his manse until 1868, when he died at the great age of 83, although, in the words of the church chronicler, he had been 'dead to the world' for many years prior to this.[16] Scott Russell was bridging a considerable social and emotional gap when he stepped off the train back into the great world of affairs and celebrity in which he now moved in London, with the image of his stricken father and the family at Errol, fresh on his mind.

Russell and Cole saw much of each other in these years; their aspirations for the Society of Arts and their journalistic activities drew them together. They walked and talked together, they drank tea together, sipped 'sherry cobbler' together, and frequently dined together—at the Adelphi, at the Garrick, at the Oyster Shop—and often in the company of Cole's many contacts in the art world—Mulready, Horsley, Redgrave and Thackeray—as well as their common friends. They were sure to meet with their ladies at Dilke's musical evenings, frequently devoted to a single composer, one time Bellini, another Mendelssohn. At one of these, at least (February 23, 1847), they met the great Scottish encyclopaedist Robert Chambers whose sister, Amelia, had recently married the German artist Rudolph Lehmann, both to be good friends of the Russells in the future. When Robert Napier, the great marine engineer, came up from Glasgow looking for pictures for his new house at Shandon on the Gareloch, Russell took him along to Henry Cole who conducted them to Sheepshanks', the principal art dealer in the city.[17] In subsequent years Cole was often a guest at Napier's mansion.

During Russell's absence on his many business errands, Mrs Russell would often be invited with her daughter, Louise, to spend a weekend with the Coles, at their home or at their holiday residence at Ryde on the Isle of Wight, Cole frequently escorting them in style there and back. These visits and intimacies were reciprocated fairly frequently over a period of about three or four years, after which they were mainly maintained by the children.[18]

From his first winter in London, Russell was a regular attender at the Tuesday meetings of the Institution of Civil Engineers at the headquarters in Great George Street, where he exchanged opinions with such pillars of the profession as R. Stephenson, I. K. Brunel, John Rennie, G. P. Bidder, Joshua Field and others with whom he was to have much to do in his career. On the subject of resistance to bodies in fluids he described the Pitot tube, praising its utility for velocity measurement (although Bidder was sceptical) and also described the dynamometer he had used to measure the fluid resistance to ships and the tractive resistance to railway trains. He curiously restricted his remarks on ship resistance to the need to consider the shape of the vessel and the size of the channel, remarking that he was speaking on the authority of ten thousand experiments made upon large vessels in open spaces, but making no direct mention of the theory he had presented before the British Association and of which at least some of his auditors had heard him speak at B.A. meetings. It is evident from the recorded discussions that Russell was moving more purposefully into civil engineering and was engaged on some consulting business, and independent experiments on the tractive resistance of rolling stock, breakwaters and tidal river control. His earliest assignment on the latter was that sponsored by the British Association in 1838 in connection with the Clyde. He also conducted a similar study of the Dee in Cheshire and did some work on the Humber. It bears testimony to the recognition he commanded that he could be elected to membership in the Institution of Civil Engineers in 1847 despite the fact that he had not graduated from the ranks of the articled apprentices in the regular way. It was less remarkable for him to be elected a member of the newly formed Institution of Mechanical Engineers in the same year. His contributions to the discussions at Great George Street ranged over a remarkable variety of topics, and were delivered with his usual clarity and aplomb. Of course, the annual meetings of the British Association and the Royal Society continued to occupy an important place in his calendar, and in 1849 he was elected F.R.S.

An opportunity to return to his profession of naval architect arose in 1847 when he was invited to join Messrs Henry, Alfred and Richard Robinson in a new shipbuilding venture on the Thames. They had purchased or leased the shipyard vacated with much relief by William Fairbairn on the Isle of Dogs at Millwall. Russell accepted the offer, and, not long after, ended his connection with the *Railway Chronicle* and *Daily News*. The railway bubble had burst. He had now to turn his mind again more purposefully to the subject of ship design and construction. The growing demands of the secretaryship of the Society of Arts, for which his own exertions were largely responsible, threatened to become an intolerable burden on top of his new responsibilities, and he therefore asked Cole if he would consider sharing the secretaryship in preparation to taking it over in the following year, 1848.[19] But Cole does not seem to have desired this and instead, when the 1848 season came round, a committee consisting of Cole, Peter Le Neve Foster and W. Harding, was formed to reorganize Russell's office work.[20]

Earlier in that year, a remark by Cole—'Russell told me of his Admiralty disappointment'[21]—suggests that Russell had expectations of an Admiralty appointment. Was he a candidate for the directorship of the new Navy School of Naval Architecture to which Dr Woolley was now appointed, or had he hopes of a contract? On May 8, Cole arranged a meeting with Russell and John Fowler, the engineer of the railway workings at Grimsby, to discuss the subject of ferry boats for operation on the Humber. As a result, the Robinson Co. was given a contract for one of these and its peculiar requirements stimulated Russell to some interesting innovations.[22] That was his first association with John Fowler, a man with whom he was to enjoy much accord in the years ahead. Cole's Grimsby Docks campaign had not been in vain, and when he crowned his exertions by persuading Prince Albert to lay the foundation stone, he was overjoyed.[23] The Railway Company entrusted him with the arrangements, which pleased him immensely and which stood the test of a snowstorm on the day, April 18, 1849.[24]

During this period, the exhibition committee of the Society of Arts had been working hard to reach their goal of a national exhibition, but, wrote Russell later, 'The public were indifferent—manufacturers lukewarm—some of the most eminent even hostile to the proposition. The committee neither met with sufficient promise of support in money—sufficient public sympathy, nor sufficient cooperation among manufacturers, to see their way to success. ... The English people were very imperfectly acquainted with the value of such Exhibitions ... they required to be educated for this object and education had to be provided.'[25]

A step in that 'education' was a modest exhibition planned for March 1847. Russell, Cole and Francis Fuller, spent three days travelling about London in four-wheel cabs calling on manufacturers and shopkeepers and entreating them to submit exhibits. Their efforts were well rewarded, for about twenty thousand people attended the exhibition and revealed to manufacturers that exhibiting could be worthwhile. As a result the succeeding exhibitions in 1848 and 1849 were heavily supported and the exhibits had to be rigorously selected.

These annual exhibitions seemed permanently established, although they were still more local than truly national. The idea of a larger exhibition continued to engross the council of the Society, however, and they now decided to try to interest the Government in providing an exhibition building in which a large exhibition of the most meritorious objects from their annual exhibitions could be held every five years. The Prince, on being apprised of the idea, doubted that government cooperation could be obtained.[26] Nevertheless, Russell and Cole led a deputation to Mr Labouchère, the President of the Board of Trade, whom they found 'friendly to the application'.[27] They were referred to the Chief Commissioner of Woods and Forests, whom they next waited upon with the request that a suitable exhibition building be provided on Trafalgar Square; but were offered instead the quadrangle of Somerset House which was even less satisfactory. They then submitted a petition to Parliament, in April 1849, asking for the use of a public building for a national exhibition of manufactures to be held every five years.

The decision to prepare to hold the first of these in 1851 was announced by Russell at the annual prize distribution of June 14. On the day previously he had received a note from Fuller, who had just returned from an exhibition of French industry in Paris, expressing the conviction that a much grander exhibition could be mounted in London by inviting contributions from every nation. On disembarking at Dover, Fuller had met Thomas Cubitt, a venerable member of the Society of Arts, who was currently building a mansion for the Queen at Osborne, and had expressed these views to him, adding that if Prince Albert would take the lead in such a work he would 'become a leading light among nations'.[28] The Prince was almost persuaded and shortly afterwards sent for Russell to explain the scheme to him. Encouraged by this, the Prince summoned Russell, Cole, Fuller and Thomas Cubitt to attend at Buckingham Palace on June 30.[29] Cole also attended the French exhibition and, on the day before the planned audience, called on the Prince's secretary 'about the exact day' of the audience.[30] In the course of this interview, the Prince came into the room and entered into a discussion of the exhibition. Cole tells us that he then asked the Prince if he had considered if the exhibition should be national or international, to which, after some reflection, the Prince replied 'International certainly', and inclined favourably to Cole's suggestion of Hyde Park as the site. By this apparently fortuitous encounter, Cole stole a march on his fellow delegates. Next day the official meeting was held with the Prince, and the first step was taken towards a great exhibition of 'all the nations'.

On July 6, Robinson and Russell's first ship, the *Manchester*, was launched, with Cole's wife, Marian, performing the ceremony.[31] In January of that year, 1849, Russell had made a determined bid to resign from his post with the Society of Arts, but he was persuaded to continue for another year while allowing his stipend to be used to engage extra clerical help.[32] Now he was well caught up in the organization of an unforeseen and unprecedented international exhibition. Events moved quickly, the Prince called another meeting at Osborne on July 14, at which

Labouchère was present, and at which the essential features of the organization were formulated. The key to success lay, as ever, in financial support. The Government ministers soon informed them that they would contribute nothing, 'not even red tape to tie up papers'.[33] Of those who now met with the Prince, Francis Fuller was the most useful in the matter of finance, particularly in his contact through his father-in-law, G. Drew, with the firm of J. and G. Munday who were now persuaded to bear the risk of the preliminary expenses and enter into a contract for carrying out the Exhibition. Russell had received some assurance of this from Fuller, and had, in his own words, 'pledged himself to the Council to carry the great scheme into execution relying upon information received from you [i.e. Fuller] ... *You* must take care that the money is forthcoming at the proper time ...'[34] On his departure on the boat from the Osborne meeting, he expressed the hope to Cole that he, Russell, 'would not be tripped up'.[35] But Fuller did not let him down and all three now set about their familiar task of canvassing 'the great manufacturing and commercial interests to subscribe to and support the undertaking'.

This time they spread their net far and wide. Cole, on complaining that he could not bear the necessary expense, was financed for the purpose by Fuller to the extent of £100 plus costs. Russell undertook to canvass support at certain European courts, whither he had to proceed on business matters, particularly in Belgium and Prussia, armed with letters of introduction provided by the Foreign Office at the Prince's request.[36] The Prince, following the advice of Sir Robert Peel, maintained a low profile in the enterprise until the substantial support of British industry was assured. To oversee this work and the organization of the exhibition, the Society of Arts appointed a special Executive Committee comprising Henry Cole, C. Wentworth Dilke (the younger),[37] Francis Fuller, G. Drew (representing the contractors), three treasurers and M. Digby Wyatt as secretary, and in accordance with a decision made at the July 14 meeting, the Prince asked the Government to appoint a Royal Commission to oversee the distribution of funds and prizes. He expressed his views on the Commission to Russell, Cole and Fuller at Windsor on October 24, proposing that the special Executive Committee be included in the Commission and that two secretaries be appointed to the Commission, one representing the Government and the other the Society of Arts. A suggested list of nominees to this Commission was submitted to the Prince by Russell and Cole on November 22, to which the Prince suggested alterations and additions. He instructed Cole to undertake the necessary negotiations with the nominees, a task on which the industrious little man embarked without delay. This gave him occasion for further communications with the Prince and Labouchère which, in turn, enhanced his position as confidant and adviser to the Prince on Exhibition matters. On Russell's suggestion, Robert Stephenson was appointed to the Executive Committee,[38] and at a meeting between Cole and the Prince on the 15th December the membership of the Royal Commission was finally settled.

Thus ended 1849 with the preparations well in hand for the greatest exhibition of the industrial arts the world had seen. Henry Cole could take much satisfaction from his progress since Russell first introduced him to the Prince in 1846. If Russell coveted a leading role, he had introduced a cuckoo into his nest.

Cole, Fuller and Russell were invited to meet with His Royal Highness on January 1, 1850, to make final decisions. The secretaries were not yet named and it is at least suggested by Cole's diary entries that he had his doubts about Russell's availability. It would appear, too, that he had communicated these doubts to the Prince who, in any event had some prejudices of his own. Certainly, Russell had much on his hands and had made arrangements to be relieved of his duties with the Society of Arts; but the suggestion that he should now summarily be passed over as Society of Arts Secretary to the Royal Commission would appear very unjust indeed. Russell was largely responsible for the fact that the Exhibition had become a possibility at all; his omission would certainly reinforce the feeling in the Executive that Wentworth Dilke and Cole were now natural allies working against Fuller and Russell.[39]

Russell was in Berlin and Fuller records that 'no small exertions were made to prevent his being on the Commission, and my belief is that he may thank His Royal Highness for being kept there'.[40] According to Cole, however, the Prince thought that Russell's absence from the meeting on New Year's day, although on account of attending to Exhibition business, as well as his own, in Berlin, indicated that he would not make the Commission his primary business and therefore proposed not to name him as secretary![41] Fuller made a plea for Russell, whether to Cole alone or in the presence of the Prince, it is not clear,[42] and the Prince said he would name him as a Commissioner. He did not rely on him for writing minutes—he did not write good English. His style was too flowing and fulsome, like a Russian despatch. His manner, too, was affected.[43] Some of this was fair comment, but, in mitigation, the Prince conceded that

'Few could draft a good minute—only Sir Robert Peel, Lord Palmerston, and Messrs Wyse and Eastlake on the Fine Arts Commission' could satisfy him on this score. He asked about Digby Wyatt the secretary of the Executive Committee, and Cole suggested his compliant friend S. Redgrave, the artist, adding that if Redgrave were secretary he, Cole, 'would see that matters went right' to which the Prince ambiguously retorted, 'I am sure you would!'[44]

Cole left the meeting under the impression that he had authority to ask Redgrave to be the Society's secretary on the Commission and to arrange for Russell to be nominated as a Commissioner. But next day when he called on Redgrave he found that the artist was out of town. He then went on to Fuller and persuaded him to agree to propose Russell for membership on the Commission if necessary.[45] Before he could do anything further, on the following day, January 3, he received a letter bearing the Prince's seal; it contained the official announcement of the Royal Commission which would that day appear in the *Gazette*. When his eye fell on the names of the secretaries he probably had only time to notice that of John Scott Russell as Society of Arts Secretary before it was arrested by that of the Government secretary—Stafford Northcote!

The appointment of Northcote distracted Cole from any other thought. He was in the embarrassing position of having mounted a campaign against Northcote's management of the schools of design which had recently come into the open with the publication of Cole's new journal—the *Journal of Design*—founded essentially to further his views. The idea of an art journal to serve as the organ of the Society of Arts had first been suggested and explored by Russell three years before,[46] with some help from Cole and Dilke, but the uneasy working relationship between Russell and Dilke had temporarily halted its development.[47] Now Cole had proceeded on his own to serve his own ends. Northcote was a gentle, uninspiring but capable administrator of impeccable background. Curiously enough, Cole specifically exonerated Northcote's ministerial superior, Lord Granville. One suspects that he had a discreet aversion to moving his attacks too far up the scale of authority or, more likely, too great a respect for the peerage. It was just as well, for Granville was a prominent Government member of the Royal Commission now announced. Later, when the Exhibition was in progress, Granville impressed Cole with his respect for authority by asking Cole's leave to take his nieces into the building. 'It was a fact one never could forget in official life,' wrote Cole.[48] The *Art Union Journal* took Northcote's side in the schools of design controversy and it is difficult not to conclude that Northcote's views were the more enlightened. In essence, he believed that a school of art should be something more than a factory for the production of cheap skilled labour.

Cole, much agitated, set out immediately to tell the Prince of his conflict with Northcote (as if the Prince would not know). He could not have enjoyed the feeling, that, after all, he was not as influential with the Prince as he had thought.

At this same time, the Council of the Society of Arts had agreed to Russell's successor. This was George Grove, 'a cheery, bright, dear little fellow, with a merry twinkle in his eye'; one of Stephenson's junior engineers with literary and other talents appropriate to the job. He was to have a considerable influence on Russell's life. Russell was still in Germany when Cole called on Mrs Russell to request the immediate vacation of the Adelphi house. 'I told her', he confides to his diary, 'I would not be a tradesman in this Exhibition and that the best must be done for the Society and that Russell must give up the house.'[49] This was the house in which, not so long ago, Cole had taken pleasure in reading Peacock's novel, *Crochet Castle*, to this admirable lady.[50] Perhaps Mrs Russell asked for an extension over the period of the Exhibition preparations.

Russell was responsible for drawing Cole into the Society and had aided and abetted Cole's interests and progress within it. Now, with that presumption which it was his wont to assume with all but men of rank, Cole arrogated to himself the Society's authority to evict his friend, even in that friend's absence.

Another curious event was about to occur within the Royal Commission. The special Executive Committee appointed by the Society of Arts to conduct the Exhibition had been incorporated as the Executive Committee of the Royal Commission, as the Prince had proposed. Now Cole persuaded this committee to resign to permit the Commission to appoint an Executive Committee of its own choice.[51] The link of the Society of Arts with the Exhibition it had worked long to promote was thus severed. Not every member of the Society was pleased with this development and some, like Webster, felt that the Society had been used and abused, its whole business sacrificed to the Exhibition.[52] He accused Cole of feathering his own nest at the Society's expense, attributed corrupt motives to Wentworth Dilke,[53] and managed to carry a motion that the by-laws be altered to exclude exhibitions from its legitimate concerns. Nevertheless they agreed to support the Exhibition and open a subscription list[54] when Russell presented his report on the Society's part in the Exhibition at a special meeting on February 8.

Despite Cole's assiduity in seeking immediate vacation of the house, Russell asked Cole his wishes respecting the Exhibition Executive 'in order that he might advocate them'. Cole was not to be drawn, 'it was a delicate question,' he said, 'on which he should speak at the proper time.' Russell told him that Stephenson had suggested that the Secretaries replace the Executive, to which Cole retorted that he would not work in a subordinate position to the Secretaries. Russell then suggested that he and Cole share the Secretaryship of the Commission, remarking that Cole's office was essentially that of Secretary. He made the curious suggestion which Cole transcribed as—'[Russell] wanted me to agree to £800 a year he having £750 for part only.'[55] But Cole, of course, had no intention of sharing his authority with anyone and he was privy to other plans—'a delicate question' indeed. When the Commission's new Executive Committee was announced on February 12, it was noted that the only change had been the replacement of the chairman, Robert Stephenson, by Colonel Reid, Head of the Royal Military College at Woolwich, an appointee of Labouchère. Stephenson remained on the Commission—although there are hints that he was upset by the indignity inflicted upon him.[56] The services of G. Drew were no longer required since his firm was now relieved of the contract for the Exhibition and he and Fuller withdrew, with the excuse that they could not devote the whole of their time to the Commission, but they were not replaced and Cole and Dilke had the field to themselves with genial Colonel Reid as their chairman.

Cole regarded the Society of Arts' new policy of non-involvement in exhibitions as prejudicial to the purposes of the Society and confided to Russell and Fuller over dinner at the latter's house in Abingdon Street on March 7—they met there every Wednesday throughout this period— that he had decided to resign his position on the Council. Russell tried to dissuade him, saying that the quarrel was not with Cole but between himself and Webster and Dilke.[57] One wonders if Russell really believed this. Despite all persuasion to the contrary, however, Cole resigned from the Council on March 12, whereupon, three days later, the paradoxical spectacle of Fuller and Russell calling on Cole to unite with them to 'turn out the old list of the Society'[58] was enacted—Cole who had packed the membership with friends whom he could now rally to the support of the Society's exhibition policy!

41

Russell contributed by distributing a pamphlet among the members to which Webster took violent exception on the grounds that it not only misrepresented him but that Russell, who was not even a member of the Society (the Secretary could not be a member and Russell could not come up for re-election before the next season) had no right to circulate any document.

There was an unusually large attendance at the Annual General Meeting on April 3, and—who would have guessed?—the Webster faction was turned out of office and 'King Cole' as some wag had it, was firmly enthroned, first as deputy chairman, then, later in the year (December 11), chairman. He did not appear to shape events—they appeared to shape him. No greater testimonial can be given a politician.

Cole was now able to return to moving Russell out of the Adelphi house—George Grove had been officially appointed Secretary and Russell's resignation accepted. Russell explained that he needed six weeks' notice and that he was not prepared to share the house with his successor.[59] Russell's requirements were not unreasonable, he had occupied the house for five years, and although Grove was about to be married he was in no pressing need of immediate occupancy.[60]

The requisite notice was not given Russell and when the matter was raised again at a Council meeting two weeks later (May 1, 1850), Russell declared that he would give up the house two months from the date of his letter.[61] Cole moved a resolution requiring Russell to give up some of the rooms, well knowing, as he must have done, that this was no more acceptable to Russell now than it had been before. Russell, however, responded to Cole with more passive resistance than Cole could have expected. Russell's situation was invidious; as a loyal friend of Henry Cole, he could expect quarter neither from Cole's opponents nor from Cole himself! One wonders if he ever realized this.

As the preparations for the Great Exhibition continued apace, Cole diligently noted whatever criticisms of Russell came to his ears—'Col. Reid complained of Russell, two different things done on two sides of the way. Russell was the wrong point of the needle. Russell was the only man that told Reid he was slow and feared responsibility.' (March 9, 1850.) 'Northcote said some of the Commissioners had found out that Russell did not speak the truth and that the chairman of one sub-committee had requested Northcote might be secretary instead of Russell.' (April 26, 1850.) 'But Northcote did not intend to serve much' added Cole. He may have recalled that it was not long since he had accused

Northcote of telling lies in the Schools of Design controversy.[62] Then (August 9, 1850), 'Steamer to Ramsgate. Met Wylde on board—spoke of Russell's jealousy and want of truth respecting the Plans; that Colonel Reid was not a man of business.' In this same period (March 1950), Cole notes a complaint by Lord Granville that 'Mr. Scott Russell is a bad Secretary—his manner is disagreeable, he is stated to have been insolent in some of the Committees'[63] (probably an allusion to Colonel Reid's complaint). Perhaps 'Puss' Granville's notorious indolence annoyed Russell.

It is very possible that Russell's criticism of Reid was justified, but much depends on how he actually expressed it as to whether Reid's feeling of offence was equally warranted. Whatever the balanced view of the matter, our evidence is drawn mainly from Cole and one derives from it the curious impression that Cole relished any lapse of Russell from grace. Nevertheless, Reid stoutly defended Russell's function against Cole when the latter was anxious to encroach on Russell's prerogatives in sending out customs letters to foreigners. 'Russell,' declared Reid (according to Cole), 'might go wrong—neglect—but he, Reid, would not interfere.'[64] He became quite angry at Cole arguing to have the duty assigned to him and vehemently declared he would make a stand against it.[65] There is a wealth of eloquence in this—and it well reveals that Russell could expect no counsel nor help from his 'friend'. It is doubtful that he realized how much damage Cole did to him, and we cannot know the half of it.

When Russell read his summary of views on prizes at a meeting of the Exhibition Executive one suspects that Cole took satisfaction in noting that the Prince 'severely criticized and did not seem to like' it. 'No one could write but Northcote' he said![66] The old prejudice against Russell's prose remained and perhaps also a prejudice against him personally. Three weeks later (June 11, 1850) Cole ingenuously confided to Lyon Playfair, and noted it in his diary, that he, Cole, still had the 'entire confidence of the Prince and Lord Granville—whilst Scott Russell appeared to have lost it.'[67]

Cole, himself, however, was feeling the pinch at this time. Playfair had been brought in, seconded from the Royal College of Chemistry, to smooth the differences and conflicts arising within the Commission (which Cole's presence almost guaranteed), and was placed in a position of confidence superior to that of all the members of the Executive. We know of the complaints against Russell because Henry Cole recorded them, but there were clearly greater sources of hostility to occasion

43

Playfair's appointment. Cole was thwarted and he did not like it. He told Colonel Reid that he would resign and Reid urged him not to do so, as did Playfair when he heard of it from Cole in an accidental encounter (there are discrepancies between Cole's and Playfair's accounts of this).[68] But scarcely a week had passed when Cole called at the Palace to inform the Prince of the strong objections raised in Parliament against the use of Hyde Park as the site of the Exhibition. The Prince, Cole records, was very nervous; it never entered his head that anyone could object. He offered no thanks to Cole for calling, which further upset Cole (possibly Cole felt responsible for suggesting Hyde Park as a site). 'Dilke,' Cole adds, 'advised me not to resign.'[69] Nor did he.

Cole certainly gave the impression of cultivating his friends entirely for his own selfish ends. This is particularly so in his dealings with Russell. Lyon Playfair, however, opined that Cole's uppermost motive was the public good. 'He was constantly misjudged,' Playfair wrote, 'because his modes of work were not always on the surface. If he came to an obstacle, it was his delight to tunnel under it in secret, and unexpectedly come out at the other side.'[70] Charles Dickens featured him in *Hard Times* (1854) as a Government Inspector of industrial schools—

A mighty man at cutting and drying, he was ... in his way (and in most other people's too), a professed pugilist; always in training, always with a system to force down the general throat like a bolus, always to be heard at the bar of his little Public-office, ready to fight all England ... he had a genius for coming up to scratch, wherever and whatever it was, and proving himself an ugly customer. ... He was certain to knock the wind out of common sense.[71]

The historian of the Society of Arts puts it more gently: 'His best friends and admirers must have wished that he had had greater regard for the feelings of others, and that he had been content to attain his objects without thrusting aside and trampling down those who did not agree with him.'[72]

By involving Cole in the Society of Arts Russell made a considerable contribution to its progress and ultimately to the Great Exhibition and all that followed from it. But it is regrettable that it led to hostility within the Society and, in particular, with Russell's own initiator, Thomas Webster.

As the great opening day of the Exhibition approached, Russell was informed that he was authorized to wear the 6th Class of the Civil Uniform for its duration and, along with all the Commissioners, was invited to participate in the opening ceremonies. The Exhibition was incredibly successful and of the greatest historical importance. When it came to an end with an almost audible sigh on October 15, the Prince sat down and wrote letters of appreciation in his own hand to Cole, Playfair, Reid, Dilke, Northcote and Russell.[73] That to Russell ran as follows:

My Dear Sir,

It has been my intention to present to you, to-day after the close of the ceremony, with a Medal as a token of remembrance of our personal connexion which began before the Exhibition could even be planned but have been disappointed by the Medalist—although I hope soon to be able to do so, I cannot let this day pass without expressing to you my sense of how much the great work which has just been completed owes to your exertions particularly in the earlier stages of its conception and arrangement.

Windsor Castle　　　　　　　　　　　　　　　Believe me always
Oct. 15, 1851.　　　　　　　　　　　　　　　　　　Yours truly
　　　　　　　　　　　　　　　　　　　　　　　　　　Albert

The anticipated honours were bestowed by the Queen—Sir Stafford Northcote, who was unable or unwilling to devote much energy to the Exhibition, and made no secret of it, was awarded the Companionship of the Bath, as were Cole and Playfair (who made immeasurably greater contributions). William Cubitt (brother of Thomas and President of the I.C.E.) and Paxton were given knighthoods; Colonel Reid was offered an honorarium of £3000 which he accepted, then declined, and was awarded a Commandership of the Bath. Dilke was offered the same honorarium and a knighthood, but declined both.[74] This may have appeased his critics in the Society of Arts. But for Russell who had contributed so much to the Society of Arts and who had been such a fertilizing force in the creation of the circumstances which made the Great Exhibition possible, and who, after all, had been the Society of Arts' representative on the secretariat of the Exhibition—nothing. He was, apart from Fuller and Drew, the only member of the executive circle omitted from the honours list. If Russell's business restricted his usefulness in the later stages (there was the design, construction and the trials of two novel gunboats for the Prussians; of the *Rhenus*, a unique towboat for the Rhine; of the *Baron Osy* for Belgian owners; of the small *Stadt Schaffhausen* for operation on Lake Constance and of some other vessels) his contributions could not have been less than Northcote's.[75] Cole curtly confided to his diary, October 29, 1851, 'J.S.R. dissatisfied that Northcote should have been made a C. of B.'. Nevertheless, the Prince gave Russell much credit and declared, in an unidentified and unlocated statement quoted by Barnaby, that it was 'by dint of Mr. Scott Russell's tact, judgement, penetration, resource and courage that obstacles vanished and intrigues were unmasked'.[76] Russell deserved his gold medal. With more prestigious credentials, according to the English social scale, he might have been more grandly honoured—but was he not very well off for the son of a mere clergyman of an impoverished and 'heathen' Kirk? At last he could give his shipbuilding work the attention it was now demanding; but he had savoured public life at its highest levels and he would never quite remove himself from its thrall. Henry Cole went on to create the Victoria and Albert Museum—Russell's creations were of a different sort.

CHAPTER THREE

Prelude to Fame

*What seems to be the law of a fluid to-day, tomorrow shows to be a
plausible fiction, or doubtful verisimilitude. . . . a clear statement of our
ignorance is often the stepping-stone to truth.*

J. SCOTT RUSSELL

While record numbers of people were passing through the turnstiles of
the Great Exhibition in the August of that memorable summer, the aristocracy of yachting at Cowes were stimulated by the arrival of a new American racing schooner ready to challenge the pride of the Royal Yacht
Squadron. Her name was *America*, and she was owned by a syndicate
led by John and Edwin Stevens, sons of the noted marine engineer, R.
L. Stevens of Hoboken, New Jersey. Both sons followed in their father's
footsteps, in the business of designing and building steamships and
yachts, and John was Commodore of the New York Yacht Club. It tells
us much about the prevailing lines of British yachts that when Captain
H. J. Matson, R.N., a yachtsman of many years' experience, inspected
the *America* in dry dock, he reported that he had 'never seen anything
like it before', that she had a bow 'of undoubted originality ... Instead
of being convex, or even straight, her bow presented a concave surface
to the water.'[1] This also reveals how little attention was given by British
yachtsmen to Russell's reports and papers to the B.A. over the previous
decade on his wave-line researches. Perhaps Captain Matson was just ill-
informed or shared the widespread disinterest of mariners and conventional shipbuilders in what they regarded as mere theory. As early
as 1843, however, J. Phipps, in Ireland, prompted by Russell's work, had
designed and constructed several notably fast yachts with wave-lines, and
had reported on their performance to the B.A.[2] Indeed Russell himself
had recently been given the opportunity to design such a yacht, named
the *Titania*, for his distinguished fellow engineer, Robert Stephenson,
which at that very moment was being prepared for racing at Cowes.

The *America* showed her paces, quickly establishing herself as a force
to be reckoned with, and a peculiar disinclination to accept the challenge, let alone to place wagers upon it, spread through the Royal Yacht

Squadron, which situation *The Times* aptly likened to the petrified immobility of sparrows and pigeons with a hawk overhead. But an opportunity arose with an open race of eighteen variously sized yachts round the Isle of Wight. This the *America* won and thereby procured the celebrated Hundred Guinea Cup, afterwards known as the 'America's Cup', the coveted trophy of many a contentious race up to the present day. That would have remained the only official race for the *America* had not Robert Stephenson accepted the challenge with his *Titania*. As Russell expressed it, 'the English engineer was chivalrously unwilling that the American engineer should leave Cowes without the courtesy of a tournament, and he entered his small craft in the lists of an unequal contest.'[3] The *America* triumphed by 52 minutes over a course twenty miles to windward and return on a breezy day, and that settled the matter. The *Titania*, according to the system of tonnage measurement then prevailing, was rated a smaller yacht, and certainly her sail area was smaller, which in itself seemed sufficient justification for her inferiority to the *America*. Most yachtsmen were inclined to attribute the *America*'s merit to the cut of her sails which, unlike those of her competitors, were as 'boards' to 'balloons'. The ballooning sails so admired by the British were more picturesque but aerodynamically less efficient on all points of sailing except in running free. J. R. Napier, being a naval architect rather than a sailor attributed the difference between the *America* and the *Titania* to skin friction, the wetted surface area of the *Titania* being about the same as that of the *America* while, of course, her sail area was less.[4]

For all of this Russell placed the blame squarely on the 'antiquated theories of yacht measurement by which the keel served as the measure of tonnage instead of the water line', in consequence of which he had been 'forced to cut two large slices off the *Titania* on each side at the loadwater-line, to make her extreme breadth come within the law of tonnage ... The *America*,' he continued,

> was not larger, had no more weight to carry, and no more water to displace than the *Titania*, but she was left with her broad shoulders in the water unmutilated, to enable her to stand up under press of sail; and she retained her full length and depth of longitudinal immersed section in the water to enable her to lie close on a wind. In other respects her lines were like those of the *Titania*—hollow water lines.

Before the wind, he explained, there was little difference between them except for the *America*'s larger sail area. On a wind the *America* stood

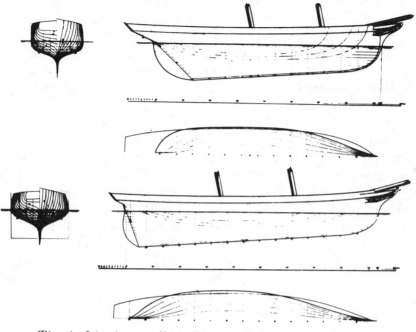

Titania I (*top*) wave-line with curtailed beam; *Titania II*
perfect wave-line

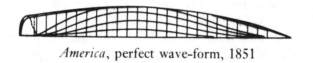

America, perfect wave-form, 1851

up under canvas by virtue of her uncurtailed shoulders while *Titania*
heeled over, consequently the *America* weathered *Titania* on every tack.
Ironically, this led to the removal of the restrictive tonnage laws and the
more general adoption of the wave-line by English yacht builders, who,
as Russell expressed it, 'called them, with rigid self-denial, "American
Lines"'.

Meantime a new class of fast ocean-going sailing ships was emerging,
generally given the name of 'clipper'. They were being built in both Scotland and North America and were to offer serious competition to steamships on the transatlantic and Far East trade. The definition of a clipper
ship and hence the identification of the first clipper is a matter of some
difficulty;[5] but there is no difficulty in distinguishing that type produced

49

by some American builders around mid-century which, because of the hollowness of their bow lines and greater length of hull, were called 'extreme' clippers. Such a length of hull, coupled to fine lines, was only made possible in wooden ships by the development of new structural devices—reinforced knees and straps, and the thickening of keelsons and decks[6]—to prevent excessive flexing and hogging. It was a relatively large vessel fashioned after the style of small fast schooners.

Scottish clippers are dated from *The Scottish Maid*, a small schooner of about 160 tons, built by Hall of Aberdeen in 1839. Russell stated in a lecture he delivered in 1852 that the Americans had found the hollow bow good for steamers and had then applied it to sailing vessels, first on their pilot boats and then, in Russell's words, 'finding it succeed there, avowed at once, in their latest treatise on naval architecture, the complete success of the principle, not even disclaiming its British origin.'[7]

The treatise referred to would be Griffiths' *Treatise on the Theory and Practice of Shipbuilding*, New York, 1851, from which Russell would note also that Griffiths had read E. G. Fishbourne's *Lectures on Naval Architecture*, London, 1846, which greatly extolled the wave-line theory. It was, according to Russell, Captain Fishbourne who first recommended wave line hulls to the Admiralty.[8]

John W. Griffiths was a naval architect and not a builder of ships, a contemporary of Donald McKay and William H. Webb, two celebrated builders of clippers, and all three had been apprenticed to Webb's father, Isaac, in New York. Griffiths' most notable ships were his earliest; the *Rainbow*, 1845, and the *Sea Witch*, 1846. The lines of the latter would have been more likely to please Russell, the entrance being long, concave and sharp, while that of the former was sharp but convex. By the time Griffiths wrote his *Treatise*, he was in no doubt that a long, sharp, and hollow entrance was necessary for speed, extending abaft the mid length, exactly as the wave-line theory specified, and in at least one other important particular he was in agreement with Russell—length was important for speed. He was also of the opinion that Beaufoy's experiments in resistance, carried out in England in the late eighteenth century, were useless, for the same reason as Russell had expressed ten years earlier—that Beaufoy directed his attention to submerged models which 'did not comprehend such forms as were actually required for the purposes of naval construction, and because the state of science was not such as to enable us, from the resistance of one form, to deduce with certainty that of another'.[9] Griffiths commended Russell for setting aside 'the musty folios of the past behind the curtains of oblivious drapery' and 'daring not only to build vessels with hollow lines, but to place the greatest transverse section abaft the longitudinal centre of the vessel'. He implied that an occasional adventurous American builder had experimented with these features but that their encouraging results had hitherto been set down as exceptions and not as the rule.[10] He did not present all the criteria of Russell's wave-line theory and mentioned, even in the 1857 edition, no more recent reference than the B.A. Report of 1838.

When *Scientific American* reported Russell's lecture of 1852, the editor asked if it were true that the wave-line was Russell's discovery.[11] Griffiths responded by stating that 'the *eye* and the *model*' had been the 'channel' through which American shipbuilders improved their designs and that they had never adopted any 'theory having for its basis mathematical inquiry—however near they may have approximated the theory of wave lines'. The yacht, *America*, he added, 'did not conform to the theory of wave-lines as discovered by Mr Russell,' and that he spoke advisedly when he said that her builder knew nothing of Russell's theory. He also remarked that the wave-line theory was regarded in America as being 'but a partially developed system', that 'merely determining the form of any line of flotation did not define the shape of the vessel'. This latter Russell preferred to see as an advantage, as he explained to the B.A. in 1849, 'The wave principle ... possesses wonderful flexibility, first from its prescribing lines *in one plane* only, and so leaving the other two dimensions in the hands of the practical constructor'[12] leaving him 'free to work out the intentions of the owners and the uses of the ships he may have to build'. Furthermore, it 'partook of the nature of a mathematical *maximum* or *minimum*', of which it was the peculiarity 'that deviations on either side of it to a moderate extent occasion deviations of magnitude that are comparatively small.'[13] It was this latter fact that led Russell and others to use the term 'wave-line' of all hollow lines and distinguish them as 'perfect' or 'imperfect' according to how closely they conformed to the ideal.

Like Russell, Griffiths had a journalistic and educational bent, and his prose also had a distinctive personal character, but there the resemblance ends. Russell could never have produced such gems as, 'The hoary head of prejudice, mantled with a guise of experience, dams up the stream of knowledge, and hurls defiance at the man who dares to assert that the fields of science are open alike to all', which garnish Griffiths' writing.

We have seen how much national pride was at issue in the matter of fast ships and there is no escaping the exultation of the American press, including the technical press, at the triumphs of the *America* and their best clippers; but the latter were closely challenged by the Scottish clippers built in particular by Steele and Stephen on the Clyde in acknowledged accordance with Russell's wave-line theory.[14] While it may be true that the 'builder' of the *America*, W. H. Brown, was not aware of Russell's work, one can reasonably suspect that George Steers, her designer, was. John Stevens at any rate had much to say to Steers on the matter and one cannot easily believe that Stevens would be unacquainted with the reports of Russell's wave-line hypothesis. Certainly Russell believed, and it was not like him to make the assertion without some foundation, that it was the advocacy of wave lines in Fishbourne's book which led to their adoption by McKay for his celebrated American clippers[15] and there is no doubt that the pursuit of wave-line forms in America, even by Griffiths, occurred several years after Russell's criteria had been revealed. The full significance and ingenuity of Russell's experimental work, however, could not be widely appreciated until it was adequately published. The B.A. reports of the years 1838–43 published only the essential criteria, and while this was sufficient for clever shipbuilders it did not do full justice to Russell's work.

One feature of all clippers, however, was not what Russell recommended—the shape of the bow. He described it as a modification of the bell bow—an inverted bell shape:

beginning about the light water-line, and flaring out all round, to the top of the bulwark, so that the forecastle occupied, as it were, the mouth of the bell. There was something graceful and majestic about the aspect of these great bows, swelling out above the breaking waves, heaving the bow of the ship by their buoyancy up to the sky, and then coming down upon the waves with such overwhelming force as to dash them into wild spray all around. It was a grand sight, but it was a costly one. While the bow was indulging the spectator in this noble pantomime, rising and falling with the struggles of its antagonist, it was, no doubt, buffeting the waves triumphantly, but meanwhile the vessel was engaged in other work than its duty. Its business was to have gone, not up and down, but forward, and this the bell bow hindered, and expended useful force in unnecessary but magnificent struggles. A bow was wanted, that should elude the waves and pass them,— escaping its enemies, not fighting them ... Believing still in the value of a large flaring-out bow, the inventors of the clipper bow endeavoured to obtain the supposed advantages of great buoyancy, without the impediment produced by so much immersion in the water, as the bell bow involved. 'For this purpose,' said they, 'let us bell the bow laterally only, but draw it out longitudinally into a fine point; thus we shall preserve its bulk, but improve its shape.' Hence the fashion came in of prolonging the bulwarks of the ship at the level of the upper deck a great way forward, even 10, 20, or 30 feet in front of the real ship, and there they were drawn into a fine point above, and joined on to the real ship about the water-line, everywhere with a kind of hollow flaring outside. By this system they certainly mitigated some of the evils of the bluff bell-bow, and they obtained what they sought—a large volume of buoyancy in the upper part of the bow, enormously in excess of the part of the bow in the water. Two classes of vessel have been much distinguished for the extent of this clipper bow. The famous clippers of Messrs. Hall of Aberdeen, and the clippers also of Messrs. McKay of Boston, in North America, introduced it largely into practice, and their vessels have had remarkable success in many respects. I attribute none of it to this flare-out bow, but to very different qualities of a practical and real kind.[16]

This was what came to be known as the 'Aberdeen bow' in Britain, but it has been argued that this shape is as much a natural consequence of the British tonnage laws of 1836 as it was of conscious design—'By raking the stempost and introducing concavity into its profile, the builders increased the untaxed length on deck.'[17] Hall carried out some interesting model experiments on this shape of hull, however,[18] but it was not originally a 'wave-line' hull.

It may be that Russell's increasing involvement in shipbuilding made him less concerned about the failure of the B.A. to publish his wave-line work *in extenso*; but these considerations no longer prevailed, in 1860, when, very appropriately, he accepted an invitation by the new Institution of Naval Architects to inaugurate their proceedings with a full presentation of this historic work. As a result of this, further studies were made of fast ships which suggested that the true criterion of the wave-line theory was that the progression of *displacement* along the bow should follow the sine curve and likewise that of the stern, the cycloidal curve.[19] To this shape was given the name wave-*form* as distinct from wave-*line*, and it could be shown that although a hull designed to the wave-line often also had a wave-form, this was not necessarily the case. The hull of the *America*, incidentally, was exactly of the wave-form and somewhat less precisely followed the wave-line.[20] It was asserted that it was the combination of wave-line and wave-form which was crucial.

Of course, speed was only one of many desirable sailing qualities and was not always the most important one. Russell's theory predicted that length was necessary for speed and also, provided the entrance was of the wave line, breadth did not matter. This was at odds with a belief held by some, particularly in America, that a slender hull was essential for speed. Russell's conclusions offered much encouragement for the use of steamships on long voyages. To be practical such steamships had to be large, and if this could also lead to higher economical speeds it indicated a development in which the sailing ship would be at a disadvantage to the steamship as long as cheap fuel was available. The iron hull was also essential to this, another fact which Russell well understood and which shaped his interest and directed his restless scientific mind.

Iron ships were initially constructed after the style of wooden ships. That is, they were framed transversely with angle iron and had a wooden deck structure. The longitudinal stresses experienced by small ships are negligible, but as hulls become longer it becomes necessary to provide greater longitudinal strength. We have noted that as early as 1835–36 Russell had experimented with a wholly longitudinal system of framing with transverse partitions, or 'bulkheads', and, in one case, also with a middle-line longitudinal bulkhead. His early wave-line steamship, *Flambeau* (1839), was strengthened with longitudinal girders but whether only along the bottom, on top of transverse frames as became general practice until the latter part of the century, or actually dispensing with transverse frames over much of the hull, is not known. The next ship to be provided with longitudinals along the bottom in this way was the *Great Britain* (c. 1840), designed by Brunel and Guppy, a very large ship for the period, 289 ft × 50·5 ft × 32·5 ft, 3618 tons displacement. This vessel was provided also with two partial fore and aft bulkheads bounding the engine room and forming coal bunkers with the ship's side. There were also five watertight transverse bulkheads for rigidity and safety.

Russell had little opportunity to develop his own ideas on longitudinal framing until he was presented with Fowler's order for a small steam screw ferry for the Humber in 1849. An interesting feature of this design was the introduction of 'partial' bulkheads, in addition to complete transverse bulkheads, to enhance transverse rigidity. The partial bulkheads were formed by a ring of deep web plates fitted between the longitudinals, see p. 55. The *Rhenus* was an exceptionally slender steam towboat (190 × 25 × 9 ft and 3 ft draught) built by Russell at this time, for service on the Rhine. On top of this he procured from the Prussian government an order for two iron gunboats, also of very shallow draught (145 × 7·5 ft deep), for service in the Baltic.

1 John Scott Russell
in about 1850

2 John Scott Russell
in about 1860

3 The Royal Commissioners for the Exhibition of 1851. Standing left to right: Charles Dilke, Scott Russell, Henry Cole, Charles Fox, Joseph Paxton, Lord John Russell, Sir Robert Peel, Robert Stephenson. Seated left to right: Richard Cobden, Charles Barry, Lord Granville, William Cubitt, the Prince Consort, Lord Derby

4 Scott Russell's first ocean-going ships: *Tweed*, *Clyde* and *Teviot*

Some iron ship structures by Scott Russell showing his
ideas before he was associated with Brunel

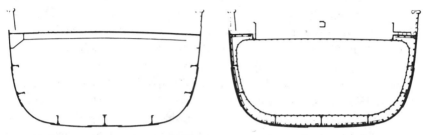

Shallow draft iron barge (1849). *Left:* longitudinal framing;
right: partial transverse bulkhead

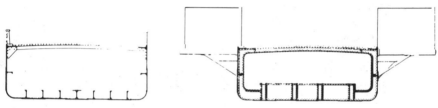

Rhenus, a shallow water towing steamer (1850)

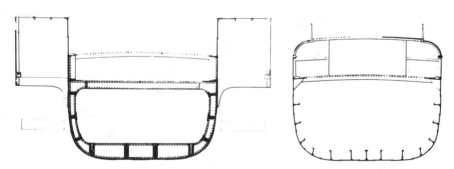

North Sea steamer (1850). *Left:* partial transverse bulkhead,
longitudinal frames, section in way of engines; *right:* longitudinal frames and partial iron upper deck

All of these ships are entitled to an important place in the history of shipbuilding but they cannot be expected to arrest the attention of the public or of the historian as they would had they been the fastest or the largest ships rather than simply the first strong, slender, steamships. The ideas, artifices and techniques developed in this work were most valuable to Russell and his specialist staff. One of the difficulties in the way of his applying the longitudinal system to all the ships he designed, at this time, was the refusal of Lloyd's to classify them for insurance. Even when this obstacle was overcome, however, the general application of the longitudinal system of iron shipbuilding could not be expected while the conventional transverse system met the requirements of strength and ease of construction, particularly the latter. A new system of construction made onerous demands of ship's draughtsmen, loftsmen and erectors and would be expensive to introduce. As Russell said in later years:

On the Clyde the men were so skilful in the building of iron ships with transverse frames, that really, I think, if I had lived on the Clyde, I should never have introduced the longitudinal system until as late as those have done who have now done it. And the reason is, because all the men, as I have said, were skilled, and all the men were instructed in building a ship, according to the lines, with iron frames; and so skilled were the men that an old friend of mine, who built iron ships there, told me that he never did anything but this:—He put the lines of the ship—the cross lines of the ship—on a great big board out in the building yard, and then all the men rushed to take their measures off those drawings; and A said, You will take the three first frames; and B said, You will take the next three; and You the next three, and so on; and every fellow settled what frames he was going to take, and all took their measures, and built their frames, and they were all paid by the number of frames they built. Now, I will put it to you, where you have a large yard of men, all drilled so as thoroughly to understand their work, is it not awfully difficult to attempt to introduce a totally new system. Therefore, I apologize, for the non-introduction, by my younger friends, of the system, by saying that they could not introduce it until they well re-educated their men, and I need not tell you that re-educating a generation of experienced men is a very difficult undertaking.[21]

It is apparent that Russell was a very busy man indeed in the years 1849–51. We have seen something of his activities in affairs of public life and business in that period and now we see something of the novel problems of ship design to which he addressed himself. The Great Exhibition was drawing to a close when his partners at the Millwall shipyard expressed a desire to retire. With the backing of Charles Geach, M.P. for Coventry, a wealthy financier and senior partner in the ironworks of Beale & Co., Russell was enabled to take over. Geach was one of Russell's fellow directors on the Crystal Palace Company which Francis Fuller and Russell formed to purchase the Great Exhibition structure and re-erect it at Sydenham and he clearly held Russell in high esteem.

The transfer had scarcely been completed when Russell was invited by Brunel to submit a tender for two iron screw steamships for the Australian Royal Mail Co. The discovery of gold in Australia was stressing the need for a fast and regular steamship service between Australia and England, and the Company had engaged Brunel to advise them in the purchase of two new steamships for the purpose. The chairman of the Company was William Hawes, a close friend of Brunel's, whose brother Benjamin married Brunel's sister. Russell wasted no time in submitting his bid which was dated February 16, 1852. He referred Brunel to the S.S. *Baron Osy*, of 600 tons, 220 h.p., '14 m.p.h. light' and '12 m.p.h. loaded', plying between London and Antwerp, and to three steamships of up to 1200 tons and 400 h.p. which he had built for the Prussian Government, '15 m.p.h. light' and '13 m.p.h. laden'. Also two for the Russian Government, one of which was the *Argonaut*, a 400-ton iron-screw steamer. He suggested 2000 tons actual capacity, securable in 1450 builder's tonnage, with engines developing 450 h.p., all for a price of £55,000.[22]

The public and professional activities of Brunel and Russell had placed them often under the same roof and they were now fairly well acquainted. Their first encounter may have occurred at the Edinburgh meeting of the British Association in 1834, but, if not, certainly at the Bristol meeting of 1836. Brunel's self-confidence was infectious and his powers of persuasion, compelling. While this led to many great technological advances, it also led to as many financial failures. Brunel's aspirations were bold and grandiose, impatient of all non-engineering restraints, and so plausible in their sanguine expectation that some of the most astute financiers easily fell under his spell. The fervour with which he incited the directors of the Great Western Railway Co. to pursue a broad gauge railway empire extending its tendrils West and North into the territory of the narrow gauge railway interests had both empires feeling very nervous. Perhaps, suggested his directors, the line was too long. It creates one of the great romantic moments of the history of engineering to picture Brunel deliberately removing his perpetual cigar and emphatically countering that, on the contrary, the line should extend some thousands of miles further—by means of a steamship service between Bristol and New York! It testifies to Brunel's powers and to the bold spirit of the early railway entrepreneurs, that within a few months of his suggesting the idea the Great Western Railway Board had formed a steamship company and laid down the keel of their projected vessel—the *Great Western*. The project had another claim to fame among Brunel's undertakings in that there were no financial crises. She cost about £53,000 (hull £21,374 and engines £13,500), Brunel making his contribution gratis.

The *Great Western's* 1838–9 season was most successful, returning a dividend of 9%.[23] The company needed little persuasion to follow up with a sister ship, and not much more persuasion to follow Brunel to an even larger vessel for which there were good engineering arguments. A 2000 ton wooden paddle steamer was initially envisaged, but this was progressively increased to 3270 tons gross with an iron hull! This apparently was too great and complicated an undertaking for Patterson, who declined even to tender, as did every other possible Bristol shipbuilder. The company therefore set themselves up as their own shipbuilders in a yard of their own and used Patterson again as shipyard manager.

Iron shipbuilding was pioneered by Grantham and Laird, on the Mersey; William Fairbairn, David Napier, Thomas Wingate, Ditchburn and Mare on the Thames; and the partners Tod and MacGregor on the Clyde. These were all producing iron ships in the 1830s of up to about 200 ft in length and 600 tons. Brunel's decision to resort to iron was not a matter of pursuing novelty. The maximum size of a wooden steamboat had been reached, the weight of the engines and their working subjected even existing wooden hulls to unacceptable strains.

The new ship, the *Great Britain*, was certainly not the first iron ship, but she was the largest of her time, the largest ship of any kind by a great margin, and novel in many ways. Her bow lines were somewhat hollow but were not wave lines.

Although Brunel recommended that the Company should accept Maudslay's tender for the paddle engines, they curiously ignored him and accepted instead a cheaper tender from a young engine designer, Francis Humphrys, the patentee of a trunk engine manufactured by Messrs Halls of Dartford. The latter, however, did not stand behind the tender and suggested that the Great Western Steamship Co. manufacture Humphrys' engines themselves, which they did, building an engine shop at the shipyard at a cost of about £50,000 and appointing Humphrys engineer-in-charge. The work was well advanced when, in May 1840, Brunel's attention was drawn to the feasibility of screw propulsion and as a result Humphrys was asked to stop work on his paddle engines and design screw engines immediately; but, in Nasmyth's words, 'The labour and anxiety which he had already undergone, and perhaps the disappointment of his hopes, proved too much for him and a brain fever carried him off after a few days illness.' The Building Committee, Brunel and Guppy, but principally Guppy, continued the work and designed and built a new engine to drive the propeller shaft through four sets of toothed chains.

The *Great Britain* was built in a dry dock and was therefore floated off, rather than launched, in July 1843, in a ceremony attended by the Prince Consort. In April of the following year she was ready for sea and was moved out of the dock, after a few mishaps, into a harbour separated from the river by two sets of locks. Unfortunately, the ship was too wide to pass through these, although, contrary to popular opinion, this difficulty had been foreseen.[24] Indeed, it is asserted that the shape of the mid-ship section of the vessel, broad shouldered and curving to the keel in the manner of the old sailing ships, was dictated by this consideration;[25] the higher the ship rode in the water, the narrower the beam presented to the lock copings. There was nothing else for it but to detain the ship a further six months while a great wooden raft was built and placed under her to raise her sufficiently to clear the locks. The morning tide of December 11, 1844, was barely high enough, but the evening tide was expected to be fractionally higher and a team of workmen was hastily recruited to tear out the coping stones and remove the road bridge spanning the lock channel. This proved to be sufficient, and with the tide at its peak and the busy scene illuminated by the light of blazing tar barrels, the *Great Britain* was successfully towed into the river by a tug.

The total cost amounted to about £171,706, a little over twice that of the *Great Western*. Just how much this exceeded Brunel's original estimate is not easily discovered, but the figure £76,000 seems to have been accepted.[26] Curiously there was no anxiety to place her in service. She was opened to the public at a charge in several ports until, on July 26, 1845, she set out on her maiden voyage to New York with only 40 to 60 passengers and 600 tons of cargo. It was all a strange premonitory experience of what was to happen to the *Great Eastern*.

In service she ran into trouble from the loosening of the propeller

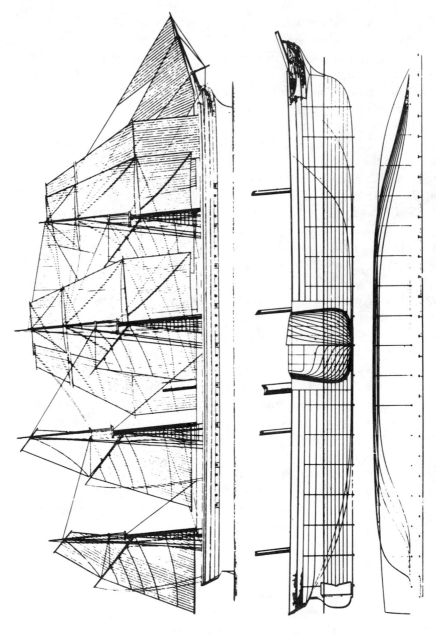

Victoria and *Adelaide*, progenitors of the *Great Eastern*

blades and the wearing of the stern bearing. All of her four round trips to New York were marred by mechanical failures of one sort or another. Then with 180 passengers on board she left the Mersey on September 22, 1846, and as a result of a navigational error ran aground in Dundrum Bay on the coast of Ireland. This prematurely ended the historic ship's transatlantic career and also that of the Great Western Steamship Company. Brunel thereafter left ships alone until he was engaged in 1851 by the Australian Royal Mail Co. for the purpose we have noted.

Russell's proposed ships were nearly the same size as the *Great Britain*, 288 ft long and 38 × 27 ft midship section, with accommodation for 200 passengers, 3000 tons laden displacement and of wave-line hull. After considering several tenders, Brunel recommended that Russell be awarded the contract, and the two ships, named the *Adelaide* and the *Victoria*, were launched complete with engines a mere six months after their keels were laid. The *Adelaide* gently entered the water on November 12, 1852, her lines, clearly novel to most of those present, being much admired, *The Times* using such terms as 'beautiful' and 'exquisite'.[27]

The ships were transversely framed, probably to comply with Lloyd's requirements, but, like the *Great Britain*, had fore-and-aft bulkheads flanking the engine room and forming bunkers with the ship's side. To this, however, Russell added a partial iron deck—an innovation of Russell's own which he later recommended to his contemporaries[28]—thus forming two great box girders running along each side of the ship and providing great longitudinal strength. The longitudinal strength of the bottom was ensured by a central box keelson along the centre line, riveted to the floor webs. There were in addition several full transverse and partial transverse bulkheads. The engines were of the oscillating type, a pair of pistons being attached to a single crank, a design to which Russell was very partial, driving a detachable screw propeller.

The relations between Brunel and Russell in the building of the *Adelaide* and *Victoria* were amicable and fruitful. Brunel's inevitable suggested modifications and requests were agreeably considered and, when adopted, presented no difficulty in being accounted as 'extras'.[29] Russell tells us that Brunel, as engineer of the Company, decided on 'the general size, proportions and power of the company's ships'.[30]

The *Adelaide* attained $12\frac{1}{4}$ knots on her trial trip, and, wrote *The Times* correspondent, 'the Admiralty Inspectors present consider the results the greatest hitherto obtained from the screw propeller'. He wrote also that 'the beauty and novelty of her proportions were the theme of general

Mid-ship sections of the *Great Britain*, *Victoria* and *Adelaide*

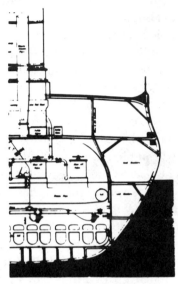

Great Britain: longitudinal bulkheads flanking machinery space, and longitudinal reinforcement of bottom

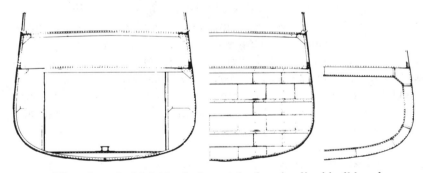

Victoria and *Adelaide. Left to right:* longitudinal bulkheads flanking machinery space, partial iron deck forming side box girders; transverse bulkhead; partial transverse bulkhead

observation'. The luncheon speeches on board dwelt upon the feat of building the ship in six months and launching her complete with machinery and rigging; that she was powered by direct acting oscillating engines and that her form 'represented the most recent theory of naval construction ... which ... enables a ship to pass through the water in the smoothest and easiest manner'.[31]

No time was lost, the *Adelaide* was due to sail to Australia on December 12, 1852; but after setting out in a heavy sea, steering difficulties were experienced with the new 'balanced' rudder which Brunel had designed and she returned to port to have the rudder changed, the decks re-caulked and some structural improvements made to the bow and gunwales. '... It is to be hoped' commented *The Times*, 'that, having secured the services of Captain Henderson, R.N., as marine superintendent, the directors will not again readily give consent to any questionable experiment in a large and valuable ship proceeding for the first time on such a lengthened and important voyage.'[32]

The voyage was something of a fiasco. Colliers which were scheduled to have stocks of coal ready for the *Adelaide* at St Vincent, St Helena and the Cape, were delayed by the stormy conditions in the Bay of Biscay and the management of the ship by the captain seems to have left much to be desired—he ran past St Helena by 70 miles (attributed to compass error) and failed to take adequate precautions with the water supply.[33] Some letters from passengers were published in *The Times* and the Company replied with an explanation and apology.[34]

Experience with the *Adelaide* contributed much to the greater success of her sister ship, the *Victoria*, which went on to win a £500 prize offered by the Australian colonies for the fastest voyage from England. She made the journey in sixty days, including two days delay at St Vincent, at an average speed of 10 knots. These two ships, Russell recorded, were among the first vessels constructed on a large scale which did not exhibit symptoms of external weakness.[35] Certainly Rolt's claim that they lacked great longitudinal strength is far off the mark.[36] They were the forerunners of a further five ships of the same class[37] and were an astonishing achievement in design, performance, cost and speed of construction, when compared to the *Great Britain*.

The *Adelaide* and *Victoria* were on the drawing board when Brunel first solicited Russell's guidance and opinion on a ship which would be sufficiently large to perform the duty of these ships without the need for re-fuelling en route. The system of longitudinal bulkheads and partial iron decks developed on the *Adelaide* and *Victoria* formed, with the longitudinal system of framing, the essential structure of the gigantic iron ship to which Brunel and Russell now gave their serious consideration—the ship which went down in history as the *Great Eastern*.

CHAPTER FOUR

The Great Eastern

My share of the Great Eastern is the purely professional one, of being responsible for the design of that ship as a naval architect, for her construction as a shipbuilder, and for the paddle-wheel engines, and boilers, as marine engineer.

J. SCOTT RUSSELL

Brunel made some preliminary calculations and sketches for a steamship to carry sufficient coal for the round trip to Australia and showed them to Russell in the Spring of 1852.[1] He had estimated that it would require a vessel of about 600 ft length and 70 ft beam. Russell records that he calculated the necessary size of ship at the request of Brunel and arrived at the figure of 20,000 tons. The requisite power for a speed of about fourteen knots worked out to about 8500 i.h.p., using the rough formulae of the time. This was in excess of what could then be delivered by a single screw, and, in the state of the art at that period, twin screws could not be accommodated; hence the proposal to employ a combination of paddles and screw and, of course, sail.[2] The paddles offered manoeuvrability, rightly seen as an advantage with such a large ship, but there were disadvantages too.

The whole conception was mind boggling. Who would be interested? The Australian Royal Mail Co. had supplied its own needs, but what about the new Eastern Steam Navigation Company which had failed to achieve its purpose of wresting the Far East mail contract from the P. & O. Co.? Russell suggested that Brunel approach them, and it tells us much about the entrepreneurial spirit of the times that they were ready to listen. They appointed a committee to meet with Brunel and Russell, but in the event, Russell attended alone, preceded by a letter from Brunel excusing his absence and affirming that Russell was 'fully acquainted' with all his plans and had 'ably assisted him in maturing them.'[3] Yates, the Company Secretary, informed Brunel afterwards that he had been 'most ably represented'[4] and, certainly, Russell must have reassured the Committee, for they recommended support of the proposals and a majority of the Board accepted them. Some, however, resigned. Perhaps they were of that wary character epitomised by the irascible Colonel Sibthorpe who had said that he would 'rather meet a highwayman or see a burglar on his premises than an engineer', an attitude for which Brunel's schemes already shared some responsibility.

Brunel now set about recruiting directors favourable to his plans, who, once assembled, 'adopted them fully' as he ingenuously remarked.[5] These plans were expounded in a typical Brunel report on July 21, 1852:[6]

> Although you will probably determine upon constructing not less than two vessels in the first instance, yet they must both be proceeded with at once, and must in fact be exact duplicates of each other ... designed and executed on such principles and with such perfection that no doubt can exist of the result.
>
> By well considering all that has been done, by selecting all that has been most successful, and by a judicious application of such results ... all this certainly can be assured ... I have, therefore, availed myself of the assistance of those most competent to afford the required information ... best able to give strength to our position by the value of their opinions, and best able to execute the various parts of the work with that experience and perfection which are essential to our success.
>
> With respect to the form and construction of the vessel itself nobody can, in my opinion, bring more scientific and practical knowledge to bear than Mr. Scott Russell. As to the proportion of power to be adopted, the form and construction of the engines, screw, and paddles, besides Mr. Scott Russell, I have had the benefit of the deliberate consideration and advice of Mr. Field of the firm of Maudslay and Field, and of Mr. Blake, of the firm of Watt and Co. I have written also to my friend Mr. F. P. Smith, to whom the public are indebted for the success of the screw ...

'The adoption of the plan being now determined upon,' wrote Brunel to Russell, 'we must proceed to determine the details and the first step unquestionably is the determination of the size and form of the ship.'[7] The intended destination at that stage was Diamond Harbour just below Calcutta on the Hooghly and there was a question of the maximum draft to permit this and whether this would be sufficient to allow the ship to be fully loaded. It was not until the next year, 1853, that the Australian run, which imposed no such restriction, came under serious consideration. By this time the dimensions of the ships were settled at 680 ft between perpendiculars, and accommodation for 3000 passengers envisaged.

The Great Ship now proposed, presented design problems of unprecedented magnitude, among which, longitudinal strength and stiffness generally, loomed large. Russell conceived the ship as a greater *Adelaide* with the addition of longitudinal framing such as he had employed on the shallow draft ships he had built. The latter indeed presented similar problems on a smaller scale. Much romantic nonsense has been written about Brunel's being the first to conceive the analogy between a ship and a bridge. As early as 1840, Russell had observed that the American builders of the slender wooden steamships, which they favoured, appeared 'to have regarded their vessel as a sort of wooden bridge, resting on two liquid butresses towards each extremity'.[8] Brunel was not the first with this idea. It is also said that he took Stephenson's Britannia Bridge as a model in designing the Great Ship. He did, but this did not suggest itself to him immediately, it evolved in the following way.

The most serious disadvantage of an iron hull was that, unlike a wooden hull, it could not be coppered and thus was prey to the accretion of barnacles which quickly multiplied, especially in tropical waters, until they drastically reduced the ship's speed. The problem was compounded in the case of the Great Ship on account of the obvious difficulty of cleaning it. Brunel proposed a double hull, the outer one being of coppered wood. To go from that to a double hull of iron and then to see the analogy with the cellular reinforcement of the top and bottom of the rectangular tubes forming the Britannia Bridge was a natural progression for Brunel as he considered how to implement his idea.

The Britannia tube, a product of the expertise of Fairbairn and Stephenson, was of exceptionally long span. It was reinforced top and bottom by longitudinal webs, or ribs, which, with an outer envelope, formed rectangular cells when seen in cross-section. Hence the term 'cellular construction'. It was one of the great innovations to nineteenth-century structural engineering. The inner and outer hulls of the Great Ship, separated by longitudinal frames, formed a structure of a similar kind. The same structure for the main deck completed the analogy with the Britannia tube. It was a considerable contribution to the design of very large iron ships. The fouling problem remained to be tackled by special paints.

Russell persuaded Robinson, one of his former partners, to invest in the project, and introduced his friend Charles Geach who replaced the last 'doubtful' director to withdraw. Brunel was now authorized to proceed as soon as 40,000 shares were taken and £120,000 (£3 per share) paid up.[9] The maximum commitment of each share was £20, giving a

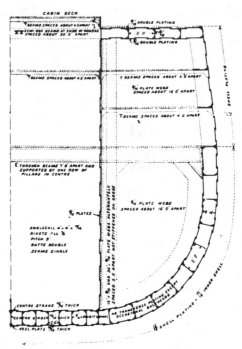

The Britannia Bridge tube (*left*) showing 'cellular' strengthening top and bottom; and (*right*) mid-ship section of the *Great Eastern* showing longitudinal framing with double hull and 'cellular' iron main deck

total initial share capital of £800,000 which was progressively to be called up as the need arose.

In anticipation of achieving this, the Company went through the motions of inviting tenders and, in May 1853, Russell's bid for the hull and the paddle engine and Blake's, on behalf of Messrs James Watt & Co., for the screw engine, were accepted.

Although the Company referred to 'tenders' received,[10] Russell's was the only one submitted for the hull. His complete tender contained the following:

(14 May, 1853)

I am prepared to build launch and deliver the said vessel complete in the River Thames, in conformity with the general conditions you have laid down, for the sum of £275,200. But if Second Vessel of the same size should be ordered within Six months after the first, the price of the first shall be reduced to £258,000 and the price of the second to the same.

In making this estimate I have taken the weight of the Ship at about 8600 tons I have also considered that I am to find the place for building the ship, that I am to find the very large and unusual plant and clenching for constructing the same. That I am to incur the expense of all works and machinery necessary for launching the Ship, or if it be found preferable that I am to construct a dock in which to build the ship and there float her out.

He tendered to supply and install the paddle engines and boilers for £44,500 and the screw engines for £53,500.

In support of his recommendation of Russell's tender for the hull, Brunel reported to the directors that it had been framed upon his calculations, and that owing to a recent rise in the price of iron it was 'somewhat, but not materially' above his own original estimate based upon the supposition of two vessels being ultimately ordered. Likewise the three tenders for the engines—received from Russell, Humphrys, and Watt & Co.—'confirmed fully' his previous calculations. He unhesitatingly preferred Russell's design for the paddle engines and advanced the additional consideration that it was advantageous to have the engines and boilers built near the ship. But, he told the directors, he preferred the extreme simplicity of Blake's (i.e. the Watt Co's) engine for the screw.[11] Privately he confided that political considerations had to be weighed. He preferred Russell's designs for both engines, but he felt bound to give Blake part of the work and hoped 'by attending himself to every detail of Blake's design' to secure all he could desire.[12] In this way, he believed he avoided what he described as 'strong party attack which might have damaged us in public estimation'.

Brunel now embarked upon the preparation of the formal contracts and specifications aided by frequent consultations with Russell and Blake who, according to Brunel's son, Isambard, 'consented to the insertion of clauses which gave the full control and supervision over every part of the work to the Engineer with very large powers of interpretation'. Russell was awarded three contracts: Hull (including launch); Paddle Engines and Boilers (installed); Cabin furnishing and decoration, rigging and Paddles and Screw.

It was arranged that the contractors would take part payment in shares, a familiar procedure in railway contracts of the time. Indeed, the competition between contractors was such that the price of the tender was often secondary to the ability of the contractor to provide funds or to take payment in shares. In this event it was usual to adjust the tender upwards to compensate; but, in the case of the Great Ship it is doubtful that such an adjustment was made. Yet the proportion of payment to be made in shares was the startling amount of a quarter of the share capital—10,000 shares.[13]

Much criticism can be levelled at Russell for his acceptance of a contract that presented so many hazards. He should have anticipated that the restless inventiveness of Brunel would lead to many changes, additions, deletions and revisions, checks and counter-checks, superimposed upon the innumerable novel demands which were inseparable from a ship of unprecedented proportions being built on a new system of construction. It was hardly reassuring that the tenders only slightly exceeded Brunel's own estimates for, even at that time, it must have been evident that several of Brunel's enterprises had overleapt his sanguine predictions. The contractor of his Clifton Bridge failed; his calculation of the cost of the Oxford, Worcester and Wolverhampton Railway was a gross underestimate; his Devon atmospheric railway was a very costly failure and the *Great Britain* steamship had cost more than he had anticipated. Bankruptcy, however, was the occupational disease of railway contractors, and in certain emergencies, railway companies had resorted to becoming their own contractors. The E.S.N. Co. made provision for taking the completion of the ship into its own hands should Russell be deemed unable to fulfil his contract. But Russell must have entertained a reasonable expectation that the E.S.N. Co. would not let him fail financially on account of the Great Ship. Above all, he was fortified by the backing of Charles Geach whom he described as 'the leading mind of the board ... especially able, enterprising, wealthy and intelligent ...' Everybody, declared Russell, had confidence in him, and, most important, Russell maintained that he for one should never have assumed the responsibilities he did had he not trusted Geach's wisdom 'to moderate the enterprise, his judgement to restrain the zeal, his clear head to direct the policy, and his ample resources to meet the vast expenditure of the undertaking.'[14] Geach, as we have noted, was already substantially behind Russell's iron shipbuilding enterprises but, most important, as partner in the great ironworks of Beale & Co., he was ready to accept shares from Russell in part payment for the iron for the Great Ship. Russell, therefore, had little reason to doubt that he had sufficient security and backing to see him through any eventuality. It may be, too, that this sense of common interest is what made him less precise in the matter

5 The longitudinals on the inner skin and bulkhead, May 17, 1855

6 The bulkheads clearly visible and upperside plating begun,
June 20, 1855. Note the absence of cranes

The construction of the *Great Eastern*

7 The outer skin has been started, October 20, 1855

8 The bow, probably early in 1856. The ribs of two ships on the stocks can be seen in the foreground

The construction of the *Great Eastern*

of defining 'extras' and less cautious about restrictive terms in the contract than was prudent.

These negotiations and the efforts to sell more shares were proceeding when, in the early morning of Saturday, September 10, 1853, Russell's works were seriously damaged by fire. The outbreak was first discovered about 3 a.m. in the forge and boiler-makers' shop. This building was roofed with weather boarding covered by tarpaulin which caught alight and rapidly conducted the fire to the adjacent buildings. Workmen on the scene manned the yard's fire pumps but overlooked the water reservoir, above the fitting shop, installed for just such an eventuality. A detachment of marines at Deptford dockyard across the river stoked up the dockyard fire float and steamed to the aid of the Russell workers fighting a losing battle in the night. Several detachments of the London fire brigade set out to investigate the red glow in the sky and mistakenly assumed that it came from Deptford. They galloped furiously over London Bridge and were very near Deptford before they discovered to their dismay that they were on the wrong side of the river! Back they scrambled across the bridge and down the other side to Millwall. One fire engine ran into a trench, eight feet deep, in the middle of the road, breaking the fore carriage and pitching all the firemen off their perches. A new river fire-float was cumbrously towed downstream and arrived about the same time as the demented fire engines, many of which took more than an hour to reach the scene. 'When it is known that these errors are not of infrequent occurrence,' *The Times* reporter observed, 'it is somewhat surprising that recourse is not had to the electric telegraph for the purpose of communicating accurate intelligence.'

The sawmill, carpenters' and painters' shops, and timber yard containing a thousand tons of deck planking, provided irresistible fuel for the flames which in two hours engulfed all the premises connected with the main four-storied brick building housing the machine shop, fitting and erecting shops, and the moulding loft and pattern stores. With it went a tragic inventory of some of the most choice and valuable plans, models and templates, including those of the projected Great Ship.

One of the two iron steamers for the North of Europe Steam Navigation Company which were on the stocks, had its bow badly buckled, and three completed sets of engines for coastal colliers, a 250 h.p. oscillating engine for a naval vessel, and machinery for a West Indian sugar crushing mill were badly damaged. The insurance surveyors declared that they had never seen such a destruction of machinery. The fire was thought to have originated in the spontaneous combustion of a small heap of coal or oily rags and floor sweepings, and it was ironical that, apart from the very inflammable roof, the shop in which it started was the least combustible of all.

The extent of the loss and damage was not declared, but judging from newspaper comments it could have amounted to £150,000, covered only partially by insurance.[15] The east half of the yard escaped injury however, and with it most of the ships under construction including Robert Stephenson's iron yacht, the first *Titania*, which was being restored after itself having been gutted by fire at Cowes in the previous year.

Russell was probably about to leave for the British Association meeting at Hull when the calamity occurred, but we have no record of his actions and reactions except that he now entertained doubts about being able to take the contract for the Great Ship. Geach, however, gave him encouragement and the assurance of his continued support.[16]

The prospectus of the Company made the optimistic claim that the ship would travel to Calcutta and back without recoaling, at a speed of 15 knots, as a consequence of which the dividends could be expected to be 40 per cent per annum. Charles Atherton, chief engineer in the Woolwich Dockyard, took the opportunity of a discussion after a paper on Ocean Steamers at the Institution of Civil Engineers, in November, to assert that it was disgraceful that the Institution should promote or countenance the public's being hooked with such gross bait.[17] Whereupon, the irascible G. P. Bidder rebuked Atherton for raising moral issues when, in his opinion, the treatment of any subject within the Institution should be restricted to its engineering bearing. Russell confined his remarks on that occasion to the demonstration of the principle that vessels of extraordinary dimensions were necessary for steam voyages of extraordinary length, and that the requirements of the merchants in Indian and Australian trade also demanded a large class of vessels.[18] Brunel, who had not been present, strenuously protested to Manby, the Secretary, that discussion of engineering work in progress should not be allowed until the matured plans were actually presented to the Institution by their promoters.[19]

By the end of the year, the necessary starting capital, thanks very largely to Geach, had accrued. It is noteworthy that the representatives of the Great Western and South Wales Railways—of which Brunel was engineer and which stood to gain from the success of the ship—were the only directors who took no more than the minimum fifty shares. The others took at least 500, Geach taking above 2000 (as also probably did Brunel) and a few such as Peto and Brassey, the greatest railway contractors of their time, who were also on the Board, 1000 each.

The contracts were formally drawn up and signed on December 22 and preparations were begun for the laying down of the Great Ship. The procedure for payment was not yet decided. Brunel preferred the usual railway practice of paying the contractor monthly, on the certificate of the engineer, in accordance with an estimate of the work accomplished. The usual procedure with ships was a lump sum payment by the purchaser at specified stages of the construction. As Russell explained it to Brunel:

> The custom of our trade is quite different from usual contracts for land-work . . . and so long as all the work as a whole is proceeding at such a rate as can be reasonably expected to produce the work finished and complete at the end of the time . . . we receive our payments regularly and calculate upon them. I also believe that the law has provided for giving ship owners peculiar claims over ships building in yards and everything belonging to them, which other property has not. However this may be, any deviation from our usual mode of receiving payments would seriously interfere with the progress and economy of the work.[20]

The actual procedure followed at this stage is difficult to ascertain but was certainly tied to the work accomplished.

Although the principal structural features relating to the strength of the hull were specified by Brunel, their detailed development and execution, not to say the origin of a good proportion of them, were the responsibility of Russell and Russell's staff. As Engineer, Brunel demanded complete control even of matters such as the site for the construction of the vessel and its launch which were nevertheless specified as Russell's responsibility. All drawings had to be approved by him and

> followed accurately until altered or added to by written authority from the Engineer. The contractor to prepare all calculations drawings models and templates which shall from time to time be submitted to the Engineer for his revision and alteration or adoption and shall be subject to his approval before being finally adopted and before that portion of the [work] to which they refer is commenced and the contractor shall furnish such copies of such calculations and drawings . . . All the parts of the ship and all details of the construction and the mode of proceeding with the work and also the means and appliances adopted in their construction to be to the entire satisfaction of the Engineer.[21]

73

This was how Brunel built railways and bridges.

This form of close and comprehensive external control had the disadvantage of prolonging the work and adding an unfamiliar note of harassment, particularly when so much of the work was entirely novel and when even the most conventional device or technique had to be handled on an unprecedented scale. Russell and his well-picked men had to accustom themselves to their unfamiliar role. Brunel, baggy-trousered and top-hatted, was a frequent visitor to the shipyard, where he brushed his perpetual cigar ash from the drawings in the design office, and jabbed a stubby finger at this and that—criticizing, demanding, and not least changing and adding. The traffic of mail to and from the yard and his city office was constant.

The decision had been made to build the ship parallel to the river and to launch her broadside-on in a controlled manner. Brunel rejected Russell's suggestion of a dry dock, on the grounds of expense (he estimated £20,000). All started with goodwill, and by the end of February 1854 the hull and engine drawings were well advanced. On March 29 Russell wrote to Brunel:

> Immediately after the signing of the Contracts, I took means to obtain possession of Ground on the Bank of the Thames suitable for the purpose of building the large ship. I was fortunate enough to obtain immediate possession of land in my vicinity suitable in all respects for this purpose [part of David Napier's yard upstream of Russell's], and so placed that the whole existing plant of my works was at once made available for the Company's Contract ... A substantial line of railway from the centre of my old works has been laid parallel to the river and along the whole length of the new shipyard; and the new yard has been entirely enclosed ... Owing to the unparalleled size of the Engines, I have had to build an entirely new erecting shop of unusual dimensions, which is now completed: I have had to sink a large iron Coffer-dam in the Foundry for casting the cylinders ... the moulds of the cylinders are now in execution, and the whole of the main parts of the Engines are rapidly advancing.
>
> I hope that you and the Directors when you consider the very short time which has elapsed since the order was given will see that I have not been remiss in taking every step in my power to secure the rapid and satisfactory advancement of the work, and I can only express my desire to avail myself of every suggestion that can be made to me of any modes of accelerating or improving the work.[22]

Brunel needed no encouragement to make suggestions, although he nearly always couched them as demands. He took much satisfaction from suggesting a slight alteration in the disposition of the plates here and there and more careful design to avoid the insertion of structural members which were superfluous to the structure but which were required to facilitate erection. This, he claimed, led to a saving 'of 40 tons of iron, or say £1200 of money in first cost!! and 40 Tons of cargo freight—at least £3000 a year!!'[23]

How inconsequential this was to seem in retrospect. The first careless rapture of designing and raising this mammoth slowly above the marsh dwellings of Millwall was soon to turn into worry and anguish. Brunel emphasized economy of material—'every part has to be considered and designed as if an iron ship had never before been built'.[24] It was very good discipline for Russell's ship draughtsmen, which would stand them in good stead, but one wonders if Russell adequately allowed for this when he estimated his contract price from the cost of his earlier ships. Brunel looked in on Dickson scaling up Russell's four-cylinder oscillating engine into the largest paddle engine ever built, and criticized this and that, although his own record in the design of engines for the Great Western Railway did not recommend him for this work.

'Pray give me an afternoon soon as I have done the strengthening of the bulkheads in a way I think will please you,' writes Russell (Feb. 1854); then 'Complete sets of detail drawings of the whole of the construction and strengthening of the general hull of the ship with the alterations which you have from time to time introduced are now completed and inked in conformity with your instructions' (May 29, 1854); 'All the calculations of displacement and capacity which you ordered have been completed and embodied in a diagram which I have sent you ... To ascertaining the weights and considering arrangements for strengthening the floors I shall give immediate attention' (July 13, 1854); 'I send a new tracing of the Boilers with the alteration you indicated in the up take.' (Nov. 30, 1854.) These items culled from a voluminous correspondence reveal the tenor of Russell's collaboration with Brunel.

In March of that year, Brunel invited tenders from Samuda, Laird, and Russell for three iron paddle-wheel steamships intended to ply between Milford Haven and Waterford. He asked for terms which amounted to the rental or charter of the vessels from the builder. Russell was the only builder ready to enter into such a deal and his price was comparable to that of his competitors, but nothing seems to have come of it.

Other work was going on in the Russell yard while the site for the

Great Ship was being prepared. There were auxiliary screw colliers, of which Russell designed and built about a dozen to replace the familiar coaling barques which plied between Tyne and Thames, and on which he experimented with several innovations;[25] the steam corvette *Esk* launched in June (one of a number of Admiralty contracts occasioned by the hostilities against Russia in the Crimea and the Baltic[26]) and the paddle steamer *Pacific* launched in September, which was intended for Mediterranean service but which successfully plied the Atlantic for a time. The *Pacific* was itself a novel iron ship, being divided into nine water-tight compartments and fitted with four new smoke-tube boilers of Russell's design, each fired by five furnaces with half the coal consumption/mile of the *Victoria*.

In preparation for the Great Ship, some hundreds of oak piles, from 12 to 15 inches square and from 20 to 38 feet long were laboriously driven into the ground. A huge covered moulding floor was prepared so that the ship's lines could be laid out full-scale and new machinery was purchased for the platers' shed and engine works. All engine castings were run on the site and the fourth and last cylinder, 6 ft 2 in bore by 15 ft and weighing 34 tons, was cast in October 1854, by which time the machining of the other three cylinders was nearly completed. The completed engine weighed 836 tons and was designed to develop 3410 i.h.p. at 10·75 r.p.m. The crankshaft was in three sections and was quite the largest ever built, as also was the propeller shaft. Indeed, it was very difficult to find an ironworks which would undertake such outsize forgings. The challenge was accepted, however, by Messrs. Fulton and Neilson, at the Lancefield Forge, Glasgow, and the result redounded to their credit. Special furnaces and steam hammers had to be installed by them, and at £40,000 they were not overcharging, especially when flaws in the webs produced two rejects. The screw engines were of slightly greater power but with higher speed and hence shorter stroke—4 ft.

Russell described his engine thus,

> It will be observed that these engines rest on four great beams, which run the whole length of the 40 ft engine room. These beams rise 14 ft above the floor, and are, like the rest of the internal work of the engine room, cellular bulkheads of $\frac{1}{2}$ in plate and angle iron. These beams are about 10 ft apart, and divide the engine into three portions; viz. a pair of oscillating engines on the left, a pair of oscillating engines on the right, and the air pumps in the centre. It will be observed that each pair of oscillating engines is coupled to a single crank-pin, an arrangement in favour of which I have elsewhere

avowed my strong partiality. The working of the engines is brought to the centre, and they are handled from a platform immediately above the air pumps, which are worked by a crank in the intermediate shaft. The two cranks on the end of the intermediate shaft differ in no respect from the ordinary crank, and carry a crank-pin on which the two engines work. It may be noticed that there is no second crank to work the paddle shafts; but instead, there is a large wheel of cast iron keyed on the other shaft, embraced by a friction strap, and into an eye of that friction strap the outer end of the crank-pin works and drives the wheels. This friction strap allows the engine to be detached at will from either or both paddles.[27]

Although Brunel had his say in some of the engine details, the credit was due to Dickson, Russell's engine draughtsman, and to Russell himself, for the engine was based on a type already designed and manufactured by him, a type which, around 1856, he extended to three pistons mutually at 120° attached to a single crank. This was a very neat and compact engine. The valves of the three cylinders were actuated from a single eccentric and a single air pump driven from another crank on the same shaft helped to counterpoise the unbalanced forces. One suspects that had Russell developed this engine earlier he would have been tempted to use it in the *Great Eastern* on account of the smaller cylinders required for the same power. The third cylinder was disposed vertically, either above or below the crank, and the balancing was remarkably good.[28]

Russell's report of October 25, 1854, to Brunel, gives us important details of progress:

Two of the four great cylinders which with their appendages form the Paddle wheel Steam Engines have been cast, bored, and faced with perfect success; the third has already been cast and is being bored; and the fourth and last is to be cast on Friday the 27th Inst. Should that be equally successful, the speedy conclusion of the construction of the Engines will have been secured, as those are the only portions which involve great risk, heavy outlay and slow execution. ... The great intermediate shaft now being forged at Lancefield is nearly completed and it is now the largest and most difficult forging ever executed. For its construction entirely new machinery has had to be constructed, and new furnaces have had to be erected. The two cranks are in hand and one of them is complete. The piston rods are in hand and one is complete. All the small portions are in a corresponding state of forwardness.

The plans of the boilers have also been completed and are now in hand. In order however that you may see the exact state of each individual part

I enclose a detailed statement of drawings, patterns, castings, malleable iron, turning and boring etc.

In regard to the Ship itself, I beg to inform you that, since my last report to you of the 25th July every part of the work has been making as rapid and continuous progress as is consistent with accuracy and good execution of the work. The whole central body comprising all the Engine rooms all the boiler spaces, all the coal bunkers, with the cabin spaces and saloons over them have been framed and carried up to the full height with the exception only of the two extreme bulkheads, which are in hand but not yet erected. This portion includes between 300 and 400 feet of the centre of the Ship comprehending nine transverse bulkheads and ten longitudinal bulkheads and the partial intermediate bulkheads. From the middle body of the Vessel the keel is being rapidly extended towards the ends, and being rivetted as we proceed. We are preparing to cover in the middle body of the Ship with the double iron deck, the whole of the iron of which is in progress of delivery and a considerable portion already on the ground. The covering in with the iron deck above we are hastening forward as fast as possible to shelter the men so as to enable them to carry on the work during the winter without interruption from the weather. We are now proceeding to work on the outer skin of the vessel for which a considerable portion of the plates has already arrived and the remainder are being rapidly rolled and delivered on the ground. As the keel is extended towards the extremities of the Vessel, we are continuing to drive piles into the foundations of the slip—to carry the weight of the extremities. We have carried the railways, formerly constructed, by means of turn tables on to transverse lines which run under the keel of the ship. ... I hope in two or three months to have a portion of the middle so far completed as to enable us to fix the four upper decks and commence the fitting of the cabins. The large punching machinery which has been constructed for punching the outer skin of the Ship is now completed along with the Steam Engine which is to drive it and will be at work upon the skin in a few days. The weights of the principal portions of the work now erected and in progress ... make 1736 tons, exclusive of deck beams, webs and considerable quantities of other plate and angle iron for general purposes of the Ship. Besides this, I estimate that the quantity now ordered and in progress of delivery is about 500 tons more. I enclose the estimated weights of the various portions of iron in the Ship, in detail.

I beg also to send you the Photographs you have ordered of the central portion of the Ship, copies of which are being prepared for the Directors. The great erecting shop containing the cylinders &c. being photographed in like manner, but the weather has been most unfavourable.

It was pioneering on a grand scale, and as each constructional problem was solved it had to be committed to paper to go forward to the Chief

Engineer for approval and often elaboration. It was not surprising that the estimated launching date now began to appear far from realistic, an ominous portent for Russell.

Nevertheless, everything was going well, when, in October, the keystone of Russell's enterprise, Charles Geach, died. It was a catastrophe for Russell, and a serious loss for the Company. The full realization of this had not yet sunk home when Russell, Yates and Brunel were involved in an unexpected diversion which cast an unwonted shadow on their relationship. This arose from an article entitled 'Iron Steam Ships—The Leviathan' which appeared in *The Observer* (November 13, 1854). This was the first substantial journalistic treatment of the Great Ship. Brunel took violent exception to some of its statements and omissions with respect to himself and the 'Great' ships, and deplored the fact that Yates was so insensible of these that he had ordered copies of the article for possible distribution. He thought that the article showed 'marked care in depreciating those efforts which he had made in advancing steam navigation', and wrote one of his long agitated letters to Yates, expressing this conviction and demanding to know who had written the article. He apparently believed it had been written by Yates or Russell—it 'bore a stamp of authority, or at least it professed to give an amount of detail which could only be obtained from ourselves.' At the same time in a letter to Russell, he practically accused Russell of writing the article. He asked whether 'it was (it did not look so) by a friendly hand who would himself rectify it!'

A reading of the offending article makes one wonder at the passion it aroused in Brunel and it seems incredible that he could think for a minute that it was by any other hand than that of a reporter whose knowledge of the history of trans-oceanic steamships was shaky and who had never been in an iron shipyard before. The reporter describes his visit to the yard and clearly states that the details of construction of the Great Ship, her speed and safety and purpose, were explained to him by the 'builder'. This evidently included an explanation of the principles from which the lines of the ship were derived. He had been told that hollow lines for speed were 'no new discovery', they had simply been lost then found again. He made no allusion to Russell's contributions to this subject. Indeed, apart from acknowledging Fairbairn's contribution to iron shipbuilding through his finding a method of joining iron 'so as to make it equal in strength to solid metal', no personal attributions are made. It is the Eastern Steam Navigation Company he congratulates. If there is marked care about anything, it would appear to be the avoidance of puffing any specific individuals involved with the Great Ship. One gathers from this that Russell himself avoided attributions in his explanations to the reporter. Thus, when the reporter referred to how the Great Ship would overcome the difficulty attending the fuelling of steamships on long voyages he wrote that he was not precisely aware to whom the credit of this bold suggestion was due but that the 'proposition was gravely started ... Mr Brunel, the engineer of the ... Company, approved of the project, and Mr Scott Russell undertook to carry out the design. We all know,' continued the well intentioned but erring writer, 'that when the *Great Western* and the *Great Britain* were built there were many prophetic fears ... as to the fate of each—and how completely they realized the anticipations of their adventurous owners.'

'I cannot allow it to be stated, apparently on authority,' protested Brunel, 'while I have the whole heavy responsibility of its success resting on my shoulders, that I am a mere passive approver of the project of another, which in fact originated solely with me and has been worked out by me at great cost of labour and thought ...'[29] Brunel has our sympathy, but it is not evident at all that the statement was 'apparently on authority'.

One wonders how Brunel could believe that he was not widely assumed to be the originator of the idea of the Great Ship. He already had a reputation for grand schemes and ideas, and his position with respect to the Great Ship was certainly well understood within the profession. At the British Association meeting held in the September prior to the appearance of *The Observer* article, Russell had presented a paper 'On the progress of Naval Architecture ...' in which he had 'complimented Mr Brunel for the engineering skill and ingenuity he had displayed in leading the way in the construction of large iron ships'.[30] The omission of some such comment in *The Observer* article also upset Brunel.

The article began with a review of the beginnings of transatlantic steamships. The writer gave the particulars of the *Sirius* and the *Great Western* and appears to have confused in his own mind the *British Queen* with the *Great Britain* and indeed calls it the *Great Britain* at one point. He is wrong in some of the particulars of this and of rival ships of the time, and remarks that she, the *British Queen*, 'has recently been sold to the Belgian Government'. She was sold to the Belgians over ten years before. She was engined by Robert Napier whose name, the writer remarks 'is now associated with the most splendid triumphs in steam loco-motion which has ever yet been achieved' (The Cunard Co.). Brunel felt left out and certainly he had some justification. It was small consolation that the *Great Britain* was called the 'parent' of iron ships and of screw propulsion (which it was not) when the writer had the indelicacy to refer to her 'ludicrous starting in life' and 'rather unfortunate termination'. One is relieved that he did not now mention Brunel in this connection. 'The same friendly hand' protested Brunel, 'would not have thrown ridi-cule, and that by a positive false statement, upon that which he at the same time admits to have been the means of almost [the writer did not say 'almost'] introducing two of the greatest improvements in steam navi-gation.'

The 'friendly hand' was certainly not authoritative. It 'believed the *Great Britain* to be the largest steam ship yet built' yet in the next para-graph states that the *Himalaya* was the largest vessel 'at present afloat', which it was.

Brunel's paranoiac reaction to this blemished article and particularly his readiness, on the strength of it, to impute invidious motives to Russell, is difficult to reconcile with his heroic image. Was he now growing jealous of Russell's increasing public identification with the ship? The public and *The Observer* reporter, after all, saw it in Russell's shipyard. The incident is important in that it first draws into focus the prestige of the Great Ship as an issue between Brunel and Russell. As far as Brunel was concerned, the ship was his, totally, in conception and execution. As in all his schemes, he drew·upon the ideas, opinions and experiences of others, but the finished work was *his*, not shared with anyone. Russell was simply the contractor, like a Brassey or a Peto. This was a matter of great importance to Brunel. Russell, however, was not merely a con-tractor, he was a practising engineer, naval architect and shipbuilder, all three. In these capacities he contributed to the realization of the Great Ship. He was, in his view and in that of many others, a collaborator. Brunel had no 'collaborators', ever.

Brunel's son reproduced his father's letter to Yates in his biography but curiously excised from it the name of the newspaper concerned. In his original draft of this book he refers to the article as containing 'perhaps the first of the many statements which have been published giving to others the credit due to Mr Brunel,' but he deleted this. Did he in the meantime read the article?

There are indications that it was this excised comment which encouraged Rolt to accept Brunel's suspicions at face value without even tracking down the offending article to read it for himself. It led him astray.

We do not know how the matter was resolved, but it was of much less importance to Russell than the crisis in his financial arrangements with the Company which was precipitated by Geach's death. He explained his problem to the Directors on December 20, 1854, and reiterated his statement in a letter to Yates dated December 28:

> The substance of my statement to the Board of the Eastern Steam Navigation Company at their last Meeting was to the following effect.
>
> The lamented death of the late Mr Geach has materially altered the circumstances in which I am placed with reference to the continuance and completion of my Contract in two respects.
>
> First, I had contracted for the manufacture of the Iron through Mr Geach with the firm of Beale & Co. of which he was a principal partner and had arranged with him to take a large proportion of payment of the Iron in Shares.
>
> Second, I had made arrangements with the Eastern Steam Navigation Company to take part payment of my Contract in shares of the Company and also to take my cash payments at periods of time which would leave me in certain contingencies very largely in advance in my expenditure beyond the sums I should have received in payment.
>
> The death of Mr Geach has rendered it necessary that I should somewhat modify the first of these arrangements and make the payments of the contract for iron quite definite as to nature, date and amount.
>
> In order to enable me to do this and also to provide for my own future expenditure on the Ship, what I have to request of the Board of the Eastern Steam Navigation Company is that they would consent to a modification of the dates and proportions of the future payments in such a manner that the exact sums of money still to be paid should be divided into certain monthly payments of definite amounts to be set against the execution of a similar definite proportion of the work to be done, so as to enable me beforehand to make the necessary arrangements for carrying on the work in the expeditious manner which the Company require.
>
> I need not add that I believe such arrangements can be made in all respects consistently with the interests and security of the Shareholders of whom I am myself one of the largest and that if I had thought otherwise, I should not have made this proposition.[31]

How the directors accommodated Russell in this matter is not clear. There is some mention of agreement to pay Russell in ten instalments of £8000 subject to progress. But if, in fact, only £65,000 remained to be paid by August 1855—as Brunel asserted—then the average monthly payment must have run to about £13,500 for the hull alone, including payments for shares.

Work on the Great Ship continued steadily; its giant form began to rise like a rust-coloured primaeval monster with platers, riveters and their helpers swarming like ants over the bare bones and armoured hide, and frequently falling to their death.

In these days, the managers of the principal departments of the works and shipyard wore frock coats and rather tall top hats. Russell was a familiar figure with, in addition, his walking stick and black velvet waistcoat with Royal Yacht Squadron gilt buttons, black satin cravat and white collar. The thumb of his free hand was habitually thrust in the armhole of his waistcoat, likewise his other thumb when his stick was dispensed with. One of his drawing office apprentices retained a pleasant memory of his 'charming personality' and considered him 'a fine gentleman'.[32] He recalled, too, an 'amusing' memory, of Russell and the Marquis of Stafford—whom he considered a great friend of Russell's—racing down the yard to the new iron screw yacht, the *Undine*, then under construction, Russell's thumbs in his waistcoat and his long frock coat flying. Later, at the launch of the *Great Eastern*, the correspondent of the *Illustrated Times* commented approvingly of Russell's elegant appearance and general urbanity which 'were a marked contrast to the style and manners of the other important gentlemen present'. This was the outward expression of Russell's temperament, but he was in no respect a dandy.

Brunel's report to the directors in February 1855 set out the considerable progress of the work and the plans for launching at great length. He accepted responsibility for some initial tardiness:

> ... as I have made it a rule from the first that no part of the work should be commenced until it had been specially considered and determined upon, and working drawings in full detail prepared, and, after due deliberation, formally settled and signed, the work did not make at the onset that display of progress which might have been made, if less regard had been paid to establishing a good system which would prevent delays hereafter, and ensure a more perfect and satisfactory result. I am not prepared to say that the work is in that state of progress which will ensure its completion within the period fixed in the contract ...[33]

This extensive report was published in its entirety in *The Times*, and if Brunel was apprehensive that the public may have been unaware of his dominant position with respect to the project and the design of the ship, he must surely now have felt that he had put them to rights. Russell is not mentioned in this report. It was also privately circulated with a dedication to Napoleon III.

Some weeks later, Russell received a letter from Prince Albert's secretary asking him to call at Buckingham Palace to speak about the Prince's wish to see his, Russell's, large ship.[34] The visit to the shipyard was arranged for a few days later, March 28, and Russell informed Brunel accordingly. Brunel, unfortunately, was unable to be present, and it appears from Russell's letter to Brunel reporting the occasion that the latter had expressed concern that his role should adequately be represented; *The Observer* article apparently still rankled. One surely could understand if Russell resented the invidious implication. Brunel's letter has not been preserved, but the following was Russell's reply:

> My Dear Mr Brunel,
> I was very sorry to find you could not meet the Prince this morning. It was, however, of less consequence than I thought or than you thought as the visit was mainly designed for the Battery in which he takes a deep interest and he bestowed comparatively little time on the Great Ship.
> I took the opportunity of explaining what I supposed he and everybody else knew, that you are the Father of the great ship and not I and to say many other things which I should not have done if you had been present. Allow me to take this opportunity once for all while on this point of saying that you may always trust your reputation as far as the Big Ship is concerned to my care in your absence for many reasons: 1st I have as much reputation as I desire or deserve. 2nd I think it much wiser to be just than unjust. 3rd I would much rather preserve your friendship (which I think I possess) than filch your fame (if I could) and forfeit your friendship which I should. *Verbum Sat*. I will never trouble you on this point again but remain
> Always Faithfully Yours,
> J. Scott Russell.

L. T. C. Rolt scoffs at the remark that the Prince's primary interest was the floating battery. Before we are seduced to this view we must recall the significance of the battery as a historic innovation to naval warfare and as a new weapon produced by Napoleon III (see Chapter 7) for use against the Russians in the Crimea. The Prince was deeply interested in military engineering matters of this kind and, not long after, himself invented an armoured gun turret which he generously suppressed in favour of Cowper Coles' 'cupola' of which he was a powerful advocate.[35] Russell's comment on the Prince's preoccupation with the floating battery, therefore, is eminently credible. As Russell rightly remarks, too, there

84

was little reason for anyone not knowing that Brunel was the 'father' of the Great Ship. Indeed, at that stage particularly, one could expect that he would be considered by all readers of *The Times* as its sole designer, constructor and planner. There is forbearance in Russell's response, an attempt to mollify but also a nuance of rebuke. The 'My Dear Mr Brunel' with which it opens has significance, for no other surviving letter between the two men bears this form of address; it is invariably 'My Dear Sir', or 'Sir', with the subscription 'Yours faithfully'. Contrary to L. T. C. Rolt's assertion, there is no distinction in this respect between letters written before and after the letter reproduced above. Was Russell attempting to disguise his annoyance or was he feeling more conciliatory than annoyed? On the crucial point of acknowledging Brunel's contribution to the conception and design of the Great Ship, Russell was as good as his word, as we shall see. His writings, indeed, are notably replete with generous acknowledgements of the talents and contributions of others.

Having had their fingers burnt, Yates and Russell were more cautious thereafter in publicity matters concerning the Great Ship, and when a reporter from the *Liverpool Courier* visited Millwall to gather material for an article in May of that year, he must have been cautioned about the situation, for, he wrote to Yates, though he had received answers to all his questions 'in the fullest and most cheerful spirit', he yet 'submitted the article to no person that [he] might bear all the responsibility upon [his] own shoulders'. Yates had the article made into a pamphlet and sent a copy to Brunel, along with the reporter's letter, for his amendment and approval prior to its circulation.[36]

There was yet another matter, however, which the Prince and Russell had to discuss. Wilhelm Bauer, an inventive Austrian engineer who had designed and constructed a three-man submarine, had left Austria in 1853 because of current political squabbles and lack of interest in his novel boat, and had attracted the interest of the Prince. The submarine was propelled by a screw operated by a treadmill and the method of submergence was first to take in water ballast until the deck was awash, then to control the submergence by inclining the vessel by means of the movement of a heavy weight in a series of dips. Surfacing was achieved by pumping out the ballast.

By arrangement with the Admiralty, Russell employed the frustrated inventor to develop his device; but it appears that Bauer's need for an interpreter and his suspicion that his drawings were being consulted during his absence filled him with apprehension. He recorded that on the last Sunday of April 1854, his interpreter drew his attention to a paragraph in *The Times* which commented on the underwater craft being designed by Russell for use against the Russians. He stated that he upbraided Russell and Fox with planning to steal his inventions. They scoffed at the suggestion and explained that the reference was not to Bauer's submarine but to one of their own.[37] A search of *The Times* has not revealed the contentious paragraph. Fox as a harbour engineer was indeed interested in underwater excavation but he was not in business with Russell as Bauer thought. The irascible Bauer fled with his model and designs to Russia although he claimed that efforts were made to prevent his leaving England. His submarine *Le Diable Marin* was launched at St Petersburg in May 1855. The cost of correcting a miscalculation was an embarrassment to the project, but it was successful. Unfortunately it struck some rocks and sank. The Russians wanted Bauer's submarine but did not want him, so he left for France where Napoleon III gave him some help but with no happier results. Bauer alleged that Russell built a submarine from his, Bauer's, drawings and that it sank with loss of life because of some essential features he had withheld. But Russell's submarine bore no resemblance to Bauer's. It was, in fact, a diving bell shaped like an inverted boat and propelled by a two-man crew walking along the bed of the sea, pushing against thwarts fixed to the underside of the vessel. The idea of blowing out the ballast tanks with compressed air, commonly used in modern submarines, was introduced, but control required a cool head and the operation a good deal of nerve.[38] Palmerston sanctioned an appropriation of £7000 for the development of the vessel and Sir Ashley Cooper-Key, Sir James Hope and Sir James Sullivan were appointed to report on its trials.

Disraeli got wind of this and wrote to Lord Derby:

Secret & most Confidential   November 20, 1855
... Palmerston is for blowing up Cronstadt having got a discoverer who builds submarine ships worked by submarine crews, & who are practising on the Thames with, they say, complete success ...[39]

According to Cooper-Key, however, the tests were not nearly so successful as Disraeli's informant suggested. There were accidental drownings and after a submersion of twenty minutes without incident on its first official test, the vessel dived again only to return suddenly to the surface 'blow like a whale' then capsize.[40] On another occasion it surfaced below an unsuspecting ship in Portsmouth harbour to the consternation of all concerned.[41] But by this time the end of the war was in sight and, further development obviously being required, the enterprise was abandoned. Russell added this to the several activities in his life on which he apparently felt committed to secrecy, for he never alluded to it.

So much then for Russell's business with the Prince. To return to the partnership between Russell and Brunel on the Great Ship, something of the issues and attitudes arising between them in 1855 may be gleaned from the following.

Russell to Brunel (February 10, 1855)

I have been confined with a severe attack of bronchitis ever since I saw you. I have been considering the subject you had written to me about, in so far as to provide for the future an authentic record of work done including exact quantities of iron delivered.

I have arranged that all the invoices of iron for the Great Ship shall in future be sent in quite separately from other work, so that you will have first the Iron Master's delivery of the iron, next the weighers receipt at the works, and I will get a regular form made out for the purpose. As for the past we have not unluckily separated the materials of that contract from the others, but we shall get a pretty good approximation to it by calculation, and such checks as we have got.[42]

Russell to Brunel (March 13, 1855)

The plates have been ordered by us, of the exact dimensions by you, and have been delivered to us in the manner customary to the trade.... The fixing and rivetting, has only been prevented from going on as fast as the preparation of the materials, by the fact of a few essential plates having been frozen up on their way.

As you are well aware that there is no difficulty or delay in the ultimate completion of the work, caused by this circumstance in as much as the fixing and rivetting are at any time, especially in summer, able to overtake easily the other work, I trust that you will not use an inevitable accident of weather, to embarrass seriously my proceedings—I have desired all possible means to be used to get these plates delivered upon which the successful erecting of all the others depends. They are the plates of the gunwale, required to give vertical strength to the iron deck, and the wales on the end of the main deck beams required to form and fix the whole skin of the sides, with truth and accuracy. The moment they arrive, the fittings will proceed rapidly.

Two additional bulkheads are ordered and their erection will accompany the extension of keel.[43]

Russell to Brunel (March 30, 1855)

On receipt of your former letter I immediately ordered the weight of the plates to be kept down. ... You may remember to have ordered a portion of the topsides connected with the iron deck to be made one inch thick instead of 3/4 of an inch, but as you have since extended the iron deck considerably, so as to have a longer hold on the sides, this thickening may be countermanded, as I do not think we have any of the plates made.

This and taking off the 1/16 from future materials may perhaps save what you want.[44]

A few weeks later, that malign fate which seemed to dog Russell, struck again. The armoured floating battery, so recently inspected by the Prince Consort, was gutted by fire on the eve of its launch, slid down the ways and broke its back. The estimated loss was about £45,000, offset in part by insurance. Brunel hastened to advise Yates to insure the Great Ship, and Russell to employ a policeman.

Brunel did not spare Russell but kept on his back. Within a day or two he was complaining about the quality of some indicator diagrams taken in connection with some steam jacketing experiments, about the progress made on the ship over the past month, about an interruption in the supply of the periodic photographs which Russell had agreed to provide, and about some other matters. To this, Russell immediately replied (May 9, 1855):

I beg to inform you that I have thoroughly examined the apparatus for taking the diagrams, in the experiments on heating steam. Our two indicators are the best that can be made, one by a Scotchman, and the other by an Englishman, both the most distinguished.

As these appear not to be satisfactory I have arranged to get the use of the Woolwich collection of Indicators, which is very large, and when I have done that I shall have exhausted all the resources I am acquainted with. Then indeed I shall be prepared for your patience being exhausted.

On the second point, that the iron-work of the Ship is not this month proceeding rapidly enough, was quite true when you wrote the note, but the deliveries of iron which reached you yesterday will have satisfied you that I also have been dissatisfied, and have been whipping-up, with what success you will there see, from the largely increased deliveries visible in the last return.

Allow me also to suggest that you will not consider occasional variations in the progress of the work as any serious dereliction of duty, but that if I am now one hundred tons under the mark, and at another time one hundred tons over the mark, I shall have the credit as well as the discredit for the whole.

Thirdly, the complete drawings of the Stern are in hand, but I wish to observe that the changes made at the Stern of the Vessel had rendered it necessary to re-adjust the lines on the floor, and that I was unwilling to give you the drawings until they had been corrected by the altered lines on the large scale. That is now being done, and you will have the Stern drawings quite accurate in a few days.

The drawings of the Masting, according to your last sketch, have been completed and sent to Ferguson, the Mast-maker, from whom I hope to send you a report in a few days.

Fourthly, I gave your last definite order to the Photographer. I shall have the copies of the last series this week. They are making beautiful Photographs, and from the arrangements made, you may depend on having copies of two views at the commencement of every month.[45]

But Brunel was not easily appeased, he dashed off an immediate retort:

Your reply this morning to my long list of complaints is an admirable specimen of an Under-Secretary's reply in the House to a Member's motion—it does not satisfy one single honest craving for information and for assurance of remedy ... I do not want better indicators than usual. ... Those made on this occasion and to which I object were absurd—like attempts at writing of a two-year-old baby—and I take credit to myself that I did not resent the insult of showing them to me as indicator cards.[46]

This is how Brunel inculcated a warm spirit of co-operation. Russell remained unruffled, and on May 18 curtly commented: 'I have duly attended to all your requirements and they are in progress. I will be glad to have an hour with you on various points either this evening from six till seven, or tomorrow morning from eleven to twelve.'

Further tests on the heating system were conducted and further indicator diagrams were procured, apparently with little complaint. On June 7, Russell recorded progress on the several experiments and reported:

I have further increased my drawing forces by putting all the drawing of cabin and interior arrangements into new hands.

Ferguson is hard at work upon the masts, spars, and general arrangements of sail and rigging, but I find his prejudice much harder to contend against than my own, as he naturally prefers to take the existing arrangements of the largest class of ships rather than invent new ones. However, I have compelled him like myself to try his hand thoroughly on your last plan of masting &c exactly as it stands.

As you are not expected home till Monday, I thought it might be agreeable to you to know all this.[47]

The idea of reducing losses due to cylinder condensation in steam engines by steam jacketing was new and it was not known whether these savings would justify the considerable difficulty of applying the principle to the large cylinders of the Great Ship. Russell felt the problem of size sufficient and was doubtless pleased when Brunel bent to the opinion of Joshua Field and abandoned the idea, although Brunel is said to have regretted it.

Reporting on the progress of the paddle engines, at the beginning of June, Russell remarked: 'As you are aware of the state of their progress, I think you will have no hesitation in certifying to the Company a payment for the Engines as considerably more than earned.'[48]

Meantime, In April, a most contentious issue had been re-opened by a correspondence between Brunel and a Mr J. W. Bull, a shipbuilder in Buffalo, New York: whether to have a 'free' or a 'controlled' launch. Bull approved of Brunel's decision to launch broadside: 'It is by all odds the safest and preserves the vessel without strain in the slightest degree,' he wrote. Since 1837, hundreds of vessels had been launched successfully at Buffalo in this way. For large heavy vessels a slope of 1 in 12 would be satisfactory with the ways 'slushed with tallow and flax seed mixed in'. On the point of launching, the ship was held by check ropes and a 'key wedge'. The wedge was knocked out and the guys cut simultaneously and levers were on hand in the event of sticking—'no earthly power can check or stop her when she once begins to move', he declared. There had been no failures, only a straining of the ways with a slightly uneven start. The displacement wave and refluence were considerable.

In the beginning, Russell's preference was to build the ship in a dry dock as was done with the *Great Britain*; but no suitable site could be found and in any case Brunel estimated that the necessary size of the dock would make it more expensive than Russell anticipated and asserted that 'Launching seemed to offer the fewest difficulties and the greatest certainty'.[49] But longwise or broadside? Most launches in Britain, then as now, were longwise and the art was well developed. But, with such a large ship, would the river be sufficiently deep or the ship sufficiently light? The decisive objection in Brunel's opinion, however, was the inconvenience to the constructors of having to cope with the great height to which the bow would have to be raised. Launching broadside on the other hand could produce such a large wave that sightseers would have to be warned from the river. Again, too, the hull could strike bottom on entering the water. It should be remembered that the absence of large cranes made it necessary to install the engines while the ship was on the stocks—introducing them through a hole in the hull—and so greatly adding to the launching dead weight. It seemed preferable to Brunel to slide the ship gently to the water's edge at low tide, by a system of winches and brakes, and float her off. It would be difficult to do this other than in a series of movements or jerks even with lubricated wooden launching ways, hence he was led to consider a mechanical system of rollers support-ing the cradles on metal runners—a 'patent slip' which could be re-erected at the ship's intended port to lift her in and out of the water for cleaning and repair. This idea seems to have been rejected on grounds of expense. Nevertheless, the apparatus and procedure demanded by a controlled launch made it a more expensive and complicated operation. It was not usual for Brunel to remark that Russell concurred with any of his ideas; but the problem of launching the giant ship weighed suffi-ciently on his mind for him to implicate Russell in his decision to 'build her parallel to the river and slide her down gradually to low water mark and float her off'. Russell fully concurred, he noted.[50] Not only so but Russell suggested the use of hydraulic jacks for this purpose which Brunel considered too expensive, although he was later to employ them.

On July 9, Brunel and Russell had a long discussion on the subject, with Bull's letters before them, which resulted in Russell coming out in favour of a free launch, while Brunel just as strongly preferred 'lowering gradually'.[51] Next day, Brunel wrote (July 10, 1855):

> We agreed then yesterday after discussing both sides that whatever the relative merits of launching without check or of lowering by degrees in all other respects we must select that plan which should be safest and that agree-ing as to the facility of the former operation we should well consider now what would be the best mode of carrying out the latter.

In other words, the safest rather than the surest mode was Brunel's choice and a controlled launch it would be. In the course of a letter to Blake, Brunel wrote with respect to the launch: 'Mr R. finally concurs in my determination, *coûte que coûte*, that which was safest and surest *must* alone be considered.'

But this was a distortion of Russell's position. The 'safest' way was

not the 'surest' in any case. Russell did not concur with Brunel's decision
to adhere to a controlled launch, his reluctant compliance with Brunel's
dictates cannot therefore be called 'lip service' as L. T. C. Rolt described
it.[52]

It is to be expected that Russell, particularly in his present circumstances, would greatly be concerned with the expense of the launch and
that he would feel encouraged by the American opinions and experience
to urge a free launch which Brunel and Russell estimated would save
£10,000.[53] Indeed, a controlled launch was an unknown novelty in comparison. If, as Rolt asserted, Russell was now dragging his heels in anticipation of extricating himself from ruin by a 'clever' disengagement plan
from the *Great Eastern* contract, the method of launching and many other
matters should have been of little account to him. Apart from anything
else, it should be borne in mind that Russell had been paid to a considerable extent in shares and that these, including the 2000 held in trust by
the Company as security for the due performance of the contract, now
representing a sum in excess of £20,000, stood to be forfeit.[54]

Brunel's way of dealing with his difference of opinion with Russell
on launching method was to give some semblance of keeping the options
open while planning the controlled launch on which he had decided.
Launching was a great art, peculiarly belonging to the naval architect
and shipbuilder; but Brunel became very preoccupied with his controlled
launch plan and virtually pushed Russell aside. He required data from
Russell, however, the estimated launching weight, the rise and fall of the
tide and the exact position of the centre of gravity,[55] and, on August 23,
was 'rather surprised' to find Russell 'less anxious to possess precise
knowledge on such points' than he was. 'I am not going to trust to chance
and must satisfy myself at once on these points which will influence the
arrangements to be made for launching', he declared. Russell had been
involved in many launches, but Brunel thought this no justification for
confidence.[56]

In the same breath, Brunel was urging Russell to accelerate progress
on the ship. On August 12, he wrote that only £65,000 remained to be
paid and 4500 tons of ironwork remained to be erected. 'I have tried gentle
means first . . . I must strengthen the dose a little. If you do not see with
me the necessity of shaking off suddenly the drowsiness of sleep that is
upon us . . . you are lost . . In fact unless . . . on Monday next we are busy
as ants at ten different places now untouched I will give up—but you will
do it.'[57]

Russell responded on August 21 with his construction schedule for the remaining work. He still considered a March 1856 launch possible:

> I beg to inform you that in consequence of your urgent representation I have carefully gone into the whole of the progress of the Iron Work of the Great Ship, with the view of making arrangements for its speedy completion. I have examined our means of execution and I find that we are now so much advanced in the work that I shall be able to add a large number of hands upon it—so as to ensure with tolerable weather the following progress...

Here Russell presented a detailed statement of his anticipated monthly progress to January 1856 and declared that, provided Brunel ordered work to proceed immediately on the stern 'where the tedious and difficult fittings of all the parts of the ship around the screw . . .' would require about six months to complete, the ship could be ready to enter the water in March.[58] Brunel probably was holding up work on the stern until he had decided upon the position of the screw. Russell enclosed estimates for additional works which Brunel had proposed[59] and stated that £37,673 in excess of the contract price would be necessary to complete the ship.

He now felt disadvantaged by the principle of being paid according to the weight of iron erected. This, he argued, took no account of the cost of changes and reinforcements over the system of construction on which his estimate had been based. 'Extras' have long been a source of contention in shipbuilding and construction contracts generally, so it is no surprise that they were as much an issue in the novel case of the Great Ship. Russell explained his point of view in reply to a letter from Brunel dated September 27 which raised the subjects of progress, payment and 'extras'. Here we find Russell's customary restraint wearing a little thin:

> I have your long letter—I am sorry you have written it because I thought we had concluded that whole matter in a conversation we had lately, and I had discharged it entirely from my mind. As your letter seems to require it of me, I am now obliged to sit down and write a long answer instead of doing my work here.
>
> You are wrong in supposing I am indifferent to the weight of the ship. I have thoroughly satisfied *myself* of its weight. I only regret that you are not satisfied. But I have ordered my people as soon as possible to cheque [sic] Mr Jacomb. [Rolt had it that Brunel had Jacomb secretly calculate the data because of a lack of confidence in Russell's calculation. There is no justification for Rolt's conjecture.] I had hoped perhaps to have seen you in

the country [i.e. Sydenham] on Sunday—to talk over many things in the future—Instead of which I must sit down and answer your last and try to become Yours most Obediently.[60]

[Then followed a review of the business as Russell saw it] I beg to state that I am quite satisfied of the true weights of the Ship as now constructed... I cannot regard the weight of the ship as so important in a pecuniary point of view as you do. I have built the Ship faithfully to the dimensions and sizes agreed upon, understood, and drawn in, when I tendered for the same. It is quite true that a redistribution of the material took place soon after the work commenced, to which I did not object, as it appeared to be made on the principle of neither increasing or diminishing the amount of materials and labour and in fact it was so, I proceeded accordingly to build the Ship, as originally agreed for, and have I hope done so faithfully and well.

Since that time and at various periods, additions have been made and improvements invented, which had no previous existence either understood or agreed. These were successively from time to time proposed and ordered by you; I generally wrote them down at the time, understood them as extras, and understood that you did so; and I have executed them as such. Of these, the amount is very considerable and I should never for a moment have proceeded with them, had I not understood them as extra. The new series of keelsons, double of the former number. The small 60 feet bulkheads between the longitudinal webs. The prolonged iron decks, are some of those.

What I have done has been to go steadily through with the Ship as it was originally, clearly understood and agreed considering that as the contract. Everything invented since I have considered as an extra, and I think I am right.

You have told me that in the contract there is a mention made of 7000 tons of iron, as an amount not to be exceeded except as an extra. I am not personally aware of the mention of that figure nor do I regard it as likely to be of any consequence. It formed no element of my original tender, and as the original tender was simply intended to be carried out in the contract (of which I have no copy) I cannot conceive that that amount can be so mentioned as to form it into an essential element of the contract.

At all events I feel that I have faithfully built the Ship as intended by both of us, when the price was settled and I cannot but think I have a right to claim as extra everything not contemplated then, but invented since.

I have also mentioned to you that I think I am fairly entitled to an extra charge for having laid out a large sum in a superior method of execution adopted for improving the strength and durability of the vessel, to that originally contemplated.

I beg further to assure you that my price for the Ship was founded on a comparison made between the cost of that Ship from an analogy with ships previously built, which did not require that I should rest so much on any assumed weights of the parts, as on a comparison of the general dimensions and tonnage of the ships themselves.

The framing for the screw engines and the spare rudder and the iron decks at stem and stern, are also points which I must regard as extra works.

In regard to current payments—If the £10,000 per month is in cash, I am content. If however it is to be subject to deduction of £2000 for shares it will not cover the current expenditure necessary for advancing the works at the rate you and the Directors expect—but will require to be £12,000 subject to a deduction of £2000 for share payments.

I think also that Martins look for the payment in October of the full amount—and that it is in conformity with the arrangement with them. You will remember that the last payment made to them was really the 25th of August payment which had stood over till late in the following month for the convenience of the Directors. If you look into it you will find this so.

In regard to the work still to be done, I can only say, that with the exception of the arch and tunnel casings all the plates have been ordered and delivered—therefore however we may differ in opinion on the quantity of work already executed there can be little difference on the amount remaining to be brought into the Yard—and if I am right in the matter of extras there is already more iron in the Ship, and the Yard, as extras than is required to complete the Ship as originally agreed for.

To satisfy you that the remaining iron for the Ship is already in the Yard your assistant need only look at the figured model and drawings and refer to the list of specifications when he will see that the plates were ordered, and to the corresponding numbers on the invoices, to see that they have been delivered.

Brunel lashed out in reply:

How the devil can you say you satisfied yourself of the weight of the ship when the figures your clerk gave you are 1000T less than I make it or than you made it a few months ago—*for shame*—if you are satisfied I am sorry to give you trouble but I think you will thank me for it—I wish you *were* my obedient servant, I should begin by a little flogging...[61]

Another memorandum, dated October 5, accompanied this letter, requiring Russell's immediate attention to matters involving the funnels, screw, screw shaft, screw bearing, paddle wheels, paddle box, and again, 'Plans for launching must be determined upon; they are deferred too long.'

Russell betrayed no hint of resenting Brunel's swashbuckling harassment. At no time did he dispense with the natural courtesy that distinguished him. His restraint probably irritated Brunel. 'I have examined your memorandum of immediate wants and shall work hard to supply them before your return',[62] Russell wrote. One may suspect, of course, that Russell's restraint was not dissociated from his apprehensions of his banker's (Martins') demand for the immediate payment of £12,000 out of a total of £15,000 said to be due. He had warned Brunel of this, as we have seen, and now (October 12) he requested Brunel to authorize the payment of the requisite sum.

Next day, October 13, Russell wrote: 'If you have any further instructions either about Screw, Paddle Box or Paddle Wheel, you will oblige me much by letting me have them if possible on Thursday next when I shall have returned from Antwerp.'[63] A new design for the paddle box was being completed and the screw height changed which would mean changes in the design of the stern post and delay in proceeding with the tedious stern fabrication to which Russell previously referred.

With some reluctance Brunel authorized a payment of £10,000; but he was not going to release more, unless Russell satisfied him on the launching preparations. He was much more concerned about these than he was about the completion of the ship. Does this suggest that progress on the ship was still consistent with a March launch? A few days after meeting with Russell, he laid it on the line:

> I must beg of you to look back to the several letters I have written to you for weeks past and the memoranda of requirements sent from time to time— and supply the deficiencies, and particularly as regards the launching you must not assume that the short conversation we had the other day on the ground has advanced the thing much—the principle of sliding the ship down on two systems of ways placed at proper points is that which I have wished and I suppose it may be considered as settled, but you must submit to me for my approval the plans of construction of these ways and the mode of sliding the ship down, and the time is arrived at which the work of the former should have been commenced, at all events I cannot of course include the cost of these works in my estimate of work done until it is done, and I must caution you that the future periodical payments must be regulated by this as well as other considerations—you know my views—let the plans be prepared immediately and something done before you apply for your next payment.
>
> It will be absolutely necessary before I can approve of the point at which you propose the aftermost ways that I should know the weights and the distance of the centre of gravity of all the after part that would over hang.

My impression is that it would bring too great a strain on the upper works as at present building and that we should want some additional iron in the top sides and I am disposed to think this desirable independent of the question of launching but I want the weights to enable me to judge.[64]

The work continued despite Brunel's irritability; but it was not the only contract on which Russell was engaged in 1855. This year saw the launch of the small screw steamer, *Kiev*, and a new, larger, Antwerp-bound *Baron Osy* as well as the ill-fated floating battery, *Etna*. The keels of two fast cross-Channel steamships, the *Orleans* and the *Lyons*, of 279 tons, were laid some time in the Autumn, and in July Russell was one of the many private shipbuilders called upon by the Admiralty to help meet the requirements for what were variously called gunboats, despatch vessels and sloops, occasioned by the war. He was given a contract for two wooden 'gun vessels 1st. class', named the *Nimrod* and *Roebuck*, each costing £17,871; then, in October, for a 100-ton iron mortar float costing about £3500, and, in November, for another two paddle gunboats, the *Bann* and the *Brune*, this time of iron. Since the principal ironworks were operating at full capacity, certain engine works and foundries, including Russell's, were invited in June by the Admiralty to tender for the immediate supply of cast iron mortars of 10 to 13 in. bore.[65] Whether Russell tendered or not is unknown, but the matter no doubt provided the stimulus for the experiments on a mortar shell with spiralled ridges which he now conducted in a field adjacent to his yard.[66] Privately he was submitting designs and ideas for a fleet of iron warships and, in addition, was supervising the secret trials of his submarine. It may have been in connection with these that he had occasion to call on the Prince at Windsor Castle on November 20.[67] A letter of this date prepared by Brunel for Russell, is headed—'Letter not sent in consequence of matters arising which I believe to be occupying anxiously Russell's attention and not wishing to add to his troubles';[68] but he did not long restrain himself. On November 30, he sent a long *Memoranda as to Launching* to Russell repeating much that had already been said about the launching procedure and specifying various measures and precautions and dimensions. He was still very anxious about the close tolerances presented by the draught of the ship and the depth of water available on various tides. Every shipbuilder who had a ship to launch was concerned about these matters and about the trim and stability of the ship when it was deposited in the water; they were not novel concerns, they were fundamental to the art of the naval architect and Russell understood the principles as they applied to engined steamships better than most, as may be gathered from his great book, *The Modern System of Naval Architecture*. But Brunel bludgeoned Russell to provide the data on which he, Brunel, could make his own calculations and set Jacomb to struggle with separate estimates of the same data as a check. 'I peremptorily require the plan of the cradle and of the ways being settled forthwith,' he pounded. 'I have made up my mind as to how they may be made but . . . . as the pecuniary responsibility rests with you [i.e. Russell] I should wish to give your plan the preference if I can.'[69]

It possibly agitated Brunel that he should be opposed by Russell and Bull on the plans for the launch, and one wonders if his experience with the *Great Britain* had left a legacy of mortification which made him especially sensitive to the spectre of failure or mishap in this matter. It was a strange premonition which impelled him. Before Russell could reply to the memorandum—within two days in fact—Brunel wrote again:

> I must beg of you to let me have with the least possible delay the correct position of the centre of flotation at the 15 ft draft-line and let this calculation be made and tested with the greatest care that no possibility of mistake can arise. I cannot stand any longer the anxiety I have felt ever since we have commenced the ship—as to our launching and having calculated myself her weight and centre of gravity at the time of launching I must have her centre of flotation—and this your people can do better than mine—but let me know that they are doing it *afresh* we must not put our faith upon calculations made a year ago by one who is now absent—and possibly made on data no longer strictly correct.[70]

Russell now responded immediately with deliberation 'I have directed an original calculation of the centre of flotation to be made as you desire immediately. I went thoroughly into the question of launching with Hepworth [his shipyard manager]. When you come down I will show you exactly how the matter stands.'[71] On the 19th December he forwarded the drawings of the cradle and ways, which seems at last to have eased Brunel's anxieties.

Although Russell had not previously built really large iron ships, the construction of the *Great Eastern* was remarkably well organized and far better generalled than the military operations of the time in the Crimea. A remarkable degree of standardization was pursued. The plate sizes were the largest which could economically be rolled at the time, 10 ft × 2 ft 9 in, made principally in two thicknesses—1 in for the shell and $\frac{1}{2}$ in. for the deck and webs. About 30,000 of these plates had to be shaped, located and riveted to place. All rivets were $\frac{7}{8}$ in diameter and uniformly pitched at 3 in. The miles of angle bar were mainly of one size—4 in $\times$ 4 in $\times$ $\frac{5}{8}$ in. It was estimated that there were 3 million rivets in the completed ship. All this was erected with primitive tackle. Hundreds of workmen, in the manner of mountaineers, hauled up their supplies and hoped to avoid falling debris and flying red-hot rivets, rivets which were held and hammered manually. There were no overhead cranes. Russell proposed a travelling crane capable of dealing with 60 ton lifts, but Brunel rejected it. The hull plating was greatly expedited by fixing each alternate row ('strake') with little or no cutting, then tailoring only the strakes overlapping these. This was an innovation called 'in-and-out strakes' which was widely adopted thereafter.[72] Myriad assembly problems and pipe arrangements on an unprecedented scale were handled quietly and efficiently. It was a splendid achievement, and time revealed the excellence of the workmanship.

The subject of payments was vexatious. Russell pressed, as we have seen, for specific amounts at specific intervals. 'I must either have payments with certainty or reduce my number of hands' he wrote to Brunel in October. But Brunel had adopted a formula which took account not only of the weight of iron erected but of the rate at which it was erected. He also took account of the iron delivered. The precise system has nowhere been recorded. In addition, Brunel reserved full discretionary powers to withhold payment for unsatisfactory attention to his demands however capricious.

Towards the end of 1855 Russell submitted the following statement to Brunel:

I do not see the return of work you recommend payment for, at all in the light you do.

I am satisfied that I should have at least £5000—on the Ship, to represent truly, her rate of progress.

The iron was I find exactly returned, none of it having been included in former returns.

My estimate is as follows

Ship	£5000–0
Paddle Wheels	1200–0
Screw and Short Shafts	1300–0
Engine	1500–0
	£9000–0

I think these are fair sums—the shafting mentioned in the return, is only the piece immediately carrying the screw itself, which I always understood was to go with the screw, and which I was told by Blake was not in his contract.

I shall be happy to attend a joint meeting if you will appoint one, with him, to settle anything on that point which you may consider not settled.

I fear the small amount and delay of this payment may do harm, which its correction in the next may not compensate.[73]

The surviving records do not enable us to determine to what extent, if at all, Brunel accepted this statement. All we have is Brunel's report to the Directors dated January 15, 1856, in which he writes:

The quantity of Work done, from December 18 to January 15, is only about 200 Tons erected. This at the full Schedule price would be 200 @ £6 = £1200 but the required rate has not been attained by about $\frac{1}{8}$th.

As there have not been above 350 instead of 400 Tons erected between November 20 and January 1 this would consequently reduce the payment according to the last proposed arrangements to £1050 and no other payment becomes due in respect of iron delivered. Indeed the result of the Stock taking shows not only that no iron has been delivered beyond the quantity previously allowed for, but that there is a considerable deficiency.

It is difficult to unravel this. 200 tons are erected between December 18 and January 15, which should earn £1200; but because the rate of erection between November 20 and January 1 was 350 tons instead of a target 400 tons, the £1200 is reduced in this proportion to £1050.

The closing sentence refers to the fact that Brunel's assistants, busy checking and estimating iron bought and erected, found that an inventory of iron in the yard left 2400 tons to be accounted for. He wrote to Russell (January 9) in great alarm and with commendable consideration:

If my fears should prove too well founded let me entreat of you as a sincere friend to meet the thing openly and to trace up the explanation and give it plainly.

Do not lose an hour in ascertaining the facts as to the quantity of iron on the ground ... Have your storekeepers made some great error? Have your people used up materials for the purpose? Whatever it is ascertain the cause at once—a day must suffice—and be prepared to lay the case frankly and plainly before the Directors—to its full extent and do not let the first intimation of the facts come through me ... believe me that my fears arise entirely from deep anxiety for you and sincere concern for your welfare.[74]

To this, Russell replied:

I have desired Hepworth to go deliberately into the inventory of plates so as to get an exact amount. Mr Jacomb can see the iron of the paddle wheels, in Mr Dickson's charge.

I have myself gone over the plates of the Big Ship and I have satisfied myself that the entire outer skin of the Ship as well as the iron deck, are in the yard.

To this I find no exception but one or two awkward plates at the ends, of which the exact shape had not been determined. I think it will be satisfactory to you to know this.

If there be an error in the estimate of plates delivered I do not think it can exist in those returns which we have made, but must be in the estimate of what was on the ground prior to our having commenced the separate returns.

Of course you are aware that the arches, tunnels and internal work remain to be ordered.[75]

It transpired after a day or two of flurry that the alleged discrepancy was not 2500 tons after all, but 800 tons. Nevertheless, this was enough for Brunel to elaborate upon, a week later, in his January 15 report to the directors:

The return made to me monthly by Mr Russell's Storekeeper gave a total of 6305 tons delivered up to December 14th. I never had any reason to doubt the correctness of these returns and I do not now believe that any mistake has been intentionally made or even intentionally overlooked ... I have had monthly returns delivered by the Storekeeper and have been assured ... that none of the iron so imported was ever knowingly used for other purposes ... and I do not see how it could have been so applied accidentally to any but a trifling extent, nevertheless a large deficiency appears to exist, the quantity fixed in the Ship at this moment may be assumed to be 4000 tons which will be found correct within 20 or 30 tons there should be therefore in the yard some 2300 tons ...

Mr Russell's Foreman and Storekeeper returns only about 1100 but I believe they have not included a quantity which is prepared ready for fixing ... I make the quantity in the yard about 1400 tons but this would still leave 800 or 900 tons to be accounted for and I am totally at a loss to suggest even a probable explanation but the result is confirmed by an analysis made by Mr Jacomb of the stock on hand ... I do not impute any intentional misrepresentations and more than that I do not believe there has been any but ... I have great cause to complain of neglect or to say the least of it of [in] attention to my orders and remonstrances. My instructions even when repeated frequently and formally in writing are too much disregarded.

I represented to Mr Russell, some ten days ago that he ought not to have

101

made preparations for building two small vessels in the Company's yard without the Directors' sanction.

I wrote last week more formally and positively notwithstanding this four more were commenced and proceeded with rapidity, a vessel which was laid down and commenced without permission directly in the line of our Ship and preventing the erection of the stem is entirely standing still and will prevent our proceeding with that part probably for 6 weeks or 2 months, Mr Russell I regret to say no longer appears to attend either to my friendly representations and entreaties or to my own formal demands and my duty to the Company compels me to state that I see no means of my obtaining proper attention to the terms of the Contract otherwise than by refusing to recommend the advance of any more money unless and until those terms are complied with—by the delivery of the materials required and by attention to my instructions and orders at the same time, then, I feel that such a course would embarrass Mr Russell and probably cause greater injury to the Company's interests.

If Brunel could see no way in which the 'missing' iron could have been misappropriated, then it was either in the ship, or in the yard, or his observations and calculations were wrong. It may be significant that the deliberations for the continuance of work on the Great Ship were based upon the erection of 1100 tons of iron—the amount estimated by Russell to be lying in the yard. What Brunel refers to as 'the Company's Yard' was, presumably, that portion of Napier's yard of which Russell had 'obtained possession' in order to accommodate the Great Ship (see p. 74). Our evidence is that it was leased to Russell,[76] in which case he had a right to use it, as indeed Yates confirmed.[77] As for the ships which Russell laid down in the Napier yard with such expedition, these were probably the first of the twelve iron mortar floats for which he was awarded a contract on December 28. The *Nimrod* and *Roebuck* must have been nearing completion, for they were contracted to be launched in the first week of February. Berths were probably also being prepared for the iron gunboats *Bann* and *Brune* if a start had not already been made on them. This accounts for the total of seventeen vessels reported ordered by the Admiralty from Russell in 1855.[78] The two Channel steamers, *Lyons* and *Orleans*, were also on the stocks and a screw steam yacht, the *Undine*, for the Duke of Sutherland, was on the drawing board.

Russell had every need to press on with these contracts, especially the naval contracts which carried bonuses of 30s per ton if completion dates were met. The purpose of the bonus, it was declared, was to offset the 'unexpected increase in the wages the shipbuilders were compelled to pay the shipwrights and other workmen'. In spite of the bonuses, however, the Admiralty later reported that 'some of the builders still lost large sums of money by their contracts'.[79] The considerable establishment of Mare & Co, went bankrupt, the failure being specifically attributed to an unrealistic bid for a number of the same iron gunboats and mortar floats of which Russell had a share.[80] Likewise the favourite navy firm of W. & H. Pitcher failed in the following year, 1857, even after building as many as 54 of these gunboats.[81] The inflation of costs and wages brought devastating consequences when the war ended early in 1856. With poor prospects in view, unprofitable current contracts and reduced credit, most of the Thames shipbuilders either failed or closed down.[82]

Burdened by the excessive commitment of the Great Ship, Russell could have been in little better case than his fellow shipbuilders. When one reads the Admiralty inspector's report of excessive rain and snow in the winter of 1855–6, it seems all the more remarkable that no reference is made to this as a serious impediment to progress. Russell explained his position to the Board of the E.S.N. Co. on January 15, 1856, the day prior to the submission of Brunel's complaining report quoted above, and tried to persuade them to take a more generous position in the matter of 'extras', reiterating his objections to Brunel's insistence on 7000 tons as the weight of iron to be erected before 'extras' could be allowed or full payment made. Russell argued that the ironwork of the hull, completed as contracted, would not exceed 6400 tons, and that 'extras' comprised those changes and refinements which occasioned costs in time and labour beyond those which formed the basis of the contractor's estimate. There had been many such extras and some had occasioned much expense. Brunel opposed this view, most emphatically, and insisted that Russell, as recently as March 1855, had not objected to the acceptance of 7000 tons as the contractual weight of ironwork in the hull on launching.[83]

Russell also averred that the mode of launching now proposed would be much more costly than he had contemplated. He now favoured, as we have noted, a free launch; but while Brunel had made some pretence at keeping an open mind on the issue, he had in fact not wavered from his insistence on a controlled launch. Now he admitted to having actually ridiculed the suggestion of a free launch every time Russell raised the subject[84] (Bull continued to urge a 'free' launch and even offered to come and give his assistance[85]). He rightly declared that a controlled launch had been considered likely from the start. This was perhaps the most vexatious of the invidious predicaments in which Russell found himself as contractor, having to accept the risks and costs of ideas and procedures for which he was not responsible and with which he was not in agreement.

The balance remaining to Russell's account under his contracts was about £40,000. In the previous August he had predicted a further £30,000 as necessary to complete the ship. He believed he had a legitimate claim for extras which, if the Company had been so pleased, would have helped to meet this additional cost. The sum of £20,000 was retained in his name by the Company, in the form of 2000 shares, half paid up, and he had an unspecified number of shares in his possession, received in part payment. These shares had little market value. The money funnelled off from Russell to meet the calls on his shares was therefore so much money down the drain until the ship could command financial confidence. We gather from a comment by Yates to Brunel that shortly after the half-yearly meeting in the previous September (1855) Russell had told the directors that unless he were paid £15,000 per month without deductions for calls on his shares, he could not go on with the works.[86] We have noted that the figure £12,000 was certainly mentioned in this connection. It was to this that the directors now alluded when they stated in their report that 'Russell's views as to payments to which he was or would from time to time be entitled' had not been 'consistent with the interests and rights of the company.'[87]

These circumstances would force Russell to concentrate all the more on his bread-and-butter contracts, a necessity with which Brunel evidently had little sympathy, despite his being well aware of it. As early as November he warned the Directors that Russell might become 'embarrassed in his proceedings',[88] and by January was predicting Russell's bankruptcy which he had the temerity to describe as 'not a creditable one'.[89] He feared, he wrote, that it would be to the ruin of Russell's character. It is difficult to understand how this could be said of a man who was so clearly a casualty of well-intentioned folly—the folly of embarking on an uncertain undertaking so completely at the mercy of Brunel's whims and egotisms and with means largely dependent on the survival of one individual who then died. Nor do we know how Brunel came by his knowledge of Russell's financial affairs. He regretted that Russell had no friend about him to give *strong advice*, the advice that he, Brunel, would have given if he were not so sure that Russell would not listen to him. This advice, as we gather from Brunel's comments to Yates, would have been nothing more generous than to go into liquidation under inspectorship while the several works on hand were carried on, with no new works or liability incurred, leaving Russell to concentrate on his engineering business. In this way, thought Brunel, Russell's works might be left in a state to survive. Russell, he said, had 'misled him more than anybody',[90] an ambiguous remark. How far, may we ask, was Russell misled by Brunel? The fact of the matter is that the financial circumstances of the time and of the Great Ship had defeated Russell and only the E.S.N. Co. or his bankers could keep him in business. One word from Brunel may have sufficed.

Russell engaged Freshfield and Coleman, the E.S.N. Co.'s solicitor and accountant respectively, to examine his affairs, and Brunel calculated that the Company as its own contractor could complete the ship for a further £75,000. In a letter to Brunel dated January 24, 1856, Freshfield alluded to a new agreement: 'Mr Scott Russell has been here and he seems disposed to sign the agreement, as modified. I fear you will find difficulty as to the variation in the weight of the iron—the modifications as to launching can, I think, consistently with the views expressed by you be made to work. It has been arranged to provide Funds for another week and Mr Yates is to accompany Mr S. Russell to the works to put things in better train...'[91]

Brunel applied his own insinuating pressure—or was it simply an expression of solicitation?—'I am anxious as ever,' he wrote Russell, 'to save you from disasters [bankruptcy?] which I think I see though apparently you do not.'[92] At the same time he requested Freshfield to prepare a certificate stating that Russell was no longer in a position to proceed with his contract. He saw no hope of achieving an arrangement by which Russell could continue. It was important that if Russell went bankrupt the Great Ship and the ground on which it stood should be secured against his creditors. It was necessary, therefore, to place Russell in breach of contract. The requisite yard space and premises had to be leased, but part of this could only be executed by the mortgagees, Messrs Martins, who we can be sure, were keeping a close eye on the situation—on the affairs of the E.S.N. Co. no less than on Russell's. Martins now moved to settle the issue by refusing to honour Russell's cheques, leaving Russell with no alternative but to liquidate under inspectorship much as Brunel had suggested. On February 4, the Scott Russell Shipbuilding and Engineering Company announced suspension of payment. Next day, the E.S.N. Co. took over the ship[93] and, at the end of the week, Russell discharged his employees, including—to Yates' annoyance—those engaged on the Great Ship.

CHAPTER FIVE

The Leviathan Languishes

*So long as she is on dry land, a ship is no ship, and it is the finishing
stroke of the shipbuilder to place her safely in the water. To this part
of his skill belong all the traditions of launching. In this the traditional
shipbuilder is truly great for science has taught him nothing.*

J. SCOTT RUSSELL

The situation was tense, Brunel was suspect, and both he and the Board
of Directors were at pains to justify their position before the shareholders,
with the allegation that Russell had asked for more than he was entitled
to. Brunel made light of the situation, referring to plans which had been
maturing to make 'at least a few profitable trials or preliminary voyages
to America', and his discretion was commended by Yates who wrote:
'I agree with you to the fullest extent, that we are surrounded with subjects which require to be delicately handled... to give little pretence for
countenancing the many unfounded Reports in circulation, and I think
your Report of itself sets all such at rest.'[1]

The Directors' Report informed the Shareholders that shortly after
the September meeting they had remonstrated with Russell on the slow
rate of progress, and that 'under the advice of Mr Brunel, a modification
was proposed in terms, based on the principle of strict inspection of the
work performed and of payments made accordingly'. They explained also
that they had underwritten Russell's final payroll on account and had
tried to avoid taking the work out of his hands; but that on February
5, 'under the advice of Mr Brunel', they had taken completion of the
ship 'under the provisions in the contract enabling them to do so'. They
also were at pains to point out that the Company held in trust 2000 shares
deposited by Russell as security for the 'due performance of the contract'.[2]

Yates explained to Brunel that the wording of the report had been
so contrived that it avoided raising any question upon Russell's Contracts
or implying that Brunel had in any way accelerated Russell's fall.[3]

The following statement of Scott Russell's affairs was published in
February 13, 1856:

Liabilities

To creditors on open balances and acceptances		113,940.	19.	10
To creditors holding security	15,000			
To estimated value of security held	6,000	9,000.	0.	0
		122,940.	19.	10

Assets

By cash balance	159.	3.	6
By book debts considered good	12,000.	0.	0
By assets consisting of materials, engines &c at works	38,802.	8.	6
Ditto Mr Russell's interest in various ships	40,000.	0.	4
Ditto contracts for vessels and machinery now constructing	9,392.	0.	0
	100,353.	12.	4
By debts under £10	118.	0.	5
	100,235.	11.	11

By shares in Gt. E.S.N. Co. upon which cheques
have been paid amounting to £22,410.

The E.S.N. Co. reserved their right of any claim which they might establish on the estate for breach of contract in case a satisfactory arrangement could not be carried out with them.

The Company's solicitor, J. Freshfield acting for the liquidators and for Russell, alluded to the destruction of a considerable amount of property as well as the delays incurred by the fire of 1853.

> The capital being principally borrowed and the premises heavily mortgaged, the Government contracts and other works, although profitable, required extended means: but, owing to the altered state of the money market, it was impossible to provide sufficient to meet current engagements, and, under these circumstances, Mr Russell thought it prudent to suspend, and place his affairs in the hands of his creditors. It was believed that if an arrangement could be made for carrying on the Government contracts and some of the other works the mortgagees would allow the use of the premises: and the creditors, by adopting the mode of liquidation under inspection, could thus avail themselves of advantages which would probably lead to an increased dividend, and prevent the sacrifice which otherwise must ensue... the assets showed about 15s in the pound, 10s of which it was believed might be realized about June, leaving the balance open to negotiation...

J. E. Coleman, accountant to the E.S.N. Co. and to the liquidators, opined that the Government contracts and some of the other works in hand could steadily be proceeded with and, in answer to questions, said that it was not proposed to continue the construction of the Great Ship, the contract passing to the management of the directors. Up to that time, he declared, no loss had been sustained in connection with that ship; 'but if the work were continued, it would, no doubt, exhibit an unfavourable result'.[4]

A set of resolutions were passed: 'The affairs of the house' were to be liquidated under the inspectorship of Samuel Beale, Thomas D. Grissell and John Jones, who were to employ all the funds, stock and assets, of the estate as necessary to complete pending contracts and works in hand and to make arrangements with the mortgagees for the use of premises and plant. A deed of inspectorship was to be entered into with each creditor and such deed would 'contain covenants by Mr Russell to devote his whole time and attention under the direction of the inspectors, for so long as shall be necessary to complete the works and contracts in hand, to liquidate the affairs of the house according to the rules of administration adopted in bankruptcy, as if bankruptcy had taken place this day . . .' Russell would be released upon the inspectors certifying that the liquidation had proceeded sufficiently and upon Russell's assigning any remaining assets for distribution among the creditors. The inspectors were also empowered to 'make Mr Russell such allowance as they think fit for his services'.

Some of the creditors recommended that the entire management should be left to Mr Russell but Mr Freshfield said that, however encouraging such a compliment might appear, it would be necessary for the general interests of the creditors to follow out the scheme as presented.[5]

Russell's financial statement does not show him bankrupt, but the prognosis was not good and Martins were of no mind to be patient. They could well have had their eye on bigger game, however. They would note how the current recession had been embarrassing many of the shareholders of the E.S.N. Co. and how the arrears on calls had reached the large total of about £149,300. They would also have heard some of the grumblings provoked by the additional calls occasioned by these arrears. We can be sure that many shareholders would now have been happy to rid themselves of the obligations of their shares, but they could not easily sell them, for there were no takers. For the same reason, the Company deemed it unwise to proceed to a general forfeiture of shares, preferring to exert whatever pressure they could on those individuals who were in a position to discharge their liabilities.[6] It could easily have appeared to Martins that not merely Russell, but the E.S.N. Co. would soon get into difficulties. If they had an eye on the Company's assets they were in a position perhaps to acquire them. This certainly offers one explanation of the squeeze exerted on Russell and of the difficulties the Company now experienced in its dealings with Martins for the lease of yard space and premises.[7] On the afternoon of March 12 another fire broke out at the yard, this time in the sawmill. The damage amounted to £3000, partially covered by insurance, and was not expected to delay the work in progress.[8]

It was arranged that Yates would 'personally take charge of the establishment, and the execution of all the works to be carried out at Millwall, assisted by Mr Russell in all the higher branches of the business'.[9]

The Admiralty contracts (4 gunboats and 12 mortar floats) were protected by provisions which gave the Admiralty the right to commandeer their unfinished ships, machinery and associated materials; but they left Russell to complete his contracts with them, with the exception of the *Roebuck* and *Nimrod*, launched on March 31 and April 21, respectively, which, possibly because they were of wood, were completed by men from the Naval dockyard at Deptford. They also, curiously enough, granted Russell a bonus for these two vessels.[10] As for the Great Ship, Russell was directed by the liquidators, and Brunel by the Company, to discuss prices for the completion of the hull. The Company did not wish to discuss the engines until agreement could be reached on the hull.[11]

Russell's estimate was submitted in two parts; one part dealing with the completion of the plating came to a total of £9775 which was about three times what Brunel thought it should be. He thought he should be given a detailed breakdown of this estimate, and Russell accordingly arranged for himself and Brunel to meet with Hepworth who was responsible for it. Hepworth informed them that he had kept no record whatsoever of his calculations and only very reluctantly agreed to justify them in greater detail. But the revised statement he sent to Russell was, as Russell feared, still unlikely to satisfy Brunel. Hepworth appears to have told Russell in no uncertain terms that he was not going to be pushed around and that they could take it or leave it. 'I think it is all we shall get from Mr Hepworth', wrote Russell when he forwarded the new submission to Brunel on March 27, and added that if Brunel wanted more or other than this, he, Russell, would go down to Millwall and do it himself, for which purpose he would call on Brunel to know precisely his further wishes.[12] The upshot was a further letter from Russell in which he made the pregnant remark: 'I find that it will be better for all of us not to force upon Hepworth this work, in a manner contrary to his own way of setting about it.' He offered his own estimate, based upon the erection of 1100 tons of plating at £6·5 per ton and 225 tons of other items at £10·5, total— £9512·5. He offered also, on behalf of the Estate, to accept arbitration where Brunel disagreed with the tenders.[13]

It was customary—even for Brunel as we have seen—to base the estimate for fabricating and erecting the ironwork at a fixed amount per ton. He had allowed Russell £6 per ton, Russell was now asking £6·5 per ton. There was no dispute that there were at least 1100 tons of iron 'on the ground', so it is very difficult with the information available to understand Brunel's estimate of £3000 when, according to his former rate it should have been at least £6600. Taking into account the inflationary effects of the recent war, Hepworth's estimate was probably not far out. Yates was for accepting it, but Brunel's back was up—he would not throw away money—and he brushed off Yates with the comment that he had no competence in the matter.[14] In the event even Hepworth's estimate was to be well exceeded. Russell, nevertheless, was anxious to continue his association with the Great Ship, and in another letter (March 31) he assured Brunel that whatever the outcome of the current bargaining, he was ready to serve:

My dear Sir,

I feel that until our constituents, on your side & mine, have come to terms on money questions, it may be necessary for both of us to advocate views which are not identical.

I have been desired to prepare a written proposition to be made to your board; stating officially the terms on which they are ready to undertake the work, as I understand, for next Wednesday.

If therefore you think that I do not now meet your views so readily as you may expect, please to attribute it to the awkwardness of the position.

When money matters are settled I shall no longer have to act in a double relation; & shall be prepared to carry out the mechanical part of the undertaking with undivided zeal and energy.

Yours faithfully

J. Scott Russell[15]

Brunel did not seek arbitration but simply reported that the negotiations had failed, and advised the Company not to continue by tender from Russell's liquidators but to retain the services of Dickson and Hepworth and proceed on their own. Yates, along with the chief inspector and the accountant, met with Russell and reported to Brunel:

5 April, 1856.

My Dear Sir,

    I went with Beale and Coleman to Millwall yesterday where we met Mr Russell, who appeared taken aback at the discussing for the first time of his real position, what have been his expectations I know not, but it is lamentable to see him now, before the Inspectors he professes himself willing to do all in his power to forward our views, but without any breach of charity I doubt his sincerity, we can retain Dixon and Hepworth from whom we may get all the assistance required for the next *3 Mo.*, after which they will be entirely at our service.

    Mr C. Freshfield will be ready to go into and arrange the heads of agreement on Monday Mg...

I am my Dear Sir
Yours faithfully,
Jn. Yates[16]

    This letter is puzzling. Russell was employed by the Inspectors—who, after all, represented his creditors. Yet here we have Yates reporting that, in the presence of these Inspectors, Russell professed himself willing to do all in his power to forward the interests of the E.S.N. Co., and that he, Yates, was sceptical of Russell's sincerity in this. It is difficult to understand why Russell should be expected to forward interests which were in opposition to those of the Inspectors for whom he acted. As for Russell's 'real' position, was it not simply that his services to the Great Ship were now dispensable? The Company had entered negotiations to retain Dixon and Hepworth, his key managers. Is it surprising that Dixon and Hepworth placed a high price on their services? This manoeuvre simply made it necessary for the Company to make its own terms with Martins for the use of whatever space, facilities and equipment were required and engage its own workmen. Russell's function could be performed by Brunel, but the demands were onerous and Brunel evidently saw some advantage in engaging Russell to ease this burden, as we may gather from a letter from Russell to Brunel three weeks later:

    Referring to our conversation on Saturday, I beg to state that I continue to feel a deep interest in the completion of the Great Ship and that if the

111

Eastern Steam Navigation Company were to propose to me to undertake the superintendence of the work of finishing the Great Ship, and her machinery for them at Millwall, I should be disposed to entertain it and that if the conditions were satisfactory I should be willing to devote my best energies to the work.

It is right however to mention that I must in any case continue for the next three months, to see that my present contracts at Millwall are properly completed, a duty which being on the same ground would not interfere with the other. I shall also be obliged some time during this year in order to counteract the ill effects produced upon my health by the anxiety and vexation I have suffered, to take one Months entire relaxation from business, but that need not be done until the work is fully organised, and the drawings and plans for carrying it on completed.

I take for granted that the completion of the Ship and Engines, is to proceed expeditiously and is not likely to extend beyond twelve months.[17]

Brunel replied immediately, offering Russell a form of assistantship on his personal staff. After some consideration, Russell answered that he conceived it to be his duty 'if the Board of the Eastern Steam Navigation Company should wish it, to afford to the completion of the Great Ship any assistance which they might see to be useful to that undertaking and which it may be in [his] power to render as a practical shipbuilder and maker of marine engines, and as having hitherto so far conducted the work in that capacity'. In this, he added, he would, of course, act entirely under the Company's and Brunel's orders and instructions. But he felt 'insurmountable objection' to leaving his 'business as Shipbuilder and Engine Maker' to accept 'simply' the position of Brunel's 'personal assistant'; he thought this 'not likely to be satisfactory to either party'.[18]

In the end, Russell was accepted by the Company in his role of 'Shipbuilder and Engine Maker' to superintend the completion of the hull and paddle engines of the ship. Arrangements for the use of the equipment and premises were completed with Martins at a price, after much bargaining, and the work was resumed on the Great Ship on May 23. Yates managed the business and made arrangements 'for keeping up a continuous propition' as he expressed it.

In the pamphlet on the *Great Eastern* published in 1858 it was stated that 'When the ship passed into the hands of the Company they found three-quarters of the work remained to be done before it was ready for launching'.[19] This statement must be evaluated in the light of the fact that Brunel accepted 4000 tons as the weight of the ironwork assembled, more than half of the estimated total. It was not Brunel's way in any case to be so far out of touch that he would not know that three-quarters of the work had still to be completed in December 1855 while he was getting excited about launching preparations.

Meantime work on Russell's contracts had recommenced. His personal estate and earnings were not involved in the liquidation. Thus we should not be surprised, except at his generosity, when we find him in the midst of his troubles in April 1856, serving as honorary secretary to a testimonial fund for Smith, the pioneer of the screw propeller, who had hit hard times, and subscribing £100 in common with some other shipbuilders, while Brunel subscribed £50.[20]

Russell supervised the resumption of work on the Great Ship in May and his correspondence with Brunel implies good and co-operative progress. In mid July, he informed Brunel that the model and drawings of alterations to the stern framing had actually been 'some time waiting' for his 'sanction to proceed with the work'.[21] But Brunel was taken ill and requested that the drawings and a report on the work be sent to him.[22] Russell obliged, also listing some oustanding items held up pending Brunel's decisions and reporting rapid progress on the hull, the engines, paddles and screw.[23] Receipt of this prompted Brunel to struggle down to the yard to 'look over the subject', whereupon he was disturbed to find much other work proceeding which, however necessary, had not been given his expressed sanction as he required. He was perturbed, too, to find that the foremen were being allowed to tackle many jobs in their own way—as was normal shipbuilding practice then and for many a long day afterwards. This he considered 'disorganized'. Not even Russell was to have power to authorise unapproved work. If in an 'emergency' such power should be necessary, it had to be reported immediately to Jacomb and Brunel and all work was to be entered in an 'order book' as it was authorized by Brunel and no other work was to be initiated. He would even stipulate which unfinished engine parts were to be 'gone on with'. As for the stern and bow drawings he had just received, they were not 'such drawings as might be given to a manufacturer and contractor to work from without further instructions'—'I must have them,' he demanded. They were such drawings, however, as foremen platers and erectors could work from with their customary discretion on the site, a discretion which they continued to use—much to Brunel's annoyance— even when the drawings or his instructions were very explicit, as in the case of some cabin deck beams which he wanted to be fixed with wood screws instead of bolts. Russell delegated much responsibility to his foremen, particularly in those 'small things' which Brunel expected also to be worked out and presented to him for approval and the list of which, he said, now quite frightened him.[24] Brunel sensed that they (Russell and Yates) were pushing ahead with the ship without as much recourse to him as he desired. He saw it as a conspiracy to deprive him of 'all proper authority'. In response to these complaints, Russell wrote to Brunel:

> ... there seems to be a discrepancy between the instructions I have received from them [i.e. the Board] and which I have endeavoured fully to execute, and the course of conduct you conceive I should have adopted.
>
> According to the instructions of the Board I was to push on the works of finishing the hull of the Ship and the engines with the greatest possible expedition. I have done so in every Department under my charge.[25]

Russell referred Brunel to a report he had just submitted to the Directors (August 28, 1856):

> It is now more than three months since I had an interview with the Board, at which they proposed that I should undertake to organize the recommencement of the Works on the Great Ship, and to superintend the completion as fast as possible of the iron hull of the Ship, and her paddle engines, in order that she might be launched early in the spring of 1857. Having agreed to undertake (as Shipbuilder and Engine builder) to superintend this work for the Company—I then mentioned that as soon as I had fully organised and set it in work, so that it could proceed without delay, it would be necessary for my health to make holiday for a month or six weeks, I now think it right to state what progress I have made in the work I have undertaken, and to mention that unless some serious reason prevent it I shall go to the Continent about the middle of next month, so that any further arrangements the Board may wish to make before I leave Town may be made. The whole of the iron hull is now in a state of rapid progress and so completely planned and organised that the workmen under the Foreman can proceed with it during my absence without further instruction.
>
> I beg to state that the whole of the engine is in rapid progress, all the parts of it are in hand and that it is going on and being completed on the original plans, so that it will be ready to go into its place in the Ship as soon as the cranes and other gear for raising it are ready, and they are rapidly going forward.
>
> On the 11th of August last I sent to your Engineer the enclosed list of drawings, which comprehended the various points he had then decided, those I think are sufficient to enable the Foreman and workmen to go on and complete the work.
>
> I beg to state that the alteration ordered by you in the height of the decks

has in conformity with your desire been rapidly carried into effect, and that the new beams and deck are going into place—

I beg to state that the arrangements of masts and rigging, and the arrangements of cabins and cabin fittings are not as I understand yet decided on, and as these are not matters in which I have received any instructions from you to act, I have done little in the matter—

I wish you to understand that I am ready to take the superintendence of that department or not, as the Directors may wish.

You requested me in re-organising the Works to endeavour to make with the Foremen arrangements of a more economical nature than they had proposed to you—I found them perfectly ready to assist me as their old Master on such terms as I should consider fair—

I accordingly settled with Mr Dickson and Mr Hepworth that so long as I remained in superintendence of the Work, they should receive from the Company at the rate of £25 per week each, to be computed from the date of recommencing the Ship, should this extend till March next it will amount to about £1000, pounds each, instead of £3000, the sum required of the Company—

I think it my duty to them to state that the rapidity, the economy, and the excellence of the work now in progress and done during the short period of three months does them great credit.[26]

Brunel now made, in his own words, 'frequent and strong vital representations' to Yates and 'strong remonstrances' to him personally about what he called the 'peculiar state of things in the works'. Yates pointed out that after September 11, control of Russell's complete works would pass to the Company along with the 'expenditure of their own moneys'. Russell's contracts had been completed with the launch of H.M.S. *Brune* on August 31. Yates was clearly reluctant to rock the boat. Brunel was maddened by this, he refused to temporise with a 'weak policy under which we have for weeks been tolerating a state of things most costly to the Company'. He deplored a 'total absence of control that fully half of the work in hand had been undertaken without proper instruction from authorized parties'. He could not approve of 'tacit acquiescence of such a disorganized system as had grown up'. He alleged intentional contravention of his orders and that Russell was rarely seen at the works to instruct or to receive instructions, refusing even to read his, Brunel's, written instructions. 'Such are the people who practically have the control in the expenditure or rather the waste of our money,' he complained. He went over Yates' head to the Chairman of the Company demanding a meeting of the Board on the matter.[27]

Yates, who was daily at the yard, could not decipher the scrawl:

Your Letter came to hand this morning and I was obliged to leave it with my son to transcribe, he has done so and brought it down to me, but it is of such an extraordinary character that I require a little time for reflection before giving an answer.

You have marked the envelope private but surely you do not intend it as such, and I cannot allow my hands to be tied by private communications of such a nature, I am therefore at present disposed to answer it as an official document.

I court the most rigid enquiry into my conduct by the Chairman and Directors, and am quite content to abide by the result.

The Chairman is in Ireland but no doubt on receiving your proposed communication he will take such steps as will ensure a Meeting of the Directors to give to your statements and mine every possible consideration.

You will hear from me again tomorrow.[28]

Russell received a similar letter and replied:

As your letter of the 15th which I have received this morning, appears to have been written under a false impression of the duties with which I was charged by the Directors, when asked to superintend for them, the shipbuilding and engine making at Millwall I have only now to express my regret that you should have written that letter.

I have endeavoured to the best of my judgement to discharge the duties entrusted to me by the Directors, with energy, fidelity, and singleness of purpose and even where I have differed with you in opinion I have endeavoured to act courteously, considerately and with deference towards you.

That these endeavours have not earned your approbation I am sorry, and must await any further instructions which my employers may choose to give me.[29]

The Committee of Works met to consider this delicate matter on September 19. They declared that in view of all the interests of the many people who had a stake in 'this World famed enterprise', they had a right to 'count on the utmost forbearance of all persons in matters partaking in any degree of a personal character'. If indeed Mr Russell had assumed to himself a 'position of action independent of Mr Brunel' it could not be founded on anything which had taken place under the authority of the Court of Directors. They hoped that the misunderstanding was one which arose rather from the practical operation of their reorganisation of the work than from the essence of their communication with Mr Rus-

116

sell. They sympathised with Mr Russell 'under the heavy trials' which he had had to encounter and hoped that his proposed vacation would conduce to his benefit and the recovery of his health.

It was then unanimously resolved

> that no portions of the works henceforth be undertaken except as shall receive the sanction of the Committee of the Works and that the responsibility and necessary authority for carrying these works into effect be confided to the Engineer in Chief, all the practical working men being subject to his authority, but leaving to Mr Yates the duties already confided to him in accordance with the suggestions contained in Mr Brunel's letters of the 23rd May last.[30]

This resolution vested Russell's functions—the responsibility of carrying the approved works into effect and authority over all the 'practical working men'—in Brunel. Russell was being 'let go'. He could not have been expected to change his mind about serving as Brunel's subordinate. Both men no doubt felt abused.

Russell went off on holiday—and business—to the Continent, taking his first steps to restore his fortunes from his office at 37 Gt George St. (the Harley Street of engineers) whence, on his return, he resorted every morning around ten. He had had a narrow escape.

In none of Brunel's undertakings was his fortune placed on the line, nor were the financial resources of his favourite servants—Gooch and Claxton. The same could not be said of Russell. Patterson, for all his admiration of Brunel and for all his many years as a shipbuilder, would not tender even for Brunel's earlier ships. He preferred to serve in the role in which Hepworth served Russell and 'on the advice of Brunel' the *Great Western* was not built under contract, 'as it would have been impossible to provide for any alterations which it might be desirable to make during the construction of a ship of such novel dimensions.'[108] What manner of man was Scott Russell, with fewer years in shipbuilding than Patterson, to accept these risks and to undertake the construction and design of such a prodigious ship as the *Great Eastern*? He would bend to the assertive authoritarianism of Brunel and patiently forbear even when he was dictated to in matters in which he had the greater competence and in a manner which must often have been an affront to his professional pride. Undoubtedly he was a man of exceptional courage, ability, patience and self control. We must also infer that he had great respect for Brunel's genius and engineering achievements. His unquestioning belief in the good intentions of those with whom he had dealings more than once exposed him to disaster. His naiveté in these matters is so much at odds with his abilities that it seems incredible, and his financial imprudence compounded by a strain of bad luck leaves us aghast. Brunel's livelihood, in contrast, was not at the mercy of his indifference to commercial constraints.

Brunel reported to his Directors that he was desirous 'under these improved circumstances of calling the attention of the Committee of Works to the arrangements which [he considered] essential to [his] being able to carry on the work efficiently and expeditiously and as economically as the peculiar circumstances of difficulty under which [they] were placed [would] admit of.'[31] So he went on. He was not referring to difficulties with the view to shrinking from them, but it was no ordinary task, he explained, for a company to 'execute work which embodies an establishment of 1000 or 1200 men consisting of engine boiler makers, carpenters, pattern makers, coppersmiths, smiths, foundry men, ship's plate workers and a crowd of labourers ... consuming a prodigious amount of stores ... an establishment greater than many of the large private engineering establishments ...' Now we are getting an insight into the magnitude of Russell's operations—the multiplicity of his responsibilities. Brunel regretted the necessity of embarking on such an undertaking. He was under the 'impression' that the Directors were uninformed of the difficulties he had had to contend with to keep some control over the conduct of the works. He was also under the 'impression' that the Directors were greatly misinformed 'as to the amount of labour ... and the extent to which every detail of the minutest description [had] devolved upon [him]'. This reads as if Brunel had not demanded encumbrance with minutiae!

Now the great and novel work was to be completed through two foremen who were not of his selection

or who felt in any way bound to him or to his interests and reputation—who had been brought up or spoiled in a school of unusual extravagance and absence of control—for they had always been in Mr Russell's time entirely their own master and the cost of everything executed in that yard had been a main cause of the enormous amount of money lost in that establishment in the course of a few years.

This report was extremely verbose, a wearisome catalogue of complaints and demands and minutiae of management. Dickson and

9 The *Great Eastern* dwarfing its surroundings at Millwall

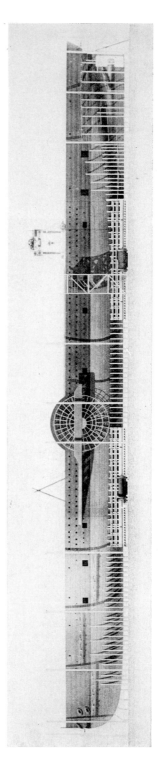

10 The *Great Eastern* from the landward side, showing her wave-line hull

11 A model of Scott Russell's paddle engines for the *Great Eastern*

12 The interior of the *Great Eastern* paddle engine rooms

Hepworth, he declared, could not be expected to study economy for the Company when they did not do it for their own master. Furthermore, he thought they were grossly overpaid—which 'could only produce a very bad moral effect upon them'. He demanded 'entire and undivided authority over these and over everybody in the yard—and above all over the ordering of work and of the materials or work required'. But cases had arisen which would 'require the decision of the Directors to make this clear'. He again referred to the undercurrent which he alleged had been at work to deprive him of all 'proper' authority, clearly considering Yates one of the conspirators. To a letter dated October 1, Yates replied: 'I neither admit your assertions nor conclusions neither will I be deterred from offering an opinion whenever I may feel it necessary or to be my duty to give one.' Were it not for the respect he entertained for the Directors, he explained, especially for the Chairman, and for their appeal for forbearance, he should probably have replied to Brunel's present and previous letters in a very different manner.

> I feel strongly that from your having failed in your attempt at a quarrel with Mr Russell you appear determined, if it be possible, to seek occasion for one with me.
> I will not, however, be provoked, neither will I swerve intentionally from the faithful discharge of my duties to the Directors, whose servant I am and to whom alone I hold myself amenable. I have always, and frequently at very great personal inconvenience, endeavoured to the utmost of my powers to meet your views and wishes, in every respect, and I assure you it is a source of painful regret to me to find that I have been so unsuccessful, and that feeling of regret is greatly aggravated by the necessity for this correspondence.[32]

The tenor of Brunel's response can be gleaned from Yates' reply of October 7:

> I have to acknowledge the receipt last evening of your letter of the 4th instant, and in reply to state that after the very extraordinary course taken by yourself at the last meeting of the Committee of Works, which was evidently the result of deliberation and pre-concert, I felt it to be my duty to express my feelings in strong terms both to the Chairman and Deputy Chairman, and upon further consideration I see no great cause for regret in having done so.
> When I undertook the arduous task of re-organising the Works at Millwall, in conjunction with yourself, I expected at least that I should have met with your support and assistance. Before entering upon those duties you yourself,

wholly unsolicited, drew up a chart for the guidance of both parties in carrying out the necessary arrangements which were approved of and adopted by the Committee of Works, confirmed by the Court of Directors and reconfirmed at the last meeting of the Court.

These propositions, Yates reminded Brunel, were that he, Yates, would manage all accounting, purchasing, stores, wages and hiring, and the execution of Brunel's orders served in writing. Brunel would see only to the quality of the work. 'To these regulations,' Yates added,

> I have faithfully adhered, by them, as manager of the Works, I am still willing to abide, but, in my capacity of Secretary, it is my bounden duty to see that no unnecessary expenditure is incurred, and although you have repeatedly put me down when venturing to advise the Directors in matters of this kind, as something beneath their notice from a 'mere Secretary', still whenever I conceive it to be my duty I shall follow the same line of policy, observing that at least, as a paid servant of the Company, my right to advise or address the Board, is perfectly equal to your own, and I trust whenever it has been my duty to advise the Board, it has been done in a becoming and respectful manner, and without assuming the form of Dictation which, you will excuse me for saying, has been too frequently the case with yourself. I have no desire to quarrel, or to be at variance with you, the interests of all parties forbid it. I desire to exercise the utmost forbearance, as I need it myself, but I will not be constantly subject to your misrepresentation, or to be trampled upon by you or any other man.

Yates wrote that he would continue to observe these provided that neither new work nor alterations involving an expenditure exceeding twenty pounds were undertaken without the directors' sanction. Also—and here Yates boldly puts his finger on a source of his and Russell's difficulties with Brunel—that the work should not be delayed in doing or undoing or 'for want of practical working plans and promptitude in decision'. He felt that if these arrangements were to be varied 'by every trifling circumstance' all further exertion on his part would be useless.

The dispute developed quickly but it moves out of our ken with Yates ready to place the whole of his correspondence with Brunel before the Directors.[33]

The relationship between Russell and Brunel held every promise of success as a partnership. Their gifts, for the most part, were complementary, as also were their temperaments. Brunel, arrogant, outspoken, direct and forceful; Russell, suave, self-controlled, courteous, intellectually and socially restless. Russell was a scientific naval architect with more than his share of inventiveness and originality, Brunel a much more widely experienced engineer with an incomparable command of its science and practice and a corresponding inventiveness and originality. It can be argued that it is his flamboyance which tends to raise his achievements above those of his greatest contemporaries; but however this may be, he was an exciting man of exceptional boldness of imagination and engineering skill. This we set against his inability to delegate work and its responsibility and to restrain his technological zeal. It is not unusual for such a mind and will as his to be unable to accept dilution of authority in a partnership, but he seems also to have been exceptionally jealous of his fame. One of his contemporaries recorded some observations which are well borne out by the evidence of these pages:

> His conscientious resolve to see with his own eyes, and to order with his own lips, every item of detail entrusted to his responsibility, brought on him an enormous amount of labour, which, on another and more easy system, would have been borne by subordinates, perhaps with equal advantage to the public. His exquisite taste, his perfect knowledge of what good work should be, and his resolve that his works should be no way short of the best, led rather to the increased cost, than to the augmented durability, of much that he designed and carried out. His boundless fertility of invention, and his refusal to be content with what was good, if he saw beyond it what was better, led often to disproportionate outlay.[34]

Russell, on the other hand, liberally delegated responsibility. Brunel would call him lax or negligent; but the *Great Eastern* might have been less of a failure if it had been completed less carefully in non-vital matters, but with expedition. Brunel ranted about uneconomical conduct of the operation: we shall look with eager expectation to what he achieved without Russell!

Brunel was not a Brassey with a talent for handling a work force of men. He could not even compete with Russell in this regard and in his need he turned to one of his disciples, Daniel Gooch, to assist him as superintendent. But Gooch may well have baulked at the invidious duty of conveying Brunel's orders to Dickson and Hepworth, who knew their jobs well and were unlikely to take kindly to being supervised in their own yard by a designer of railway engines. Brunel was certainly not blind to this difficulty,[35] and Gooch appears to have declined the duty.

Brunel turned his attention again to the launching ways and made the fateful decision to attach rows of iron plates to the underside of the cradles running parallel to the axis of the ship to provide a surface on which they would slide along rows of ordinary railway line to the waters edge. He thought by this means to avoid the binding of wood on wood. On January 19, 1857, he accepted the tender of Thomas Treadwell with whom he had done business on the Great Western Railway. Treadwell was given six months to complete the job, for it was now planned to launch the ship in August 1857.

At the General Meeting in February, 1857, it was announced that the total calls on shares amounted to £606,019 on which arrears amounted to £192,000, of which only £64,000 was considered recoverable. Included in the arrears were the calls due from Russell who still held a considerable number of shares.[36] It was announced that during the negotiations to take over the ship's completion, 'as well as on all subsequent occasions, the Directors felt it right to state that every assistance was afforded by Mr Russell and the inspectors under his estate'. Next day, however, the shareholders received a printed circular from one of the directors, Robert McCalmont, who was engineer of the N.W. Railway, asserting that the sanguine statements of the Board were made 'with the knowledge that there is no intention of attempting to complete her at present, the idea being that the ship should be got into the water in a state not approaching completion, and that the inadequacy of your means should be left unproclaimed or at least not grappled with until that time.' With £450,000 already expended, he declared, £60,000 would be needed in addition to the present share capital (estimated to be about £100,000) to complete the ship, i.e. after launching. He thought that the Directors should be restrained from spending any more money or making further calls unless the requisite sum be raised at once. He believed that expending money on the ship without the means to complete her was 'no better than throwing it into the sea'. Others, however, were sure that the funds could more easily be raised once the ship was in the water.

As the Great Ship slowly moved towards completion, more and more sightseers trooped round the yard at lunchtime each day and excursion steamers cruised to and from Westminster Bridge, loaded to the gunwales when the sun shone. Whether the creator of the giant iron hull was I. K. Brunel or the man, Scott Russell, whose name was attached to the yard, did not greatly concern this mass of people. There was no inaccuracy in Scott Russell's being alluded to as the 'builder' of the Great Ship in a leading article in *The Times*, April 18, 1857, except that Russell was now no longer supervising its completion and Brunel was not mentioned. Russell took the opportunity to clarify the matter in a letter to the editor:

Your interesting observations on the great ship now building in my yard at Millwall, in your leading article of this morning, have induced me to beg the favour of your communicating to the public some additional points of information, which I have no doubt they will find interesting.

I hope you will pardon me for saying that your mention of my name exclusively in connexion with that ship may be interpreted injuriously to the rights of others who have largely shared in whatever merits or responsibilities belong to the undertaking. In justice, therefore, to my own feelings and to their rights, I wish to communicate the following facts:—

My share of the merit and responsibility is that of builder of the ship for the Eastern Steam Navigation Company. I designed her lines and constructed the iron hull of the ship, and am responsible for her merits or defects as a piece of naval architecture. I am equally responsible for the paddlewheel engines of 1000 horsepower, by which she is to be propelled.

But Messrs James Watt and Co., the eminent engineers of Soho, have the entire merit of the design and construction of the engines of 1500 horsepower which are to propel the screw.

It is, however, to the company's engineer, Mr I. K. Brunel, that the original conception is due of building a steamship large enough to carry coals sufficient for full steaming on the longest voyage. He, at the outset, and long before it had assumed a mercantile form, communicated his views to me, and I have participated in the contrivance of the best means to carry them into practical effect. I think, further, that the idea of using two sets of engines and two propellers is original, and was his invention. It was his idea also to introduce a cellular construction like that at the top and bottom of the Britannia bridge into the construction of the great ship. It will be seen that these are the main characteristics which distinguish this from other ships, and these are Mr Brunel's. Her lines and her structure in other respects are identical with those of my other ships, which are constructed like this on a principle of my own, which I have systematically carried out during the last 20 years, and which is commonly called the 'wave' principle. In other respects, also, her materials are put together in the manner usual in my other ships.

I think, too, there are others whose names and services in this matter the public should not forget whenever the great ship is mentioned. The mercantile difficulty appeared at the outset, and this has proved itself since, to be quite as great as the mechanical difficulty of the undertaking. So unusual an enterprise could not have been carried out without ability, enterprise, and prudence, to the credit of which the board of directors, represented by their chairman, Mr H. T. Hope, and their secretary, Mr John Yates, are entitled in a high degree. And there was one of them who bore the burden and heat of the day, and at the outset of this undertaking was one of its most able and zealous supporters, the late Mr Charles Geach. I think I am justified in saying that without him it would never, as a mercantile speculation, have been undertaken by many of those who have undertaken it; that on his aid and exertions many of us probably, and certainly myself, relied mainly for the successful issue of the undertaking, and that his untimately death materially increased the difficulties of that undertaking, both to the directors and to the constructor of the ship. Let not, therefore, his share of any merit that may belong to the undertaking be forgotten.

In conclusion, permit me to add that my share of the merit and responsibility ends with the construction of the hull and of the paddlewheel engines, which have now been nearly completed by my assistants, Mr Dickson and Mr Hepworth. The launching of the ship, the rigging and masting of the ship, her cabins and her outfit are not mine, but are executed entirely under Mr Brunel, Captain Harrison, and the other officers of the company.

This can be taken as the testament of the construction of the *Great Eastern*. One could not expect this kind of public acknowledgement from Brunel, not even a private one.

A booklet published in London in the following July bore the title: 'The Great Eastern Steam Ship, a description of Mr Scott Russell's Great Ship, now building at Millwall...'[37] and contained the statement that up to that time it had 'been generally thought that the Great Eastern steam ship had been designed by Mr Brunel, but the candid and straightforward letter of Mr Scott Russell, published in the Times of April 20th corrects that impression, and gives to all concerned in her original design and construction, their due share in the great work.' The contents of this booklet appear to have been contributed by Russell.

There were some shipowners, like W. S. Lindsay M.P., the historian of merchant shipping, who regarded the enterprise with a sceptical eye. When asked by Brunel to what trade he, Lindsay, would apply the ship, Lindsay said with a laugh 'Turn her into a show'.[38] This must have been very discouraging to Brunel, but he was comforted by occasional visits from his old friend and rival Robert Stephenson who ingratiated himself by abusing Dickson with whom he probably discussed the design of the paddle engines. 'I dislike his face immensely,' Stephenson wrote to Brunel, 'I felt that it was an imperative duty to treat his suggestions irreverently.'[39] Rolt quotes this to emphasize Brunel's difficulties; others might think it does no credit to Stephenson who was, in fact, something of a snob.[40]

By mid 1857, Russell had sufficiently come to terms with his creditors to lease the unoccupied part of David Napier's yard[41] with a view to re-establishing himself as a shipbuilder. The details of his liquidation settlement were never published and, along with so much else, have been lost beyond recall. It is a gross exaggeration to say that Russell had a miraculous recovery as a shipbuilder. At least a full year elapsed before he was able to lay down his first keel in the new yard. His old shipyard lay vacant after the removal of the Great Ship and its engines until it was taken over by the Millwall Ironworks & Shipbuilding Co. formed by C. J. Mare who had failed at Blackwall. This was a more dramatic restoration of fortune than Russell's.

In July, the Directors reported that the launch would be in September and the anticipated final cost £620,000, of which £159,162 remained to be spent. Martins made trouble about the extension of the lease but finally agreed to allow the Company the use of the yard from August 12 to December 15 for £2500.[42] Yates warned Brunel to launch on October 5 or they would be in the 'hands of the Philistines'.[43] Costs were running at about £2000 per week in wages and materials. Treadwell had required more time to complete the launching ways however—a familiar experience among Brunel's contractors. Rolt does not blame Treadwell nor accuse *him* of delaying tactics. He blames Russell's failure to place the sub-contract soon enough, yet Brunel received Russell's designs in December 1855!

By the end of October the Great Ship was a splendid sight in her new paint, standing grandly in the fog, ready to meet the sea. But Brunel was not so ready, he needed more time to rehearse the launching procedure and test the equipment, he would not be hurried.[44] He dashed off another distraught letter to one of the directors:

> Our finances are indeed in a gloomy state and here again I feel that I have been somewhat cruelly treated—the enormous expenses of the last few months and particularly of the last few weeks are and must be thrown upon me—whereas full 50 or 60 per cent of them, I should say more—but that you even would not believe me—are the result merely of the attempt to carry on such a concern as this without an experienced manager of Works.
>
> I have for weeks seen our money running away faster and faster each day with less and less result—100 men increased to 200 with half the work done— there was no help for it but to rush on with eyes shut in the hopes we should reach the end before we were quite exhausted—we have fortunately done so, but it will not be fair hereafter to saddle upon my responsibilities the

enormous cost of the work—you know of course that I have nothing *whatever* to do with the employing of men—settlement of wages or any expenditure whatever.[45]

So, it was Yates to blame, also the Directors for firing Russell, and Russell for copping out! It is difficult to avoid the conclusion, however, that Brunel brought it all on himself. He, no one else, forced the issue with Russell and he—and Yates—missed Russell. If Brunel had been able to employ the looser rein which Russell and his men required to get on with the ship in their own way, compromise a little on his ideal of perfection, and share a little of his glory with an able partner, the ship would have been finished sooner and, with lubricated wooden launching ways of proper bearing surface, in the water sooner, to the advantage of the suffering shareholders and the tortured resources of the Company.

But Brunel had spoken of expenditure too soon, the Great Ship was not yet in the water. Brunel expected the ship to slide down the iron rails under its own weight, about 12,000[46] tons to be moved 200 ft down a slope of 1 in 12 to low water mark. He had commissioned some friction experiments from his former assistant William Froude (who was to achieve fame for his ship testing tank) which reassured him of the feasability of his plan. Froude seems to have discovered the subtle fact that friction declines with velocity.[47] If the hull should not move from rest when the restraints were removed or if one end should move more easily than the other, force could be applied through cables at the bow and stern, which were threaded through pulleys attached to lighters moored in the river thence to steam winches on land at the bow and stern of the ship. These could be assisted by two hydraulic rams of 100 tons and 150 tons force respectively. Too rapid, or excessive sliding, could be controlled by two great chain cables respectively attached to the forward and after cradles and wound round great drums restrained by band brakes. The tension in these brakes was exerted as desired by squads of men hauling on holding-down tackles pulling on levers attached to the brake bands. Slack in the chains was taken up by rotating the drums by means of manually operated geared winches.

The launch was begun as planned on Tuesday, November 3, 1857, after a night of feverish activity during which, according to the *Morning Chronicle*, Brunel, Russell and Harrison were engaged with 1500 workmen making the necessary preparations by gas light. Brunel directed the launch by making appropriate signals to the fore and aft 'controllers' from a platform attached to the ship at deck level. The controllers were

Hepworth and Dickson respectively, mounted on platforms adjacent to the great drums. Brunel had not much opportunity to rehearse the proceedings nor to carry out all the tests he would have desired, but he had recently conducted a similar operation on the Saltash Bridge. It was to be a cautious process—a little movement at first to try everything, then perhaps more and so on—and not necessarily all on the one day.[48]

The directors, with an eye on the depleted coffers, opened the launch to the public, selling about 3000 tickets, unknown to Brunel who was most upset when he found out for he wished to feel unencumbered by the expectations of the public. He was afraid of ridicule in the event of a hitch, but there was nothing for it but to carry on.[49] There was a christening ceremony in which Miss Hope, daughter of the Company chairman, officiated. Then, all systems ready, the dog shores were knocked down and the crowd waited expectantly. Nothing happened for a few minutes, then suddenly the forward cradle slid a distance of about six feet. The signal was given to operate the after winch to give the after cradle a start.[50] With a grinding roar the after cradle suddenly slid about fifteen feet, the men who had been winding in the slack of the brake chain had not disengaged the winch handle and were sent spinning into the air like matchwood. All were injured and one was killed. Brunel took this opportunity to suspend the launch for that day, the worst was happening! Prince Albert arranged a visit to the scene through Russell (he always negotiated visits to the ship in this way)[51], then, with no fanfare, the launch was continued. This time, to general consternation, the great hull obdurately refused to move. Launching now became an operation of pushing day after day, foot by grinding foot down the ways with as many hydraulic rams as could be procured—a total of 21 in the end.

Robert Stephenson, now in very poor health, came to lend moral support to his great contemporary, a little put out at not having been invited earlier. He advised Brunel to forget Russell (it is not known what Russell may have said or suggested) and ignore the taunts of the press. All through the winter the pushing and heaving was continued, until at length with substantial movements in January 1858 the Great Ship was deposited at low water mark to await the high tide which floated her off on January 31. The event caused great excitement on the river, both banks were crowded with cheering sightseers, the Deptford bells pealed merrily, all kinds of craft assembled, and the river steamers heeled over as their eager freight crowded to the rails on the viewing side. The launch had taken about three months of anxiety, prodigious effort and, not least, embarrassment—for the public had laughed. But no engineer could laugh. Here was heroism and the paradoxical triumph of failure. The Great Ship was launched at last, and if Brunel felt exhausted, he was not more exhausted than the Eastern Steam Navigation Company. The cost of the launching operation alone turned out to be £120,000—more than 40 per cent of the original tender for the construction of the hull, and far in excess of the £14,000 originally anticipated by Brunel and Russell. Nearly £750,000 had been spent on an iron hull containing some incomplete machinery, and there was no money left to fit it out and complete it for sea. Indeed there was a debt of £95,000. Nor does this sum include Brunel's fees, or the salaries of his staff. From the time the Company undertook the completion of the ship Brunel drew no fees and met the salaries of his men out of his own pocket.[52]

Several Lords and gentlemen,[53] no doubt Russell included, were aboard the *Great Eastern* as it was towed to moorings off Deptford. Brunel could not complain that he did not now get his share of glory—all to himself—and his busy pen nowhere recorded any hint of appreciation of any help or any debt to any other mortal soul; perhaps he felt this only just.

Our sympathy and admiration for Brunel blind us to the fact that the launch of the *Great Eastern* was an engineering failure. Russell explained it thus:

> The launching arrangements... were duly carried out by the owners of the ship as originally designed, but with the addition of a set of iron bars on the upper surface of the ways, and another set of iron bars on the lower surface of the cradle. When abandoned to the sliding force of these bars, the ship slid a few feet until the lubricating stuff was rubbed off, and then the rails simply bit one another as the wheels of a locomotive engine bite the rails, and then held the ship firmly in its place: so firmly, that not only was the inclination of 1 in 12 with the whole weight of 12,000 tons of ship on it unable to move it down the inclined plane, but some thousands of tons of additional pressure by hydraulic rams were unable to force it down into the water in a less period than some three months from starting.

Russell's analogy of the wheel on a rail is not exact but what he is saying is that the iron bars bit into the iron rails, and this is probably correct over those regions in which the bearing stress was particularly high, due to concentrated loading, deformation of the ways, and skewing of the ship. This is borne out by one observer's comments—'some portions of rails bear unmistakable evidence of the terrific pressure to which they have been subjected'. It was probably not a simple matter of excessive friction,

128

although that, too, cannot be discounted. The results of Froude's experiments misled Brunel. Russell, in a crude experiment of his own with a loaded railway truck on an incline, with wheels locked, claims that he satisfied himself that there would be difficulty in the launch, but there is no record of his communicating this to Brunel or anyone else. Brunel, in any case, would feel fortified by the reassurance of Froude's more careful simulations. Russell went on:

> Had the surface on which she was carried been simply the ordinary plank surface well lubricated with tallow and grease, the phenomenon of launching the Great Eastern would have been no other phenomenon than the ordinary launch of a large ship. The area of the ways covered by the two cradles was nearly 20,000 square feet, and that surface was far more than sufficient to conduct the weight smoothly and gently down into the water in the manner of an ordinary launch; but it was the destiny of the Great Eastern to be the victim of experiments which had nothing to do with her original design, or her ultimate purposes.[54]

CHAPTER SIX

Completion of the Great Eastern

The fitting of the ship is as extensive a portion of the shipbuilder's art as her construction; but how much of all the utensils, and fittings, and conveniences, and equipage, and furniture, he finds himself, or receives from others, is a matter of usage, understanding, contract; not of fixed or inevitable routine.

J. SCOTT RUSSELL

The Eastern Steam Navigation Company now, in the first months of 1858, considered the steps to be taken to complete the essential work on the *Great Eastern* and the passenger accommodation sufficient to serve the 'few profitable trials or preliminary voyages to America' first mentioned in the Company Report of February 19, 1856. John Fowler, who was rapidly coming into prominence, and who was later to enjoy a degree of immortality with Sir Benjamin Baker as co-designer of the great Forth Bridge, was engaged to advise the Company. Fowler, Brunel reported to the Directors,

recommended strongly that an opportunity should be afforded to Mr J. S. Russell to associate with himself some practical and substantial men engaged in the different branches of work now required and who from their practical knowledge would be able themselves to arrange a general plan for the completion of the ship and who should enter into a contract with the Company for such entire completion in a given time and for a given sum or at all events at a cost within some definite limits. Mr Fowler expressed his belief that such a combination could be effected and that he Mr Fowler could thus be the means of reconciling the numerous parties alike interested in the success of the ship but having as he represented very [different] views as to the course to be followed . . . I expressed myself perfectly ready to aid in any such plan and conceiving that if it could be brought about it would have the effect he hoped for of producing a union of interests and feelings which . . . would in this case displace a state of antagonism and ill feeling which was represented to exist . . . I promised my loyal and zealous support it being clearly understood that the obliteration of all this ill feeling was to be a positive condition . . . I have since then had several interviews with Mr Fowler and have made such suggestions to him as I thought might assist in the task he had undertaken and I believe Mr J. S. Russell has been engaged in examining the whole of the work on board the Ship with the view to framing calculations . . .[1]

In addition to Russell, Fowler called in L. S. Lucas and the three had a discussion with the E.S.N. Co. Board. Brunel observed to Fowler that the part he had allotted to Messrs Lucas was small and to Russell very large. He had doubts about this unless Russell could 'bring his mind to go into the matter with very different feelings from those which, at all events very lately, governed his mind and actions'. He asked Fowler if he thought he had effected this change. If not, he feared that Russell would submit an offer that would 'hardly be acceptable'.[2]

The ill feeling to which Brunel refers was not all on the part of Russell. Some members of the Board had become disgruntled with Brunel and the management of the Company and were ready to oppose all plans suspected of proceeding from his advice. Brunel thought it apparent 'that a confidential officer of the Company communicated everything to others and intrigued with others'.[3]

Fowler assured Brunel that he would not propose 'any interference with his, Brunel's, position,' and Brunel requested that this be stated in writing.[4]

Meantime the directors had been authorized to raise £220,000 to pay off the debt and finish the ship. The Millwall yard had to be vacated and the intermediate crankshaft (replacing earlier rejects) was being turned there night and day. There were few lathes of sufficient size in the country. The directors declared that, assuming an average speed of 16 knots (the design speed of the ship was 14 knots) the ship could cross the Atlantic in seven days and that provisional arrangements and deals had been made with the N.W. Railway (with a railhead at Holyhead) and the Grand Trunk of Canada (with a railhead at Portland, Maine) and others who stood to benefit, which would underwrite the service, and for seven voyages the estimated earnings amounted to £309,000 for an expenditure of £185,050—profit £123,950![5] But the bait proved less than adequate and the response was slight. By July, two factions had developed, one, led by the Chairman, J. A. R. Campbell, M.P., favouring either auction of the ship or power to accept an offer, and the other, led by Magnus, favouring the formation of a new company to buy out the old.[6] Already the ship was being eyed by some as a means of laying a transatlantic cable.[7] Here was a ship which could be available at a bargain price.

Whatever happened, the shareholders would lose. The financial editor of *The Times* wrote that it could be little honour for men to point to costly monuments and say 'We executed that at such and such an outlay and at the ruin of a thousand families who were told that it would be accomplished at a third of the amount'.[8]

The Magnus proposal prevailed and the new company, to be called the Great Ship Company, was formed in November 1858,[9] offering £1 shares and having purchased the 'strongest and fastest ship afloat ... larger than the united tonnage of seven of the largest ships in the world, for the bargain price of £160,000'.[10] £2.50 of the new stock was exchanged for £20 of the old, £140,000 was to be called for completion of the ship and £30,000 would be held in reserve.

Brunel was re-engaged as engineer and Yates as secretary. The great engineer, however, was now seriously ill with nephritis, diagnosed by none other than Dr Bright after whom, as its discoverer, that disease was then called, and was advised to winter in a warmer clime. He and Mrs Brunel, their son Henry and their doctor, accordingly took off for Egypt trailing a startling collection of stores and supplies. We are left with the characteristic picture of Brunel wedged against a paddle box of the ship that conveyed them across the Mediterranean as it tossed in a rough sea, observing the periodicity of the waves and the paddle revolutions, while his doctor languished seasick below decks! He was doubtless reluctant to leave his great ship, but there was every prospect that he would return before work could be re-commenced. He had left a detailed specification for the contract and had insisted on its terms being strictly adhered to. It was announced at the end of January 1859 that £300,000 had been subscribed and that 'No money would be wasted in the mere frippery of decoration, though at the same time all the fittings would be of the most substantial kind'.[11] The work was to begin on February 15, and had to be completed five months after. This, said the *Illustrated Times*, meant that the long expected trial trip would take place about mid July, when it was intended to run out from Weymouth to the middle of the Atlantic.

Brunel's specification discarded many of his planned novelties and it may be that Russell's counter-specification discarded even more of what was extraneous to the immediate purpose. The important thing was to have the Great Ship on her way as soon as possible. Russell declined to bid on Brunel's specification but undertook to finish the ship in six months to his own plans and have her 'fitted in every respect for sea as a first class vessel', for £125,000, with a premium of £1000 per week for earlier completion and a penalty of £10,000 for every week overdue! There was to be no charge for 'extras'; all questions and differences between Russell and the Company were to be referred to arbitration, and the arbitrators were to be empowered to award him compensation where they deemed the directors to have given orders for the execution of work not covered by the contract.[12] Russell was a bold man indeed to face the hazards of another venture into uncharted ways. Again, too, a proportion of the payment would be in shares.

Wigram and Lucas submitted a higher bid based on Brunel's specification, which Brunel understandably pressed the Board to accept, but a majority of the Board, led by its most influential stockholders, Samuel Beale, one of Russell's liquidators, among them, favoured Russell's proposal and believed him to be in the best position to get the ship off to sea in the short time specified. This, of course, was in accordance with Fowler's recommendation. Before the formalities were concluded, the great 40-ton wrought-iron crankshaft for the paddle engine was loaded on a barge and floated out to the *Great Eastern* at her moorings off Deptford, where it was hoisted aboard by means of a new floating derrick. The completion of the paddle engines and associated piping and auxiliaries was Russell's primary task along with the completion of the remaining iron and wooden structural work. The remainder was subcontracted by him to various firms of specialists—Ferguson, the masts; Westthorpe, the rigging; Hall, the sails; Crace, the interior decorations, furnishings and hotel fittings; Watt, the screw engines, and so on.

Brunel's representatives, Jacomb and Brereton reported assiduously to their chief, but they in no way substituted for him. After his return to England in May 1859, he visited the ship nearly every day and freely exercised his prerogatives as Engineer.[13] He received careful reports of the screw engines from the Watt Company and pressed Russell for like reports of the paddle engines but with less response than he demanded. This should not surprise us, nor that Dickson surreptitiously gave the engine its first whirl in the wee sma' hours of July 25 when no one was about. However unsatisfactory Brunel may have regarded Russell's communication with him on this matter, the great paddle engines were a success, were ready on time and did their duty well throughout the career of the ship. A. L. Holley, a distinguished and widely experienced American mechanical engineer, rhapsodized over them: 'Nothing could exceed the smoothness and steadiness with which the paddle engines operated.

I never saw better fits in steam machinery.'[14] Then, later, on the trip to Holyhead, after criticizing the screw engines he declared:

> But what shall I say of the paddle engines? Oh! that Messrs. Allen, Copeland, Quintard, Smith and Collies, and all our engine designers and builders were here to see them. Four great oscillating cylinders on one shaft, and you would not know they were in motion, save for the light rush of steam at their centres. There is no pounding of boxes and valves, or general rattling jar, thump and spring, as is too common in oscillating engines.[15]

On August 8, Russell held a banquet aboard the ship to celebrate its 'completion'. *The Times* correspondent proclaimed that it was 'only doing bare justice to Mr Scott Russell's exertions to say that no other man in the Kingdom could have fitted the vessel in the same time, and there were not a few who believed the task would prove too much even for his energy'.[16] This was probably no more than the truth and it is all the more remarkable that the work had to be accomplished while a continuous stream of inquisitive visitors, as well as dignitaries, was conducted over the ship daily. This was a source of revenue which the directors were unwilling to forgo. They had profited from it while the ship was on the stocks at Millwall and they never missed an opportunity to replenish their coffers in this way wherever the ship happened to lie.

The distinguished guests to the banquet were entertained to a demonstration of the engines—they called it a trial—and the result, according to *The Times* correspondent, 'was considered by all the engineers on board to be satisfactory in the very highest degree, and far beyond what could have been expected'.[17] The engineers present included Sir John Rennie, Joseph Locke, M.P., Whitworth, Brereton, Jacomb, and Robert Stephenson, M.P.

The healths of Mr Brunel and Mr Scott Russell, 'the engineer and builder of the ship', were given, to which Scott Russell replied 'regretting the absence of Mr Brunel, explaining his own share in the construction of the great ship, and bearing high testimony to the share of his colleague as the originator of the great idea'.[18] No further details of this speech were printed in *The Times*.[19]

All were in high spirits and the managing directors were probably very relieved that everything had gone off so well and the state of the ship apparently so far advanced. But there was still much to be done, at which no shipbuilder could be surprised.

On August 20, over Magnus' opposition, the directors were auth-

134

13 Scott Russell (left) and Brunel (with cigar), probably taken on the first day of
the launch of the *Great Eastern*, November 3, 1857

14 The first abortive attempt to launch the *Great Eastern*, November 1857

orized to issue the 30,000 reserved shares 'to send the ship to sea free of debt'. The Chairman declared that the ship's engines 'worked well', and that 'it was expected that in a few days *the ship would be handed over to the company* [italics mine] by the contractors, when three engineers would report upon her state'.[20] The three engineers appointed to serve as arbitrators, were Fowler, Hawkshaw and J. R. McLean (also spelt McClean). Magnus was very critical of the management of the Company and pounced on every opportunity to attack the Chairman of the Board and his deputy. Russell, too, as the recipient of their contract came in for a share of this. Jackson, the Deputy Chairman, declared that he had lived 'a hell upon earth' on account of Magnus' conduct and that 'if the contract had been given to any other than to Mr Russell, the ship would not have been ready in six months. The Chairman had done everything that was possible to forward the vessel; he even slept on board, such was his anxiety to see that all went well'.[21]

The sailing date was fixed for September 3, and Russell was convinced that the work would never be completed unless the ship actually set out on its voyage. Anyone who has experience of the last-minute chaos that invariably attends the departure of a new ship from its fitting out basin cannot be surprised at the confusion that reigned aboard the *Great Eastern* as her departure date approached. Take into account, too, that she was not moored to a dock served by dockside cranes but was anchored in the smelly river, accessible only by boat and lighter. With but a week remaining, *The Times* correspondent informed his readers that:

> Among the other things that have yet to be done . . . The capstan deck forward has also to be planed, the entire deck caulked, and an access made to the bearing for the screw shaft. Some kitchens have to be fitted up, and cooking ranges fixed, and several of the cabins to be painted and furnished. Accommodation is also ordered to be prepared for 450 passengers to dine in the 80 feet saloon aft. Several berths have yet to be fixed, and 150 additional sofas provided. The yards have also to be crossed and the sails bent, and the steering apparatus to be fixed in place and tested. All these items seem to make a vast amount of work yet to be done, but . . . if it was necessary, not the least doubt is felt that as far as these matters are concerned the ship could be made ready for sea in from 24 to 36 hours at furthest. The new steering apparatus will, perhaps, take a few days to fix and regulate. This simple but most ingenious invention is due to Mr Lungley, the shipbuilder of Deptford. By means of this Captain Harrison, or the officer of the watch on the bridge, will be enabled to steer the ship by a signal indicator with as much certainty as if he guided the wheel himself.[22]

135

On the last day, the final 'dock' trials of the paddle engines took place in Brunel's presence. These seem to have passed off without complaint, but at mid-day Brunel felt very unwell and had to be carried ashore. On arrival at his home in London it was discovered that he had suffered a stroke. Brunel was never again to see his last great work.

The great day found

> decks and saloons lumbered up with bales of bedding, piles of furniture, and masses of crockery; smiths were 'busy closing rivets up' ... plate from Elkington's was being stowed away, men were busy hanging costly chandeliers from Defries's. Everyone seemed in a hurry, and struggled and stumbled amid a confused mixture of shavings and forges, anvils, guns, anchors, cables, barrels and hawsers ... it seemed hard to believe that the chaos of sofas, dinner furniture, mirrors, chandeliers, and carpeting would ever be in their proper places by morning ... Mr Parry, to whom the contract for furnishing the fittings of the ship has been entrusted, worked with the most indefatigable energy, and during a few short hours immense progress was made.[23]

Departure was delayed for four days, however, as a result of difficulties connected with Board of Trade clearance, or so it was said. Even on the night before the actual departure, great quantities of equipment were being hauled aboard in the moonlight while, according to the *New York Times* correspondent,

> Below, were all the sights of a great hotel or rather of a condensed town— a directors' meeting in one room, social and business parties in others—one saloon full of tea-drinkers, another of newly arrived guests, and others in the hands of decorators ... below, several hundred men are receiving their pay, still lower, and a furlong distant, the crew are piling up stores—and so on *all the way down*

Nevertheless, as the dawn's eerie light spread over the river estuary on September 7, the *Great Eastern* slipped her moorings one by one, and an escort of four tugs led her down river commanded by Pilot Atkinson, with Captain Harrison at his elbow and Scott Russell on the bridge 'to direct the action of the engines'.[24]

A full list of the passengers (at £10 a head) would make fascinating reading. It comprised a great concourse of ladies and gentlemen and their families. These, in addition to the workmen and crew, were milling around the ship from an early hour.

The news travelled fast that the Great Ship at long last was on its way and soon the banks of the river, the windows and roofs of the houses by the water's edge, the tops and yards of vessels in the docks and every vacant space 'became instinct with life' and loud cheers greeted the giant along her triumphal way to the sea. Such a sight was observed by some of us many years ago when the *Queen Mary* was edged down the Clyde, her stately form assuming massive proportions as she dwarfed the high tenements by the river. So must the *Great Eastern* have appeared to the people of her time. The number of masts and funnels alone was an index of immensity to the spectators of 1859, and the *Great Eastern* had no less than five of each as well as an obvious expression of power denied her giant successors, great paddle wheels.

As *The Times* commented, however, the enthusiasm of those on board was tempered 'by the absence of the eminent man to whom the conception of the ship was due—Mr Brunel'. He was now very ill.

The passage was not without adventures, the most alarming of which was the breaking of a hawser attaching the leading tug to the bow as it tried to swing the ship round to avoid a barque and schooner obstructing the 'fair way'. Only Russell's judicious use of the engines kept the ship from being thrust aground by the current.[25]

She anchored by Purfleet for the night while swarms of crowded craft sailed round her and the band played interminable *Rule Britannias* and *Conquering Heros* until darkness fell. Next day, the reporters noted, the Marquis of Stafford and Lord Alfred Paget came aboard, and the ship continued on her way to the same cheers and feverish interest as of the previous day. The next anchorage was at the Nore light, where the Great Ship, now entirely under her own steam, arrived at noon.

Next morning, in high spirits, some eighty men hauled on the capstan and raised anchor to the rude music of a reed pipe. Captain Harrison beat time and cheered on the work and some jovial gentlemen added their shoulders to the task—Scott Russell, J. A. R. Campbell, Herbert Ingram, M.P., and Lords Stafford, Mountcharles and Paget.[26]

It was a dull overcast day with a strong running sea as the *Great Eastern* proceeded on her way to Portland with the Downs of the English Channel coast ever in view. Towards six o'clock, the skies cleared and the welcomed change in the weather enticed the distinguished company on deck from a repast in the saloon. They had scarcely settled in their various ways to enjoy the scene when suddenly 'with the mingled roar and crash of a battery of artillery and a line of musketry', up shot the forward funnel thirty feet in the air in two parts amid a cloud of steam and smoke and a shower of splinters and pipes. When the resulting

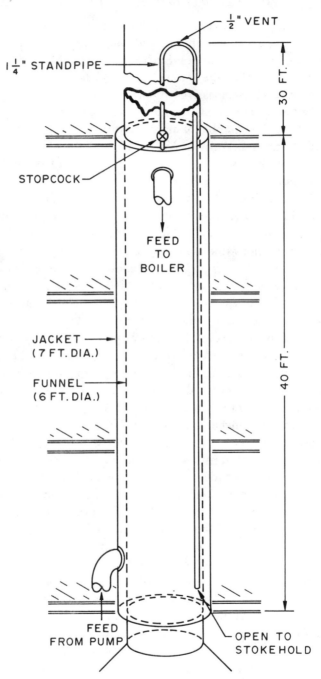

Great Eastern funnel feed-water heater

138

confusion subsided—and it took some time—it was seen that the ship was in no danger, but that the grand saloon and adjacent accommodation had been much damaged. The furnaces served by the fractured funnel blew back into the boiler room while several stokers lay injured, five fatally, in the wreckage. The many engineering guests on board were quick to lend a hand, then examine the damage and postulate the cause of the accident. It was clear that the feed-water heating jacket encasing the forward funnel had exploded.

Only the two forward funnels were encased with feed water jackets. Each jacket, constructed of half-inch iron plate, extended from the boiler room to the deck for a distance of about forty feet, forming a long thin six-inch annulus with the funnel, which was about six feet in diameter. The feed pump delivered to the base of the jacket—or heater as we shall call it—and the boiler drew its supply from a point near the top. To obtain sufficient head to force the feed into the boiler against a maximum boiler pressure of from 20 to 25 p.s.i. a one-and-a-quarter-inch stand-pipe was extended about thirty feet upwards from the top of the heater. This was then bent over on itself and led back down so that any overflow would be conducted to the stokehold. To prevent a possible syphon effect, a half-inch hole was cut in the bend at the top of the pipe. The feed pump kept the heater topped up. A relief valve on the pump delivery chamber ensured that the pump would not deliver while the water in the heater was at a selected maximum level. The heater also could be by-passed so that the pump delivered directly to the boiler.

The heater served the very useful dual purpose of shielding the adjacent accommodation and woodwork from excessive heat and increasing the thermal efficiency of the plant by retrieving some of the 'waste heat' carried off by the flue gases. Robert Napier, who patented this style of feed heater, had abandoned its use, as had some others who had tried it, but it was nevertheless widely employed. The most serious hazard to which funnel heaters were subject was the formation of steam within them if the supply or outflow should be held up. A vent or safety valve could release any build-up of pressure but the heater could dry out, in which case a sudden influx of water could conceivably lead to an explosive generation of steam, either immediately or later depending on the temperature of the overheated surfaces.

It is very doubtful that the stand-pipe fitted to the *Great Eastern*'s feed heater could have provided an adequate vent in this case, especially in view of the length of the pipe. Certainly the half-inch hole at the top would not have helped much. The indications are that these eventualities were not expected, nor does it seem to have been thought necessary to fit a vent or safety valve to funnel heaters of this type. In two previous applications Russell had not fitted the heaters with vents or safety valves,[27] but it is not known if the heaters in these cases could be by-passed and, of course, the temperatures and heat in the *Great Eastern*'s flues presented greater hazards. Both Russell and Blake opposed Brunel's wish to use these heaters on the *Great Eastern*, but Brunel designed and ordered them for the paddle engines when the Company replaced Russell as contractor. Their design and presence, therefore, for good or ill, were Brunel's responsibility.

A complication in the case of the *Great Eastern* was that a stopcock was inserted between each heater and its stand-pipe to facilitate a modest test under water pressure. The cocks were not afterwards removed and were thus a potential danger in that they could be closed by inadvertence or design. Sometime after the departure of the ship from the Thames, these cocks were closed for some reason and by some person unknown. As long as the connection to the boiler was open, the pressure in the heater would not exceed that in the boiler even if no water were being fed, and, of course, as long as the feed water was being fed through the heater there would be little danger. The donkey engines driving the feed pumps gave trouble and apparently were able to feed the boilers directly more easily than they could via the heaters. This suggests that the head to be overcome in topping up the heaters was greater than that presented to the feed pumps by the boilers themselves. Partly for this reason and also to supply colder water in an attempt to reduce priming—both reasons were given—the heaters were by-passed and closed off.

John Dickson, Russell's engine works manager, accepted responsibility for fitting the stopcocks to the stand pipes. He explained that he did not remove the cocks after the hydraulic test of the heaters because he thought that in the event of fracture of a stand-pipe the cock could be used to prevent water damage to the accommodation served by the ventilating space which surrounded the jacket. At the inquest, Dickson declared that he was ready to swear that McLellan, the chief engineer of the ship, had in fact asked him to leave the cocks fitted and that Brunel had expressed no objection.[28]

The inquest into the deaths resulting from the explosion was concerned with determining who and what was responsible for the explosion and whether there had been an act of negligence. The culprit faced the charge of manslaughter. Of greater concern to the directors and the contractor was the responsibility for the repair of the damage. The Company took the view that the engines were the responsibility of their respective builders until the Company had the opportunity to consider their functioning on the cruise to Holyhead. This, the Chairman said, was the understanding with Russell—there was no contractual obligation. They were withholding payment of the final instalment until the contract was fulfilled to their satisfaction. It had been arranged that the engine builders should appoint the chief engineers responsible for the entire working and control of the screw and paddle engines. He asserted that Russell gave all necessary directions for the management of the paddle engines from the time of coming aboard to leaving. Brunel had expressed the opinion that a river trial was inadequate and the Chairman said that Russell must have known this was Brunel's view whether it was in writing or not. Indeed, it had to be said to Russell's credit, that he was no less determined to give his engines a thorough workout.

Russell's case was that the final dock trial in the presence of Brunel was all that was required by his contract. He and Blake had asked the Company to allow them to recommend the entire staff of both engines, but the Company had allowed them only to recommend the four head engineers of each engine. These four, for the paddle engines, in order of rank, were: Messrs Arnott, Marshall, Patrick and Gerard, and after the final dock trial these had left Russell's payroll and joined the ship's Company. They therefore reported to their chief engineer, Alexander McLellan. Russell pointed out that he was not responsible for the complete contract of the ship, but only for certain parts of it. If it had been his trial trip, he went on, he would have been accountable for all operating and entertaining expenses accrued during it, yet clearly the Company had accepted these. His attendance on the cruise from Deptford to Portland, he declared, arose from his deep personal interest, and the engines were never under his charge on that voyage. The presence of his engine works manager, John Dickson, was likewise explained. He was present on Russell's invitation and had likewise volunteered every assistance in his power. Mr Arnott and staff, he emphasized, 'had most undoubted charge under Mr McLellan'.

A strenuous effort was made by the Company's counsel to show that Russell's contract to finish the vessel had not been completed and hence, presumably, to prove the Russell was responsible for repairing the damage to the ship.

Russell maintained that his position on the bridge was to advise the pilot or captain on engine matters and to transmit instructions regarding speed to both engine rooms. Captain Harrison first said that if Russell had not volunteered to operate the indicator to the engine room from the bridge, he should have appointed his officers to do it, then later, 'If I had known that Mr Russell was only volunteering his assistance on the bridge, I would not have allowed him to take the position he did, or any one but my own officers'. He expressed outrage on learning from the evidence that, unknown to him, Russell and Blake had agreed between them to avoid over-taxing the engines. The fact however that Captain Harrison or anyone else assumed that Russell was in charge of the paddle engines, just as some others, seeing Dickson in the engine room or over-hearing his giving directions, thought Dickson to be in charge, did not prove anything. The evidence of the ship's engineers themselves brought out that they regarded McLellan as their chief although he had told some of them before the cruise started to take instructions only from those in charge of the engines. It turned out, however, that most regarded Arnott as that engineer in charge, although each had his own province of responsibility. Dickson stated that McLellan certainly conducted himself as chief engineer in the engine room, gave orders to get up steam, regulated the water and 'tried the brine'.

Brereton, Brunel's deputy, acting Company Engineer, explained that the height of the column of liquid in the heater stand-pipe regulated the pressure in the jackets. He explained that previous to being lengthened, the stand-pipe 'was too short, and the water ran over too soon'. He could not 'say that there was any engineer in charge of that cock', but he deponed that Dickson 'was the engineer who was responsible for the action of the paddle engines', and that 'it did not occur to anyone to ascertain that the cock was open before starting'.[29]

Fourth Engineer Patrick testified that he had seen neither McLellan nor Dickson give orders from the time they set out, and that he regarded Arnott as in charge. It was he, Patrick, who, on his own initiative, had shut off the feed to the funnel jackets. He alleged that Arnott was present two hours later when, in answer to a question, he had informed Dickson of his action. None had thought to check the vent cocks. Dickson, because he had no mind of them, Arnott because he had not heard Patrick's statement.

Patrick told the court that immediately after the explosion he went to Arnott and asked him if there were something which would obstruct

142

the passage from the casing to the stand-pipe and Arnott had replied that the stand-pipes were fitted with cocks but that they were open, 'but he said at once "Go and see"'. *The Times* report had it that 'Witness took a spanner and went to the second funnel casing, where he found the cock shut, and instantly opened it. There was a great rush of steam...'

John Arnott, who gave his evidence most uneasily (according to *The Times* reporter), deponed that he was in charge of the engines when the explosion occurred, and that Mr Patrick was under his orders. The latter did not report to him that at twelve in the day he had shut off the feed from the funnel casing and turned it direct into the boilers. Had this been reported to him, he would at once, knowing that there were cocks in the vent tubes, have ascertained that they were open and the steam escaping. He had not been aware that the feed had been shut off from the casing at all. He did not give Patrick any instructions to open the cock of the second funnel after the explosion. Both cocks were open when the ship left Deptford. He and Duncan McFarlane, who had customarily been charged with supervision of cocks on trial trips under Russell, had made a tour of the various connections prior to the departure of the ship from Deptford. He found that both cocks were then open. He could not recollect what had made him so particular in checking these cocks beyond that it was usual to examine all the cocks on feed pipes before starting. The jacket had been used before and the cocks examined before. He did not know that the donkey engines would not work and that that was why they were obliged to abandon feeding through the funnel jacket.

Samuel Brittain, one of the assistant engineers of the paddle engines said that from nine to eleven on the day the ship left the Nore the donkey engines had great difficulty in 'forcing the water through the water casing into the boilers' when the boiler pressure exceeded about 18 p.s.i. He reported this to Mr Dickson who then adjusted the escape valve of the donkey engine. When this proved ineffectual Mr Patrick 'came down and turned the feed off from the casing direct into the boiler'. The reason for this was not that the boiler was priming, he said, only one of the after-boilers was priming slightly. He did not see any steam or water escaping from the vent during the whole voyage. This was, to some extent, in contradiction to McFarlane's evidence that he had seen the steam blowing off from the vent pipes up to the day of arriving at the Nore, after which he was appointed chief auxiliary engineer and had no occasion to observe the vent pipes. This change of responsibility was undoubtedly a factor in leaving the cocks unsupervised. Dickson declared that two of the donkey engines were certainly out of order and priming of the boilers caused defects among the others. Any one donkey engine was sufficient to feed the boilers, he said.

Russell thought it must be taken for granted that all believed when the feed to the funnels was shut off that the cock at the top of the tube was open. It was quite proper to shut off the feed from the casing to the boilers. Boilers always primed when they left the river, and priming was a source of great danger and inconvenience to the boilers. That was checked at last by throwing in cold water to the boilers, and it became desirable, therefore, to shut off the hot water from the casing, and let in cold water from the donkey engines, which was done. He did not know of the presence of the cocks in the stand-pipes, though he agreed with Mr Dickson that it was always a wise precaution ... The cock was not necessary where it was, though he thought it a useful precaution in case the stand-pipe broke. In previous ships on which he had fitted heaters of this type no provision at all had been made for the release of any build-up of pressure within them.

The Coroner in summing up thought that there was sufficient evidence to justify the jury in coming to the conclusion that Mr Dickson had acted carelessly in not attending to the condition of the cocks when he knew they were there. Mr Arnott also knew of the cocks and he was bound to examine them from day to day, and he was therefore, the Coroner thought, almost fully as culpable as Mr Dickson. The jury, he averred, would have to solve the difficulty upon the most contradictory evidence. The jury, in returning a verdict of 'accidental death', found that the explosion had been caused by the closing of the cock but that it had not been shown who had closed it. The engineers, they declared, had used insufficient caution.

It is instructive to consider on whom the responsibility would have fallen if the design of the heater had been ruled unsafe—as unsafe it was. The closing of the cock on the stand-pipe was not necessarily the cause of the failure of the heater, there were conditions under which it may have failed even with the cock open, as we have noted. Then, too, it was ascertained that the cocks were open on departure from the Thames and no one had ordered them to be shut. On whom would the responsibility have fallen had the cocks been found to have been shut by some un-authorized person—as, indeed, they could have been? The donkey engines were used to operate not only the boiler feed pumps but bilge pumps and other service pumps. Indeed the bilge and feed lines were connected and sea water was used—startling facts for the modern marine engineer to contemplate. In the light of this, one can appreciate the force of Russell's suggestion that the inlet to the funnel jackets could have been clogged (this would have appeared as a malfunction of the pump), then, when it was cleared, a gush of water would impinge on extremely hot surfaces and generate steam with explosive energy.

No questions were asked about foaming or spilling from the stand pipes when the ship began to draw sea water. This could have caused some inconvenience and led to the closing of the cocks.

The *Great Eastern*'s 'trial trip' was by no means a normal one. There was no single shipbuilder meeting the specifications of his client in the usual way. The Company sent their ship to sea under the command of her captain but, apart from that, with no system of management or clearly defined responsibility.

The whole matter was widely reported in the press. *The Engineer* (September 23) felt it was no more than Russell's due to give an impartial view of the conditions upon which his liability depended. They did this, they said, because *The Times* had 'allowed certain officious correspondents to prejudice Mr Russell's position by making *ex parte* statements in its columns, and neglected afterwards to publish explicit contradictions which were sent it, and which had since appeared in *The Daily News*'.[30]

The Times, however, did publish two of these contradictions, one by Russell and another by his old friend Francis Fuller, from which we can gather the kind of *ex parte* criticism to which Russell was publicly exposed:

Sir,—I observe in *The Times* of to-day letters ... pretending to contradict my evidence and Mr Dixon's regarding the part I took, and the part I did not take, in the management of the paddle-wheel engines...

I frankly admit that I communicated probably 100 messages, in the course of the voyage, from the bridge to the paddle-engine room.

I as readily admit that my chief assistant was in the paddle-engine room, giving all the assistance in his power to carry the orders I transmitted into effect.

I equally admit that my son Norman assisted me in transmitting some of those messages, and that he counted for me the strokes of the engines, and reported to me every five minutes their condition and speed.

It is perfectly true that at one time the screw-engines went faster than the paddle-wheel engines, and at another time the paddle-engines faster than the screw.

John Scott Russell

But all your correspondents have omitted to state (what they could equally have stated if they were competent witnesses and wished to be just), that I transmitted the same number of orders in the same manner to the screw-engines, which were not made by me, and where no engineer of mine was assisting.

The fact is I merely worked the telegraph, and transmitted the necessary instructions to both engines from the pilot and the captain, in such a manner as would best give effect to their wishes, and cause the vessel to perform the evolutions they desired.

But is it just or fair to argue from such circumstances that I was in responsible charge of the working of both sets of engines? I am sure Mr Blake will not say I was responsible for his engines because I concerted telegraphic arrangements with him.

I may further state that I did not go into either engine-room, and I could not even see the paddle-engines work from where I stood. My engines, and, as I imagine, those of Messrs Watt and Co., were in the hands of the Company's engineers serving under the ship's articles. Out of 170 persons, servants of the Company, employed on the engines and boilers, only four were appointed by the Company on my recommendation, and an equal number on Messrs Watt and Co.'s recommendation.

Had the paddle-engines remained my property; had they been worked on my responsibility; had the trial trip been in any degree mine, I should have taken upon myself the entire and absolute control of the whole paddle-wheel and boiler department, and should not have permitted any one to touch either engines or boilers who had not been absolutely appointed by me, and been solely responsible to me. As it was, the Company refused my offer to recommend to them competent persons for the entire staff of the paddle-wheel engines and boilers, and only accepted my recommendation for the appointment of their four first engineers.

The management of the engines and boilers being thus placed in the hands of the Company's own servants, all I could do was to render the utmost assistance in my power, as every maker of engines naturally would do, when he had the opportunity, in a work of extraordinary magnitude.

I remain, Sir, your obedient servant,

J. Scott Russell

Weymouth, Sept. 20.

Francis Fuller wrote that, in common with every other passenger, he saw Russell on the bridge receiving directions from the captain or the pilot and communicating these directions to both the screw and paddle-engine rooms. He heard Russell give only one order independently of those communicated to him by the captain or the pilot, and that was to ask a man not to empty a large box of wood shavings to windward of the engine room. Fuller asked Russell why so much coal and dirt was left to blow about on deck and Russell replied that he could not interfere as the ship was in charge of the captain. Mr Ingram, one of the directors, was appealed to about the subject because passengers were tramping the dirt into the saloons and spoiling the beautiful carpets, and Ingram said he would see to it. Fuller also refuted that Russell was being sought at one stage through his son to give orders to the engine-room. Fuller was present on the occasion when Norman was asked about his father and, contrary to the assertion of the correspondent, nothing of Russell's being required to give orders was said or he would have heard it.

The press reaction generally was one of marvel that the ship had survived such a violent assault with so little damage, testifying to its prodigious strength. Everyone associated with the ship got a fright and the shock was not lessened by the fact that fate struck when the euphoria of success was at its height, crowned by the tragic news of Brunel's death. The equation was obvious—the troubles of the launch and the explosion during the trial trip had been too much for the indomitable spirit of Brunel.

In *The Times* report of Russell's testimony he was quoted as saying, in answer to a question, 'that, except in so far as the late Mr Brunel was the originator of the idea, he was the builder and designer of the great ship, and the contractor of the paddle engines'.[31] No other report included this statement and, indeed, it reads like a parody of Russell's usual statement on this issue. However, the statement as it stands was for the purposes of the inquest and, in that context, was as close to the truth as may be. It would, of course, make him responsible for the design of the heater and that could well have been to his disadvantage. This isolated and dubious quotation would not have commanded our attention had not Rolt found among the Henry Brunel papers the copy of a letter referring to it from Patterson to Claxton. Patterson was the Bristol shipbuilder who served as shipyard manager, under Guppy's committee of works, in the building of the *Great Western* and *Great Britain*. In this, Patterson wrote:

> I am sorry to see Mr J Scott Russell taking all the credit to himself as respects the *Great Eastern*. Mr Brunel spoke of a 1000 ft. ship to me at the time the *Great Britain* was building and at the same time expressed his dislike of the old-fashioned way of framing ships. He would have all the framing in the direction in which the diagonal ribbon lines are in the framing of a

wooden ship and this plan of framing he has carried out in the great ship and he has in almost everything then proposed now carried out and I am quite sure all credit for all arrangements in that ship is due to Mr Brunel . . .[32]

Patterson evidently was unacquainted with Russell's usual statement on this issue, expounded in detail in his letter to *The Times* in 1857, and knew nothing of Russell's own experiments in longitudinal framing or his ideas on naval architecture. As the man who refused to serve as constructor of the *Great Britain*, a ship about one-eighth of the size of the *Great Eastern*, it ill became Patterson to be so ready to denigrate Russell. But it reveals the extent to which Brunel hero-worship inflamed its devotees against Russell as apparent inheritor of his prestige with respect to the *Great Eastern*.

The temptation for Russell to exploit the association of his name with the *Great Eastern* was understandably strong. He had skirted bankruptcy, and his original shipyard was but a memorial to lost hopes. To restore his fortunes he needed all the shipbuilding prestige he could acquire. If Russell succumbed to the temptation under these compulsions, it would deserve our sympathetic toleration; but his lapses were, in fact, very few while his counterbalancing acknowledgements were very numerous, no small thing in the circumstances.

The explosion damage was estimated at £5000, but its side-effects were damaging to Russell in a more sinister way. Immediately prior to the explosion the shares had risen to a premium after being occasionally at discount due to the contractors unloading their shares received in payment.[33] Now the shares had lost their value and the finances of the Company were anything but comfortable. The shareholders were restive and the directors yielded to the temptation to deflect some of this ire upon Russell who consequently now became the Company scapegoat for all ills. A. L. Holley remarked:

> When anybody wanted to find fault, I noticed that Scott Russell was the victim. If the ship did not go fast enough, Scott Russell's engines were to blame, *of course*. Nobody seems to remember that the screw is the chief power, it having six boilers to work it, instead of four, which are all that Scott Russell's paddle engines have, and that each screw boiler is larger than any paddle boiler. The London *Times* must go out of its way to an extent which is now getting to be more than ridiculous—it is contemptible—to misrepresent every feature and function of the ship which can throw discredit upon Scott Russell.

Holley goes even further, and we must weigh his remarks with respect, for he was an engineer first and foremost with no axe to grind, who conversed with everyone connected with the Great Ship. He makes the remarkable statement:

> As far as Scott Russell is concerned, I may say, *and can prove* [italics mine], that there would not have been any *Great Eastern* had it not been for his untiring efforts and engineering genius and skill. The best evidence of it is the barking of the dogs, now that he is gradually coming out of the trial with honour from those whose appreciation is worth having.[34]

Russell repaired the damage under difficulties at Weymouth and Portland and reinforced damaged parts of the boilers. The Company advanced the requisite £5000, without prejudice, pending clarification of liability. The Board of Trade surveyors demanded replacement of the damaged boiler plates but Russell argued that his repair would serve the ship until it reached Holyhead where a more acceptable—though not necessarily better—repair could be effected.

The *Great Eastern* left for Holyhead on October 8, 1959, with 'Scott Russell and his assistants' in sole charge of the paddle engines. This time, only the managing directors, Board of Trade inspectors and invited engineering and naval representatives were on board in addition to the authorized workers and crew—the party was over. The journey was uneventful and the engines ran smoothly, the paddle engines developing 2900 i.h.p. and the screw engines 4700 s.h.p., with a speed of about 14 knots—the exact speed, as Russell pointed out, that Brunel had aimed to achieve. Captain Harrison ordered a speed trial of the ship under each of the two engines separately. Neither engine-builder, however, was willing to subject his engine to the forcing that such a test might promote, especially when the locked propeller would offer resistance to the paddle engine and the locked paddles to the propeller engine, perhaps leading to unfavourable publicity. The labour of disconnecting the paddles or propeller from their engines was offered as an excuse. Neither Russell nor Blake wished to accept responsibility for the repair of damage to their engines incurred by any trial which demanded more than their intended duty[35] and the engines had already operated continuously for nearly two days—a long spell for their 'running-in'. Holley reported that

> The screw and paddle builders worked in great concert, as did their machinery till the latter part of the day. Then when Mr Russell was sick in his room, one of the screw engineers tried to misrepresent and tamper

with an experiment in a manner calculated to throw discredit upon the paddle engines. The fact is, nothing perfectly satisfactory can be done till *all* the machinery is in the hands of the company.[36]

Interested parties, however, were anxious to discover the respective contributions of the engines and just prior to reaching Holyhead, the screw engine operator agreed to the trial, but Russell remained obdurate.[37] By the time the ship headed out to sea on October 12 for another trial, Russell had yielded to the arguments of his friends and the desired tests were conducted.[38] These showed that the paddles could drive the ship at $7\frac{1}{4}$ to 8 knots with the screw locked and 9 knots with the screw free. The corresponding figures for the screw were 9 and 11 knots. This result met with general satisfaction. A. L. Holley was strongly of the opinion, an opinion which was widely shared among the knowledgeable, that the ship was under-boilered.[39] This was as much Brunel's responsibility as Russell's.

On reaching port, Captain Harrison told Holley that he was 'ready to cross the Atlantic in her tomorrow'. Holley added that as far as he could learn,

> the few things objected to by the Board of Trade could be easily remedied. The ship and engines [were] substantially alright, and there [was] nothing to be done to insure safety and economy which [could not] be accomplished in three weeks at least, provided they do not as heretofore, interfere with the work by jamming the ship full of visitors. The decoration and fitting of some passenger and freight compartments [was] not yet completed, but these [would] not be needed.[40]

Scott Russell 'and his friends', Holley indicates, were anxious to proceed with the trip to America, indeed this was the feeling of the majority of the directors, but the Chairman of the Company was afraid that the New Yorkers would not visit the ship in cold weather—so much did exhibition fees now dominate the thinking of the management—shades of Lindsay's prophecy! The *New York Times* correspondent, however, disagreed—'the ship just as she is, is one of the most wonderful sights and studies in the world, and it is pretty certain that November blasts would not keep our people away from her.'[41]

The fanatical dissension within the Board and the continuous impediments to the maiden voyage of the ship made it difficult for the management to do other than resist Russell's demand for payment of the remaining money due under the contract, even if they should have been willing to meet him on this.

150

Now, at Holyhead, in mid October, the trial trip completed satisfactorily, and regardless of the need to proceed without delay on the preparations for the trip to America, the Company exposed the ship again to thousands of sightseers who 'ransacked every nook and corner'. There was, or course, a commitment with the railway company for this. Magnus' faction engaged William Patterson to survey the ship and give a report—hopefully one which would help destroy the management and deny Russell his payment. Patterson brought along his fellow shipwrights George Bayley and John Jordan, to help him. All were well experienced in the construction of wooden ships.

The adverse report was delivered some weeks later—'the hull was not completed as a first class passenger ship . . . in her present state it would be imprudent to send her to sea on a lengthened voyage.'[42] With a few exceptions, they continued, the cabins were not equal to the requirements of a first-class passenger steamer—'inferior in materials, workmanship and furniture'. The most substantial criticisms were that the decks were of inferior wood and not tight, that there was inadequate or no heating, inadequate ventilation, and insufficient steering gear. Some of these were design deficiencies and were thus not chargeable to Russell as the finishing contractor completing the ship as designed. Others were chargeable to him or his sub-contractors, and others again, such as the heating, finishing and decorating of certain cabins and saloons, were excluded from Russell's contract pending a decision regarding the intended service of the ship.[43] The extent of Russell's responsibility could only be decided by those who were aware of all the facts and of the terms of his contract. We must accept that the three engineering arbitrators, Fowler, Hawkshaw and McClean, were in such a position, and when, in August 1860 they awarded Russell £2,000 in excess of his final payment of £6000, and rejected the Company's counterclaim, that they did so advisedly.

Meantime, at Holyhead, on October 16, the first of the sightseers was Prince Albert. Captain Harrison did the honours for the Prince, while Brereton and Jacomb, Brunel's mute lieutenants, followed up in the train of directors. The contractors were not presented. The directors of the North Western Railway Company entertained the directors of the Great Ship Company to a grand banquet in appreciation of the heavy excursion trade now attracted to their Holyhead branch line. They ran twenty excursion trains every day, the fare including admission to the ship. The banquet presented an opportunity, however, to attract the interest of influential members of the Government and of Parliament to an enterprise of national importance. The Directors were now making a bid for a Government subsidy. But, in his reply to a toast, W. E. Gladstone, the Chancellor of the Exchequer, poured cold water on these hopes: 'I believe,' he said, 'in the principle on which we have long acted in England, although it has been greatly departed from in late years—viz. that the assistance of the Government should never be extended to private enterprise unless under circumstances of rigid and extreme necessity.' Scott Russell was present, but he was no longer on the roster of speakers.

The *Great Eastern*, now completely under its own crew, left for Southampton at the beginning of November and Scott Russell was reported as saying that Southampton was so situated as to render it the best port for the arrival and departure of the *Great Eastern*, both with regard to freight and passengers and was also a place where a dock for her accommodation could be built to the greatest advantage.[44] Subsequent history has endorsed this view and its expression at the time inspired a particularly generous reception of the ship at that port, marred by the drowning of Captain Harrison when his gig capsized on making for shore.

The feed pump deficiencies were rectified and, despite the results of Patterson's survey, A. L. Holley saw only 'some minor and inexpensive, but at the same time very essential, matters in reference to the comfort of the passengers' prerequisite to crossing the Atlantic. The management of the Company, however, was under siege from Magnus and his supporters within the Board, and the resentful shareholders without. They tallied up their debts as about equal to the £26,742 of shares yet to be issued[45] and for which, thanks to the funnel explosion and adverse criticism from within their own ranks, there was little market. Even if the arbitrators decided against Russell, the Company could only expect to be relieved of paying him his final instalment, for it was unlikely that he would carry out any more work on the ship. They did not have funds to pay him in any case nor to supply the deficiencies of the ship preparatory to her maiden voyage. There was a threat, too, that should the ship sail to New York instead of Portland, the Grand Trunk Railway Co. would sue for breach of contract. It is intriguing to note that two of the directors, Brassey and Jackson, were also directors of the Grand Trunk. At the end of November, the Magnus faction published their adverse surveyors' report of October 2, and thereby inflicted even more injury to their property than the explosion had done. The conflict was now in the open with a vengeance. Guedalla, one of the faction, held a private shareholders' meeting to prepare the attack on the management of the Company. He urged the shareholders to retain their shares—it is difficult to see how they could do anything else—and told them that he believed the arbitration would be in Russell's favour. He particularly inflamed the assembly by declaring that although £10,000 had been paid for coals for the recent voyage, £20,000 had been paid for wine![46] Dissenters in the audience disputed this, claiming only £4000 as the wine bill. The directors were asked to explain their position before the January meeting. It did not help matters for the directors to have to reveal that they had now mortgaged the ship for £40,000 from what they described as 'friendly sources', for six months at $7\frac{1}{2}\%$.[47]

They now bent to the demand for a committee of inquiry, and in their surrender, the Chairman and Vice-Chairman, Campbell and Jackson, quarrelled over an anticipated knighthood which was not conferred on either.[48] Jackson defected to Magnus' side and magnanimously tendered his resignation to make way for Magnus and a nominee of his own, Mr Bold.[49] Campbell, now deserted and beleaguered, tried to justify himself in a report to the shareholders, throwing all blame on Russell and other directors. The 'engineering neglect' which caused the explosion, he said, was responsible for the postponement of the maiden voyage to America. Russell's recent liquidation had 'induced' him to prefer a new contractor, but, for the good of the ship, he had allowed his personal reservations to be overruled by Messrs Beale, McCalmont and 'several of the old and influential shareholders, representing collectively with their connexions, more than half the capital'. They agreed to accept Russell's tender because he 'was the only engineer who would undertake to complete the paddle-wheel engines, on which a large amount of money had been already expended', and because 'his tender differed from all others in embracing entire completion as a first-class ship, and being willing to give good security for the proper completion of all the work.' He asserted that he had no personal interest whatever with the tendering parties.[50]

All the pent-up frustration and resentment of the shareholders overflowed at the general meeting on January 11, 1860; one likened it to a bear-garden and, in the words of *The Times*, 'many personal observations were freely indulged in, apparently to the great satisfaction and amusement of the meeting'.[51] Holley described a florid clergyman, with red hair, undoubtedly the Reverend Mr Nicholson, who 'ever and anon popped up . . . like the hammer of a piano when the key is touched' with the most bitter and violent opprobrium.[52] The picture emerging for Holley was one of 'salaries and commissions, banquets and jobbing, patronage and facilities for bulling and bearing the stock . . . scrambling and abuse, recrimination and jealousy'. The interests of the shareholders, he lamented, went to the wall. Limited liability companies, he believed, were on trial during the *Great Eastern* exposure of incapacity and jobbing.

A week or so afterwards, Russell made a noble bid to restore sanity and a sense of proportion. He circulated a report among the shareholders, boldly printed on gilt-edged paper, informing them of the assets of their property. In conclusion he summarized his remarks thus:

> Such, then, are a few of the sea-going qualities and money-earning capabilities of our ship; and you will thus see that all the qualities and powers of the vessel originally promised when she was designed have been borne out by experience. She has proved handy and manageable . . . She has realized the speed for which she was designed, and which is such as to enable her to reduce the time of a voyage to Australia from 59 days to 39 days . . . She has been proved to afford comparative immunity from sea-sickness, along with the comfort and luxury of a first-class hotel . . . yet we are told that our property is a bad one, and must be laid aside as unseaworthy.
>
> It has been stated that the ship is not now completed throughout her whole extent. Of course she is not. She was not meant to be entirely completed until after her return from America, when her permanent station and trade could be determined. Originally she had been designed to accommodate 3,000 passengers, or 10,000 troops; but for the purpose of going to sea on her trial trip to America, she was only to be completed for 675 passengers. Only two compartments of her length—one of 90 and another of 60 feet long—were completely fitted for passengers. The rest of the ship remains as intended, almost entirely unfitted, or provisionally fitted only, for temporary purposes.
>
> . . . You have been taught to suppose that you and I have opposite interests. Do not believe it. My interests can never be separated from those of the Great Ship. I am proud to have been her builder. I expect yet to earn great reputation by her; and I am, like yourself, a large shareholder. It is, therefore, my interest, even more than yours, that your property in the ship would turn out valuable. It is true you owe me money for work done, but we are not, therefore, enemies. I want no more for my work than three honest and able arbitrators, to whom you and I have both referred the matter, shall pay in due time. Let us both, therefore, set about turning our mutual property to account, for our mutual good.

Then, in a final clause he enunciated, as none of the businessmen on Board seemed able to do, the unquestionable desiderata for success:

> As a fellow shareholder of the ship, let me tell you what is now wanted is the best possible management of the ship. Steam shipping property is not easily managed; but, if you can agree upon men of ability, experience and success in the management of steam property, to take the entire practical control of the executive part of our business, you will not be disappointed with the result.[53]

This excellent advice, no less than the example of conciliation and practical composure which he set, was ignored and though they did not know it at the time, in ignoring it the last hope for the success of the *Great Eastern* melted away. 'If the ship were given to me,' Holley wryly remarks, 'it would be as fatal a present as that of a white elephant in Siam.'[54] He was convinced that the only hope for it was the acceptance of offers to charter her for twelve months by a Mr Lever on terms advantageous to the shareholders. He saw no prospect of the Company managing the ship properly. Neither the new nor the old management of the Company showed any disposition to accept Lever's offers.

The outcome, after two further meetings was a new Board and the rejection of dishonourable imputations upon the previous Board. The new Board included the Marquis of Stafford, two sea captains and Daniel Gooch, in response to the desire for the inclusion of more 'practical' men. None was experienced in the management of a steamship line.

It was suddenly discovered that the Board of Trade requirements were much less than at first anticipated and the extravagant strictures given so much publicity largely without foundation.[55] £30,000 would send the *Great Eastern* on a voyage to America.[56] Messrs Lungley of Deptford quickly completed the necessary work and the *Great Eastern* sailed to New York, on July 12, 1860, with Mr and Mrs Daniel Gooch, Norman Scott Russell, A. L. Holley, and Zerah Colburn among the few passengers on board. Scott Russell, who had originally intended to sail on the maiden voyage, remained at home.

The ship was still in America when, early in September, the arbitrators pronounced an award of £18,000 in favour of Russell, an amount greatly in excess of that for which Russell would have settled earlier. This announcement, thought *The Engineer*, should be heard with pleasure by professional engineers everywhere.

For months past, [it went on] the designer and builder of the finest ship in the world had been one of the best abused men in England ... because it suited the commercial ends of interested parties to hound on the daily press against him ... and because a few professional persons, forgetting temporarily the responsibility of the undertaking, pronounced *ex parte* judgements upon portions of the great ship with a critical severity which they would shrink from having applied to works of their own ... Although we have had occasion to differ with Mr Scott Russell, he is nevertheless one of the last men whom the scientific press of this country ought to see unfairly treated ... men willing to sneer at those who are incomparably superior to themselves never are wanting. But the truth is, the world owes very much, and the profession still more, to every man who, like him, brings an original and powerful mind, well stored with scientific knowledge, to the advancement ... of steam navigation.

Notwithstanding the unassailable authority of Fowler, Hawkshaw and McClean, the new Company managed to obtain a stay of execution of the award, alleging that the arbitrators had exceeded their jurisdiction, whereupon Russell brought specific actions against the Company. One, for the payment of the arbitrators' award; two, in respect of additional work done beyond the contract and for interruption by reason of the Company exhibiting the ship to visitors during the progress of the works; and three, for damages by reason of the Company's blocking the transfer of certain of his shares in the Great Ship Company. The upshot was a verdict in Russell's favour. The litigation, however, extended into April 1861, and on the 25th of that month a sheriff's warrant was executed on Russell's behalf, taking possession of the ship and its stores, then lying at Milford Haven. This was argued to be necessary since the ship was the only security for Russell's claim. A final ruling by the Court of Common Pleas three days later ended the matter by confirming the award to Russell and ruling out the possibility of appeal. Thus ended Scott Russell's connection with the Great Ship Company, and, on the face of it, his saga with Brunel's great dream. But the Great Ship did not leave its creators unscathed, nor even to rest in peace.

The subsequent history of the *Great Eastern* is no less eventful than that of its creation. The ship was never employed on the duty for which it was intended nor was it successfully used on transatlantic service. Its management was inadequate to the task and was embarrassed by one or two mishaps, the most serious of which was the mishandling of the ship in a storm, either due to incompetence or inadequate steering power, or both, which led to the ship's being caught in the trough of the waves with paddles inoperable, the rudder post fractured and the screw obstructed by the loose rudder. Control of the rudder was retrieved, on the suggestion of an American engineer among the passengers, by winding a coil of rope round the stump of the rudder post and the ship limped into Cork in this condition with the baggage reduced to a slurry in the hold. She was later auctioned off to a syndicate who planned to use her for the laying of a transatlantic telegraph cable in 1866 and 1867 and this, it seems in retrospect, was the historical contribution for which she was uniquely created. She was used to lay a further cable across the Indian Ocean then finished her days as a showboat. She was scrapped in 1898, on the Mersey, by which time transatlantic liners of comparable size were being built in Britain and Europe, owing much, for their structure, to the heroic precedent of their great prototype of half a century earlier.

The respective contributions of Russell and Brunel to the design and construction of the *Great Eastern* are easy to catalogue in broad outline, but their mutual influences one upon the other are not so obvious although they must have been considerable. Both, too, in turn, owed something to others. Russell claimed the ship 'as a piece of naval architecture'—that is, its lines, its sea-going qualities (speed, stability, etc.) and the great paddle engines and boilers. Then, in addition, he established the system of construction which, in turn, influenced the structural features broadly established by Brunel. The latter insisted on authorizing everything, but this did not give him any proprietary right to the ideas which he merely approved. Brunel and Russell had a community of interest in longitudinal framing, but the actual techniques employed owed much to the draughtsmen, foremen and workmen on the job. Russell names these in his great book. It is to Russell and his assistants—and he was good at picking them—that honour is due for overcoming the unprecedented problems set by the gigantic size of the ship and its novel structure.

The *Great Eastern* constituted one of the most dramatic engineering adventures of the nineteenth century and unites the names of I. K. Brunel and John Scott Russell, willy nilly, in perpetuity.

CHAPTER SEVEN

The Iron Warship

Have we a fleet able to chase from the seas all the fast ships which our enemies will send out to destroy our commerce by sinking our merchant ships? Have we a fleet of fast iron-armoured men-of-war, sufficiently armed to penetrate the ships of our enemy—sufficiently protected to resist his guns—sufficiently fast to choose our own time and place for the fight—sufficiently buoyant to carry fuel and stores into any ocean where we require their service, and to engage and defeat the enemy in his own waters, instead of in ours?

J. SCOTT RUSSELL

During 1858 and 1859 while the *Great Eastern* was awaiting completion at her moorings on the Thames, Russell was moving to re-establish himself as a shipbuilder from that portion of David Napier's yard he had purchased in 1857. Business was not good, but he did pick up an order for two luxury iron steam yachts of extremely shallow draft which he launched in 1858. One, *El Rey Jaime II*, was for the Sultan of Turkey, and the other, *Cleopatra*, for Hama El Pasha of Egypt. This was the third *Cleopatra* Russell constructed for the same owner. Both ships called for the application of his longitudinal structural system, partial and complete bulkheads, iron deck, etc., and both were powered by his neat three cylinder oscillating engine on a single crank and paddles. *Cleopatra*, a long, slender barge-like craft, reached a speed of 15 knots and sailed to Egypt under her own steam.

Early in 1859, the Admiralty gave him an order also for a shallow-draft iron paddle-steamer for the Indus flotilla. Orders for five more were placed with other builders but only Russell's performed to specification.[1] Also launched by Russell in this year was the 17-knot paddle-steamer, *Thunderer*, said to be the fastest of the day,[2] a steam sloop *Prince Consort*, and a 400-ton wooden auxiliary screw gunboat *Donna Maria Anna* for the Portuguese navy (August 14). The period found him also actively consulting with the Admiralty over the design of the *Warrior* on which construction began at the Thames Iron Works, in June 1859.

The *Warrior* has a prominent place in naval history, being the first iron-hulled, armoured, sea-going warship. A ship, as one historian puts it, which was 'utterly different from anything ever seen by anybody ... Nothing in the least degree comparable to such a revolutionary step in British fleet architecture is to be found in the whole records of the Constructor's and Surveyor's department at Whitehall.'[3]

The superficial indications are then, that at this time Russell was making a fair start on a recovery of his fortunes. It was no doubt progress on a shoestring with advance payments, and his materials and ships serving as security. We have no details of this or of the extent of his encumbrances.

There were also stirrings, in 1858, to mark the tenth anniversary of the Great Exhibition with an exhibition in 1861. Dilke and Cole initiated the proposal and persuaded the Royal Society of Arts to appoint an executive committee, of which Russell was a member, to wait upon Prince Albert and present the scheme to him. Russell characteristically drew up a plan for the exhibition which Dilke and Cole studied. The preparations however were soon referred to the Commissioners of 1851 who held in trust the funds accrued from the Great Exhibition and soon a new executive committee was formed under Cole of which neither Dilke nor Russell was a member. It was just as well, for Russell's hands were full.

The background to Russell's association with the *Warrior* began as far back as 1851 when he first contemplated an iron-hulled and armoured steam warship. In this he was prompted by his conversations with R. L. Stevens, the eminent American steam shipbuilder when the latter was visiting England with his yacht, the *America*. Stevens told him of the results of a long series of experiments conducted by him for the U.S. Government on the resistance of iron plates to shot. Three years later, events in the Crimean War drew attention to the subject. The wooden gunboats of the time were an unequal match for shellfire and the unsinkable bastions controlling access to strategic channels in the Baltic and the Black Sea. In anticipation of this the French had begun to plan the construction of shallow-draft, heavily armoured floating batteries, said to be the brain-child of Napoleon III himself. These were protected by an armour cladding of 10 mm iron plates which had been found to be effective in range tests. The French ironworks could not supply sufficient armour plate for the ten batteries thought requisite, in time for the campaign of 1855, whereupon the British allies agreed to share the task. Orders were immediately placed—one, the *Etna*, with John Scott Russell;

the *Meteor* and *Thunder* (launched April 17, 1855) with Messrs Mare; and the *Glatton* and *Trusty* (launched April 18 and May 3) with Messrs Green; all Thames shipbuilders.

We have noted the fate of the *Etna*, destroyed by fire on the eve of its launch, May 3. As Russell looked wryly on the hulk of iron armour lying partly in the river, its timber linings charred to a cinder, he thought he could turn the accident to advantage by using the armour on a proto-type armoured corvette or frigate of his own design: a fast, well armed, sea-going ship, not another clumsy floating battery.

The design Russell produced was of a completely iron ship constructed on the longitudinal system with an outer skin of thick iron armour plate backed by wood. The lines and proportions, of course, were based on his wave-line theory. He had a model constructed to his drawing and submitted both model and drawing to Sir Baldwin Walker, the Surveyor of the Navy, on November 15, 1855, with the following covering letter:

> This model and drawing show the internal arrangements by which the greatest strength is to be produced.
>
> They were designed by me for the construction of a shot-proof corvette. You are aware that from the beginning I have been a believer in the shot-proof quality of vessels made of iron plates of great thickness.
>
> About five years ago the eminent steam shipbuilder of America, Mr. R. L. Stevens, communicated to me the result of a long series of experiments made at the expense of the United States Government by himself, the chief practical result of which was that iron plates of five inches thickness were absolutely impenetrable to the heaviest shot fired by the largest guns in the service, the heaviest charge of powder, and the shortest distance.
>
> The model I submit shows the manner in which I propose to build a shot-proof corvette which would possess all the qualities of our present steam corvettes, but would be of larger size and armament, and of perfect impenetrability.
>
> When I first made this design and mode it was my intention to have taken out a patent for such construction, applicable to war vessels in general, but as a patent involves publication, of which other countries would be able at once to avail themselves, I thought it better to keep my secret and to submit the matter at the proper time, in confidence, to our own Admiralty, and which accordingly I now beg leave to do.
>
> I beg, at the same time, to express my conviction from what I have reason to know, that if such vessels be not built by us, they will speedily be built in other countries.

Sir Baldwin Walker discussed the proposal with Russell and was reasonably impressed. The time was not auspicious, he feared, for placing a revolutionary idea of the kind before the Admiralty, but he would take the first opportunity to do so. Russell enquired after the fate of his design on each occasion he met Sir Baldwin over the next three years and submitted further proposals until, late in 1858, Sir Baldwin asked him to prepare a larger version of his design while at the same time the Surveyor's department under Isaac Watts prepared a similar design and invited some other shipbuilders to do likewise.[4] Sir John Pakington, now First Lord of the Admiralty in Lord Derby's new administration, gave Russell a ready ear. The news from France of course was disquieting. Napoleon III, unlike the British Admiralty, had no doubt about the virtues of armoured warships and had appointed Dupuy de Lôme to design a fleet of armoured steam frigates, of which the *Gloire*, laid down in 1858, was the first. A Parliamentary committee was promptly established to examine the relative strengths of the British and French navies and, early in 1859, recommended that Britain should accelerate the conversion of her remaining sailing ships to steam and go into the whole question of iron-clad vessels.

The Admiralty was due a great deal of credit, Russell declared, for the manner in which it settled upon the design of the *Warrior*, and in this his opinion was no doubt fortified by the fact that it was a design compounded of his and the 'Department's' which was accepted and executed.[5] The requirements of the *Warrior* were long range, high speed (at least 14 knots) and good sailing qualities. Her armour had to be proof against 68 pounder artillery and she had to be able to accommodate a battery of 48 guns and to ram. As laid down, she was a fully rigged three-master 380 feet between perpendiculars, 58 feet maximum beam, $26\frac{1}{2}$ feet load draught and a corresponding displacement of 9140 tons. Her 1250 n.h.p. engines were the largest installed in any naval vessel up to her time, and the two-bladed 10 ton, $23\frac{1}{2}$ foot propeller was the largest hoisting screw ever made. The armour plates, $4\frac{1}{2}$ inches thick, were forged under a steam hammer and, backed by wood, protected 280 feet of her central hull, where her armament was disposed in broadside array. She was subdivided by watertight bulkheads, transversely and longitudinally, and was of wave-line form. Her extremities were not armoured nor heavily loaded, to avoid undue stresses due to the fine lines, but they were honeycombed with watertight compartments. The longitudinal framing facilitated the incorporation of a stout iron ram stem, a tactical feature to which the

161

current ascendancy of armour over gunfire lent much importance. So important indeed that, in 1870, Russell declared to his fellow naval architects: 'There is a new warfare. It is no longer, "Lay her alongside", but "Give her the stem", which will be the order of battle.' This was not Russell's idea, it was the thinking of the most erudite naval tacticians of the period. To accomplish this he predicted fleets of high speed twin-screw warships reinforced to ram.[6] The *Warrior* anticipated this.

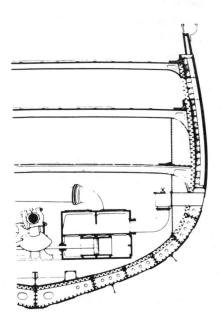

HMS *Warrior* mid-ship section: longitudinal frames; transverse webs; iron decks, and longitudinal bulkheads flanking hull; side armour.

When she was laid down in June 1859, there was by no means universal approval of the departure from wooden hulls. The debate, in which Russell took a prominent part, went on. The Admiralty's decision to make such an uncharacteristic and wholesale break with established practice was therefore all the more laudable.

It went hard with Russell that despite his contribution to the design of the *Warrior* and his several submissions to the Admiralty, his bid for the contract was rejected on account of price and time. He protested that his pioneering rôle entitled him to some special consideration, but the Surveyor advised the Admiralty that Russell was not alone in 1855 in thinking that vessels of this class would be introduced into the Royal Navy, and that none of the

> main features of the plan which had been adopted originated with him with the exception of omitting the protecting plates from the bow and stern and introducing transverse shot-proof bulkheads for the protection of the midship part of the vessel. All the other features such as fine lines for speed, general arrangement of the skin of the iron hull and the extensive introduction of longitudinal iron webs and iron decks were in such general use that any constructor would it is believed consider himself free to adopt them if he felt inclined to do so. Fine lines for speed cannot in fact be regarded as having originated with any one individual. It has been gradually developed from the earliest date of steam navigation.[7]

In other words, Russell's pioneering contributions were not protected by patent and the Admiralty felt no sense of obligation to one of its most valuable and imaginative advisers. Russell, over a period of years, had submitted a whole range of designs of armoured ships embracing all the various sizes.[8] In conducting this campaign in secret he unfortunately committed his advanced and original designs to sterility, and, in the end, to plagiarism. He called the *Warrior* a 'noble design', and claimed that he could be permitted the liberty of saying so, because, as he explained: although the design of that ship may be in some respects called mine, yet in other respects equally the design of the Surveyor's Department; and I feel quite ready to do justice to their merit in that design, as I am sure they are to do full credit to me for such parts of it as originated with me.'[9] Fine lines may not have been patentable but systems of hull construction could have been and since have been patented. Russell, however, felt that he owed it to the nation to avoid the revelation which patenting involved. We shall note how Sir William Armstrong dealt with this problem to his advantage with respect to some dubious gun patents.

The Admiralty gave the contract to the Thames Iron Works which had taken over Mare's old yard. If they beat Russell's tender in price and time they did so to their cost, for they defaulted in time and had the frustration of having their final payment withheld as penalty.[10] The large sternpost and the novelty of the construction—pioneered on a greater scale by Russell on the *Great Eastern*—proved more than they bargained for, even had the Admiralty not introduced changes during construction. Russell accused the Admiralty of deliberately seeking the default of inexperienced builders,[11] but, nevertheless, with respect to the builders of the *Warrior* 'he had the greatest pleasure in bearing his humble testimony to their excellent construction of the Admiralty design.'[12] Regardless of the Admiralty's posture in the matter, the *Warrior* was regarded as very much a 'Scott Russell' ship within the profession, and Charles H. Jordan, assistant naval architect of the Thames Iron Works, tells us that he was entrusted with the drawing of the hull details on the strength of his former experience with the longitudinal system of construction while in the employ of Scott Russell.[13]

The launch of the *Warrior* in December 1860 was impeded by the cold. The grease froze on the ways and six steam tugs took an hour to haul her into the water. Shipbuilding was a great adventure in these days and the, unthinkable sometimes actually happened. The *Warrior*'s measured mile performance of 14·3 knots set a record for fighting ships which was not exceeded for some years, not even by her sister ship *Black Prince*, built by Napier on the Clyde, which, although practically identical to the *Warrior*, remained consistently slightly slower. The same crowds which congregated to watch the progress of the *Great Eastern*, now mustered to watch the birth of the most powerful warship in the world. When her long, black, hollow-lined form slipped among the stubby, wooden hulls of the Channel Squadron at Portsmouth in 1861, she looked, as one said, 'like a black snake among rabbits'. She owed something to the precedent of the *Great Eastern* which owed much to Brunel as well as to Russell and both in turn owed a great debt—freely acknowledged by Russell—to the pioneering work of Fairbairn in iron structures.

In the same month as the *Warrior* was laid down, the Admiralty compensated Russell for the loss of the contract by giving him an order for four wooden steam gunboats propelled by screw.[14] It was an ironical twist for the advocate of iron hulls.

An earlier instance in which Russell aided the Admiralty with iron ships occurred at the time of the *Etna*'s loss and warrants comment. Admiral Napier's much trumpeted expedition to the Baltic had come to an ignominious halt. As Russell expressed it, 'our admiral's noble ships could plough the deep but could not plough the bottom of the shallow Baltic, and he had no vessel of such draft of water as would enable him to command the fortress he was to destroy'. Whereupon Russell on behalf of the Admiralty, arranged the purchase of the two iron gunboats he had designed and built specifically for service in that sea, in the period 1850–1. This matter was raised in the House of Commons, and in a letter to *The Times* (May 11) Russell advised the public that these particular gunboats were 'of a description and power for which no vessel in [the British Navy was] at all a match', and that certain experienced steam officers in the navy, as well as Captain Claxton, had 'spoken strongly to some authorities in favour of the immediate construction of this class of vessel for use in the Baltic and on the Danube'. They were exceptionally well armed and could fire two eight-inch shell guns from platforms at bow and stern, parallel or transversely to the keel—a unique arrangement for the time.

These ships, the *Nix* and *Salamander*, were built to the order of Prince Adalbert of Prussia, who asked Russell to design for him a class of gunboat carrying twice as much armament as any vessel of her size in British service, travelling at least two knots faster and drawing not more than seven feet of water. These requirements were amply met, and, in addition, the lines, fore and aft, were identical so that the boats could steer with either end foremost, a great help in manœuvring in shallow waters. This was the prototype of a class and design of warship which, constructed of wood, saw much service in the American Civil War. By the time the transfer was made, however, the Russians had installed underwater defences at Cronstadt, and so the gunboats were despatched to the Crimea where, named the *Recruit* and the *Weser*, they were of great service, under Cowper Coles' command, in the Sea of Azov.[15]

The advent of the steam-powered iron warship caught the Admiralty naval architects at a disadvantage. The requisite knowledge and expertise lay with the civil shipbuilders, and while Russell and others lent their advice and were ready to design and construct, the Admiralty's naval architects felt the need for wider avenues of communication with their civil contemporaries. Sir William White, drawing on information give him by Sir Nathaniel Barnaby, relates that the formation of an institution of naval architects had been talked about by Dr Woolley, former principal of the defunct School of Mathematics and Naval Construction at Portsmouth, and some of his former pupils, but that 'it needed someone familiar with the workings of other great technical Associations to bring such mere wishes to a living issue. In Mr Scott Russell, a leader was found, and a most capable leader he was.'[16] Early in 1860, Russell invited Woolley and two of the more gifted of Woolley's former pupils in the service of the Admiralty, Edward Reed and Nathaniel Barnaby, who were both to become distinguished Admiralty Controllers, to meet with him at his house at Sydenham to draw up the necessary plans. The time was right and Russell was ready, even offering to guarantee the initial expenses. E. J. Reed agreed to serve as Secretary and one of his first duties was to invite fellow naval architects and shipbuilders to join the founding body and establish the criteria for membership. An inaugural meeting was promptly called and Sir John Pakington, the former First Lord of the Admiralty, was appointed President. Russell was appointed a Vice-President, and the Institution began its proceedings at the premises of the Royal Society of Arts, in April 1860, with the first of a series of three papers by Russell on the Wave-line Principle. Russell attended every annual meeting of the Institution until his death and rarely listened to the reading of a paper without contributing to the discussion, sometimes, indeed, a little too volubly. It is important to notice that he was highly esteemed and regarded even with affection within the Institution he promoted.[17]

The initial reaction of merchant shipbuilders was cautious, they had more inhibitions to overcome than had the Admiralty men and evinced no enthusiasm for a professional forum devoted to the discussion of new developments and mutual problems. While, likewise, Russell may not have cared to reveal his secrets to his business competitors, he certainly took genuine pleasure in their successful application of his wave-line principle, although he gained no pecuniary advantage from this. He had, for instance, gladly testified before a Parliamentary committee to the feasibility of a proposed 17-knot all-weather service between Holyhead and Dublin to be conducted by a fleet of four wave-line ships designed by Oliver Lang, jnr., and his enthusiasm was sincere, when, on the bridge of the first of Lang's elegant wave-line creations, the *Leinster*, he saw her 'driven at the highest speed against a head sea, in the heaviest storm ... I saw this vessel enter a wave on one side,' he rhapsodized, 'and come out on the other leaving nothing behind but a small portion of the paddle box: and the passengers down below were not conscious of anything beyond the ordinary inconvenience of a sea voyage.'[18]

Russell's purpose was greatly assisted by the general usefulness of some of the matters discussed at the first meetings of the Institution, none more so than the vexed question of Lloyd's conservative attitude to technical innovation. One great practical result of the discussions was the prompt decision by Lloyd's to classify any ship incorporating novel features provided the builder submitted his plans and paid for a continuous and special survey.[19] This at least was progress, if rather late in the day for Russell who had been a considerable innovator, particularly with the longitudinal system. Lloyd's would not classify Russell's longitudinal ships although they did underwrite a few of them under privately arranged terms.[20]

Another naval development with which Russell had some connection and which formed the vital subject of many a discussion at the new Institution was the armoured cupola or gun turret. Captain Cowper Coles took out his patent in the year of the *Warrior*, 1859, and the Admiralty and the War Office financed the construction of a prototype by Russell. It was removed to Woolwich Arsenal early in 1861 to be mounted on the *Trusty* for experiments.[21] Some ten years were to elapse, however, before a proper turret ship was authorized. Although Russell submitted a design for an ironclad mounting twelve guns in rotating turrets,[22] he did not claim to be a pioneer of turret ships, but he had a good deal to say about their special problems.[23]

Meantime, Russell was once again nearly tripped up financially. He received the award of the *Great Eastern* arbitration in April 1861, but does not seem to have been sufficiently prompt in settling a debt of £1000 claimed by one John Dickson (his former manager?) for work done to that ship. On September 26 of that year, while Russell was on one of his European jaunts, Dickson's lawyer presented a petition for Russell's bankruptcy with the incredible assertion that Russell had left the country to escape his creditors. Clearly he had not shaken off his obligations. The petition was granted and Russell had the trouble of appealing against this on his return. The judgement was reversed, October 9, and Dickson was paid through Freshfield & Co., Russell's solicitors. But Harry Lester of Lester & Perkins, ship repairers, whom Russell had engaged to repair the *Great Eastern's* explosion damage also conceived a claim against Russell and challenged the Dickson settlement on the grounds that it was a case of a creditor's compounding with a bankrupt to receive preferential treatment over other creditors. He also was granted his bankruptcy petition, whereupon Russell produced evidence that Lester, who was the son of his former master shipwright[24] and had been one of his apprentices, was in fact in debt to him. He had now to prove, nevertheless, that neither he nor his agent had paid Dickson but that a third party had done so without their connivance. The judgement went in Russell's favour and this second attempt to force his bankruptcy was quashed; but not before some damage had been done to his economic credibility.[25]

His order book was again empty and he now 'retired from the commerce of shipbuilding' having constructed upwards of a hundred ships.

The last ship to leave his slip was the 600-ton auxiliary screw iron clipper, the *Annette*—what he called his 'pet Annette'—launched in December 1861. It was appropriate that this ship should incorporate so many of the features he had pioneered and developed—longitudinal framing, partial and whole longitudinal and transverse watertight bulkheads, iron deck and 'wave' lines.[26] The screw was retractable by means of a neat mechanism of his own design.

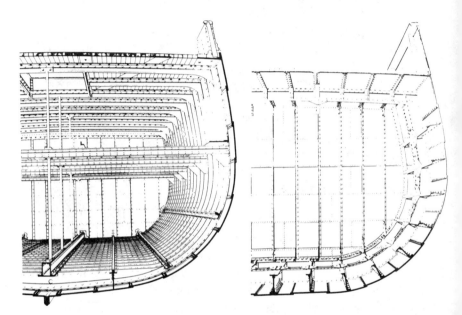

Conventional transverse framing (*left*), and Scott Russell's longitudinal framing in the auxiliary screw clipper *Annette*, 1862 (*right*)

Now he fell back upon his consulting practice, began to prepare a book on the state of the art of naval architecture, and continued his vigorous advocacy of an iron fleet. The issue, iron v. wood greatly complicated the prevailing controversy over Britain's naval preparedness in the face of French advances. Some asserted that France had no intention of engaging in hostilities with Britain and that Britain's numerical strength of 'wooden walls' was an adequate shield in any case. Pakington was at the Admiralty only long enough, 1858–9, to order the *Warrior* and the

Black Prince, before the Liberals came into power and returned Somerset to the Admiralty. The new *Warrior* class of 9000 tons displacement carried the same armament as a 5000 ton French frigate. Could not the same money have purchased several smaller ships of equal armament? Could the *Warrior*, 120 feet longer than the largest three-decker, be accommodated in the basin at Portsmouth? Why so long? Above all, could thin iron plates really be as strong as thick wooden timbers? Did not iron splinter and sink? So it went on.

Russell thoroughly examined the whole subject in a booklet entitled *The Fleet of the Future, Iron or Wood*? published in 1861, and of course strongly advocated iron. The large and strong party in the Admiralty and elsewhere who conceived strong objections to iron-hulled ships of war was led by the prestigious artillerist Sir Howard Douglas. Sir Howard, then an octogenarian, had long sedulously opposed the introduction of iron ships to the navy and had long been heeded. He was given the floor of the Institution of Naval Architects at an early session[27] and Russell followed with what E. J. Reed described as 'one of the ablest speeches ever delivered upon iron ships'.[28] Sir Howard was quite demolished by Russell here and elsewhere, and some felt Russell had been too severe on the old man.[29] But Sir Howard on his part had injudiciously cited the *Great Eastern* as an 'awful roller' which had not attained her intended speed.

The occasion indeed found the man. When it came to explaining unfamiliar scientific or technical phenomena, none excelled Russell. His skill as a propagandist, for himself no less than for his causes, is well illustrated by his letter to *The Times* to correct the statement of a previous correspondent that Dupuy de Lôme had been a pupil of Russell's. In this Russell at once subtly equated himself to de Lôme, underlined his French connection and emphasized the progressive attitude of the French rulers to naval progress. He and de Lôme were of about the same age and standing in their profession, he wrote. It was 'unfair' to call de Lôme his pupil. They had long been on terms of 'free and open professional intercourse', but in this he had received at least as much benefit as he had given. M. de Lôme had 'also carried out original scientific researches on a large scale with the ample means placed at his disposal by the wise liberality of the French Admiralty. These researches had led him to important practical results', which he, Russell, considered as valuable as anything he might ever have communicated to de Lôme.[30] This was no more than fact yet it comes across as something more.

169

Within a year, news from America of the indecisive slogging match between two armoured batteries, the *Merrimac* and the *Monitor*, seemed to settle the question forever. Russell quickly revised his booklet, making it very largely an examination of the British naval establishment, the history of its resistance to change and an advocacy of the immediate planned and progressive building of a new fleet.

He did not pull his punches, and produced in consequence probably the most entertaining of his writings. Only his apprehension of the serious danger threatening his country, he declared, induced him to publish views which would 'provoke the hostility of parties and persons who wielded a vast power, influence and patronage'. He was indeed to suffer for it.

Recent governments had certainly granted larger appropriations to the navy and many new warships had been and were being built—but, with two exceptions, they were of wood

> ... we hastened to increase our stores of timber; we covered every slip in our dockyards with new wooden ships of the line; we multiplied our gigantic unfightable frigates; we replaced our rotten and decayed gunboats by new wooden gunboats. And while Louis Napoleon, in a country prolific of timber and where iron is nearly an exotic, is resolutely abandoning wood and taking to iron, we are as resolutely ransacking our forests, importing timber from all countries of Europe to such an extent that in these seven years we have nearly doubled the cost of timber by the excess of our demand, and have known the agents of Government so put to their wits' end for a stern-post of oak, that they have rummaged the growing forests of England for a live tree big enough for their purpose, and have had to cut it down with the green leaves growing and send it afloat as part of Her Majesty's wooden fleet with the live pieces still contesting with the salt water for exclusive possession of the cells of the wood. Such was our love of wood and our hatred of iron that we, in an iron country, possessing resources so great that no shape or size or quality of thing in iron could be demanded that could not instantly be produced, still cling to wood; and in exact proportion to the conviction on the mind of the Emperor Napoleon on one side, arises our dogged determination to shut our eyes to the two great facts on the other. We had twenty millions to spend as well as he. In the same seven years in which he spent twenty millions, we spent thirty millions, but ours all upon wood, with one exception in iron, and his all upon iron, with an exception in wood.

What, too, was the Emperor's way of setting about his plan?—

> ... he did not search for a First Lord of the Admiralty who had sound Tory principles [Pakington], or an accomplished nobleman of pure Whig descent

[Somerset]. He did not look out for a Surveyor of the Navy [Sir Baldwin Walker] who never in his life had either mastered the science of naval architecture, or even possessed the practical experience of building a ship, or even a jolly-boat. He did not appoint by seniority the most aged shipbuilder in the dockyard to stand at the head of his profession [Isaac Watts], and be designer of ships for the navy. He did as any practical man would do in his own business; having got a difficult thing to do, which had not been done before, which had no precedent to guide it and no authority for an example, he looked out simply for the man of most talent—of best scientific acquaintance with the principles of his profession—the man who had shown most capacity for a new career—in short, the man who seemed most fitted for his work—and he found his man in an officer of the dockyard in Toulon, comparatively young, but who had already ventured to break through the official routine of his profession, who had studied the principles of naval architecture in books of science under professors of naval colleges (which exist in France, though not here), who had travelled to England and made himself acquainted there with the most modern plans of iron shipbuilding, and the most improved forms of modern ships. This man the Emperor Napoleon had the sagacity to find out and the wisdom to select contrary to all routine, and placed him at the head of the department for constructing the future fleet of France.

The Admiralty, nevertheless, decided to investigate the resistance of iron to shot, changed their minds, then at the *Excellent*, the naval depot at Portsmouth, authorized what Russell contemptuously referred to as 'make-believe experiments'. The Emperor, he said,

had succeeded in making iron plates resist shot. The Admiralty set about the contrary problem, how to make iron plates not resist shot . . . as if the only object had been, not to find out the one wise way in which iron plates could resist shot, but the many foolish ways by which they might be made not to resist shot . . . and all this time the lavish expenditure on wooden ships has gone on.

How much credit Russell could take for Lindsay, the shipowner's, resolution in the House of Commons on 11 April, 1861, that further construction of large wooden vessels should cease, may never be known; but we can be sure that he and his supporters, well acquainted with Russell— Sir Morton Peto and Sir Joseph Paxton—were well fortified with a knowledge of Russell's views.

Somerset made excuses. He was not responsible for the Admiralty over the past seven years, and his own actions were at the dictates of Parliament—'waiting for something to turn up' said Russell. But now thirty million pounds was available for the reconstruction of the fleet—'shall we spend the money on the establishments or on the fleets?' asked Russell.

If you ask those men who have spent the last £30,000,000 without giving us our fleet, what it is best to do with the money, they will tell you by all means maintain the establishments: first spend the money on the dockyards, and afterwards, if you can, on the fleets... The great establishments, the dockyards, are the great vehicles of expenditure. No machinery can be more effectually organised for the purpose of spending the money and not providing the fleet than the dockyards... In this respect the expenditure of the last seven years is faultless... But look at the result. All those mountains have produced the glorious result of two ships of the line!

But even that is too much. The establishments could not and did not produce the two ships of war composing the fleet of 1862. They were not built in the dockyards, but in the country; in short, the Government bought them, they did not build them...

If you do buy your ships, you will have one comfort at least—you will know what they have cost, and you will know when you have got them. In your establishments you never know what they have cost, because you never will allow the cost of the establishment to go into the cost of the work done. And you never know what is done and what is not done; and, further, you know by dire experience, that as much or more may be spent on undoing, lengthening, and enlarging, cutting down and altering, as on building...

If you want your ships, therefore, buy them. Buy them at the market price, in the open market; buy them, but not at the cheapest price; buy them, but not at the lowest tender; buy them of the men who know their business, who do good work, who supply good materials, and who in return ask fair prices. If you do this you will sometimes be cheated by stumbling on a dishonest contractor; you will sometimes be deceived by the dishonesty of your own officers and inspectors; you will sometimes have your contracts badly done, by the tendency of parliamentary influence to send government work to quarters where the votes of members have been used to influence the giving of contracts. This is evidently and notoriously the case in all government contracts.

But, from the very nature of this particular class of contract, it will be exempt from most of these injurious influences. Like the present contract for marine engines, they will be on so large a scale as to challenge much attention and scrutiny.

Russell's history of Somerset's tenure at the Admiralty from 1859 to 1862 would be relished by Captain Halsted, Coles, Reed and other professional advocates of the cause, but in inverse ratio, we imagine, by the Duke or Lord Clarence Paget his secretary. They found the fleet of the future fairly commenced, wrote Russell, and plenty of money was voted for its prompt execution:

They had only at once to order two more *Warriors* from the funds already voted, and we should long ago have possessed the three finest and fastest steam-ships in the world. The beginning of 1861 would thus have seen us in a much better position than the beginning of 1862 now finds us. The Duke and his Admiralty had a brilliant career before them, if they had been equal to the occasion; they had a country anxious above all things to maintain its naval supremacy—they had a rival hastening with giant strides to dispute the supremacy—they had a House of Commons eager to wipe out the blot of parsimony by liberal votes for the defence of the country—the members of this House were only anxious that the Admiralty should be up and doing. The country, in short, found itself in a critical emergency when the Duke of Somerset was called to the head of the Admiralty, and the question by which the Duke of Somerset's administration of the navy must mainly be tried by is—what did the Duke of Somerset in this critical emergency do for the safety of the nation?

The answer is simple and sad. The Duke doubted—hesitated—pondered—and did nothing. For Lord Clarence Paget it must be said that he did not display the bad qualities of his chief. He did not either much doubt or much hesitate, but in the thing in which he was most profoundly ignorant he acted with most decision—most precipitation, and accordingly what he did with impulse and energy he did wrong. It ought to be known that the Duke negatively, and Lord C. Paget actively, designed the *Defence* and the *Resistance*, two vessels, in regard to which there is but one question, whether they are or are not fit to cope with one of the old wooden fleet they were meant to supersede, not whether they could defend us from the attacks of the *Gloire* or assist the *Warrior* in resistance to an invading enemy, but merely whether they could safely encounter in a tolerable sea one of our old-fashioned wooden frigates. That is the total triumph of this administration.

Let us just see how they came to be built. They were made out of the money left by Sir J. Pakington to provide a fleet of *Warriors*, and here let me once more do justice to the scientific constructors of the Admiralty. In these trophies of the Duke of Somerset, they had little hand and no heart. They knew beforehand that these ships were unworthy of the nation; they did all in their power to prevent their construction, but failed...

The *Defence* and *Resistance*, the offspring of the Duke's doubts, and Lord C. Paget's doings, are probably the two worst designed ships that have ever floated, and as their history is calculated to be most instructive and practically useful, I shall give its salient points.

These precious twins were begotten nearly as follows:—The Duke says he had grave doubts about the *Warrior*, and that he found himself embarrassed with money enough to build a third *Warrior*. He thought, moreover, that £400,000 was a terrible sum of money to waste on *one* ship. Embarrassed with this doubt, he applied to the undoubting Lord Clarence, propounding the modest question as to whether, with so much money, their Admiralty could not add two iron-coated vessels to the navy instead of one. 'Nothing easier,' said Lord Clarence, 'let me try my hand on it;' and Lord Clarence did accordingly try his hand. And lucky for him it was that he had no doubts and implicit reliance on his own skill, for a less courageous man would have been disheartened by his first steps in the attempt to make two ships out of one. His first inquiries in the technical department of his office were far from encouraging. The conversation we may suppose to be as follows:

Lord Clarence. Now, Mr Constructor, I want you to draw me out two ships with all the same qualities as the *Warrior*, only smaller, and to cost half the money.

Constructor (humbly). My Lord—I am sorry—but if you please—it can't be done.

Lord C. (overcoming official resistance). But it must be done. There is a minute of the Board, and I am to see it carried out.

Con. But, my Lord, it is not in the nature of things. We tried before we designed the *Warrior* to do it in little, and we found it could not be done, and so we were obliged to go to the size of the *Warrior*, and we should have gone further if they would have given us the money.

Lord C. Oh, never mind what you did,—it is what you are to do now that I am concerned about. Can't you make a vessel of half the tonnage of the *Warrior*?

Con. Yes, sir.

Lord C. What will that be?

Con. 3000 tons, my Lord.

Lord C. Can't you take half the engine-power? What will that be?

Con. Yes, my Lord, that makes 600 horse-power.

Lord C. Then take half her length of armour.

Con. That makes 120 feet.

Lord C. And let her carry half the number of protected guns.

Con. Yes, twelve.

Lord C. Well now, sir, go and design that vessel. There's half your weights to be carried in half your tonnage, and I know about displacements well enough to know that the ship will carry them.

Con. No change in principle, my Lord?

Lord C. No change in principle.

Thus was the design ordered. We shall now see how the design was approved.

Of course it took some time to put these data into shape according to Lord Clarence's requirements; and under his lordship's parental watchfulness the design came out. The hideous abortions, which we will now call Lord Clarence's twins, were at length produced in the shape of a drawing to be approved by the Lords of the Admiralty.

The Board, however, require the scientific department to sign the drawings, and before that signature some further conversation was necessary.

Lord C. Well, are the drawings ready?

Con. Here they are, my Lord.

Lord C. Now, let me see; so you have got her to the tonnage I wanted, after all?

Con. Yes, my Lord, very near; we have taken a very little more, which we wanted for displacement.

Lord C. Good; that does not much signify. How about the guns? Have you got half the guns?

Con. Very nearly, my Lord. We had to take one off each side, to suit the displacement.

Lord C. Can't that be helped?

Con. No.

Lord C. Well, never mind, we can screw them in somewhere—somehow. Well, what is your next difficulty? Have you got in 600-horse-power?

Con. Yes, we have got them in.

Lord C. And how about coals? You know I am very particular about coals.

Con. My Lord, we have got half the quantity the 'Warrior' has.

Lord C. What, no more?

Con. No more, my Lord.

Lord C. And how far will that carry her? As far as the 'Warrior?"

Con. Not nearly, my Lord.

Lord C. How much short?

Con. Eleven miles out of every fourteen.

Lord C. Well, in days how much?

Con. Five to seven.

Lord C. What, five days' service for the *Warrior's* seven? That will never do. You must make it more.

Con. We can never do it, my Lord; she has already got her ports too low.

Lord C. What, lower than the *Warrior*?

Con. Yes, my Lord, two feet lower.

Lord C. What? the guns carried two feet nearer the water? I said she should be the same as the *Warrior.*

Con. But your Lordship will do me the justice to remember I said it could not be done.

Lord C. But I told you it was an order of the Board, and must be done. But about the coals: I can't see that half the coals should not carry a ship of half the size over the same distance as double the coals carries twice the size of ship.

Con. It is on account of the slower speed, my Lord.

Lord C. What! slower speed? Why should the speed be·slower?

Con. It is, my Lord, slower in the proportion of 11 to 14.

Lord C. But the Board did not order that. How do you get that?

Con. By calculation.

Lord C. Oh, but that is matter of opinion. Now, I think she will go on as fast as the *Warrior.* I am a sailor, and if I had the command, I should make her do it. But won't the ports take in the water?

Con. Yes, my Lord, they will.

Lord C. Then why don't you put them higher?

Con. Because it would make her a worse sea boat than she is.

Lord C. You don't mean to say that she is not a good sea boat?

Con. I fear not, my Lord.

Lord C. Then why did you not make her so?

Con. Because she is not big enough for her purpose, my Lord.

Lord C. But why should she not have good qualities? I like the look of her.

Con. We have done the best we could.

Lord C. Well, I like her look, and I think I can set my opinion as an experienced seaman against yours.

Thus was the design discussed by the Secretary and the constructor, and now, of course, Lord C. had to take his design into the Board and get it approved.

Duke of S. Well, have you got the new design at last?

Lord C. Here it is, your Grace.

Duke of S. So they have not found it impossible, after all?

Lord C. Very nearly, your Grace; if I had not stood by them and made them do it, it would not have been done.

Duke of S. Well, there can be no reason why a ship half the size should not be built just as good as another ship twice as big, can there?

Another Member of the Board. Of course, if the Board choose to order a ship half the size, they can have it. We never found any difficulty with old Seppings.

176

Lord C. Well, then, here is the ship. Will the Board please to order one or two?

Duke of S. Two, certainly. We have got money for two, have not we?

Another Member. Money for one *Warrior* or two half the size.

Lord C. The money and size are a little over half.

Another Member. That don't matter; we can take the balance out of the reserves.

Duke of S. Well, then, let the minute be—design approved—tenders to be taken immediately for two—to be completed as soon as possible. Are you quite sure, Lord Clarence, that the design is all right?

Lord C. Quite sure, your Grace; I have looked into it myself. It is all right: the same sort as the *Warrior*—half the size—half the power—half the armament—half the money, or very nearly so. I ought to tell you, my Lords, that there is a little difference between the constructors in the office and me. They don't think she will be either as good or as fast or as high out of the water as the *Warrior*; but that is matter of opinion; and I, as a seaman, think I have as good a right to my opinion as they have to theirs: and I can't see why a ship of half the size, with only half the armament, and with half the power to drive it, should not go as fast and carry her weights as well as if you doubled it all.

Duke of S. That sounds like reason.

Old Sea Lord. It is only the prejudice of these landsmen.

The plans are carried off by Lord C., and he orders the constructor to push on the designs for specification and tender immediately.

Thuswise—though not probably in these words—were the *Defence* and *Resistance* ordered by the Board, and just so were they executed by the builders.

Russell's was not the only voice to be heard on the issue of the iron warship, but it was the most vehement, articulate and most expert. One must judge from some of the comments of the time, however, that the public ear was more readily given to the reported opinions of Sir William Armstrong the armaments baron, or William Fairbairn the authority on iron structures; but it was Russell who set out the technical arguments in detail for the benefit of the lay Members of Parliament and, unfortunately, to the embarrassment of the Somerset Admiralty.

CHAPTER EIGHT

The Middle Years

John Scott Russell ... a man of attractive manners and of rare eloquence ... and as a public speaker and as an eminent engineer and naval architect, he will long be remembered by the professions and scientific associations to which he belonged as one of the most brilliant of their members.

The Engineer, June 16, 1882

At last, unencumbered by the vicissitudes of an uncertain business, Russell could devote himself to consulting work and to the various professional concerns and causes to which he gave so much energy and devotion. The battle for the iron warship was won and an Institution of Naval Architects had been founded which now lent status to a formerly disorganized and subsidiary profession, and into which, as its presiding force, Russell now threw himself heart and soul. He was hardly less assiduous in his support of the Institution of Civil Engineers of which he had been a Member of Council since 1857 and of which he was elected a vice president in 1862. He was also a founder member, Member of Council and past vice-president (1855–6) of the Institution of Mechanical Engineers, and no committee of the B.A. on naval matters was complete without him—the committee on steamship performance 1857–62, which convened in the London house of the Marquis of Stafford; the committee on tidal observations on the Humber; the committee to make further studies into the resistance of water to floating and immersed bodies on which he was joined by those incomparable authorities or rivals in the subject, W. J. M. Rankine, J. R. Napier and William Froude. Russell superintended the experiments conducted by the latter committee on various hull shapes drawn through water. He also served on the committee appointed in 1866 to analyse and condense the data collected by the Steamship Performance Committee. On this he rubbed shoulders with Fairbairn, Rankine, J. R. Napier and Thomas Hawksley—excellent and congenial company, engaged on the kind of work for which he was best fitted, albeit gratuitous and doing little to replenish his impoverished pocket.

The 1860s saw Russell in his prime, a familiar figure wherever scientists and engineers foregathered and well known to many eminent men in public and professional life at home and abroad. Even the ill-fated Archduke Maximilian of Austria had occasion to offer him his best and heartfelt thanks for some pamphlets sent to him,[1] perhaps those dealing with the fleet of the future. The Great Exhibition planned for 1861 was postponed to 1862 on account of the Franco-Austrian war and the untimely death of the Prince Consort. It was a shadow of its great predecessor. When the subject of a monument to the Prince was raised, Russell sent a letter to the Queen recommending that the monument to Frederick the Great in Berlin be taken as a model—as indeed it was—although the Queen's secretary in thanking him, was good enough to tell him that this 'had already been suggested more than once'.[2]

Russell was nowhere more influential and constructive than in the company of his fellow naval architects, shipbuilders and naval officers in the Institution of Naval Architects. The full members of the Institution, the professional naval architects, were very much in the minority at these assemblies, being outnumbered by the naval men and other 'Associates' who had more understanding of seafaring than of ship design. A study of the transactions, however, reveals the truth of K. C. Barnaby's observation that

> Scott Russell was always amazingly tactful and courteous in handling the remarks and the attacks of admirals, captains and commanders who came to the meetings. He would single out some sensible remark for praise and either ignore the rest or gently point out an alternative explanation. If he found nothing to praise, he would thank the speaker for his interesting views.[3]

Another notable instance of Russell's tact was in the matter of his dispute with Lloyd's. He led the attack on Lloyd's conservative approach to innovations in iron shipbuilding, yet when, on the occasion of Grantham's paper on iron ships in 1862, the feelings of the two chief Lloyd's surveyors present were much ruffled by the onslaught on their policies, Russell to everyone's surprise threw oil on troubled waters.[4]

The desirability of a school of naval architecture had long been on his mind and he quickly set about recruiting the influence of the Institution to this end. The need had recently been impressed upon him more personally in the education of his son, Norman, whom he had sent to the *École Impériale du Génie Maritime* in Paris. He discussed the subject and presented some proposals to the Institution in a paper 'On the

179

Education of Naval Architects in England and France' at the fourth session of the Institution, March 28, 1863. In this he contrasted the systematic education of naval architects in France with the unorganized system of student-apprenticeship prevailing in Great Britain.

Curiously enough, there had been Admiralty schools of naval architecture founded at two earlier periods of alarm which were discontinued when the crises passed. The first was established in 1810 then abolished in 1833, because, said Russell, 'its pupils advocated the cause of science and professional skill as opposed to empiricism'. But some of these pupils served the nation well when, much against the inclination of the naval establishment, the fleet had to be transformed from sail to steam. Then another attempt was made within the Admiralty to organize the education of naval constructors in 1844, by the founding of the School of Mathematics and Naval Construction. Dr Woolley was appointed Principal in 1848 and numbered among his pupils several who were to become well known in the profession, Edward Reed and Nathaniel Barnaby among them; but the effort was short-lived, being brought to an end in 1853, at the very time that much was beginning to be said about the use of the profits of the Great Exhibition for the erection of a central institution 'for the dissemination of a knowledge of science and art among all classes'. This was also the moment at which the Government Department of Science and Art was established with Lyon Playfair as 'Secretary for Science' and Henry Cole as 'Secretary for Art'.

Now, in 1863, having fired the first salvoes in a campaign for a new school of naval architecture, Russell energetically led a committee of the Institution in planning the curriculum and selecting the lecturers, recruiting also the influence of their president, Sir J. Pakington, to the cause. Pakington has not been very respectfully treated by political historians, but whatever his foibles he was usually on the side of the angels.

There was, of course, much to be said for the way in which British mercantile shipbuilders had developed their craft, supported by the private researches of many engineers and naval architects and the large-scale investigations sponsored by the British Association. A particularly fruitful co-operation between shipbuilder and applied scientist developed on the Clyde involving J. R. Napier, Denny, Elder, Rankine, and Kelvin, from which the shipbuilders of all nations benefited. Nevertheless there was a strong case for a more purposeful academic preparation of naval architects, a case which Russell presented with his customary flair and persuasiveness.

A short time after Russell had read his paper on education before the Institution, Henry Cole visited the Russells at Sydenham. In the afternoon he escorted Mrs Russell to the Crystal Palace where they examined the cast of the new gates, then returned for dinner. Over dinner, Russell described his plan for a Naval College, and Cole notes in his diary that he had advised him 'to get the Government to pay on results rather than means'.[5] Russell later alluded to 'payment by results' as 'a shopkeeping principle utterly inapplicable to the very nature and essence of education, which is a process of moral and intellectual culture, and of a nature utterly foreign to the barter and sale of commodities.'[6] Perhaps Russell would have liked Cole's support, but nothing in their past relationship could have suggested that Cole would exert himself for someone else's idea, even a friend's, unless he saw a way of appropriating it to himself.

In the September of 1863 Cole met Admiral Robinson while on a visit to Robert Napier's house at Shandon on the Clyde. Robinson, an admirer of Russell, raised the subject of the school of Naval Architecture and, according to Cole, revealed that the Duke of Somerset, then First Lord of the Admiralty, was willing to have one, but not that Scott Russell should manage it.[7] Thus Russell's attack on Somerset's naval policy came home to roost. It was characteristic of Russell's fate that Somerset had been returned to the Admiralty just when a more friendly incumbent might have seen him in charge of his own school.

We have no authority, of course, for assuming that Russell would have liked to become Director or Principal of a new school of Naval Architecture other than the obvious fact that he had much to recommend him for the role. His well recognized expository powers, wide international contacts, command of several languages and great practical and theoretical experience and knowledge could not fail to place him in the front rank of candidates. But, the ways of humans are perplexing and brilliance sometimes blinds as well as illuminates. One senses that this was bound to be the case with Russell; but with Somerset at the Admiralty, there could be no doubt. Russell would appear too big to handle. Nevertheless he had the qualities of dynamism and leadership to promote the school with expedition. A place was made for it at the South Kensington museum and the first pupils—twenty of them—were enrolled in November 1864. The Government placed it under the jurisdiction of the Science and Art Department, and thus under the direction of—Henry Cole! Dr Woolley was the first Director General, Merrifield the first Principal. To complete the irony, Russell's great book was published only a few months later—

The Modern System of Naval Architecture for Commerce and War. The three volumes measure $28 \times 20 \times 2$ or $1\frac{1}{2}$ inches, a *Great Eastern* of books, published in August 1865 by Messrs Day and Son, Lithographers to the Queen to whom, by gracious permission, it was dedicated. Doubtless the size of the volumes was dictated by the large scale of the many drawings which Russell used to illustrate his text in the manner of architecture books generally. It is a beautiful and erudite work, a great pleasure to read, but, as Sir Westcott Abell says, 'It is a pity that its mere size tends to prevent easy access to the mass of data it contains'.[8] The writing and preparation of the *Modern System* occupied a great deal of Russell's time in the early 1860s. Merrifield helped prepare it for the press and contributed certain mathematical analyses of strength and stability and the calculation of areas and volumes. It is a monument to Russell's mastery of his subject, his originality and his capacity as a teacher, a veritable Bible to the naval architects of his time. Its printing and publication required also his financial support and this in a perplexing way was to have fateful consequences for Russell, as we shall see.

If he was disappointed at not being more closely identified with the school he promoted, he betrayed no hint of it, and at the annual meeting of the Institution in April 1867, at a time when he was facing great troubles, expressed warm and generous approval of the achievements and progress of the students and staff of the new college.

It was a time of transition for the navy and there was much to talk about on the subject of naval craft—structure, armaments, armour, speed, turrets—and Russell was deeply involved. Despite the controversial nature of many of the issues, Russell was so courteous in argument and urbane in address that he made few enemies on this account. His elegance, self-assurance and aplomb contrasted incongruously with his tortured financial history and this may have fed the fires of antipathy in some. In an age when wealth was an incontestable index of success and status, he was at a decided disadvantage.

One group of people certainly found him maddeningly insufferable; this was the Brunels and their friends. They saw him as the conceited usurper of the celebrity arising from the Great Ship. This was aggravated by some, including a number of engineers, sympathizing with Russell, seeing him as the victim of Brunel's appetite for fame or even of his jealousy.[9] Russell nowhere on record maligned Brunel. He certainly criticized Brunel's quest for novelty at the expense of viability and graded experiment, but he was not alone in this. Some, however, and undoubtedly

Brunel's sons among them, would have been most sensitive to his statements that the accidents to the *Great Eastern*—and the *Great Britain*—arose from Brunel's infatuation with unproved novelties. This theme pervaded an address he made to the businessmen of Bristol in April 1863, on the subject of 'Very Large Ships', which holds great interest on several counts. The businessmen had reason to honour I. K. Brunel's memory, but their predecessors had resented and resisted his pushing them to what would have been greater and greater expense to accommodate his increasingly large ships. Brunel, on the other hand, felt his Company greatly betrayed by the failure of the Bristol dock trustees to enlarge their accommodation and, not unreasonably, objected to the increased harbour dues which persuaded the Company in the end to desert Bristol and use Liverpool (which received large Government subsidies) as their ocean terminal. This was the background to Russell's address, an address intended for the businessmen of Bristol, not engineers or naval architects.

It was, Russell said,

> Mr Brunel who urged on the inhabitants of Bristol the construction of the *Great Western*, who afterwards urged on them the construction of the still greater *Great Britain*, and who many years afterwards proposed to me that we two should undertake the construction of the *Great Eastern*. We must all regret the premature extinction of that sanguine mind. Mr Brunel was essentially a man of large views in every thing; we may say that greatness was his *forte*, and it may, perhaps, be said also, with truth, that greatness was his foible. The *Great Western* was a big ship in her time, and in consequence she did what no other ship had done before. The *Great Britain* was a great ship full of great blunders, and I fear that some of these helped to take away with her that trade from Bristol which it had been intended to bring there. The *Great Eastern*, the largest of all his conceptions, has read us all a lesson.[10]

His thesis was that while the *Great Western* was 'one of the most prudent and well-conducted enterprises in the history of great ships', no single ship could begin a 'new line of Steam Navigation'. The ship which ought to have been the second *Great Western* was one which, instead, was 'as unlike her as it was possible to conceive'—the *Great Britain*. Thus the company had all the disadvantages of two experimental vessels. This is incontestable. Excuse is offered by the historian of the *Great Britain*[11] that Brunel could not get immediate support for a sister ship for the *Great Western*, but he nevertheless went to a very much larger ship which took two or three years to enter service. This ship, the *Great Britain*, Russell went on, was not only larger, she was a 'museum of inventions', her shape an imitation of Sir W. Symond's new and empirical form of ship;[12] she was altered from paddle to screw, a new kind of chain gearing had to be employed and she had to be sold at a 'disastrous bargain' to ply in the trade of a rival port, divested of her 'ingenious' engines and new screw gear, to become a 'new ship of slow speed and auxiliary power'.

To try all these experiments at once, he declared, 'was to unsettle everything and settle nothing; and no one can now say that he is a bit the wiser for anything the *Great Britain* taught him, except that no one will ever build a *Great Britain* over again.'

This makes sacrilegious reading today and it is not entirely correct. The shape has indeed the appearance of a modification of that favoured by Symonds but it arose no less empirically from the need to pass the ship through lock portals which were narrower than its maximum beam.[13] It is true that there were problems in service with the screw and the chain drive and that she was far too large for Bristol dock facilities. Russell did not hold it against her that she ran aground, but when the company failed, she was indeed purchased at a bargain price for use as a sailing ship on the Australian run, her engines being replaced by a more efficient power unit, used as an auxiliary to move the ship through the Doldrums. Meantime the Cunard vessels crossed the Atlantic with regularity, safety, increasing speed and, with aid of the mail contract, with profit. No one built a *Great Britain* again; but it is largely due to her being a 'museum of inventions' that she owes her immortality. Russell might have extended his cricitism to the City of Bristol for chasing the *Great Britain* out of Bristol. The City, however, had some excuse for their fear of where Brunel would lead them. Russell believed in building from proven ideas and isolating the unknown variables in a progressive series of ships—the Cunard idea—but he would have denied us the exciting speculative engineering leap into the future represented by the *Great Britain*, which we enjoy as long as our money is not involved.

As to the *Great Eastern* he accepted a share of the 'blunder' of not settling on a pair of slightly smaller ships, although these ships would not have been able to do exactly what was expected of the larger ships. It was certainly better in his opinion to have at least two smaller ships than one only of the larger size. Then he considered it a blunder that the directors—he did not say Brunel—'resolved to complicate the business of launching a ship of large size with the double experiment, first, of launching her themselves, without leaving it to the shipbuilder [he considered launching very much the shipbuilder's art, *The Modern System*, vol. i, p. xxxii, note 7] and second, of launching her in a way contrary to all precedent, namely, on iron rails, instead of upon wooden ways.' On the subject of novelty, with respect to the *Great Eastern*, he had been determined, he said, 'that no new inventions should be tried at her expense'. The scaling up of proved engines, boilers, hull lines and longitudinal system had appeared to him to do justice 'to the great experiment of large size', and no other experiment was therefore allowed to be 'mixed up with it'. No accident had ever happened to the ship through these items. The three serious accidents to the ship had all occurred, he claimed, through experiment or untried novelties—metal launching surfaces, funnel feed-water heaters, and a new design of rudder head. He had designed the rudder and its fixtures in a manner which he had found successful in practice but had been excluded from designing the rudder head and steering gear, which the Company 'wanted to have done in a way of their own'. This rudder head fractured in a storm 'by which the ship was as nearly lost as a ship could be' while his rudder 'stuck to its place', and took the ship to port.

This reads more arrogantly than the context allows. Russell's point was not that he was a better designer than Brunel but that it was safer to develop from the lessons of experience when commercial viability depended upon the result. As he was saying this, Russell was writing for the naval architects of the future that 'When the history of steam navigation comes to be written, a large share of the merit will have to be awarded to Mr Brunel.'[14]

CHAPTER NINE

Fate and Fortune

The truth is sure to come out some day, somehow or other.

J. SCOTT RUSSELL

The French scare which had accelerated the reconstruction of Britain's fleet eased in Britain as another, resulting from the Civil War in America, took its place. This war excited much partisanship at all levels of British society, but while victory for either side was uncertain, the British Government, despite its greater economic ties with the Southern, or Confederate, states, was discreetly unwilling to become involved. The Northern, or Union, forces, while in industrial resources stronger than their Southern opponents, were obliged to supplement their production of armaments by purchases in Britain. The Confederates, on their part, had to maintain lifelines with Europe, not only for armaments but for all manner of industrial products and to pay for them with cotton. All of this required ships, especially steamships, which could outsail or elude the blockading fleet of the North. Preferably they had to be of sufficiently shallow draft to run up the Southern coast close to shore, and paddle rather than screw steamers had the advantage of more easily pulling themselves off any shoals on which they should run aground. In addition, it was Confederate strategy to harry the oceanic commerce of their Northern adversaries, and for this they needed fast armed cruisers.

J. D. Bulloch and J. H. North were posted by the Confederate Government to England in May 1861 charged with the task of making the necessary purchases of ships and letting the necessary contracts. They had been instructed, too, to familiarize themselves with all aspects of naval armaments, and North, in particular, was ordered to find out all he could about the *Warrior*.[1] It is reasonable to suspect that they soon would be referred to Russell for advice, for no one could have served their purpose better, and indeed, our suspicions are confirmed by the fact that Bulloch's first attempted purchases were of Russell's two fast ships, the *Victoria* and *Adelaide*,[2] on the Australian run; but these overtures proved abortive. They, and other agents, combed the seaports for the requisite ships

186

and managed to outfit some as raiders with such effect that strong pressure was exerted on the British Government by the Union side to see that the posture of neutrality was upheld, particularly by closing ports and dockyards to the arming and commissioning of ships of war. Both sides, however, made purchases of arms, particularly of naval guns, but conducted these with as much discretion as possible in case of protest and embargo. Armoured warships, called 'rams', were ordered by the Confederates, two from Laird of Birkenhead and one from Thomson of Clydebank, which were well on their way to completion by the end of 1863. These posed a considerable threat to the Northern ports which were vulnerable from the sea. The Massachusetts Government under Governor Andrew became alarmed and planned the fortification of Boston harbour and its approaches. Accordingly, around July 1863, they sent a Colonel Ritchie to London with a sum of money to purchase with all due secrecy the necessary guns or gun barrels and ammunition for this purpose. He placed his orders with the usual suppliers.

One major manufacturer of heavy guns, Armstrong, did not come into the reckoning for he was exclusive supplier to the British Government. The Armstrong patents, the essential feature of which was a rifled steel barrel prestressed by shrunken outer coils of wrought iron, were claimed by both Blakeley[3] and Treadwell.[4] Thus, when the War Office proved and accepted Armstrong's design, contentious litigation was forestalled by his presenting his patents to the Government which promptly obtained an Act of Parliament to forbid their disclosure. Armstrong's works at Elswick, on the Tyne, were then incorporated as a state arsenal under Armstrong's managership to supply Armstrong guns exclusively to the British forces, while Armstrong himself was appointed Engineer of Rifled Ordnance, a post which placed him in virtual control of the selection and production of guns. Other manufacturers complained that their guns were not only denied a fair trial but that their patents were in danger of being pirated by Armstrong under the Government screen. Armstrong's outspoken belief that patents were undesirable and unnecessary did nothing to calm their fears and had *Scientific American* exclaiming, 'Not content with appropriating the ideas of others right and left, he would have larceny legalized by the world'.[5]

After about four years, the Government and Armstrong bowed to mounting criticism, aided by failures in the Armstrong breech-loader, and, in February 1863, dissolved their special arrangement, whereupon the Elswick works, greatly extended at public expense, reverted to

Armstrong 'at a valuation'. Now the Armstrong Co. had to face a reduction in its output of 50 tons per week, and the fact that its dubious patents were still legally the property of the British Government.

Armstrong's partners and professional servants felt that they had been stupidly and shabbily treated by the Government,[6] and his principal legal adviser, Stuart Rendel, son of his old friend, the harbour engineer, J. M. Rendel, and brother of his partner, George Rendel, urged upon Armstrong that it was his patriotic duty as well as a duty to himself to maintain the prestige of his guns by taking foreign orders. Sir William replied

> that he had made a great flourish over the gift of his patents to the Government at a time when he certainly might have obtained a very large sum for them; that, though he had not accepted money, he had taken a knighthood, a C.B., and a well-paid office; and that, therefore, he could not possibly, as soon as he had left office, start upon the supply of his guns to foreign powers.[7]

Nevertheless, Sir William relented and told Stuart Rendel that if he could obtain any orders for Elswick he would grant him a commission of 5 per cent.[8] In June 1863 Rendel got into cautious communication with the Confederate agents, no doubt through Mr Gilliat their London banker of whom he was an intimate friend, and from whom he accepted an order for two or three 150-pounders for the rams then under construction. There is no record of his having taken like initiative with the Union authorities at this time, although he was also friendly with Benjamin Moran, Secretary of the American legation.

Russell conducted business with and counted several good friends on both sides whom he frequently entertained of a Sunday at his hospitable board. There, in the country garden at Sydenham, thoughts turned to the possible peaceful resolution of a conflict which the more noble spirits of both sides deeply deplored. One of these friends was the eminent American mechanical engineer A. L. Holley who arrived in October on yet another visit to England, this time to investigate for Winslow and Griswold, of Troy, New York, the new Bessemer process of steel manufacture, and to acquire the American patent rights.[9] In the previous year he had been engaged by Edwin Stevens, a pioneer of armoured ships whom Russell first befriended on the occasion of the *America*'s challenge at Cowes in 1851, to glean information on British ironclads, ordnance and armour. The material he had then garnered now formed the basis of a book he was preparing.[10] In November he took the opportunity to accompany Russell to the British Association meeting at Newcastle where the latter presented a paper on the application of gun-cotton to warlike purposes.[11] The Confederate consul at Liverpool reported that Scott Russell's 'name in such a connection [carried] much weight with it'.[12] The conference participants were conducted over the Armstrong ordnance works at Elswick which gave Russell an opportunity to introduce Holley to Captain Noble, Armstrong's ballistics expert, with whom Holley made arrangements to supply sketches of American guns in return for the same of the Armstrong guns. On leaving, Russell remarked to Noble that if he were interested in pursuing business with the American Government, Holley would be a good man for his purpose.[13] Noble did not act immediately, but about a month later, indeed, on Christmas Eve, he called on Russell at Great George Street in London, to obtain Holley's address (as he alleged), insisting that he did so on his own initiative and without the knowledge of Sir William Armstrong who was not personally to be involved.[14] Russell, according to Noble, explained that he acted for the American Government in procuring and inspecting war materials[15] and undertook to approach the Americans on Noble's behalf with a proposition that certain Armstrong guns could perhaps be had for a very favourable price. According to Russell, Noble told him that two 150-pounders were in store and ready for immediate delivery.[16] This fits the facts, for there were two or more 150-pounders ordered by the Confederates through Stuart Rendel for one of the rams which were now being impounded by the British Government.[17] The matter was one which required most discreet handling for there was no telling what the Government would now do to emphasize its neutrality. Noble left Russell with particulars and prices of the main sizes of guns available and their ammunition.[18]

Russell kept an appointment with Mr Adams, the American minister in London, on the afternoon of December 30, the matter of the guns providing a convenient opening gambit for his principal business, which must have been very unexpected. This was to discover if Adams thought a peace settlement was possible. He told Adams that excellent men of each side were in the habit of congregating at his house on Sundays as on common ground, where they talked constantly and freely of the practicability of a settlement. 'He asked me,' confided Adams to his diary,

> whether I thought there was any such feeling of hate among the population
> of the North as to render conciliation out of the question. I replied that so
> far from it the main thing to be apprehended from any opening of the kind

would be too eager a rush towards it. The great point to gain by the war was emancipation. It would not be wise to approach the question of restoration until that was put out of doubt. Mr Russell remarked that the condition of affairs was so dreadful in the south, and was viewed as so desperate, that he had good reason for supposing some disposition to exist favourable to some graduated form of emancipation. If that was so, I replied that the great obstacle to reconciliation was in the way of removal.

... Mr Russell asked me my opinion of the probable way it could be initiated. I said by the people acting in the States to overrule their leaders at Richmond. He intimated the leaders would not be wise to act themselves. The lesson had been frightfully severe and most of them felt themselves subdued by it. I answered that I could not see any safe way of dealing with the quasi government.

... He repeated that the central power was well inclined. He intimated that he had better means of knowing the actual state of things there than he thought I could have. To the world, they still held up a bold front, but within was despair. Whom he could refer to as giving him this information I can only vaguely conjecture. His affinities would lead him among the tribe of military and naval agents like Bulloch, Sinclair, Maury, Huse and the rest.

Thus was initiated a curious but none the less serious—and almost successful—attempt to negotiate peace in America: one which came to light only with the release of Adams' diaries in 1927.

That evening, his mind full of the mysterious conversation he had had with Russell, Adams took his customary stroll and detoured from his habitual route to call on Colonel Ritchie and tell him 'confidentially' that if two of the largest sized Armstrong guns were unwanted 'they could perhaps be had'.[19] Ritchie immediately wrote to Governor Andrew:

> Our minister Mr Adams has been given to understand in a private manner, that if we wish to secure two of the largest size Armstrong guns, we can probably have them at once. Of course the business must be managed with great secrecy and caution. The English Government would never allow the sale and exportation of these guns and Sir William Armstrong long since parted with all his rights in his own inventions and patents to the Government. There would probably too be a great public outcry if it were known that any of these guns had been allowed to go abroad and not only all the public enemies of the Armstrong monopoly but all the other inventors of new guns would seize upon such a transaction if known to create new difficulties. Mr Scott Russell I believe was Mr Adams' informant and Mr Adams referred him to me, thinking the matter of so much significance that he came here himself to tell me of it.

190

... as far as I can gather there are two muzzle-loading 600 pounder Armstrong guns which do not belong to Government and which are offered to us ... The offer does not proceed as we understand, at present, from a desire to *sell* us the guns, but from a desire that we should have the guns, at cost, and test them ... I am so closely watched here that I must, if I do anything, have as little apparent connection with this business as possible.[20]

'Friends of Armstrong's,' he wrote, 'who sympathize with us are anxious that we should have some of the guns to test,' and as the guns could be 'had at once and are cheaper than those we contemplated buying', he felt greatly tempted. Further, 'the sellers will themselves ship the guns'.[21] 'I am most positively assured,' he added, 'that there will not be any possibility of any delay in the delivery!'[22]

Ritchie apparently interpreted Adams' allusion to 'two of the largest guns' as referring to the 600-pounder which was indeed the largest gun produced by Armstrong. The two guns available, however, were certainly not 600-pounders; they were 150-pounders. Meetings between Russell and Ritchie then ensued, at which the whole subject was discussed.

On January 6, Ritchie wrote to his superior that he could 'have at once—1 – 150 pdr., 1 – 300 pdr., and 1 – 600 pdr.' and six of each calibre in three months and probably at lower prices.[23] Russell's personal advice, he added, was that he should take at once two of each smaller calibre and one 600 pdr.

Neither Ritchie nor Noble knew anything of Russell's main purpose in calling on Mr Adams. Russell's conduct of the gun deal is fully consistent with his later assertion that he had taken it up with Adams as an obligement to Noble. It appeared a very innocent and simple function which Russell performed and he would have been amazed had it then been suggested to him that this was going to lead him into a greater personal calamity than his financial failure with the *Great Eastern*. Because of this it is necessary to trouble the reader with the essential details of the transaction. The delivery dates, method of payment and what constituted 'delivery', as set forth in the correspondence, were all to become crucial issues, and not least the nature of Russell's function in the matter. All this because the agreed arrangements were, in the event, not adhered to and because Russell once more got into unexpected financial difficulties during their protracted course.

On January 8, 1864, Russell reported to Noble the encouraging response to his overtures. He considered an order for one gun of 'each of the three sizes' nearly concluded if they could be delivered at once,

191

and that there were good prospects of a larger order. He asked for an immediate quotation for the guns and their projectiles and for half a dozen or a dozen of each sort of gun with delivery time.

Noble replied immediately (January 9, 1864):

My Dear Sir,—Many thanks for your letter of the 8th inst. With regard to immediate delivery, I imagine that the Amer. Gov. would be satisfied if the guns and ammunition were ready by the commencement of the summer campaign, and this, I think, we could undertake to do.

I have had a long consultation with Mr Rendel on the subject, and he thinks the guns could be ready as follows:—One 150-pounder in two months; one 300-pounder in three months; and one 600-pounder in four months (of course several of the 150-pounders and 300-pounders could be ready in four months, if required). About the ammunition, there would be of course, no difficulty.

... The success of such large guns depends in action, in a great measure, on the carriages on which they are mounted [Here followed prices of carriages]

... We should prefer to have nothing to do with shipping the guns, but we could deliver them at any port. I need hardly say that we should be glad to give fuller explanations and further details to you or anyone you may send down to make enquiries.

I may add that the above prices include a commission of five per cent.

Here we have the almost casual introduction of the subject of an honorarium at the end of the letter in a way that supports the assertion made later by Russell that it was gratuitous and not a matter of prior agreement. It was of course, the same commission as that offered Stuart Rendel.

Three days earlier, Russell was able to warn Noble (January 12) to expect the order which he, Russell, had suggested to Ritchie—two each of the 150 and 300-pounders and one 600-pounder—it being understood, he remarked, that 'all these will be ready at the times mentioned'. He also alluded to the manner of payment:

Looking at the question of cost, it appears as if the total order would amount to £13,555.

It is intended, on giving the order, to place securities in my hands to that amount, which securities I will exchange with you for the Bill of Lading ...

As I said before, further correspondence and some delay will be necessary concerning the larger order, but I have reason to expect it in one month hence. I shall also require from you exact drawings of the guns and carriages, and also of the ammunition. I need not say that the use to be made of them is the instruction of the educated persons who will have to use them, a point in which you yourselves would be equally concerned.

Ritchie was under some difficulty in mustering payment for the guns. He had used all of his appropriation and now, as he explained to the bankers, Messrs Baring (January 13):

... At this point, I am unexpectedly offered supply of guns from a new source. The quality of the guns, their size and character, their price and above all, the fact that they can be delivered speedily, recommend this offer, and it will not be possible to secure any guns from any other source, at the same prices or at any prices within certainly 8 or 9 months.

I think it of the utmost importance not to allow this opportunity to escape me ...[24]

With Baring's help he organized some of his own funds to meet the order pending a reasonable expectation of reimbursement from his Government and with some support from C. F. Adams who held out hope of the American Government's accepting responsibility should Massachusetts be unwilling to provide the necessary funds.[25] It testifies to Ritchie's enthusiasm for the deal and to the need, as he saw it, for prompt action.

Next day, Russell wrote to Noble to confirm the order (January 14):

My Dear Sir,—The order is confirmed, as advised in my last.

I shall, in a few days, be able to inform you of the deposit of securities for payment, but you may date the order from the receipt of this, and go on with all your might.

I have promised for you that you will neither fail in time nor in quality.

Captain Noble immediately replied, asking for an 'official' order but hedging a little on the matter of schedule and, most important, proposing different terms of payment (January 15):

My Dear Sir,—I have received your two letters of the 12th and 14th instant.

Will you be kind enough to send us an order that we can enter on our books for the guns and ammunition, so that we may treat the matter in our usual manner. In giving the official order I would merely specify 'for a foreign government'.

... If we are fortunate we shall be able to complete the guns in the time I named to you, and no exertions shall be wanting on our part to ensure their completion scrupulously at the time named. At the same time, as you

193

know, we are very particular in the examination and inspection of every part of the gun prior to its being put together, and if any part had to be rejected there might be some little loss of time in replacing it. With regard to quality, I have no hesitation in pledging myself that the workmanship will be un-exceptionable.

We shall give you drawings, as you request, of guns, carriages, and ammunition, and shall be prepared to give every necessary explanation.

The terms of payment we are receiving from continental governments are, one-third at commencement, one-third during progress, on certificate of in-spection, and one-third on completion. The same terms will be proposed on the present occasion.

I shall be in London at the end of next week, and shall be happy to give you every information you may require.

Russell replied immediately, spelling out the order in detail—to a total of £13,960, and closing with the comment: 'Unobjectionable securities, payable to my order, have this day been deposited in safe keeping, and I will hand them to you in the manner stated in my letter of the 12th instant. You will see the total amount of the payment is £13,960, being greater than the sum formerly mentioned.'

Noble now tried to insist on the terms he had proposed and his letter crossed with one from Russell holding promise of a larger order. Captain Noble to Mr Russell (January 18):

My Dear Sir,—Your letter of Saturday has made the number of guns, projec-tiles, &c., required perfectly clear, and the only question remaining open is that of payment.

I mentioned to you, in my last, the terms which we are now getting abroad, and I am assured that the firm cannot consent to any material alteration in these terms.

I shall be glad to hear that the arrangement proposed in my last is agreed to, but should you require a personal interview, I shall be in town, and wait upon you on Saturday next.

Mr Russell to Captain Noble (January 18):

(Private and Confidential)
My Dear Sir,—Confirming my letter of the 16th instant, I have now to state that the order will, in all probability, be extended up to the larger numbers quoted in your letter of the 9th instant, but that it will probably require three weeks before the special messenger can return to this country.

. . . You may enter the order, already received, as for one of the Northern Powers, not specifying which, in case political complications might arise.

Mr Russell to Captain Noble (January 19):

> My Dear Sir,—The terms, the agreement, and the payment were all con-
> cluded before the receipt of your last two letters, my only basis being your
> letter of 9th instant.
>
> The terms I required were that perfectly good securities, payable to my
> order, should be placed in safe hands in London to the full amount of the
> order. That has been done, and so done, that both the names of persons,
> and the nature of the transaction, is the most secret and confidential that
> its nature permits.
>
> I am prepared to give you perfect satisfaction, personally, both as to the
> soundness of the securities, and their safe custody.
>
> The moment you have finished any part of the order you will receive a
> corresponding payment.
>
> If you are dissatisfied with the arrangements I have made, please to let
> me know at once, as the contract was originally designed (by the parties for
> whom I am acting) for other hands [Russell if bluffing here], and the work
> must be executed immediately.

Captain Noble now explained (January 19) why he was asking other
terms of payment:

> The transaction has a good deal more risk attached to it than ordinary
> commercial contracts, for should an embargo be placed on exportation of
> warlike stores, or should political complications arise, the loss in such cases
> might fall on us. Besides we are receiving similar terms from our own and
> other governments.

By Russell's original terms the full payment for the complete order
would be made on receipt of the bill of lading. That is, when the goods
were delivered at the dockside ready for shipment. This was required
to be not later than some time in May—four months from about January
14. In his letter of January 19, however, he says, 'The moment you have
finished any part of the order you will receive a corresponding payment',
an ambiguous statement depending greatly on what was meant by a 'part'
of the order. In the context, it is probable that Russell, and presumably
also Noble, saw the order in three 'parts', corresponding to the three delivery dates (which were verbally agreed as March 14, April 14 and May
14). Did the order still include delivery for shipment? This is not clear.
The arrangement was very casual—fatally casual in the event, for there
was to be disagreement over this issue.

Noble called on Russell several times in London between the 23rd
and 27th of January,[26] and they arrived at some understanding; but there

was no written confirmation of it. Russell regarded the letter of January 14 as the contract, but Armstrong took a different interpretation of the delivery terms, supported by the implication of a letter of January 30 from Noble to Russell, which listed the equipment required for a battery to take the field immediately on disembarkation and which quoted the prices for delivery *at the works.*

The American minister informed Russell at this stage that someone had made a confidential enquiry of the Secretary of the American Embassy whether any agent of the American Government had been in Britain with authority to make a contract for Armstrong guns. Russell told Noble of this and asked if the enquiry could have come from any one connected with his firm. Fortunately, he added, the Secretary had been kept ignorant of the subject. He mentioned it, he said, only to show the need for the greatest prudence on the part of all connected.[27] Noble replied that he had learned that the investigator was a 'gentleman in connection with' his firm and assured Russell that it would not occur again.[28] The most obvious inference is that the company was anxious to ascertain the source and authenticity of Russell's contract.

What Adams did not tell Russell was that the 'investigator' was Stuart Rendel and that he had spoken to him. It is possible that Rendel did not know about the transaction and had simply called in pursuit of an order. He expressed mistrust of Russell, however, whereupon Adams declared his readiness to enter into any other arrangement 'which would assure all parties against risk'.[29] Apparently Rendel had acted independently of Noble; perhaps he wished to filch the contract for himself or perhaps he was suspicious of the arrangements for payment. However, once apprised, Armstrong asked Rendel to return to Adams and remove all suspicions injurious to Scott Russell which he may have aroused.[31]

Russell supplied Armstrong with the particulars (shown opposite) of the drafts deposited with Barings in his, Russell's, name.

Russell passed on Armstrong's prices to Ritchie without adjustment. His whole remuneration was contained in the 5 per cent commission allowed by Armstrong. The documents show Russell's exerting himself on behalf of his American correspondent on the one hand and helping the Armstrong Company procure as large an order as possible on the other. Armstrong was happy not to be directly involved with his client in the circumstances and visited Russell to express his approval of the arrangements and thank him for his efforts.[31]

Settled by acceptances of Baring, Brothers & Co, of January 16th, 1864, at 4 months:

No. 1	£ 900	[150-pdr. supplies
2	1100	1 – 150-pdr.
3	1100	1 – 150-pdr.
4	1620	300-pdr. supplies
5	1800	1 – 300-pdr.
6	1800	1 – 300-pdr.
7	2040	600-pdr. supplies
8	3600	1 – 600-pdr.]

Towards the end of February Noble reminded Russell that he had given no instructions regarding gun carriages, to which Russell replied that he was daily expecting instructions, and again emphasized to Noble: 'I have no doubt they will be anxious to make the shipments at the time intended'.

Ritchie, indeed, had been disappointed at the modification in schedule, but the delivery dates seemed reasonably acceptable—

2 – 150 pdrs. and stores	March 14
2 – 300 ,, ,, ,,	April 14
1 – 600 ,, ,, ,,	May 14

All the Bills held by Baring were to be passed to Russell with Adams' approval, on the production of the acceptance certificates and it was agreed between Russell and Ritchie that it would be best to ship the complete order in one operation to avoid possible embargoes by the British Government.[32] So matters stood at the end of February 1864.

By this time Russell was involved in a plan to set up his son, Norman, as a shipbuilder at Cardiff, on the strength of a contract for a steamer, or number of steamers, from the Spanish Royal Mail Co. It is altogether too suggestive for us to overlook the coincidence that at this time Bulloch, the chief Confederate agent, in a letter to S. R. Mallory, the Secretary of the Confederate Navy, referred to the proposition of his 'friend'—'a prominent English gentleman', that 'under cover of a previous and bona fide contract with a foreign government for a number of mail steamers', he be engaged to build one or more which might afterwards be delivered to the South. 'The vessels were to have been of iron purely as if for commercial purposes,' a fact which, Bulloch thought, on account of fouling difficulties, made them unsuitable for cruising.[33]

This person also, Bulloch remarks, was one whose name 'was

associated with a contract from the War Department' but from which he had retired for reasons which Bulloch believed he had communicated to 'the Secretary for War'. Unfortunately a search of the records has failed to reveal this correspondence.

The new yard occupied a spacious site on the River Taff under the name of the Bute Iron Works, and the keel of the first ship was laid down in July.

During this period, Russell continued his negotiations as an intermediary striving for an acceptable formula for peace. He felt sufficiently encouraged by Adams' reaction to his initial approach to call on him again on January 12, 1864, when he found Adams on the point of going out on his customary evening walk. He offered to accompany him and they walked together in the dark through and in Regents Park as far as York Gate and back, then parted at the south end of Portland Place.[34] Russell began by telling Adams that he was in a position to know the mind of Jefferson Davis as well as Adams might be likely to know that of President Lincoln. He asked Adams if terms could be made on the slavery issue, but accepting that, what would be the opinion of the U.S. Government on the disposal of the southern debt? Adams replied that he would have to sound Washington on this. Russell was prepared to suggest, for example, a complete prohibition of the right to possess slaves and the granting of freedom to all children from birth. He added that if the principle could be mutually agreed upon, he would take the responsibility of sending a special messenger to Richmond and he hoped an armistice might follow, pending negotiation. Adams counselled caution and asked Russell to wait until he had an answer from Washington, which would take about six weeks.

Adams then wrote to Seward, the American Secretary of State, remarking that Russell was 'an Englishman of character, whose acts of service to the government of the United States had been repeatedly brought to his attention'. He was also, Adams continued, a friend of the Confederates.[35]

Adams was personally very anxious to see the war brought to an end before it had driven an irreconcilable gap between the contending societies, North and South. But he did not wish to see the North compromise excessively on the slave emancipation question. Russell's comments held promise of reasonable and acceptable terms, and the prospect of peace was of such moment to Adams that he resorted to the greatest secrecy in his dealings with Russell. He told Seward that not even his secretaries knew of his interviews with Russell, and that no record of the deliberations was being made in the archives of the legation.[36] We have seen how secrecy in the matter of the arms deal was important to both the Americans and Armstrong. Now we can see how equally important—if not more so—it was for Russell and how, indeed, he would be disposed to treat the arms negotiations rather as an obligement than as a source of profit and why he tried to serve the Americans well.

Adams could think of nothing else for a time. Russell's communications seemed more and more singular, and gave rise to a number of questions which clamoured for an answer. Who was it that prompted Russell? Was it a Confederate plot to put the North into confusion in the forthcoming presidential elections, to promote the success of a candidate disposed to yield too much for the security of the North? Surely, thought Adams, there were easier ways, less circuitous and awkward, to set about proposing terms.[37]

On February 1, 1864, after discussing the gun contract, Russell again launched into the 'peace' subject. He explained that he had offered to take a part in the attempt at reconciliation and that although he had encountered opposition he had persevered and overcome it. A person whom he did not name had taken the trouble to consult with everyone connected with Confederate operations in England, and, at Russell's urging, also in France, and had obtained general assent. This person was ready to carry the agreed plans to both the Confederate and Federal authorities; but once in Richmond he would have to find another channel of communication with Washington. Russell and Adams found themselves no nearer to a solution of this problem after two or three hours 'colloquy' on the subject. The former removed Adams' apprehensions of a plot by pointing out that the election would be over by the time their peace approach was made.

Seward's reply to Adams' letter arrived just prior to February 20, on which date Adams read it out to Russell. The United States needed assurance of the responsible character of the parties behind the proposal and the terms had to be defined and clarified. Russell said that he was not discouraged by this reply and that it was more or less the best he could have expected. He departed and returned three days later with written proposals and disclosed that the agent was ready to proceed to Halifax in the next Cunard steamer if he could obtain a safe conduct through Federal lines. Some modifications to Russell's proposals were thought necessary and these were attended to in the 'material plan' which he brought for Adams' comments on February 29. He now undertook to compose a final draft and address an identical note to each party explaining the origin and purpose of the transaction and defining the precise limits of the responsibility of each.

Adams explained that he could not arrange a safe conduct without knowledge of the identity and credentials of the emissary, as well as a guarantee that he would not be the bearer of any papers or information or letter 'that could furnish an advantage to the insurgents at Richmond'. He asked this only as a protection to himself. 'Mr. Russell said he had not thought of that before but he saw its importance. He would consult his friend on that point.' He disclosed that the name of that friend was Yeatman, a man who had enjoyed close personal relations with Jefferson Davis.

A draft of the final proposal and covering letter was shown to Adams on March 3, and met with his approval. Russell returned two days later with the 'paper of Agreement', as Adams described it, signed by himself alone, together with his covering letter in duplicate, also signed by him. He affirmed that Slidell and Mason, two very important officers of the Confederate Government approved of the arrangement as did everybody associated with them on the European side of the Atlantic. There was no further action until Russell again called on Adams on March 21 to tell him that Yeatman had not been able to get away; but was going to proceed on the 26th. Meantime he had been notified of the general approval of Mr Davis and promised every facility to place the proposal before the people of the South and the authorities of the United States. It still remained, however, to establish a line of communication for the emissary. It was indispensable for each side to avoid the suspicion of playing false to its own friends. Could some neutral agent, perhaps an Englishman, be suggested? But Russell knew of none competent to conduct 'so delicate a duty'. Adams suggested Judge Wayne of the Supreme Court, a Southerner who had stayed with the Union, and Russell on his next visit, March 25, was able to confirm the selection of Judge Wayne, and the travel plans of Mr Yeatman. A second agent had been deemed advisable and a Mr Ellitson had been appointed. Russell asked Adams if he would be prepared to furnish Ellitson with funds for the trip as their personal resources were negligible. Adams readily agreed to do so. Then, wrote Adams, 'Mr Russell concluded by remarking that our agency was now over. I added that in my opinion we all might feel under great obligation to him for his earnest and disinterested efforts to aid both parties.'[38]

200

The 'delivery' date of the 150-pounders and their stores had been exceeded by nearly three weeks when, on April 4, Russell called on Adams to inform him that Ellitson had departed in the steamer as planned and that Yeatman had preferred to take his chance on a fast blockade runner, which explained why Adams' son Charles Jr, who returned to America aboard the steamer did not find Yeatman aboard. Adams had entrusted Charles with a letter for Seward which the latter accepted without any obvious reaction.[39] On being told that the bearer was cognizant of the letter's contents, Seward

> remarked generally, that he had but little faith in the matter, that he had made some inquiries about Mr Yeatman and the result was that he found that Yeatman had borne in Washington the reputation of a flighty, visionary character, and his impression was that, though doubtless well enough intentioned himself, he was being made a tool of by the Confederate agents abroad.[40]

Adams read to Russell the relevant passages from a letter he had received from Seward, in which Seward expressed appreciation of Russell's initiatives but some doubt about the authority and influence of Mr Yeatman. The general tenor of the letter was unenthusiastic and the doubt about Yeatman's influence disturbed Russell.[41]

Thomas Yeatman, a native of Tennessee, was personally acquainted with Jefferson Davis. He was very wealthy and on the very eve of hostilities had offered Davis his support with one hundred loyal men raised and equipped at his own expense.[42] He had personal as well as patriotic reasons for promoting an end to hostilities. His brothers were split in their allegiance, North and South, and his wife, a Massachusetts woman, had separated from him on the issue.

Adams complained that Yeatman in his letters to Seward had singularly misrepresented his (Adams') role in the affair. Russell consequently thought that 'a summary or recapitulation of the faults attending the whole transaction, pointing out the exact deviation from it caused by the actions of Mr Yeatman' was due to both Adams and him, and he proposed to bring this to Adams next day, May 20. But he found it desirable to go over the series of papers sent by Seward before proceeding further, after which he apparently decided to send a letter to Yeatman instead, explaining the present position of the question and how it had been left by the government at Washington. Russell called on Adams to obtain his approval of this letter.[43]

Immediately after his April meeting with Adams, Russell had written to Noble for a progress report, reminding him of the required operational data and gun carriage drawings, and affirming his intention to inspect the work. Noble then replied that the 150-pounders were nearly ready and, with Armstrong, called on him in London, whereupon they agreed to meet at Elswick, but Armstrong's frequent absences made this difficult to arrange until May 16, a week after the 150-pounders were 'tested and browned', and two days prior to the date on which the drafts fell due and which should have seen the whole order of five, not merely two guns completed. Russell left Elswick with a financial statement embracing the completed work and a proportion of the work in progress, in the prospect that he might be able to arrange payment for both. He made it clear that, although he would make an effort to oblige, much depended upon the wishes of his 'American correspondent'.

At the end of his discussion with Adams of the Yeatman affair on May 18, Russell explained the situation of the gun contract and showed Adams Armstrong's statement of the work completed and partially completed. He asked Adams what disposition he would incline to make of the drafts which now fell due. 'I said,' recorded Adams,

> that with respect to a payment on account I should be willing to pass over to him, as the person to whom they are payable, a proportion of the notes tomorrow. With regard to the remainder I should like first of all to see and consult with Messrs Baring ... It was finally settled with them that I should retain any of the notes I did not want to pay out at once, as long as I thought proper. The retention would make no difference.[44]

He reported the decision to Russell next day and, in his own words, 'surrendered to him four of the eight notes left in my hands, being an amount falling about ten per cent short of the foot of the account. We passed the requisite vouchers on each side.'[45]

The actual drafts passed to Russell were numbers 2, 3, 5 and 7, originally intended to cover the two 150-pounders, one 300-pounder and the 600-pounder stores. This was a disruption of the payment plans and was £688 short of the £6729 required to meet the statement. It was the closest approximation the possible combination of the drafts permitted.

Russell cashed the four drafts, but whatever transpired or passed through his mind he decided to adhere to the original plan of paying for each 'part' of the order on its completion. This certainly avoided impending confusion. It would have been a different matter had he been able

202

to cash all the drafts and pay out in whatever portions he chose from his own account. He therefore now asked Noble for an invoice restricted to the 'two guns completed, and the whole of the ammunition completed' separate from all work in progress, and to have the contents of this invoice packed and marked 'J.S.R. London'.[46] This invoice amounted to about £3250 and when Russell paid this and withheld his 5 per cent commission he was left with a cash balance of £2810 in his possession. It was mid May and he urged Noble to be good enough to push on with the remaining work for which he would send the money as fast as it was completed. 'I am sorry to tell you', he emphasized, 'that the unexpected delay in the completion of the order has caused considerable disappointment, as the supplies are really wanted for immediate work.'[47]

This part of the transaction first raises the question of Russell's function. If he were the agent of either of the parties it was his duty merely to pass the funds from one to the other. If he were a contractor or middleman he was entitled to use his own funds and make payments as he saw fit. Indeed, if these payments had been required before Ritchie's drafts fell due, he would have been obliged to draw from his own resources or from advances by the bank. Russell's actions were those of a contractor. If the bank had now failed, it may well have been held by the Americans that they had in fact paid for the complete order since the payee of the drafts should have cashed them on maturity. Russell was apparently willing to take this risk and accept Adams as the authorizing agent. The evidence is that he did not think much about his liabilities, having at this stage no reason to doubt his own or the bank's solvency.

The whole order should by now have been completed and on its way to the dockside; but it was to become increasingly delayed. Of the 300-pounders, which should have been ready by mid April, one was invoiced on July 7, and the other, August 8—about three and four months respectively overdue, and even at that they had not been tested. These invoices included supplies associated not only with the 300-pounders but with the 600-pounder, and although the 600-pounder was not yet completed it was actually included in the August invoice in anticipation of its being 'ready in a week's time'.

Noble made much of the fact that the 150-pounders and stores were awaiting shipping instructions. The original plan had been to ship the complete order as a unit and it was Russell's expectation that Ritchie or his appointee would help to see the order out of the country.[48] He apparently held to this plan and received no representations to the contrary from Ritchie. The impounding of the Confederate rams and a turn to the advantage of the Union forces had probably taken the urgency out of the transaction. There was surely all the more reason, now, for the Armstrong people to fear a cancellation of the order, and it was understandable therefore that they should try to crowd all the remaining part of the order into the August invoice, ready or not. Russell met with Noble, then, in a letter dated August 16, informed him that he was unable to settle accounts since 'the holder of the securities' had left town on a pleasure trip. This was true; Mr Adams, the American minister, and his family were on a touring holiday in Wales from August 5 to September 2,[49] a fact which could easily be verified. The Armstrong people now showed more impatience for payment than Ritchie showed for his guns. Russell acted promptly on Adams' return on September 3 and as a consequence cashed drafts 1, 4 and 8. Again it would be a matter of reaching a total close to the foot of the bill. Ignoring his commission, he had now drawn £9110 from the drafts to meet a bill for £9544. Adhering to his agreed procedure, he asked Armstrong (September 9) for a revised invoice excluding the 600-pounder. This left the two completed 300-pounders (£3600) and sundry supplies (£2344). He explained that it was 'in order to carry out the instructions of my correspondent abroad'. When Armstrong complied, Russell sent him a cheque for the guns and, much to the Armstrong Company's expressed disappointment, promised to settle the supplies invoice on his return from a journey a week or so later, and this he did (September 24). All had now been paid for except the 600-pounder gun and some remaining supplies.

Russell had now drawn about £12,160 from his American source and had remitted to Armstrong, including his own commission, about £9194, leaving an uncommitted balance of £2966 still in his own hands and a final draft of £1800 still uncashed.

So far, the Armstrong Company had no grounds for complaint. The payments were not unreasonably delayed. It could seriously be placed against Armstrong, however, that the agreed delivery dates had been grossly exceeded. The guns had not been ready for that summer campaign for which Captain Noble himself had presumed they would be required. The Armstrong team were now anxious and while Russell was settling the invoices, just described, they declared the 600-pounder ready and submitted to Russell a final invoice (September 22) for this and the remainder of the supplies, to an amount of about £5228. Noble informed Russell that the 'whole stores' now awaited his instructions.

Russell now wrote to Ritchie (September 26) about shipment of the guns, saying that unless otherwise advised he would act on his own best judgement.[50]

The peace negotiations were already a thing of the past. Yeatman had returned to Virginia and Russell suspected Yeatman's hand to be in various articles looking peaceward in Richmond papers.[51] At the end of the year, Charles Adams wrote to his father: '... I am very curious to see the Diplomatic Correspondence of this year. Will the curious Scott Russell diplomatic fiasco see the light? I think it ought, if only to prove that we have ever been ready and almost eager to discuss schemes of pacification brought forward with even a shadow of authority.'[52] It did not come to light until the Adams diaries were released, but if it had, would it have shown what Charles thought it would? Or would it only have revealed, as it did to his father, 'the prevalence of personal quite as much as political apprehensions' on the part of Lincoln and Seward. Had it been otherwise John Scott Russell would have been the instrument of a great service to the American people and to humanity.

Instead of being extolled as a hero for bringing peace to a war-torn nation, Russell now found himself embroiled in difficulties associated with a troublesome gun contract which he felt he had originally entered into as an obligement. Noble pressed for payment of the final invoice and Russell informed Adams, who invited him to call on October 21, that the contract was now completed and agreed with him upon a mode of shipment. Adams was to consult Messrs Baring and write to Ritchie.[53] Russell, Adams noted in his diary, 'was rather inclined to talk upon other matters', but there was no time to spare. Nevertheless, he had managed to tell Adams that he had had a long conference with the director of *The Times* on the subject of the caste of that paper towards Americans and that he flattered himself with the notion, of which Adams saw no evidence, that the policy had since been modified.

Adams talked to Barings about shipment of the goods on October 28[54] and on the same day Russell wrote Noble:

My Dear Sir,—I have returned from a short absence, and hasten to answer your note.

I am waiting for final instructions as to payment, shipping, and orders for further items, for which I wrote since I saw you, as I said I should. When I receive instructions, I will lose no time in communicating further with you, taking delivery of the last invoices, and paying for them. I hope to make more satisfactory arrangements for shipping than we last spoke of.

On November 3, Russell again wrote to Noble:

> My Dear Sir,—I find I forgot to ask you also for drawings of the gun car-
> riages. If you could make me these drawings at once for the three sizes I
> would send them out by the next mail, and I think it is not improbable they
> might bring an order by return of post.

Armstrong was not, apparently, very anxious to pass on the gun carriage drawings, no doubt preferring to have an order for the carriages.

Next day Russell handed over his last invoice to Adams who thereupon authorized him to draw the final draft for £1800.[55] Russell, however, did not cash the draft until December 13, nearly five weeks later.
He was distracted meantime by the launch on November 17 of the first
ship from his son's yard on the Taff. This was the *Mallorca*, an iron paddle
steamer with a guaranteed speed of 12 knots. She was certified A1 at
Lloyd's as an 'experimental' ship, being constructed on Russell's longitudinal system, and registered to sail under the flag of the Spanish Royal
Mail from Barcelona to Majorca. It is an odd fact that the *Mallorca*
appears in the Mercantile Navy list of 1865 with Russell as the 'registered
owner', although not so in Lloyd's Register, and that a local historian
writing within living memory of the event recorded that 'it was a great
day when they launched . . . the splendid paddle steamers . . . the *Majorca*
and the *Mallorca* . . . perhaps the most beautiful and highly finished
examples of the shipbuilders' art ever attempted in the locality.'[56] It is
puzzling that the report of the *Mallorca's* launch in the *Cardiff Times*
(November 18, 1864) makes no reference to a sister ship, nor was a
Majorca registered anywhere. One suspects some sleight of hand to transfer a ship to the Confederates. It was Confederate practice to have their
blockade runners registered in an individual's name. Despite Bulloch's
initial disinterest in iron ships, he was ordered by his chief to be grateful
for any suitable vessels,[57] whereupon he had immediately purchased, 'on
the stocks', the *Owl*, *Stag*, *Bat* and *Deer*, steel paddle-steamers of the
same overall dimensions and power as the *Mallorca*—230 ft × 26 ft and
190/180 h.p., but launched in August and September[58] and during the
same period he had a further ten of slightly varying sizes laid down to
his order, also with steel hulls.[59] Had Russell anything to do with any
of these designs one wonders?

Russell cashed the final draft on December 13 but took no steps to
settle the account. Then, early in the new year (January 4, 1865) he received a curt letter from 'Sir W. G. Armstrong & Co.' threatening to

make application to Messrs Baring directly if Russell did not settle the final invoice by January 11. Russell immediately replied that he had been awaiting the gun carriage and gun drawings which he had requested and which might have brought an order for carriages and enabled them to accompany the guns. He said he would at once take measures for shipment of the order and would make the final payment immediately on the 'delivery of the goods for shipment', by which he meant delivery at the Liverpool docks. Armstrong, however, maintained that the agreement was for payment on delivery at the works, in which case the final remittance had been legally due in September last—provided the guns were in fact completed and tested which later events showed was not the case. Russell did not agree, but asked for, and was supplied with, the weights and dimensions of the necessary crates.

Russell's view of the terms of the contract could have been genuine; the letters support both interpretations. But he was also short of the necessary funds as events were to prove. He doubtless had sunk money in his son's shipyard which does not seem to have built another ship, and if the Confederates owed him money, he was out of luck, for they were now losing the war; he was also financing the printing of his great book— *The Modern System of Naval Architecture*. These are his involvements of which we have knowledge.

Ritchie's understanding of the 'delivery' plans was that originally it had been intended that the sellers themselves would ship the guns 'because, as represented they could not have any direct dealings with us'. It was supposed, he continued, however, that he or some other agent would be present to give directions, and the *delivery* of the guns was to be at the foundry—all costs of moving them and shipment to be at the charge of the customer.[60] This was nowhere in writing, but was consistent with the correspondence.

The Armstrong men made enquiries of Adams who then wrote to Ritchie urging immediate shipment of the guns and stating his belief that some active measure should be resorted to, recommending Ritchie's presence in England to expedite matters. Ritchie immediately wrote to Russell (February 1), complaining bitterly about the delay and informing him that unless the guns were shipped at once 'someone would be sent out to look after them'.[61] Since Russell was not in the pay of the Americans, it is difficult to understand why Ritchie thought Russell could be threatened into arranging shipment. Did they intend to pay him for the shipping arrangements? To this Russell replied (February 17) that arrangements had been made to ship the guns immediately in three detachments. He also described the great difficulties he had encountered,[62] but exactly what difficulties cannot be known to us unless his letters to Ritchie turn up.

Armstrong's men must now have suspected that Russell was requiring time to pay. Their patience ran out, however, and, on March 22, they told Russell that they were placing the matter in the hands of their solicitor and declared that they had now ascertained that Russell had 'long since' been placed in a position to pay and that they felt it their duty to communicate 'with the persons for whom, as we now understand, you intended the goods'. They were now also slapping on a 5 per cent charge for interest and storage.

Russell did not acknowledge this letter, but ten days later (April 4), wrote directly to Captain Noble:

> My Dear Sir,—I am happy to say that I believe I have, at last, arranged the matter of the shipment of the pieces and stores, a matter which has proved infinitely more difficult than I had any idea of when the duty devolved on me.
>
> Will you be good enough to communicate with the Traffic Manager of the North Eastern Railway, asking him to send you such wagons as you think will form the fittest conveyance to Liverpool of the first batch of guns and ammunition, comprising the two small guns and forty tons of ammunition belonging to the invoice, dated May 21st, 1864?
>
> Will you let me know what the time required by the railway would be to deliver these on the rails in Liverpool Docks, and at what cost? I need not say that they ought to be carefully covered and protected.
>
> It is intended that the whole shall go in three or four successive shipments from each of which we shall gain experience.
>
> When I hear from you I will let you know the day on which they should arrive in Liverpool. If they could be in Liverpool by Saturday morning next they might be shipped at once, but I fear that may be impossible.

Noble replied that the matter was now in the hands of their solicitor but that if the balance were remitted within the week they would stay proceedings, to which Russell responded (April 7):

> My Dear Sir,—I am sorry to find that you refuse to ship the stores which have already been paid for.
>
> As soon as the stores not yet paid for are delivered for shipment I shall pay for them as I have already informed you.
>
> I confess that it is somewhat disheartening to me, who am unexpectedly

208

mixed up in the matter of shipment of your guns, &c., in a transaction which I originally undertook at your urgent personal request, to feel that in this difficult and delicate matter I not only receive no help from you, but am thwarted at the very moment when your prompt assistance would have enabled me to close rapidly the whole transaction.

The refusal to ship the stores that are paid for will not accelerate the payment for the others, but merely cause unnecessary delay while I write for further instructions.

Armstrong must certainly have feared that Russell would refuse acceptance of the final gun. It was long overdue, even had it been ready, as he alleged, in September, which it could not have been if indeed it were the same gun that now lay untested at Elswick. He could not, too, have failed to notice the approaching end of the war—the guns were probably no longer needed! The Armstrong team took the view that Russell was in possession of funds intended for them. On the matter of delivery, they believed that they had now 'delivered' the whole order. They therefore decided to put a lien on the goods paid for until the final invoice was cleared. On April 8, the day prior to General Lee's surrender, as it happened, Armstrong's solicitor, Mr Dees, wrote to Russell an ultimatum that since 'the balance now remaining unpaid was due so long ago as September last' and since he, Russell, had been 'placed in a position to pay it at that time' (which was not precisely so), the Company would avail themselves of their legal remedies if there was any further delay in payment.

Russell either now regarded it as his duty not to settle the account or was unable to do so. He reported his predicament to Ritchie (April 7) in a letter which contained the disturbing comment: 'I am stopped from shipping by the refusal of the manufacturers to deliver the stores which are already paid for because I refuse to pay for the others except on delivery, a course in conformity with your views. I fear trouble with them and unless you come out yourself I do not see my way through it.'[63] In the same letter, Russell quoted £962–4–11 as the amount required to clear the guns out of England—£319–10–2 remaining in Baring's hands, from an additional appropriation which is something of a mystery, leaving £642–14–9 to be provided. At the same time he consulted his own solicitors, Messrs Freshfield, who counter-attacked as follows on May 5:

Mr Scott Russell considers that not only has Sir William Armstrong, under the circumstances, no claim upon him, but that, on the contrary, he has very considerable claims upon Sir William Armstrong. He regrets that you have been instructed to apply to him in the manner indicated by your letters under acknowledgement, and he desires us to express a hope that, on consideration, Sir William Armstrong will see that it is neither his interest nor his policy to proceed in that spirit ...

After studying the material in Armstrong's hands, Dees responded (May 20):

The correspondence, I find, is long and full of details, and not worth my having it copied out for you, but Mr Russell will not dispute my assurance to you that there is not a word in it of any claim on his part against my clients, and any notion of the existence of such a claim is unfounded.

The short state of the case is that the goods were all ready in September last, that Mr Russell had then received the money for the purpose of paying for them, and that nothing remains to be done but to pay the money and take them away. I feel assured that you will give Sir W. G. Armstrong & Co credit for the utmost reluctance to take a step which must necessarily have the effect of disclosing a state of things not creditable to Mr Russell. I trust you can arrange the payment without my bringing an action.

When Ritchie appeared on the scene towards the end of May he found that Russell, in fact, was anxious to settle with him but required time to do so. Governor Andrew of Massachusetts told Ritchie that were he not approaching the end of his term of office he would have tried to sue Armstrong. In the circumstances he advised that they proceed on the premise that Russell was Armstrong's agent and therefore Armstrong's responsibility;[64] but Armstrong took exactly the same position in reverse.[65] Both discovered that this was not as easy as they had expected. Several of Russell's statements in the correspondence with Noble imply that he was an agent of the Americans, and he was most assiduous in protecting their interests but they did not pay him, while Armstrong gave him a commission. Was he, then, a trustee or a principal (i.e. contractor)? Russell had not given any thought to the matter but he asserted that he was not an agent. Armstrong had the audacity to urge Ritchie to sue Russell, but himself began bankruptcy proceedings. He was soon advised that he had no case in bankruptcy against Russell as long as the goods were still in the possession of the company.[66] Nevertheless, he kept the threat over Russell's head while the lawyers slowly searched for a compromise.

At a meeting between the three lawyers in August, it was revealed that Russell's only 'available means' with which to settle with the Americans (he acknowledged no debt to Armstrong) was his share of his recently published grand treatise on Naval Architecture. His contract with the printer gave him title to 250 copies and he willingly transferred his rights to 125 of these to settle the debt. At the publication price of £42 per set, the books were estimated to be worth about £5250 to set against £5227 of Russell's debt to Ritchie or the £4966 required to clear Armstrong's final invoice.

In a letter to Armstrong's lawyer, dated August 22, Maynard & Co. acting for Ritchie offered in exchange for the 'whole of the goods', half the sum remaining unpaid and an equal share of the proceeds of the books when realized. He also made the pregnant remark 'that it would be better to take the books while we can get them'.[67] To this Dees immediately agreed, with the modification that Ritchie take all the books and pay Armstrong £4000, which was not a bad deal, if deal there had to be; but 'get the books at once into our possession', he prudently concurred.

The necessary documents of transfer were immediately executed. But complications were arising in Massachusetts. Further financial appropriation had to await the election of a new governor and in any case, Ritchie was now advised that the guns were not wanted at any price! Sell them back to Armstrong on favourable terms, but in any event dispose of them in Europe, Ritchie was ordered. The gun market, however, must indeed have been poor, and probably it had leaked out that the 600-pounder was an unsatisfactory gun, for Armstrong rejected all offers of re-purchase. At length, as 1865 came to a close, Armstrong accepted Ritchie's first offer of August 22, 'one half the sum remaining unpaid [£2614]' and 'dividing equally the proceeds of the books when realized'.[68] To complete the transaction, Russell was required to sign an order authorizing the delivery of the 'warlike stores' to Ritchie 'or his order', which surely is important in confirming recognition of Russell's status as a principal. It was now January 3, 1866, and all parties were glad to see an end to the business. But they had dallied too long; the printer now took possession of Russell's consignment of books, alleging a 'breach of contract' on Russell's part; its exact nature remains unknown.

The books however had legally been Ritchie's property from the day Russell had transferred his rights to them six months previously; but Ritchie was in no position to enforce his title to the property any more than to the guns which were also legally his. The new administration in Massachusetts was anxious only to rid itself of the nuisance and was much put out at having to budget for a further £2614 for guns in which it had no interest. Nevertheless this appropriation was grudgingly authorized

211

and payment was made to Armstrong in May 1866. It was a perverse twist to the settlement over which Russell was powerless and which harmed him more than anyone. Ritchie had the annoyance of remaining in Europe to find a customer for his unwanted guns. Armstrong came off best, but he had not finished with Russell, he would yet have his pound of flesh.

CHAPTER TEN

The Defence of Honour

In my own life I have no secrets. It is only in the business of other people that I keep secrets.

J. SCOTT RUSSELL

With the immense prestige and power enjoyed by the successful industrialist in the nineteenth century went no dearth of friends, adherents or supporters, ready to avenge his wrongs. Sir William Armstrong did not need to accuse Russell nor appear to wish to do so. During April 1866, an insidious rumour began to circulate among certain of the engineering elite at Great George Street that Russell had misappropriated funds intended for the Armstrong Company. A principal source of this rumour was Charles Manby, honorary secretary of the Institution of Civil Engineers, who appears to have been apprised of the story by Brunel's elder son, Isambard. Isambard was a lawyer, mainly in the service of the established church, and a brother-in-law of Captain Noble. His brother Henry had served for a time as an engineer-in-training with the Armstrong Company but was now a pupil in the office of John Hawkshaw. Curiously enough, in later years Stuart Rendel wrote that the ill-fated arms deal arose from C. F. Adams consulting Russell about the procurement of Armstrong guns on the advice of 'Mr Brunel', i.e. Isambard (Jnr).[1] The evidence, as we have seen, does not support this. Nevertheless, Isambard and Manby were responsible for carrying Armstrong's (or Captain Noble's) story to two former Presidents of the Institution of Civil Engineers, and Members of Council, George P. Bidder and John Hawkshaw.[2] These august gentlemen appear to have been very disturbed that in the circumstances Russell should continue to hold office as a Member of Council and Vice-President of the Institution. Bidder apprised Russell of what was being said and urged that he clear himself—how and to whom he did not specify—while Hawkshaw informed the President of the Institution, John Fowler. Fowler, however, requested that the accusations be presented to him in writing.[3] The conspirators—for that is what they now became—did not doubt Russell's guilt and had the assurance of the 'facts' which they knew Sir William Armstrong was pre-

213

pared to state when appealed to.[4] Isambard made frequent visits to Manby to hear how things were going. He felt that when the 'time for moving' came no pressure should be left unapplied, since Russell had a 'firm friend' in the President, John Fowler, who, he thought, would stick to Russell till the last.[5]

On May 12, 1866, Bidder and Hawkshaw wrote to Sir William as follows:

> Dear Sir William,—Will you oblige us by a copy of the statement regarding your late transactions with Mr Scott Russell?
>
> Our object is, in the case we are so advised, to bring it under the notice of the Council of the Institution of Civil Engineers.

Does the wording of this letter not suggest that a prepared statement was known to exist? However, Sir William took two days to oblige and when during this period he briefly encountered Isambard he declared 'with much emphasis "That matter is coming to a head"'. 'That night,' wrote Isambard to Manby (May 15), 'Noble turned up ... and was full of the subject and told us the whole story over again ... the story seems too plain to be Evaded.'[6]

When Bidder and Hawkshaw received Sir William's statement they copied it and sent it to Russell all on the same day, inviting Russell's comments. This statement gave Armstrong's account of the case and clearly implied Russell's criminal confiscation of the money. Russell did not ask his correspondents their authority to conduct this investigation, nor did he ask them to declare their purpose. He wisely asked instead for a copy of the letter which had been sent to Armstrong. On being told of this, Isambard asked Manby what he thought Russell was up to. 'Was it merely to gain time and tide over the remainder of the session?' Or was it to learn how Bidder and Hawkshaw came by their information?[7] Isambard cannot impress us as a lawyer. When Russell received the requested letter from Bidder he immediately replied (May 17, 1866):

> Sirs,—I have this morning received from Mr Bidder a copy of the letter of the 12th inst., written by himself and Mr Hawkshaw to Sir William Armstrong.
>
> This letter explains the object and intention with which you obtained the documents you sent me on the 15th instant, viz. 'to bring them under the notice of the Council of the Institution of Civil Engineers.' Had you continued to withhold that letter from me, I should have written to you in ignorance of the purpose to which you intended to put my answer.

15 The departure of the *Great Eastern* from the Thames, September 1859

16 The collapsed funnel of the *Great Eastern*

17 The *Etna* floating battery destroyed by fire, May 1855. A hose
is still playing to the right of the ladder

I now feel that I ought to reserve my judgement as to the manner in which I shall deal with the documents you have sent to me, until I learn what the desire and intention of the Council may be. Should they desire to undertake and assume the responsibility of conducting the examination and settlement of the matters that have been the subject of dispute between Sir William Armstrong and myself, I shall not be slow to furnish them with such information as may be at my disposal.

In the meantime, without raising the question whether in the transactions between us, Sir William Armstrong or myself is in the wrong, I will observe that the statement handed to me as a statement written by Sir William Armstrong is partly true and partly untrue. The most important facts are entirely omitted, being those facts which prove him to be in the wrong. An alleged conversation is adduced as fact, which, as far as I am concerned, is utterly untrue. The written statement professes to be a true statement of the case between us; but it is partial, garbled, and so framed as to lead to conclusions that are false and impressions that are unjust.

I also remark that Sir William Armstrong himself directly contradicts the statement which Mr Bidder volunteered personally to me. Mr Bidder assured me that Sir William Armstrong had publicly and in the clubs circulated a statement similar to that which has now been sent to me in writing. This statement of Mr Bidder Sir William Armstrong expressly contradicts, saying, 'it has not gained publicity by any act of mine'. I must therefore throw upon Mr Bidder personally the responsibility of the inaccurate statement he has made.

Bidder was quick to deny implicating Sir William in circulating a statement; but did not deny circulating it himself (May 21):

Sir,—I make no other comment on your letter of the 17th, except in the most unqualified manner to deny that I told you that 'Sir W. Armstrong had publicly and in the clubs circulated a statement similar to that which has now been sent to me in writing.'

I did inform you that it was a common rumour in the clubs that you had misapplied a sum of money received for account of Sir W. Armstrong and Co, to the extent of some five thousand pounds, and had appropriated it to your own private use.

Meantime Isambard wrote to Manby: '. . . I suppose our friend is considering what to do. Is there any chance (it has been suggested) that he will now come forward—the money being provided by F[owler] and say I am ready to pay if you are ready to deliver the goods . . .'

Bidder passed the correspondence with Russell and Armstrong to Charles Manby for further action. Manby forwarded it to Sir William on May 24, and received a reply in which Sir William reiterated his sore point—'Mr Russell's letter contains no denial of the only important fact in the case, viz. his having received and wrongfully retained the large sum of money referred to in my statement.'[8] He also offered to produce the business correspondence with Russell if further 'evidence' were required. Russell was not informed of this.

It must have seemed curious to Russell, after all the apparent urgency and zeal with which these enquiries were made, that no formal complaint was immediately submitted to the Council of the Institution nor even when the new session began after the intervening summer. But his adversaries had not abandoned the matter, and were fortunate enough to supplement their brief with a letter supplied by Colonel Ritchie at Armstrong's request. Ritchie was fretting in Paris and London about the poor market for guns, blaming Russell for it all and feeling very amenable to join in the attack on Russell without a bleat of resentment at Armstrong's high-handed contribution to his troubles (September 18):[9]

My Dear Sir William,—I have listened carefully to your statement made to Messrs Bidder and Hawkshaw, under date of the 14 May last, of the facts of the transaction in which, on our respective sides, we have become unfortunately involved with Mr J. Scott Russell, and I have also heard read with surprise his reply, denying the truth of your relation. As you desire my testimony, I deem it my duty to affirm that your statement of Mr Scott Russell's proceedings, in so far as they came under my cognizance, are perfectly correct. Mr Scott Russell, at the interview I had with him when I came to England in June, '65, to investigate the inexplicable delay in the delivery of the ordnance, after alleging various trivial pretexts, at last fully admitted that he had used the money for his own purposes, and could not replace it.

You are at liberty to make what use you see fit of this note.

This was a handy secret weapon with which to assail Russell at the proper time.

It must be asked why a formal complaint was not now laid before Council and why, instead, Bidder preferred to communicate the Armstrong statement privately to selected members of the Institution. The inescapable conclusion is that Bidder was not primarily concerned with the honour of the Institution at all. He, and his collaborators, sought only the destruction of John Scott Russell. Perhaps they suspected that Russell had too much support on the Council; but even if Russell did not have this support it could be expected that the Council would seek to dispose of the matter quietly. The actual course of action pursued by Bidder and his collaborators suggests why that, too, would not have satisfied them. They appear to have seen their ends served only by the fullest public 'exposure' of their quarry, an exposure which they clearly placed before the harmony and honour of the Institution, and one which they could achieve with greatest effect by opposing Russell's re-election to Council in the presence of a large assembly of the membership at the Annual General Meeting. Stuart Rendel was kept busy compiling a detailed account of the case,[10] and Isambard was again expressing anxiety that his visits to Manby would be noticed. 'W. Froude will call on you at noon tomorrow,' he wrote at one point. Froude was not only competing for Russell's fame in the field of ship hydrodynamics, but was intimate with the Brunel family and a close friend of Bidder's.

These attitudes are clarified in a letter written by Henry Brunel to William Froude after attending the presentation of a paper by G. H. Phipps on the resistance of ships, in March 1864. Henry had a romantic interest in Froude's sister and often did work for him. Phipps, to Henry's disgust, had 'praised and buttered' Russell throughout (this is not evident in the published paper). Henry found it 'positively sickening' to see how Russell basked in this and he expected him to 'burst with vanity some day'.[11] Clearly, Henry expected Froude to share his feelings.

The A.G.M. was scheduled for the evening of December 18, 1866, and as the occasion approached, Russell's antagonists tried to recruit support for the assault. Zerah Colburn, a member of the Institution and editor of *Engineering*, seems to have got wind of something afoot and, in an editorial, warned the members of the Institution that it was the intention of a particular clique to obtain control and 'circumvent the usual course of official rotation'.[12] Colburn made it clear that the clique to which he referred was that which had blocked Fowler's attempt in session 1865–6 to purchase new premises for the Institution—Bidder, Gregory (a current Vice-President), Manby (the Secretary) and Hawksley—with such acrimony that the subscriptions were cancelled and the proposal abandoned. The Institution later purchased the back premises of the offices belonging to Bidder and G. R. Stephenson adjacent to the old Institution building, for the sum of £7000. 'But for the opposition of one of the gentlemen [Bidder] who now asks nearly £2000 for his one-third share of a back yard,' then wrote Colburn, 'the Institution might have possessed the freehold of one of the finest sites in Westminster.'[13]

If we replace Hawksley with Hawkshaw (there may be a misprint), the 'clique' to which Colburn referred certainly comprised those who now sought to disgrace Russell. Fate seemed to play into their hands when Russell and Fowler went off to the Continent on railway business offering little likelihood that they could be present at the A.G.M. Russell, however, did return for the meeting, moved either by simple prudence or as the result of a tip-off, and was present on that occasion when Bidder rose, with evident self-satisfaction,[14] to object to Russell's re-nomination to the Council 'on the ground,' he went on 'that a correspondence had come to his knowledge ... [which] gave evidence that Mr Russell was deficient in these qualities of honour and integrity which ought to categorize a member of the Council'.[15] He produced some letters which he wished to read to the assembly, but, to his astonishment, he was halted by a tide of outraged sensibilities which welled up. He seemed actually to have been taken aback by so many expressions of resentment at the 'irregular, inconsiderate, and indecorous' way the subject had been introduced.[16] Clearly, if honour and professional ethics were at issue, Bidder himself had transgressed, and, of course, without a proper investigation justice could not be assured. Amidst the *fracas*, Bidder protested that the matter had been brought to the knowledge of the Council, but several Council members denied this, one of whom, Abernethy, declared that although he and others had been individually invited to read the letters, he had refused to do so, or to listen to accusations of any kind which were not brought before the Council in a regular and tangible form.[17] Here indeed was the voice of dignity and right. The anonymous observer who wrote an account of the occasion in a letter to *Engineering* asked Bidder if he expected 'that a crowded and tumultuous public meeting was to sit down and investigate the various shadowy charges arising out of a long correspondence? ... was his intention merely to bespatter his opponent with mud and to hold him up—pending a proper investigation—to public opprobrium as a person destitute of common integrity?'[18] The answer, of course, was 'yes'.

The editor of *Engineering* asked why the charge had not been examined and disposed of in Council, without having to be dragged up at a general meeting. 'It would be useless to appeal to gentlemanly feeling,' he added, 'with one who stood up to make the most damaging accusation—virtually as much in public as if the meeting had been one in St James's Hall ...'[19]

Russell declared that he welcomed the fullest inquiry, and that he was glad to find someone who was willing to identify himself with the damaging whispers of which he had heard, if not accept their paternity.[20] In this deplorable way, the matter was at last referred to Council, and Russell was re-elected to the Council with the tacit understanding that should the charge against him be proved he should be invited to resign or be expelled.

The editor of *Engineering* thought that Fowler should return to examine the charges. But Fowler, now in Italy, did not or could not do so. Council, with some notable absentees, met three days later under Vice-President C. H. Gregory. Russell objected to the shortness of notice and asked for an adjournment until January 8, a request which was reinforced by a telegram from Hawksley objecting to the business 'being thus hastily entered upon'. But a motion to begin the inquiry had either been carried prior to the arrival of the telegram or was afterwards carried (6–2)—the sequence is not clear—upon which the chairman tabled Armstrong's written statement, copies of which had already been supplied by Bidder and Hawkshaw to each member of Council 'to facilitate the investigation'. A unanimous resolution was then passed to have the Armstrong statement transmitted to Scott Russell with a request that he furnish Council with a written reply not later than January 5, 1867; the meeting then adjourned until January 8. (The members present at this meeting were: Gregory (in the Chair), Cubitt, Scott Russell, Abernethy, Barlow, Bateman, Beardmore, Brunlees, Hemans, Murray and Vignoles.)

Isambard's anxiety now became whether 'the Council should take the correspondence put in to be an adequate statement, receive Russell's answer and adjudicate without having before them the very important details Rendel can give'. He thought the attack on Bidder by *Engineering* 'very scurrilous', a surprising measure of Isambard's sense of ethical propriety. Russell set about writing his own version of the affair in accordance with Council's request and submitted it at the meeting on January 8, 1967. Before this was accepted and read, however, an attempt was made to quash the proceedings with the motion: 'that the correspondence laid was insufficient for proceeding'. When this was defeated (4–6), another motion (probably proposed by Hawksley) 'that Council proceed if and as counsel learned in the law shall advise', was also defeated (5–6), which was particularly regrettable. Russell's submission was then read and ordered to be distributed to the Members of Council.

Isambard was in a fever of anxiety that the assault would not be pushed home. He 'spoke very strongly' to Noble and George Rendel

219

(Stuart's brother) who, he was relieved to find, were ready to act even if Sir William was not. The documents were ready.[21]

At another meeting, two days later, three motions were proposed with the evident intention of lending some order to the proceedings—the first, 'that Russell answer specific charges' was not even seconded, probably because notice had been given of the second which required 'that before further proceedings a definite charge of indebtedness or fraud ... be made and that further proceedings be restricted to the charge'. This, however, was defeated (3–5). A third motion, that 'Armstrong and Russell be requested to furnish additional documentary evidence' was also defeated (4–5). (The members attending this meeting were: Messrs Gregory (Chairman), Hawksley, Scott Russell, Abernethy, Bateman, Beardmore, Brunlees, Harrison, Murray, Vignoles and Sir J. Rennie.)

It was decided that Armstrong and 'a witness' as well as Scott Russell be requested to attend a meeting of Council on Tuesday January 22 at 11.30 a.m. (later postponed to February 5) and that Armstrong be asked to present at that time the correspondence of the whole transaction which he had offered to provide. 'I hope you can be there,' Isambard wrote to Manby, 'it would be most important to keep the chairman firm.'[22] The chairman, of course, was C. H. Gregory.

The inquisition was now on, by the narrowest of margins and with many judicial imperfections. Armstrong, adopting a posture of detachment, was too powerful to be hurt and Bidder's shocking conduct of the matter was allowed to pass without official censure.

HONOUR'S DEFENDERS

It is difficult now, and many found it difficult at the time, to believe that Bidder and Hawkshaw in their pursuit of Russell were motivated only by an outraged sense of honour. There was some suggestion that Fowler and Russell had superseded Bidder as consultants on the St Gotthard railway line under circumstances which Bidder resented.[23] The facts were disputed,[24] but Russell certainly surveyed and selected part of that line and Fowler was consulted upon it by the Italian Government. More significantly, Bidder, according to Colburn, conducted a notorious feud against Russell. They certainly had very little, if anything, in common. Russell was as kindly and elegant in manner as Bidder was brusque and uncouth. More than one clash between them can be found in the proceedings of the I.C.E.[25] A simple illustration of their contrasting styles is provided by their respective reactions to some erroneous conceptions evinced in a paper on 'High Speed Steam Navigation' presented to the I.C.E. in 1857. Russell gently remarked that he had some difficulty in arriving at the exact ideas of the author on several points. 'In some instances,' he explained, 'the phrase employed was "that the resistance was as the square of the velocity;" in others, "that the indicated horse power was as the square of the velocity."' Responding to the impulse of the teacher, which was always strong in him, he went on to explain why power had to be proportional to the cube of the velocity. Bidder, in contrast, curtly remarked: 'the employment of other arguments with a gentleman who contended that the power was not as the cube, while he admitted the resistance was as the square, would be as useless as to attempt to hold a conversation with him in a language which he did not understand.'[26]

Bidder's obituary explains that 'The very frankness and single-mindedness of his character made it impossible for him to disguise his opinions'. There are many indications that although he was cheerful to his friends he was particularly ill-tempered and belligerent, doubtless a legacy of the lionizing to which he was subjected as a 'calculating boy' in his early life, being exhibited at fairs and the like by his stonemason father as a mathematical child prodigy. His exceptional talent for mental arithmetic was first brought to light when, as a mere boy of seven, he settled a dispute between two neighbours about the weight and price of a pig. He 'performed' for several distinguished people and John Herschel and Thomas Jephson of Cambridge arranged to maintain him at Camberwell Grammar School, but his father managed to remove him after a year for the further commercial exploitation of his talent. After a visit to Edinburgh, Sir Henry Jardine raised a subscription to place the young and ill-educated Bidder with a private tutor and later to maintain him at Edinburgh University where he made the acquaintance of Robert Stephenson during the latter's term there in 1825. This was a fruitful event which was to result in his entering the employ of the Stephensons who made good use of his computational facility in the wrangling which took place before parliamentary committees in the celebrated 'battle of the gauges' and in the fight for the supremacy of the Hudson railway empire. He was one of Robert Stephenson's closest friends and associates and benefited greatly from the liaison. He persuaded the Stephensons and some others to join him in founding the Electric Telegraph Company, which, with Charles Wheatstone's help, became a giant. This was only one of his many profitable business interests deriving from his activities as an engineer.[27] His most notable engineering success was the planning and design of the Victoria Docks in London which were constructed by Brassey. In his later years, we are told, Bidder's 'massive head, with its plentiful covering of white hair, conveyed the impression of an intellectual Jupiter'.[28]

While Bidder was anxious to involve the Institution in the Armstrong–Russell affair which to all intents and purposes had been settled at law, he had more than once taken the position that even spurious projects designed to deceive the investor should be unnoticed within the walls of the Institution except in their 'scientific bearing and relation'.[29] Censure or approval, too, of Government policy was to his mind improper within the Institution and it was an allusion of Russell's to Admiralty policies which provoked one of the latter's public brushes with Bidder.[30]

It is ironical that Bidder should join with the Brunels in hostility to Russell, for not only was Bidder an energetic antagonist of Brunel's in the 'battle of the gauges'—as was Hawkshaw—but also he can hardly be said to have displayed much honour in the competition arranged between the Gooch and Stephenson locomotives which Brunel proposed to help decide the issue. This competition took the form of a time trial with various loads drawn over about fifty miles of the respective railways. Bidder opposed Brunel's suggestion that the trials be performed simultaneously and insisted that the latter's engine run first. This was done. Then the narrow-gauge trials were held. In these, the engine was timed from a flying start with hot water in the tender, and prior to the return journey a portable boiler was used to provide an artificial blast to liven up the furnace. What would the Brunels have said if this had been Scott Russell's doing? Who too would they have accused when sand was found in some of the bearings of the broad-gauge waggons? The broad-gauge engine triumphed in spite of the craftiness of its opponents and this perhaps helped to dissipate bitter feelings.

Bidder, along with Manby and others in the Stephenson circle had been servants of the celebrated 'railway king', George Hudson, whose great virtue, thought Manby, was that in his flight from the avenging wrath of his creditors and duped shareholders he did not betray those whose favour he had bought or the notables he could have implicated.[31]

Hudson was ultimately saved from destitution after his failure by some former friends, undoubtedly some of Russell's accusers among them, who subscribed to purchase for him an annuity of £500 a year.

Russell was much less culpable than Hudson. He ruined no one but himself. But Hudson had people in his power and his silence was worth rewarding.

If Hawkshaw had ulterior motives in associating himself with Bidder in the assault on Russell, they may have to be sought in his competition with Russell and Fowler on the subject of cross-Channel transportation linking England and France. Hawkshaw was engineer for a railway tunnel scheme, while Russell and Fowler, between 1865 and 1867, were the engineers and proponents of a fleet of train ferries. Russell designed the ferries and Fowler the landing stages. The proposal was well supported by certain promoters and reached the stage of an application for an Act of Parliament to authorize it, but there was little agreement among the rival railway interests. Meantime the pros and cons of tunnels, bridges and ferries were argued in parliamentary committee rooms and in the press. In these circumstances, an attack on Russell had the effect of a devious attack on Fowler.

Certainly in earlier years, Fowler was on the best of terms with Hawkshaw but not as 'thick' with him as he was reputed to be with Russell. Russell and Fowler had much to commend one to the other and their relationship was a good one from the start. They must have seemed a formidable pair—both had considerable public presence and in other respects their attributes were complementary. Fowler was as wealthy as Russell was penurious, as imperious as Russell was urbane and as successful in business as Russell was unsuccessful. If Russell derived benefit from his friendship with Fowler, the latter was the first to profit by it. During his first substantial railway contract in 1850 Fowler received a serious setback which could have been disastrous to his career.[32] His bridge over the Torksey River was condemned by the Board of Trade on account of its novel tubular girders. It was Russell who drew the case to the attention of the Institution of Civil Engineers and successfully pressed for the intervention which led to the raising of the ban. Fowler went on to succeed to the mantle of Robert Stephenson as monarch of Victorian railway engineers, and to that of Brunel as chief engineer of the Great Western Railway Co.

There was a belief current in Manby's circle that it was Fowler's money which had backed Russell in starting afresh after the *Great Eastern*. An interesting light is shed on these relationships by Henry Brunel in a letter to Froude, in 1863, describing his consultations with Manby regarding the engineer to whom he should become indentured. Manby narrowed the choice to three—Hawkshaw, McClean and Fowler—the three arbiters, incidentally, of Russell *v.* the Great Ship Company. He hinted that Fowler, who, he said, was not generally considered a gentleman, would not long continue as engineer of the Great Western Railway. He was not actually acquainted with the interior of Fowler's offices but from what he had heard he did not consider them very eligible for a pupil. He believed also that Fowler indulged somewhat in surveying lines on his own account for speculative purposes. Fowler's style of work was not the kind with which he thought it desirable for Henry to be mixed up. He therefore recommended Hawkshaw but since the latter was friendly with Fowler it seemed to him desirable that Henry should give the following reason for applying to him: 'as Mr Fowler and Scott Russell are great friends and as with a regard to my father's memory I cannot keep too clear of Scott Russell I prefer not to connect myself with Mr Fowler.'[33] This, Manby believed, would be conveyed to Fowler by Hawkshaw and while it may have served some purpose in palliating Fowler, at the same time as expressing disfavour at his alliance with Russell, it could not have done much for Hawkshaw unless there were some unexpressed consideration which would make it right with him. Henry Brunel was finishing his indentureship with Hawkshaw when the attack on Russell was set afoot within the Institution. Fowler, of course, was president and holding court, as his biographer described it, every Tuesday evening prior to the Institution's weekly meetings, as he had often done in the past, with his fellow councillors and engineers. Hawkshaw, Bidder and Russell and, in earlier years, Stephenson, Brunel, Locke and Rendel, Snr, are named as frequent guests by Fowler's biographer.[34]

All of this elite corps, with the exception of Russell, had built fortunes as surely as they had built the railways and docks of a transportation-hungry world. It was usual for them to aspire to big houses, estates, sea-going yachts and art collections. If any had lost by the railway mania, it was not they. Russell, however, was not a railway man, had not risen from the ranks of the indentured apprentice and engineering assistant to superintend a whole railway contract. He was not really one of them, yet he was in line for the presidency of their institution and he had moved the specialized study of naval architecture from their forum into a new institution of which only ship designers and builders could be members and of which he was also senior vice-president. Did none resent this? Did none resent the contrast between his status and his means? Did he not fall short of Samuel Smiles' criterion of success? Yet Russell, with his maddeningly superior graces and tact, could mix with lords and princes as though he had been born to it. Here were circumstances which could attract something less than fervent support from colleagues in the Institution.

If Fowler 'seemed to attach an undue importance to material success',[35] as a friend said of him, his esteem for Russell can only be explained by his 'almost exaggerated respect for intellectual ability'.[36] It has also been said of Fowler that he was a man of the 'strictest integrity with whom the sanctions of right conduct were practical institutions'.[37]

It would be too much to say the same of Sir William Armstrong on whose behest such ardent zealots for honour assailed Scott Russell. Armstrong combined a commanding personality with a studied aloofness, 'a curious note of romantic melancholy' and 'a remoteness in his temperament which impressed people'.[38] He was originally articled as a solicitor in his native Newcastle, becoming a partner in the practice by the time he was thirty years of age, and although he had no training in engineering he conceived some ideas on the improvement of hydraulic machinery. With formidable business acumen and not a little of that spirit which distinguished his Border forbears, he pushed his way on to the English industrial scene in the late 1840s, armed in particular with a very useful hydraulic crane. He had a strong backer in the well-known harbour engineer, J. M. Rendel, who put orders his way for hydraulic harbour machinery and who, by drawing his attention to the deficiencies of British guns in the Crimea, stimulated his interest in heavy guns. Armstrong did not so much invent a new gun as develop new manufacturing techniques which made some existing ideas more practicable. We have noted how he avoided the difficulties which would have arisen from the publication of his gun 'patents'.

His principal partners were George Rendel, his engineering manager, and Captain Andrew Noble whom he introduced in 1860 as joint manager. Noble was an accomplished ballistics authority who had been secretary to various Government committees on ordnance, including the one which recommended the Armstrong gun. He was a prodigious worker, and has been described as 'ambitious, able, coercive, tenacious and choleric',[39] qualities which could not fail to commend him to Armstrong and which ensured his ultimate succession to Armstrong's throne.

It was when the Armstrong breech-loading gun and Armstrong's special position with the Government came under a torrent of criticism in 1862, that another of the Rendel family, George's barrister brother, Stuart, was first engaged to devote his energy, ambition and legalistic lack of scruple, to the public and private defence of Armstrong and his interests. This activity led Stuart Rendel first into a directorship of the Armstrong Company, then into Parliament (where he was, strangely enough, a radical Liberal) and, ultimately, to a peerage.[40]

It was a hard-hitting world in which Armstrong moved, and if Scott Russell had lived longer he would probably have looked wryly on the charges of corruption and conspiracy levelled at Armstrong and the Ordnance Department as a result of large naval gun failures in the period 1886–9. This scandal even touched a member of the Queen's household who, enquiries revealed, had stock in Armstrong's firm.[41] Sir William led in the formation of the Employers' Federation to protect their interests against the trade unions which he abhorred, and he epitomized for working class leaders that type of international armaments baron who had a vested interest in war.

On Armstrong's resignation from his Government post he was given a golden handshake to the amount of £65,500[42] for leaving a well-salaried position to take over a ready-made ordnance works. When Scott Russell defaulted in the payment for a gun he never received and which was long overdue, Armstrong's aloofness and wealth should not deceive us into thinking that he was above plotting to destroy Russell in retribution. But he left the execution to others. It was well said that he 'had the gift, so important in British public life, of not seeming to try too hard'.[43]

THE COURT OF HONOUR

Armstrong's 'written statement of the case' presented the superficial details in a way which, Russell claimed, distorted the nature of the transaction, concealed its origin and misrepresented its motives. In the reply which Russell submitted to Council, he dwelt on these points, explaining how a member of the Armstrong firm called upon him 'to solicit, as a great favour, that he would give them the benefit of his friendly advice and assistance to help them to restore work to Elswick and credit to Sir William Armstrong'. He was induced to help, he added, 'as a mere act of friendliness to a brother member of the Council of Civil Engineers'. He had for many years made artillery a study; guns on his plan had fired larger shot than any then existing and he was therefore known to one or two departments of the British and foreign Governments as having made great guns and gunnery a private study. He communicated to some foreign correspondents, he said, that he was 'enabled and could undertake to place in their hands cannon of large sizes within a fixed time and that one of these correspondents at once accepted the terms'. He was assured, he declared, that two of the guns 'were already well advanced in construction, that preparations for the next two were forward, and that the fifth was within reach, as the works, having little else to do, could bring ample force to bear on the work.' But Sir William Armstrong utterly failed to fulfil his contract and the extreme period of the whole contract elapsed without the fulfilment of any one condition of it. Here, he thought, the transaction should have ended; but he was still bent on helping Sir William and he believed that the guns were still of some use to his correspondent although their value to him was much reduced.

After accepting and paying for the two pairs of guns Russell accepted no more of them, but Sir William had tried to force his acceptance 'by failing and refusing to give the drawings and instructions required abroad, in order to prepare the carriages and to prepare for using the guns; and he ultimately refused to deliver up the guns already paid for, and by these means attempted to force acceptance of the remainder.'

Lawyers, he explained, now settled the case by mutual compromise. Sir William had decided to injure the man he had wronged and had now formed a plan for doing so by importing into this matter before the Council private affairs involving his, Russell's, relations to other persons. He was probably referring to Ritchie and Adams and his obligation to honour the confidence in which he had conducted his affairs with these men, his clients. He continued:

For my part, I have lived on the principle that everything I have ever done may with my full consent be printed in the newspapers, for in my own life I have no secrets. It is only in the business of other people that I keep secrets. I shall therefore now frankly state as much of my own private affairs to this Council, as is necessary for my own justification, taking care to avoid the names and affairs of other people.

Long after this contract of mine with Sir William Armstrong was made, and should have been completed, I suffered heavy disappointments and losses. Ever since my connection with the *Great Eastern* broke down my fortunes, I had striven hard to restore them; but three times had I to risk my all for her completion, and I have been left poor. During 1865, sources of revenue I had a right to reckon on became dried up, and property I had earned became first locked up, and then depreciated, I may add in matters over which I had no control. This was the case at the time, when it was my desire and my duty to balance accounts with some of the persons with whom I had business. I wished to balance accounts with a foreign correspondent. I suddenly found that, although I had property, I had not money enough for this purpose. Without delay, I at once told him so. But I assured him at the same time that, although I had lost money, I had set vigorously about earning it over again, and that in the meantime he might rely on my doing all in my power to diminish any inconvenience he might suffer, to guard him against ultimate loss, and to balance accounts with him as soon as I was able, and I afterwards transferred to him £5000 of my locked-up securities. Since then I have been working hard to build up my losses again.

In all this, in my immediate and frank admission of my misfortunes and losses to my creditor, in giving the best security in my power to him, and in my efforts to earn money to make up my losses and pay my debts, I feel that I have nothing to be ashamed of, although I may have to regret the loss of hard-earned money, the inconvenience to myself and my connections, and the opportunity my poverty gives to my enemies to misrepresent my conduct and impugn my motives.

Finally, Sir William would make you believe, that in this matter I had sought and he had offered, that I should undertake the business for remuneration by a commission. That is not so. No remuneration to me was ever asked or offered.

Sir William Armstrong's original proposition happened to include a discount or commission of five per cent. That sum, instead of going into my pocket, would have been far from sufficient to pay the costs and insurance and other disbursements and contingencies of the transaction, had it gone on as contracted for. The discount of five per cent, was a mere element of open account, and had I accepted remuneration, it would have been very different in nature and amount.

This letter of Russell's and the written statement of the case by Armstrong to which it was a rebuttal, were supplemented by the transaction correspondence supplied by the Armstrong Company. These were together intended to form the documentary basis of the inquiry to be conducted by the Council of the Institution of Civil Engineers. But Armstrong and his partners were not content to let the collected letters speak for themselves; they had encouraged Stuart Rendel to compose a point by point guide to the correspondence as they saw it. This was entitled a 'Paper of Particulars', and was enclosed with the copies of the correspondence distributed to the Members of Council shortly prior to the first 'hearing' on February 5, 1867. Furthermore, the correspondence included the letter solicited by Armstrong from Colonel Ritchie. This was a telling blow against Russell in the circumstances, for Ritchie could not be challenged.

When Russell entered the sombre council chamber at Great George Street on that bleak February morning he must have felt grievously assailed. Looking round he would see among his fellow councillors—those who were present—faces he identified as hostile and faces he regarded as friendly. Some members would feel uncomfortable, some resentful, some unctuously satisfied. These were his professional colleagues, his peers, before whom he was now going to be obliged to defend himself against calumny. The official circulation of Rendel's 'Paper of Particulars' was a scoop for his adversaries, and the result among the uncommitted must have been a bias against him.

It was hopeless to take exception to the admission of the new document as part of the evidence of the correspondence. There was no judge or jury to take heed. It was a prejudicial act which, no matter any ruling to the contrary, was irreversible. Russell was rightly incensed at the admission of the new document—it was 'a false step and a very unfair one' he protested.

The chairman, Gregory, assured Russell that the Council was trying to act justly and with delicacy and that whatever the impression made on their minds by the Paper of Particulars they were open to receive any proof Russell could bring to the contrary. The burden of proof was therefore on Russell and no specific charges were laid.

Should Russell have taken this opportunity to withdraw his consent to the investigation? Hemans interjected that if Russell were dissatisfied with the course the Council were pursuing, it was not too late for him to withdraw, and that he for one should feel most happy if that were the result of the meeting—but Russell could not withdraw without loss and he was anxious to clear his name. He would have reason to regret that he had not insisted on legal representation and on a more legalistic procedure with specific charges.

Gregory said that they wished only to elicit the truth. Russell replied:

> The truth is sure to come out some day, somehow or other; but permit me to call Mr Gregory's attention to the fact, that when you make an inquiry it is the truth that you can bring forward at the time, and not the truth which may remain behind, which must decide the question. Therefore, I have not only to take care that what I say is the truth, but there may be truth remaining which I am not able to bring forward. Having said what I have upon the subject of this document, I am still at a loss how to regard it. I shall proceed

229

to ask Sir W. Armstrong questions, not upon that document, but upon this correspondence which he has placed before you, and which I understand was the thing to be produced and to be proved. Only I repeat the statement, that I think it would be very wise on the part of the Council to put themselves right, if they still can do so, with reference to the admission of this *ex-parte*, and one-sided and unauthenticated statement which they have printed and circulated.

At last, persuaded to question Armstrong, Russell began by establishing that the bills of exchange by which the Americans paid him became due on May 19, 1864. Then, instead of pursuing the subject on the contract and the delivery dates, to which this was a logical introduction, he abruptly turned to the portion of Armstrong's statement dealing with the 'abortive' settlement. He referred Sir William to the part of his statement in which he wrote: 'Mr Day alleged that he had a prior claim to the property arising from breach of contract by Mr Russell, and he therefore declined to give them up . . .' In this he had underlined 'prior claim' and 'declined'. The 'property' were the copies of Russell's great book.

Mr R.—Will Sir William be good enough to state why he has underlined those words, and what were the conclusions he drew which induced him to do so?

Sir W. Armstrong.—It merely points out the effect which the letter had upon my mind.

Mr R.—Will Sir William explain what the conclusions were which led him to underline those important words?

Sir W. A.—It is simply meant to indicate that the offer of 125 copies of your book was abortive, and that Mr. Day declined to recognize it on the ground of a prior claim, and therefore it was declined.

Mr R.—Does it follow from that that he had truly any prior claim?

Sir W. A.—That was my impression upon the letter.

Mr R.—Does Sir W. Armstrong say that I am personally responsible, and ought to be held personally responsible, for some other person having stated something which may not have been true?

Sir W. A.—I have not said so.

Mr R.—That could be the only view attached to these words, if Sir W. Armstrong does not make me responsible for the statement.

Sir W. A.—What statement?

Mr R.—The words in this letter, 'prior claim' and 'declined', which are underlined.

Sir W. A.—I mean what I say in the passage of my statement . . .

Mr R.—It is this question I ask: Do you mean the Council to take it as

18 *HMS Warrior*

19 A model of the three cylinder oscillating engine on a single crank

20 Sydenham 1866. On chairs from left to right: Arthur Sullivan, John
Scott Russell, Mrs Russell, George Grove, Rachel Russell. The three
in front are not identified, but Norman Russell may be the figure
on the left

21 The Vienna Rotunda in 1873

a fact that there existed any such prior claim, and that, therefore, I had given an order upon Messrs Day, which was not a valid one? Is that the inference you put forward as the ground of it? It appears so in your statement, and it has value only in that case.

Sir W. A.—I state that you gave an order which was futile, and which produced nothing ...

Mr R.—... The inference sought is that I gave you an insufficient transfer, or rather fraudulently represented property which I had no right to.

Sir W. A.—You must not put words into my mouth. I did not use the word 'fraudulent', or anything approaching to it.

Russell continued doggedly but vainly, this way and that, to extract a definite allegation from Armstrong—did he, or did he not impute moral blame for the abortive order? If, said Russell, he had given the books to Sir W. Armstrong, knowing the existence of a lien, or a lien for any debt whatever on the books, he would have done a dishonest act. Did Sir William accuse him with this or not? Armstrong at length conceded that there was little if any moral blame to be attached to Russell for that part of the transaction. He did not know how far Russell knew the facts which made the order abortive. Russell asserted that since he had legally transferred his title to the books to Armstrong, it was Armstrong's duty to insist upon their being surrendered to him by the publisher.

Hawksley ended the long round of shadow boxing by remarking that Russell surely could be satisfied with Armstrong's answer that he did not attribute any particular blame to Russell on this part of the transaction. Sir William Armstrong, he said, did not attempt to prove that the printer had a legitimate lien and to that extent Russell could content himself with the advantage he had gained.

No specific charge or accusation was laid to be answered, there was no official accuser, the moral obliquity was simply implied and, when challenged, Armstrong innocently protested that no such implication was intended. He was there only to answer questions. Yet the Council was obviously conducting an investigation—for what? Presumably, and it was never declared in so many words, to determine if Russell had been guilty of unprofessional conduct in the transaction with Armstrong. In this case, only two questions could give rise to such a charge—whether or not Russell had prior knowledge of his publisher's lien, assuming that the lien was valid, on the books which he surrendered in settlement of the debt, and whether or not Russell had been in a position of special trust, an agent for either party, as distinct from that of a vendor or 'principal', in the transaction which he negotiated. The first question was disposed of as we have seen, but whether or not in Russell's favour was at the discretion or prejudice of the individual member of Council. No moral obliquity in this question was proved.

It was left to Russell to perceive the implications and to challenge them; the Council made no effort of its own to direct the investigation. Having, as he might have believed, disposed of the question of the printer's lien he did not turn to that of his being an agent or principal. Instead he returned to the subject of delivery and what we may call the counter charges and tried to establish that he had a right to remove the goods already 'delivered' to him at Armstrong's premises and marked with his initials, and that Armstrong had wrongfully withheld them.

He drew attention to the paragraph in Letter No. 2—'We should prefer to have nothing to do with the shipping of the guns, but we could deliver them to any port.' From this the discussion proceeded to the establishing of the letter of January 14 as the contract. Whether delivery was to be at the works or at the port was an open question, but, Russell asserted, 'Sir William had refused to do either'. Hawksley observed—

> I would just say, I do not think the letter of the 9th January makes any contract on the question of delivery, and the contract for delivery must be gathered from what subsequently took place. As far as I can put these letters together, I believe it to be a contract to deliver in the yard of Sir W. Armstrong, but that he takes upon himself the obligation of packing the goods, and he would have seen them sent to any port.

Bidder interrupted with a question prompted by a possible implication in Russell's statement that Armstrong had sought advice from Russell regarding the construction of artillery. Armstrong denied receiving professional advice from Russell, and Russell was 'very happy to corroborate' this and state that he had never said otherwise to anybody.[44]

Next day, Russell returned to the subject of the refusal to deliver and elicited from Armstrong the explanation that he had suspected Russell of stalling on the matter and of not being serious about making arrangements for shipping the goods and that he had been guided by his solicitor to withhold them pending a settlement. Russell let this subject drop, although he was to return to it. His case deserved a trained lawyer to press this point. Armstrong on the other hand was himself a lawyer. It is interesting to note the Confederate agents' resenting Whitworth's retaining 'goods' *not* paid for. In a letter from Bulloch to North, dated

September 10, 1864, we find: 'A letter from Whitworth this morning announces that the goods are ready, but that it is contrary to his rules to forward goods until they are paid for. This, after keeping us waiting for them for some months I regard as a subterfuge for delay.'[45]

Russell turned to asking Sir William when he first circulated defamatory reports on his, Russell's, conduct. Sir William denied doing so. Then, asked Russell, 'how is it that Mr Bidder told me that accusations had been circulated by you or your firm assiduously in various quarters in London ...?' Bidder promptly denied this.

Sir William said that he could hardly conceive the possibility of its remaining a secret when so many persons were necessarily acquainted with the facts; but he denied any knowledge of persons connected with him circulating reports. He denied that he was an accuser or that he was there to prove anything, he was simply a witness to the facts of the transaction as set out in his submission.

Russell returned to the subject of delivery dates and made much of the reluctance of Armstrong to furnish the gun-carriage drawings as requested. From that he drifted on to the circumstances under which he had entered into the contract. He tried in vain to get Armstrong to admit that it was of his, Armstrong's, seeking and that Russell's help in placing a contract with the Americans was of the nature of an obligement for which Armstrong expressed gratitude.

Next day, Members of Council were given the opportunity to question Sir William. Hawksley perceived the crucial issue and tried to elicit the status of Russell with respect to the contract—was he an agent for either party? With whom was the contract made? Armstrong regarded Russell as an agent for the transaction, but not the agent of the Armstrong Company. Russell of course asserted that he was not the agent of either party and we know, although some may have suspected otherwise at the time, that his only remuneration was Armstrong's five per cent commission, a commission which Russell insisted was awarded gratuitously.

Bidder asked some questions to bring out that Armstrong regarded Russell's function as one of checking the articles and of certifying payment of which he, Russell, was merely the channel. Also that Colonel Ritchie had not complained to Armstrong about the failure to deliver on time, and that he would not have felt himself justified in taking proceedings against Mr Day, Russell's publisher, to compel the delivery of the books in accordance with Russell's order. Armstrong said that they no more thought of proceeding against Messrs Day than they should think of proceeding against a banker in the event of a cheque being dishonoured. He said also that Ritchie's lawyer was a very sagacious man and that had he seen a reasonable probability of putting the order into force against Messrs Day, he could have done so. This, of course, was intended to imply that Day had legal title to the books transferred by Russell to Ritchie; but it did not prove it, and there were other reasons which made litigation unattractive to the Massachusetts government.

In reply to questioning by G. R. Stephenson, Armstrong said that it was all along understood that Russell was to have the commission for his trouble; that it was 'no doubt' an agreement made between Noble and Russell, and that he had no reason to know that Russell was remunerated beyond the five per cent.

Bidder asked if Russell could tell them what became of the 250 copies of his book which Messrs Day assigned to him. The chairman disallowed the question, but Russell nevertheless answered that he 'may have received 12 or 25 copies'.

The investigation could well have stopped there. It had been conceded that Russell had made a legal transfer of his share of the books, and that he was a principal and not an agent. He was guilty of insolvency, but was that a crime or a moral delinquency? It must have been obvious, too, that the Members of Council were not regarding attendance at the hearing as obligatory. Nevertheless a further three days of this strange proceeding were endured, February 18–20, at which Captain Noble appeared.

Russell began by trying to elicit from Noble the circumstances under which the contract for guns had been obtained. The Captain, however, was no more forthcoming than Sir William had been on this subject. They were clearly determined to give Russell no credit. Noble held to his explanation that he had called on Russell only for Holley's address. Russell asked him if he had seen Holley's book (published in 1865) and if he could say whether there were drawings in it of Armstrong guns. Curiously enough, Noble could not say whether Armstrong guns were illustrated in that book, he had but 'glanced' through it! How many could believe that? Russell could not get Noble to answer whether Holley approved or disapproved of the Armstrong breech-loading gun. Holley in fact was very critical of Armstrong and his guns. Russell's objective is not clear. Perhaps he was leading up to establishing why he could not have recommended Holley as an emissary in an order for Armstrong's guns.

Much time was spent on the subject of what letter or letters constituted the contract and on the vexed question of the importance of delivery dates. It was easily shown that once these dates were not met, Russell exerted no further pressure *in writing* for completion nor made any issue in writing of the breach of the contract.

The chairman proposed an adjournment to allow those who were not present to ask questions, in effect, to ask questions upon an examination which they had not heard. Hawksley strongly objected and the suggestion was withdrawn.

The most important questioning was from Hawksley and Vignoles on the subject of the payments and again on whether Russell was Armstrong's or Ritchie's agent and again on Messrs Day's lien on the books.

HAWKSLEY—Mr Scott Russell and Messrs Day engage between each other in some way with respect to this big book. It seems that Mr Russell is to be paid in books or some other way for his copyright, and 250 copies is apparently the number he is to have, or the proceeds of them. Then Mr Day says, 'I will hold these for you and to your order, reserving to myself the right of pre-emption for twelve months at a price, less 10 per cent., of £42, valuing the books to himself at £38 per copy. This agreement is *bona fide* made between the parties a year previously to this transaction. Then there came these unfortunate events. It is then discovered that Mr Scott Russell has no available assets except his right in these books. Thereupon a claim is made upon Mr Russell that he shall give up all he has. In some way the number of copies of the books becomes reduced to 125, and Mr Russell gives an order, which I must call a valid order—he gives an order upon Messrs Day to deliver the books (on the terms of the arrangement then existing between them and Mr Russell), to the solicitor of one of the parties for a mutual advantage and benefit; but Mr Day, taking the law into his own hands, says, 'Oh! I have a prior claim against Mr Scott Russell for breach of contract.' But I may state in the presence of Captain Noble that the person to whom the order passed, had right of action of *detenue* against Mr Day for the recovery of the books, the order for them having been given by Mr Russell for value received. I say Mr Russell, having given this order for the books in the absence of any notice from Mr Day of prior claim, it was a perfectly valid order, and could have been recovered by the parties against Mr Day.

HAWKSHAW—I differ from you on that.

VIGNOLES—It is evident there was a formal agreement with Mr Russell that Mr Day should give up the books on the same conditions as had been agreed with Mr Russell, viz., a right of pre-emption within twelve months at 10 per cent. less than the nominal price. This was an agreement of a year's standing.

HAWKSLEY—Yes.

VIGNOLES—Mr Day is bound to show that Mr Russell had, in the meantime, done something to vitiate that agreement.

HAWKSLEY—Quite so.

VIGNOLES—I think the feeling of the Council is, that the order was given by Mr Russell *bona fide*. I think so myself. I believe Mr Scott Russell gave the order for the books with a *bona fide* intention; and the reason for refusal to comply with the order must have been from some previous circumstance which we have not had before us further than as an alleged breach of faith. We have had no account of unsettled claims or balance of current account as between Mr Russell and Mr Day, previous to this order for the books having been given. For my own part, I should have been pleased if Mr Day had been here himself.

NOBLE—Perhaps my answers on this point had better be expunged.

HAWKSLEY—There is a great mistake in the comparison between this order and a cheque upon a banker. The banker is the agent of the drawer of the cheque, but Mr Day is not the agent of Mr Russell; he is only the holder of the goods, and if he holds the goods to order, an action would lie against him by the holder of the order if he did not deliver the books ...

VIGNOLES—The other side have assumed that Mr Russell gave an order which was not *bona fide*.

NOBLE—The matter with respect to the books was entirely handed over to Colonel Harrison Ritchie, and he was to hand us over half the proceeds if they were realized.

Vignoles and Hawksley were the only members to indulge in much questioning and, of course, they were among the few who attended the hearing every day. They were the only ones, also, who exhibited much legal acumen, Hawksley in particular. On the subject of Russell's status—agent or principal—Vignoles, in questioning Noble, said:

'Your allegation is, that Mr Scott Russell received money from someone else which he did not pay to you ... you were content to be paid by the drafts of Mr Scott Russell. You might have been paid direct ...'

Noble replied that they 'always expected to get the money through Mr Scott Russell'.

'Then,' remarked Vignoles, 'you must have regarded Mr Russell as your principal ...'

One of the problems which arose was the nature of the compromise in settlement of the debt. Was the compromise between Armstrong and

Ritchie only or did it embrace all three parties? At one stage Hawksley exclaimed to the chairman 'You ought to have a legal assessor present. I shall always throw that in your teeth.'[46] This seems to hark back to the motion to seek legal advice defeated by one vote at the meeting of January 8. The hearings closed with some desultory questioning on the present state of the business and on the payments made by Russell. The latter reminded the Council of a request for details of the proof of the guns, and Captain Noble took an opportunity to declare that he was not an accuser of Mr Russell.[47]

Another troublesome item in the case was the question of secrecy. While Captain Noble agreed that the Americans had an obvious need for secrecy, he declared in answer to questions that even as a representative of the Armstrong Company he had been indifferent to secrecy and denied seeking it.[48] This may have been true for himself but it was not true for Armstrong as Stuart Rendel revealed.[49] When Ritchie called at Elswick to discuss the difficulties which had arisen with the contract, Armstrong expressed the opinion that 'Scott Russell intended from the beginning to cheat both parties—and get hold of the money—and that he represented himself as the agent of the other party and enforced upon each the necessity the other was under of observing secrecy to prevent the parties coming together.'[50] This is a peculiarly malicious fabrication, but at least admits the need for secrecy on both sides. The allegation that Russell intended from the beginning—or at any time—to cheat both parties is preposterous. Had the contract been completed as undertaken, there would have been no opportunity for 'cheating'.

The proceedings closed with a request that Russell lay a 'reply' before the Council at his earliest convenience. Russell said that he desired to meet the wishes of the Council as far as possible. Meantime he had to return to the Continent for at least a week.

Captain Noble's reply to the questions regarding gun production at Elswick during the period of Russell's contract was received. This stated that the two 150-pounders were proved between April 24 and May 5, 1864. The 300-pounders were not proved and the 600-pounder was not proved.

Russell read his final statement, the so-called 'reply', as requested, at a special meeting of Council on March 12, and this was printed and circulated to the members of the Council. The new points which he introduced were that the evidence had confirmed that the guns initially offered to him were afterwards sold to other people. He pointed out that although he had paid for the 300-pounders they were not ready for delivery as they had not been proved, and he did not know if the 600-pounder was ever finished but he did know that it had never been proved and never accepted by him. It had been established that he was a principal and not an agent of either party and he had settled his debt with his American customer: he owed nothing to Sir William Armstrong who had defaulted in all terms of the contract.

It was intended to reach a verdict at a meeting of March 25, but this was not possible and the meeting was adjourned until April 2 when there was, for the first time, almost a full turnout of the Council. The members present were: C. H. Gregory (Chairman), Cubitt, Hawksley, Abernethy, Barlow, Bateman, Beardmore, Brunlees, Harrison, Hemans, G. R. Stephenson, Vignoles, Lord R. Grosvenor, Lucas, Bidder and Hawkshaw 'Honorary Councillors'. The members absent were: J. Fowler, J. Rennie and Murray.

Of the sixteen Members of Council meeting to pass judgement on Russell, only three, apart from the Chairman, had heard all the evidence and were present at all times when participation was vital—Hawksley, Brunlees and Vignoles. Cubitt and Hemans each missed one out of the six hearings, and five attended only on three random days of the six—Bidder and Hawkshaw (who would have been as well at home), Barlow, Harrison and G. R. Stephenson. Lord Grosvenor, Bateman and Beardmore each attended two of the six, Abernethy and Lucas none at all. Rennie, Fowler and Murray took no part in the business.

When Fowler returned from abroad in March, he resorted to legal advice to determine whether he should take his proper place as chairman of the hearings. The advice, based upon a misunderstanding of the nature of the inquiry, was that he should not. Certainly, if the chairman were to serve in the capacity of a judge or jury, it would have been wrong of him to enter the scene after much of the evidence had been heard. But in this hearing it was the Members of Council who served as judge and jury, and indeed, as we have noted, the verdict itself was voted upon by members who had not attended all the hearings or not even attended any. Fowler did not offer his friendship with Russell as a reason for disqualification and clearly friendship with one or other of the parties could have disqualified most of the Council. But he may have felt this. It is not known how Russell regarded Fowler's decision. It was probably in Russell's best interests.

In the event, it would seem that Russell simply could not win. To have occasioned an investigation was enough and Russell must have seen the writing on the wall when first Hawksley, then Bateman conveyed suggestions from the Council that it would be best if he would resign. This he refused to do. Then, again at the request of the Council, the President communicated to him the following:

> That, without committing the Council collectively or individually to an expression of opinion ... it is the unanimous opinion that it would be best if Mr Scott Russell could be induced to resign his position as Member of Council; and that the President of the Institution be requested to communicate in person this Resolution to Mr Russell in the most delicate manner, with such necessary individual observations as may induce Mr Russell to fall in with these views of the Council

In his reply, March 26, 1867, Russell wrote:

> Dear Mr President ... As you have not personally taken part in the matter pending between Armstrong and myself, I shall be quite ready to confer with you on the propriety or impropriety of my remaining a Member of Council; but that must be *after* the Council have given their decision on the question before them—whether I am chargeable with moral blame? Aye or No.
>
> Nothing short of complete acquittal can now be so good for me, as that this miserable proceeding should change its shape from secret calumny to open hostility, and that full publicity should be given to all the circumstances and persons concerned in it.

Russell was perfectly right; but what a quandary for the Council. Could they afford to have full publicity given to what Russell rightly called the miserable proceeding? Open hostility instead of secret calumny?

A motion to enter in the minutes the offer made to Russell and his reply thereto was carried 7–4. Then a further motion was tabled that, 'The Council ... recommended that Mr Scott Russell do retire from the Council'. To this, the three following amendments were then proposed:

1. That the transactions between the parties resulted in a debt, which was subsequently satisfied by a compromise.
   That inquiries into the conduct of Members in regard to transactions not connected with the affairs of the Institution, and other than such as are lawfully cognizable by reason of some court of competent jurisdiction having publicly adjudicated upon them, are not within the scope of the Charter of the Institution, and, consequently, that the proceedings had

239

in the present case ought not to constitute a precedent for similar future action.

2. That the transactions between the parties resulted in a debt, which was subsequently compromised; but the Council are of opinion that a reference in regard to transactions not connected with the affairs of the Institution are not within the scope of the Charter, unless after adjudication by one of the competent courts of the empire; and consequently, that the proceedings in the present case ought not to constitute a precedent.

3. The Council, having inquired into the statements alluded to in the Resolution of December 18th, and having received the reply made thereto by the Member of Council referred to in that Resolution, are reluctantly compelled to report that they do not deem that reply satisfactory.

This motion with the third amendment was passed 9–4.

A Special General Meeting of Members and Associates was called for April 10, to hear and consider the decision and recommendations of their Council. The debate was 'very stormy'.[51] As one member saw it, 'the majority of the meeting, knowing little or nothing of the matter the Council then reported upon (in terms sufficiently vague) were indisposed to be hurried into adopting a motion which followed very quickly upon the report, but ... were glad to see in the second amendment [rejected by their Council, see above] a way to escape from a painful dilemma.'[52] The obstacle to this, however, in the view of this correspondent, was Russell's attack on the motives of the majority of the Council; this apparently made it difficult for many to vote to Russell's advantage without at the same time supporting his aspersions on members of Council. The issue becoming one of choosing between the Council and Russell, the result could be predicted. Some of Russell's friends appealed to him to withdraw his severe reflections with an 'amende honorable', but he refused to do so. Challenged by a member of Council either to withdraw those imputations or to move 'that the papers and evidence laid before the Council be printed and circulated to the members and associates' he chose the latter.

The Engineer had it that Russell 'was required to apologize, and did apologize to Mr Bidder for the absurd and disgraceful statements he made regarding that gentleman; to the members of the Council and to the general body.'[53] But this is nonsense; the editor of *The Engineer* was not present and the evidence does not support him. It appears, too, that on the day before the meeting, Russell sent a copy of Armstrong's accusation of May 14, 1866, and his reply of March 16, 1867, to certain members of the Institution, each copy marked 'private and confidential'.[54] One of these members transmitted his copy to the editor of *The Engineer*, who promptly published it in that week's issue. Zerah Colburn, the editor of *Engineering* severely chastized him for the 'unauthorized and scandalous publication' of 'a private and confidential document, involving the honor of a member of Council of the Institution of Civil Engineers'.[55] He doubtless relished the opportunity of a duel with his rival and former employer no less than the heaven-sent opportunity to rid himself of the constraints by which he had been bound to silence. He was a member of the Institution, had been present at the meeting, and had received a copy of Russell's circular. In his editorial of May 10, he published the first of what was to be a series of commentaries on the case with an admirably concise statement of the particulars of both sides. On May 6, Isambard wrote to Manby about a 'paper' which had been prepared by Stuart Rendel for a meeting of Council, but which he criticized for the absence of a reply to Russell's final statement; a reply which would endorse what Isambard had persuaded himself to believe—that Russell had no case at all! Isambard need not have worried, for, after an animated debate at the final General Meeting held to decide Russell's fate on May 14, the motion, 'That the report of the council be received and adopted' was carried by an 'overwhelming' majority.

The editor of *The Engineer* declared that he had no right to be dissatisfied with the decision. The Council had spared no pains and their report 'left nothing to be desired'. *Engineering* took the view that the Institution, as a body, was bound to accept and adopt whatever report the Council might make, the only alternative being that of 'breaking up the Institution by rejecting the report, and accepting the instant resignation of the Council, or a majority of Council at least'.

Isambard, now feeling much assuaged, wrote to Manby:

... The proceedings seem to have been very satisfactory as far as they went but I cannot think they ought or can stop there. Considering both his present position and also his conduct *during* this enquiry the case seems to me removed from that of an ordinary member of the Institution even granting that the papers did not disclose a transaction of more than ordinary turpitude. I hope therefore that something will be done. You know I think why I am anxious that this gentleman in particular should have his due. He is in the habit of asserting his belief and Mr Fowler (and I presume his other friends if he has any) does not scruple to repeat the assertion without dissent that my Father was guilty of the basest conduct towards Russell. Although I am

241

aware that no one whose opinion is worth having would credit Russell's assertion that my Father deliberately ruined him from jealousy. Yet there is an outside world who are influenced by such men as Russell and Fowler and anything which strikes at Russell's credit reduces his importance with them.[56]

Here at last we see something of the personal prejudices which influenced the outcome of the Russell inquiry—the Brunel interests coinciding with those of the Armstrong and anti-Fowler factions—a fatal confluence for Russell. With such considerations at work in the forming of men's judgement we can understand why so many did not feel it necessary to attend the six main hearings.

Henry Brunel's transcript of the hearings bears a number of his pencilled annotations. At Russell's initial statement that he had arranged the contract to help Armstrong out of his difficulties, Henry wrote: 'Likely! A man like Armstrong to apply to such a conceited Jackanapes as Scott Russell, a man bursting with bumptiousness of the most offensive nature ... in such a case ridiculous.' We know more about this than Henry, but he is right in so far as Armstrong personally left others to make the overtures on his behalf. As for Russell's remark that the *Great Eastern* had broken him, Henry exclaims: 'Yes, you rascal you left filth half an inch thick under the splendid carpets laid on the decks of the *Great Eastern* and perjured yourself in the examination concerning the explosion of the water casing.' This is a glorious *non sequitur*. It comes as no surprise that in the circumstances some of the contractors would literally sweep dirt under the carpets; but the ship sailed out of the Thames almost on schedule and Russell had not designed the water casing. As for other remarks of a like kind by which Henry released his blind hatred of Russell—'very slippery customer indeed', 'what a double dealing rascal', etc., we are now well able to evaluate the events for ourselves.

Knowing what we now know, who can accuse Russell of vindictiveness or exaggeration when he embarrassed the members of the Institution by declaring 'that the whole accusation of Sir William Armstrong, promoted by Mr Bidder and backed by their associates within and without the Council, is a gross misrepresentation, having for its object the indulgence of personal ill-will, the gratification of professional jealousy and promotion of party interests in the Council of the Institution'?[57]

Colburn again devoted much space to the subject in the May 24 issue of *Engineering*. He reiterated that he did not see it as a case for imputations of dishonesty.

242

Mr Bidder invited the suggestion, inferred the dishonesty, forced the whole subject, against the objections of the Council, upon a general meeting, and has obtained what will be considered as a verdict against the person thus accused by implication.

Whatever may be Colonel Ritchie's case, it has been settled by the lawyers as a debt, and Colonel Ritchie has preferred no statement, and has neither given nor deposed any evidence either way. As one upon his trial, Mr Russell was entitled to the full benefit of every doubt, and all the evidence is consistent with his honest behaviour, unless the fact of insolvency of itself constitutes dishonesty, which few, we think, will admit. That it would have been altogether better had he in no case applied any of the drafts to any other use than paying for the guns for which he stood liable, none can doubt for a moment. But that in doing so he did anything which should exclude him from association with gentlemen is very doubtful; for we know that all merchants (and Mr Russell acted in that capacity) treat all payments to them as part of their assets, and trust, for meeting their engagements, not to specific sums in hand or payable to their order, but to their general solvency. Mr Russell no doubt trusted to his general solvency until he found his regular sources of income drying up, and that his misfortune or error of judgment had grown into a scandal and flown all over the town, with the effect of curtailing, if not destroying, what had so long been a lucrative professional practice.

While we know that the general body of members could not act otherwise than they have done—refer a direct attack upon the honour of a vice-president to the council, and, when they had reported, adopt their report—we are convinced that there are but few members who do not concur in thinking that the matter ought never to have come before the Institution, and that although it would be difficult to frame a rule against such an abuse, the past president [Bidder], who acted as prosecutor, has so far acted improperly. That we have heard the last of this painful case is doubtful, and all friends of the Institution may have further and lasting cause to regret that it was ever raised within its councils.

In the next number of *Engineering*, Colburn continued in a more emphatic vein—

Never was a case heard and adjudicated upon more insufficient evidence. . . . For it was held, in the face of all the evidence, that Mr Russell acted as an agent, and in a position of special trust, whereas any barrister would have made it perfectly clear that he acted as a principal only, and that the default in payment arose, not from any breach of trust, but from insolvency alone . . . in Scotland a verdict of 'not proven' carries acquittal; but here the conclusion of 'unsatisfactory'—which may mean an inability of comprehension on the part of the court—is reckoned, practically, as equivalent to condemnation.

We doubt if there be twenty engineers who do not now believe that Mr Scott Russell has been *tried* and *condemned*, and that, too, upon a case wherein any other court in the world would of necessity have acquitted him.

If we are to submit to the arbitration of Mr Bidder's new 'court of honour' (or was it Mr Harrison's term), let us have counsel, and a judge, and a judge's charge, and a jury who shall *hear* every scrap of evidence; and let us have a verdict of 'guilty' or 'not guilty', but not an empty sham of 'unsatisfactory', which may mean anything or nothing, but which will be taken by the thoughtless as equivalent to 'guilty'.

It is irrelevant to ask here which is the purer man, Mr Bidder or Mr Scott Russell? If we were to go by the rumours of Great George Street, it would not, however, take long to decide. We protest, only, against the obtrusion of private scandals upon the Institution of Civil Engineers. We insist that the Institution is neither a court of honour, of law, of bankruptcy, nor of divorce. In this case, if any one is to be removed from the Institution, it should be, not the accused, but the accuser. The accused has not, so far as has been proved, done anything of which the Institution should take cognisance, whereas the accuser [Bidder] has taken advantage of his position to propagate a deplorable feud, in which he is notoriously suspected of having had a personal interest in the defeat of the individual whom he has accused.

... Sir William Armstrong has no case whatever except in the courts. All that he can say is that he did not obtain full payment for guns which were not completed at the appointed time, and which, in point of fact, were never delivered, and which, notwithstanding large payments upon account, he is understood to yet hold in his possession. For these guns still in his possession, so far as known, Mr Scott Russell had paid nearly £10,000 upon account.

Until, then, Colonel Ritchie is brought forward, and proves a distinct breach of trust, there is no case whatever against Mr Scott Russell, except in insolvency. Any barrister would make this clear, in five minutes, to any jury in the land. And the empty verdict of 'unsatisfactory,' in a case heard upon incomplete evidence, before a self-constituted tribunal, and in the absence of counsel and of the ruling of a judge, may be left to take its fit place as a reproach upon the whole body of the Institution of Civil Engineers, who have, in this case, arrogated to themselves functions of which they are wholly incapable, and which they should never again attempt to exercise.

The editor of *The Engineer* passed no further comment until June 7, when with a swipe at Colburn he wrote a long editorial in support of the right of the Institution to conduct such an inquiry.[58] He said it was a right retained and exercised by all institutions to assure itself that a member is what he pretends to be. Any moral delinquency, he went on, affecting the professional reputation of a member constituted a legitimate subject of inquiry. An attempt had been made to prove that as no crime had been committed, Russell's conduct had been 'perfectly orthodox'. 'It is simply indisputable,' he asserted,

> that Mr Russell received from Mr Adams a sum of money handed to him in the faith, founded on Mr Russell's assertions, that it was to be devoted to a specific purpose, and that this money was not devoted to that purpose, our readers will easily be able to apply a fitting name to the action without our aid.

The battle was now joined by some correspondents, and Colburn reviewed the whole case again in greater detail.[59] At the same time the editor of *The Engineer* endeavoured to arrive at an 'absolute decision', a matter in which he, at least, found no difficulty. He was disgusted that Russell had refused to resign. It was the obvious course for a gentleman. Then he made the curious comment, if Russell had 'no imputation to make as to the character of the decision, he should have at once withdrawn'. But, Russell we recall, surely made such an imputation. However, the editor claimed that 'only some half-dozen' of the members present at the fateful special general meeting—or, as he expressed it, of the total membership of the Institution—voted against the adoption of the report. Yet still Russell would not resign from the Council which had 'condemned' him. 'Who can read the concluding paragraph of Mr Scott Russell's reply,' the editor asked, 'and not feel that it admits the whole allegation made against him? "I owed a balance," he says, "which I never denied, but wished to repay. He accepted the securities I offered, and closed the matter (!). For the subsequent value of those securities I am not responsible." (!!)'

With such admissions, *The Engineer* thought that it mattered not whether Russell were an agent or a principal. Alluding to Colburn's argument, it went on to say that

> the public are told that 'until a distinct breach of trust is proved, there is no case whatever against Mr Scott Russell, except in insolvency!' What! Is this the code of morality in which English Civil Engineers are to be instructed by so-called professors of engineering? ... It was not in such a spirit that our contemporary, *The Lancet*, dealt, the other day, with a most painful case which occurred in the medical profession. In that case a charge had been made against an eminent practitioner, not of pecuniary fraud, not of the misapplication of money to his personal purposes, but simply of unprofessional treatment of a patient.

John Scott Russell

One correspondent made the following interesting comments:

What is the charge against Mr Russell? That he did not pay for certain guns which he had bought—not because he fraudulently evaded payment, but because his pecuniary circumstances had in the mean time so changed as to deprive him of the power! Henceforth let it go forward to the public that the Institution of Civil Engineers is an irresponsible court of inquisition, which visits with its censures members who are unable to pay their debts. What would the House of Commons say to such a rule if sought to be enforced upon its members? We never heard that the notorious and habitual impecuniosity of Richard Brinsley Sheridan and Charles James Fox, and even of William Pitt—whose debts, amounting to six thousand pounds, Parliament voted the money to pay after his decease—were regarded by any one as disqualified thereby even for the highest offices in the State. And is this gnat to be now strained at by a Society of Engineers—composed chiefly of railway men, who are at least popularly supposed to be quite capable of swallowing the camel? Pitt's poverty was, after his death, made the subject of the highest panegyric by his rival, Fox. And with reason. For it would have been easy for a man who had the whole resources of the State in his hand to have died disgracefully rich. Whatever may be said of some of Mr Russell's assailants, the stigma of wealth does not attach to him; and let those who blame him for his poverty remember that such a condition has its precious compensations. No one can accuse him of having enriched himself by bribes—of having, while the recognised protector of a company's interests, leagued himself with contractors to fleece his employers for his own benefit—of having used official information to enable him to dabble successfully in shares—or of having acted a part in the various other forms of railway obliquity of which the world now hears so much. Let every member of the Institution of Civil Engineers say as much, and let the public believe the declaration if they can.[60]

The forcible expulsion of Russell advocated by *The Engineer* was pursued by a nondescript group of members. Their proposal was placed before Council, in accordance with the by-laws, at a special meeting on June 18, 1867. Sufficient doubt was expressed as to the applicability of the by-law to the Russell case. Legal advice was sought and Thomas Hawksley, great-hearted as ever, incurred considerable personal expense in the preparation of a contrary case for submission to Council. He was unable to attend the next special meeting on July 15, 1867, however, and asked the councillors to postpone discussion of the matter as he had been assured on authority that the by-law was legally inoperative for the purpose of expelling a member for alleged misconduct in relation to matters not connected with the affairs and concerns of the Institution.[61] Less than half the Council were present, but they rejected Hawksley's request by four votes to three,[62] and the expulsion proposal was submitted to counsel, thence disappeared. Russell's antagonists were appeased, no doubt, when the nomination slate at the Annual General Meeting of December 17, 1867, showed two vice-presidential vacancies—one of them created by Russell's apparent withdrawal—and for which Messrs Harrison and Vignoles were nominated.

The handsome figure of J. Scott Russell was never again seen, nor his elegant utterance heard, in the chambers or councils of the Institution of Civil Engineers.

CHAPTER ELEVEN

A New Start

*Our first great want is a minister of public education, and the fear is
that even when we yield to a great public necessity, and appoint him,
we may merely be finding a place for a man instead of the man for the
place.*

J. SCOTT RUSSELL

Throughout the period embraced by the 'Court of Honour' in the Institution of Civil Engineers, Russell made visits to the Paris exhibition in his
capacity as a juror. Along with the other British jurors he received an
invitation from the Schools Inquiry Commission which had recently been
established, under Lord Taunton, to assess the condition of English educational resources. This action had been provoked by an open letter from
Lyon Playfair to Taunton in *The Times* in which he warned that the continental nations were gaining great advantages over Great Britain in consequence of their superior systems of education. Playfair was primarily
interested in education in science while Russell and his two fellow
engineering jurors, Fowler and McConnell, saw the greatest need to be
the education of the skilled craftsmen and shop foremen and manager
categories. They did not agree with Playfair that 'little inventiveness' and
'little progress' in the practical arts had lately been made in England but
they agreed that continental manufacturing progress was proceeding at
a greater rate. As Russell expressed it: 'it was not that we were equalled,
but that we were beaten, not on some points, but by some nation or
another at nearly all those points on which we prided ourselves'.[1] Fowler
made education the theme of his presidential address to the I.C.E. in
May, a meeting which found Russell in Paris with his daughter Rachel
and son Norman. McConnell thought, as did Russell, that technical
education was a matter for Government intervention and that 'there
ought to be mining schools in South Wales, Staffordshire and Durham,
and machinery and engine schools in Manchester, Glasgow, etc.'[2]

Russell's response to the Commission ran as follows:

I have come to the conclusion that the higher class of education given in
each of those countries to the workmen in its skilled trades, as well as the

248

superior professional education given to the higher classes of men employed in technical professions, is everywhere visible in the works exhibited by those countries ...

The fourth great International Exhibition has afforded an excellent opportunity for marking the relative progress of different countries in the arts, manufactures, and trades which contribute to the wealth and power of nations. We have especially noted the progress of other nations in those mechanical and constructive arts and trades in which, in 1851, England exhibited pre-eminent excellence. We have to record that in many of these some other nations appear to have made much more rapid progress than ourselves, so that we are *relatively* falling off. And we especially note that our falling off is not in unimportant departments, but in some of those which had formerly constituted our staple excellence.

We have to specify that those branches in which other countries have now shown more rapid advancement are some of our own great manufactures of steel and iron, steam machinery, locomotive engines, and tools and manufacturing machinery in general. We do not say that in all of these other nations have excelled us; in some they have not yet equalled us. But what we do feel, and therefore frankly state is, that their progress has, in the last sixteen years since the first Exhibition of 1851, been remarkably greater than ours.

There are other branches of arts and manufactures in which possibly the reverse is the case. Glass and pottery, and the arts of design and construction of beautiful patterns, both in form and colour, have made remarkable progress throughout England during the same period; we therefore confine our present remarks to the mechanical and constructive arts, not commonly called fine arts.

Dissatisfied with our national progress, we have naturally turned our minds to search for the cause of the progress of other nations and for the cure of our own deficiency. We find that during these years some nations have been occupied in diligently promoting the national education of the various classes of skilled mechanical workmen, for the purpose of giving skill to the unskilled and rendering the skilled more skilful. We find that some nations have gone so far as to have established in every considerable town technical schools for the purpose of teaching all the youths intended to be craftsmen those branches of science which relate most nearly to the principles of their future craft. ...

Besides these local schools, other countries have technical colleges of a very high class for the education of masters and foremen in engineering, mechanics, merchandise, and other practical and technical professions.

We have not failed to notice that it is precisely those nations which have been systematically giving a course of preparatory training and education to their population in their skilled trades that have shown the most marked progress in national industry in these successive Exhibitions.

Prussia, Switzerland, Belgium, France, America seem to make progress in proportion to their excellence of educational training—Prussia in steel, iron, and general engineering work; Switzerland in scientific engineering, machinery, and watch and telegraph work, and in textile manufactures; Belgium in metal working and mechanical trades; France in metal work, and in steam engines, engineering structures, naval architecture, and steam navigation. All these nations seem to exhibit growing skill and progress in proportion to the excellence of the education and training they give to their manufacturing population.

It becomes, therefore, a serious national question for England and the English, whether they have or have not been wise in neglecting to take adequate measures of a national character for the complete technical training of all the youth destined to skilled trades and occupations. By this training we do not on the one hand mean elementary education, nor on the other hand do we mean any substitute for a practical working apprenticeship. We mean a schooling midway between the elementary day-school and the workshop, which the youth should enter after he knows reading, writing, and counting, in order to learn to apply his reading, writing, and calculation to the purpose of acquiring such knowledge of mathematics, mechanics, mineralogy, chemistry, drawing, &c., as shall fit him more aptly and perfectly afterwards to learn and to profit by the teaching of the workshop and the office. It is unquestionable that apprentices to trades, coming into the workshops with this preparation, will make greatly more rapid and certain progress than those who enter direct from the elementary school.

But in England we can scarcely as yet be said to possess such schools. Certainly they are not uniformly distributed over the towns of England; and it seems that in no country have they thriven or even existed except when organised and sustained by nations at large, acting through their Governments.

We have therefore to recommend to the serious attention of the British nation the consideration of the importance of establishing a national system of technical and trade education.[3]

The writing of this coincided with the harsh blow dealt Russell by the Institution of Civil Engineers and the auctioning of some of his household effects to meet the clamant demands of his creditors. He was also arranging to sell his house and move to the Continent with his family.[4] In June his daughter Rachel, wrote to Arthur Sullivan the composer, to whom she was secretly affianced, that things were 'to be settled somehow now' and that they would remain in their present house, 'for some time at least'. Her father and Mr Tennant were walking round the garden, she wrote, 'hatching plots to destroy our destroyers'.[5] Mr Tennant may well have been the son of Sir James Emerson Tennant, author of *The Story of the Guns*: both were lawyers. This tragic business cast an uncharacteristic gloom over the whole Russell household.[6]

While Russell's financial and personal calamities were no novelty among the ranks of contractors, they were in bizarre contrast to his abilities, not to say genius, as a naval architect, engineering scientist and educator. His contribution as an educator within his profession, in the broadest sense, was immense, as also was his contribution to his country through her naval and marine engineering. One would like to know more about his involvements and setbacks in the period 1864–7, the sources of revenue which 'dried up' and the property he had 'earned' which became 'first locked up, and then depreciated ... in matters over which [he] had no control'.

The brevity of the life of the Bute Iron Works on the Taff is all the more remarkable in view of the apparent boldness of the enterprise. It was ostensibly the bid of Norman Scott Russell to set himself up as an iron shipbuilder, but more likely his father's bid to set him up. The yard seems to have been abandoned after the *Mallorca* was launched, then sold to one of the Maudslay family in 1869, from which date Norman's name ceases to appear among the members of the South Wales Engineering Society. One suspects that this was the rock on which his father's resources again foundered and where the money which could have cleared Ritchie or Armstrong was locked up. He was, or had been, also the owner of—or had a share in—some ships. One of these ships was probably the *Baron Osy* which plied between London and Antwerp; another was a collier plying between Cardiff and Rouen which was lost without trace in the height of summer on account of overloading. But Russell does not tell us more.[7]

The newspapers that summer were full of reports of the *Great Eastern's* laying of the transatlantic telegraph cable, for which duty it had been purchased for a song by Daniel Gooch (Brunel's former assistant) and two other directors of the previous company. They acted under the influence of Cyrus Field, the promoter of the telegraph,[8] and Gooch received a knighthood for this act of enlightened self-interest.

Meantime Russell had the good fortune to be approached by directors of the Swiss North-East Railway to design a ferry to carry laden freight and passenger trains between Romanshorn and Friedrichshafen on Lake

Constance. He left for Zurich towards the end of August escorting his wife and daughters, Rachel and Alice, as far as the Allée Saal Hotel at the health resort of Sangen Schwalback. There they tried to recover from the stresses of the past year in health-giving baths of rusty mineral water, and in exercise and conversation, while 'Papa' went about his business. After three weeks, during which she continued to lose weight, Rachel, with much relief went on to join her father in Zurich, to 'do work for him' and keep his clothes in repair,[9] while the others returned home.

Russell, of course, had already designed a ferry for the English Channel, but the Swiss ferry presented the additional problem of extremely shallow draft—six feet being the maximum allowable— a not unfamiliar complication in Russell's experience. He obtained the requisite strength by constructing the central portion of the hull in the form of a box girder with longitudinal framing and supported the engine and waggons of the train on a central iron deck connected to the hull through two vertical side walls which also supported an upper promenade and conning deck. Each end of the hull was designed as a bow with rudder attached to simplify docking and each paddle could be driven separately. Russell later explained to the Institution of Naval Architects, in the way that was peculiarly his own, how this enabled his ferry to be berthed without steerage way:

> My captain refused to command my ship. Every captain said the ship was impossible. I am ashamed to have to confess that I had to navigate the ship myself the first time; and having done so, it was *Kinderspiel*! Now the secret of all that is in one word, the power of steering without the rudder. If you cannot steer without a rudder; you must go a pace, you must go a steerage pace, you must go so as to have steerage way in all circumstances; and you must rush into your harbour, in order to get in somehow or other. I have done that a thousand times with most excellent captains. I have seen this, that in order to keep steerage way, we have been obliged to go into narrow harbours at a pace which sometimes has shipwrecked the ship on the pier, which always incurs very great danger, and which always requires the highest courage a captain can possess. Therefore, I entirely agree with the captains, that they could not handle an ordinary ship in these harbours in extraordinary circumstances. But this was our point; by the engine alone we can steer the ship without any way whatever. And what is the rule I have made for these ships? I will tell you. The rule for these ships now is this, that they never go into harbour at a pace which will give steerage way; that they stop and reverse just before they come to the entrance, and stop and reverse so that they are at a dead halt when they get the paddle-wheels between the two

piers. I need not explain to you that at a dead halt there can be no collision. In this dead halt the captain calls down, 'Left, forward three!' He gives no order to the right, and 'Left forward three!' turns the ship round along the quay. That is how it is done. Now, all these things are impossibilities to the captain who has not seen them. But once a captain has seen them, it is that German word '*Kinderspiel!*'

The ferry was built by Escher, Wyss & Co. and launched in 1868. It went into operation in February 1869 and ended its days in 1882. This was Russell's last ship, although it served as a model for another ferry built by Escher, Wyss & Co. for the Lindau–Romanshorn route.

On his return to England in January 1868, Russell was invited to join a committee formed by the Society of Arts to advocate and plan a radical reorganization of the educational machinery (it would be wrong to say system) of the country in the direction of greater social equality and more scientific education supported by local government rates.[10] This committee arose from a conference held under the auspices of the Society on January 23, to which were invited all concerned with education for industrial development—mayors, professional societies, employers, university teachers. Among those present were Lords Granville and Russell, C. W. Dilke, Cole, Playfair, Huxley and Rankine. They did not favour polytechnics after the German pattern, but rather, new liberal colleges with new preparatory schools. Student proficiency they believed should be tested by examination and endorsed by the award of appropriate certificates which must be recognized by employers. Science, they asserted, should figure prominently in the curricula of the middle and upper class schools, and the abysmal lack of primary education among the artisan class had first to be rectified before progress could be made.

The subject of education was close to Russell's heart as we have seen. His concern for the education of 'English mechanics' is on record from the closing of the Great Exhibition in November 1851,[11] at which time he urged the Institution of Civil Engineers in vain to take the necessary initiative. In March 1868, Russell joined Playfair on the platform at a conference on education in Edinburgh, organized by the Royal Scottish Society of Arts following the lead of its sister body in London. Russell opened the conference by proposing the resolution that it was 'desirable and necessary that the principles of science should form an important element in the tuition of all classes of the community'. In speaking to this he reiterated many of the arguments and suggestions he had so eloquently expressed elsewhere. His experience of the state of education in some of the continental nations, he said, led him to conclude that Scotland had lost the proud claim to be regarded as the best educated country in the world—the population had doubled but the number of schoolmasters had not.[12]

Some of his auditors may have read the unsigned articles on primary education in Germany and Switzerland which appeared in the *Pall Mall Gazette* earlier in the winter, beginning with 'A German Village School' (December 1867). These were by Russell. The anonymity was not an oversight, he specifically requested it for reasons which are not obvious to us.[13] Nevertheless, he had no such reservations with his long article, 'Technical Education a National Want', which appeared in the April (1868) number of *Macmillan's Magazine*.[14]

In discussing the educational structure of the United Kingdom, it is necessary to distinguish between Scotland and England. Scotland long enjoyed a universal system of primary education based upon the church parish, had four universities open to scientific studies as well as several colleges of arts and science and one technical university—John Anderson's—which went through various evolutions. This was the environment and resource from which sprang Scott Russell, no less than Lyon Playfair, James Nasmyth, James Watt, William Rankine, and the Napiers, to mention only those whose names frequently appear here. No such universal educational suffrage was enjoyed by the people of England, although science and engineering were being cultivated notably by the new London University colleges and Owens College, Manchester. This state of affairs was not adequately corrected until about the last decade of the nineteenth century, but already in 1868, education for the industrial society had become a *cause célèbre*. On June 17, after the triennial Handel Festival at the Crystal Palace, conducted as usual by Michael Da Costa, Cole dined with Mrs Russell. In the course of their conversation she told him that he would do everything himself and not let others help him, 'evidently', Cole remarks in his diary, 'alluding to Russell and technical education'.

Russell threw himself into his new cause with all his wonted enthusiasm and presented his proposals and arguments in detail in a book entitled *Systematic Technical Education for the English People* which was published by Day & Co. early in the next year, 1869. It was ironical that Cole, originally an opponent of state intervention in education, should now be head of the department administering the schools of design and the School of Naval Architecture. He listened to Russell and acted on some of his ideas such as the use of the recently vacated Greenwich Hospital for a technical university, the School of Naval Architecture being transferred there in the next year, but he would not join forces with him. In March 1869 he notes in his diary that he was reading Russell's book,[15] but does not comment upon it. Shortly after, on April 19, there is the following entry in his diary:

'Scott Russell came to ask me to agitate for technical education with him. I declined as incompatible with my office. He observed, "You will not sacrifice the good you are doing to the uncertain." I said "I thought you would say so." '

The point of this is obscure; but what is obvious is that Russell did not seem to learn that he could expect nothing from Cole, and that he was little other than a source of ideas and a rival in Cole's view.

The idea of state intervention in anything, not least in education, was anathema to nineteenth-century England. It is not surprising, therefore, that despite the rising cacophony of learned voices demanding a national system of education, it took a tragically long time for Government to accept the full responsibility. Russell advocated, as a first step, the founding of a 'Ministry of Public Education', with, at its head, a man who, 'himself possessing high education, has patriotically devoted time, thought, and deliberation to the subject'. He deplored that it was 'part of our political system that fitness for the special duties of the place is reckoned a minor qualification'.

'The first duty of this minister,' continued Russell, 'would be to select as members of his council, not political agents, not official place-men, not men having nothing better to do; but to choose from every branch of technical science and technical profession, the men most distinguished for the combination of high scientific knowledge with extensive practical skill and experience.' The first of 'our national technical establishments,' he declared, should be teacher-training colleges to supply trained teachers for the system of colleges he proposed.

This system comprised a central technical university, situated in metropolitan London; less advanced technical colleges 'placed in every centre of local industry', and a lower class of college or trade school

for every 20,000 inhabitants in town districts, and for every 10,000 in country districts; and either in the same building or in a different one there should be technical schools in the evening, as complete in their course of instruction for the working men, as in the morning for the youth of the district; and to these schools should be attached a library, museum, and reading-room, similar to that of the colleges, only more elementary, and on a smaller scale.[16]

Russell estimated that there would be fifteen tech nical colleges, and a thousand trade schools, the whole costing the exchequer one million pounds per annum, for Russell believed that the direction and support of these colleges should be the responsibility of the central government—'the eccentricities of local government would be intolerable and wasteful'. But local government representation on the governing bodies would be desirable, he thought, to ensure the special educational needs of given localities would be adequately catered to.

On the subject of state responsibility, Russell's bold remarks must have raised many an eyebrow although about seventy years later they would have sounded platitudinous:

> How well the system of national organisation has succeeded, even in England, may be seen in our post-office system. How ill the want of system has succeeded, which abandons the organisation of services common to the good of the whole community to the disorganisation which leaves private individuals to further their own interests under pretence of supplying the common wants, may be seen in the present chaos which the railway enterprises of England now present to the civilised world—of national interests destroyed, national repuation lowered, and national wealth squandered. Who will be found to deny that a little of the same forethought, the same systematic balancing of national and local interests, the same wise parsimony, which have procured for other countries railway systems adequate to their wants at one-half or one-third of the cost, and with none of the shame or humiliation which attends the disclosures of our mismanagement, could also have procured for us the supply of a perfect system of railway communication, as well organised and economically administered as our post office;—shall we allow it to be said that we have a national preference for private adventure and individual gain at the expense of the community, to self-denying organisation, and prudent forethought for the public welfare?[17]

Russell suggested model curricula in detail and proposed a system of course units of three years—'each course of three years is perfectly organised by itself, and in each period a course is begun and completed'. A succession of these course units was to extend from primary school to university. Each pupil leaving on reaching his appropriate ceiling. Rigid specialization was to be delayed, for, as Russell well understood, 'eclecticism in education is, perhaps, the wisest of errors; for the final decision of life and of individual bias is not always irrevocable at 16 ... In the first period therefore the literary student cultivates science, and the scientific student literature, but in the relation of predominant to subordinate.'

Among his special curricula he included 'Domestic Economy' for girls. Society was not yet ready for women in science and technology, despite the increasing number of outstanding female pioneers in these professions, of whom Mary Somerville, godmother to the daughter of Russell's good neighbour and friend at Sydenham, Mimi von Glehn, was the most distinguished.

The Society of Arts introduced Domestic Economy to its certificate system and it is interesting that it was in cookery that a national teachers' training school was first introduced. This, at South Kensington in 1873, was intended to supply teachers for local cookery schools and for service in elementary schools.

On August 18, 1875, a letter was published in *The Times* publicizing this development. It drew attention to the fact that 'The Education Department' counted instruction in cookery as attendance at school, and paid 4s. for each girl who passed an examination. This was signed by Henry Cole. Two years later we find him reading a paper on 'Elementary Education through Domestic Economy', to the Congress of Domestic Economy at Birmingham.[18] His conversion from opponent of state support of education for the working classes to open advocate was complete.

Meantime Russell sought another channel of Governmental influence and managed to draw together a committee in 1871 for the purpose. Two M.P.s, E. T. Gourley and J. M. Carter, lent their support and Gourley wrote a private letter to Gladstone, but to no avail.[19] The technical education movement would not be rushed. The system of technical colleges which did develop in England and Scotland over the next fifty years bore a striking resemblance to that so vigorously advanced by Scott Russell. Where others had been content to talk, Russell provided a complete blueprint, specifying the requirements of buildings, curricula and resources. Furthermore, he was one of the earliest to place the emphasis in the proper place for most durable results—compulsory elementary education, the trade school and post-secondary technical college.

A few months after giving Russell the cold shoulder, Cole noted in his diary that he had upbraided Playfair for not agitating for Scientific Education,[20] and that he had met with 'Dr Watts of Manchester, Chadwick, Whitworth and P. Le Neve Foster' to 'discuss agitation in the Provinces for Technical Education'.[21] He also helped Whitworth to realize his desire to establish academic scholarships; but he only listened to Russell. It is yet another of the curious facts about Scott Russell that his contribution to the technical education movement is usually overlooked by its

257

historians, Professor Armytage being a notable exception. Although Russell's fellow naval architects, engineers and colleagues in the education movement listened to him with interest and respect, Britain's rulers were not ready to implement a comprehensive scheme of the kind he proposed. He was just too early.

CHAPTER TWELVE

The Sydenham Set

Those evenings were amongst the happiest of my life.
SIR ARTHUR SULLIVAN

Carried along, as we have been, with the momentum of Russell's professional and public activities in the two decades following the Great Exhibition, we have had opportunity to catch but a glimpse of the social and domestic life which formed such an important background to his endeavours. It is possible, without loss, to write about his great engineering contemporaries with scarcely an allusion to how they lived at home. Brunel's courtship and marriage acquires interest from its application of his promotional bent to a project of romantic love, and it casts a warm light on his character to see him as a music lover and jovial toper; but his wife and family were incidental to his life and existed largely without him. Fowler liked the company of artists, but it was he, not his family, who drew them into his circle, and, of course, although Telford was the patron of poets and artists, he had no family and preferred the company of young men. This was not the case with Russell. Russell's wife and family had a dynamism of their own which adorned and refreshed his love of social discourse at his table and his convivial garden strolls with favourite guests.

He was physically energetic if not athletic as a younger man, enjoyed sea voyages without sickness, rowed with pleasure on lakes and rivers, loved travel, and, in his fifties, with that rotundity so esteemed in his time for the way it supported watch and chain, sat stuffily of a summer's day in a garden chair with top hat to protect his fast receding hair line, scribbling and thumbing through sheaves of paper to the accompaniment of the lively laughter and chatter of his daughters and their friends, the sound of the mallets on the croquet lawn and a singing voice or piano from an open window.

Little could he have thought when he reluctantly vacated the secretarial apartments of the Royal Society of Arts at the Adelphi in 1851, that his genial and merry successor, George Grove, would play a more beneficent role in his domestic life than anyone who had yet, or would ever again, come within its compass.

The gigantic glass conservatory which had housed the Great Exhibition had to be moved from Hyde Park where all was to be left in its original state. The destruction of this novel and historic structure was a sad prospect after the glories it had seen and there were many suggestions for its re-erection elsewhere as a permanent exhibition and museum building. When it became clear that the Government had no desire to involve itself in such an enterprise, a group of six enthusiasts formed a company to purchase the structure and re-erect it, with some modifications, in the sylvan environs of Sydenham Hill. This, the Crystal Palace Company, included Samuel Laing (Chairman), Francis Fuller (Managing Director), John Scott Russell, Samuel Geach, and Sir Joseph Paxton. They procured the building for £70,000, and on Russell's suggestion offered Grove the post of secretary at a guaranteed salary of £600 per annum for ten years, with liberty to accept any private engineering practice that he could conduct without prejudice to the interests of the company. Grove was, at the time, under contract to inspect permanent-way materials for the Great Northern and East Indian Railway Companies. He was also revealing his exceptional scholarly versatility in translating Guizot's *Études sur les Beaux Arts*. This translation was published early in the next year, 1853, the precursor of that impressive series of literary and musical endeavours which displaced engineering in his life. Grove is best known as the editor of the great *Dictionary of Music and Musicians*, the earliest annotator of the Beethoven symphonies, the author of erudite concert programme notes quoted to this day, and the first Director of the Royal College of Music. This is by no means the sum total of his contributions to music and musicians—or to literature, for he was editor of *Macmillan's Magazine* for some years in the 1870s.[1] He saw the possibilities latent in the appointment to the Crystal Palace project and readily accepted it.

If Russell was slow in leaving the Adelphi house after occupying it for five years, he was not much slower than Grove who had occupied it for scarcely two. Significantly enough, Henry Cole was not drawn into the Crystal Palace enterprise, although he confided to his diary that Paxton had said to him that he, Cole, was the proper person to be manager.[2] This office, of course, was performed by Francis Fuller who had developed a hearty distrust of Cole and who was now one of Russell's best friends. Cole, on his part, was appointed Secretary for Art in charge of the schools of design and the South Kensington Museum (later called the Victoria and Albert Museum) built from the profits of the Great Exhibition. He later offered Grove the keepership of the museum, but Grove declined.[3]

One of Grove's first duties as secretary of the Crystal Palace was to engage Tennyson to write an ode for the ceremonial opening which took place on Saturday June 10, 1854. He intended to invite Berlioz to set this ode to music—which reveals his impeccable judgement in these matters—but Tennyson could not write the ode and a rendering of God Save the Queen by Miss Clara Novello, supported by a choir of 1500 voices and a band of 1600 instrumentalists, had to suffice. A battery of guns in the park at the same time fired a royal salute. It was very impressive, and even the policemen spontaneously disregarded their regulations and stood bare-headed and enthralled.

When the Queen had completed a formal progress round the building, she returned to the main transept, whereupon the Hundreth Psalm was offered to the vaulted expanse, followed by the inevitable Hallelujah Chorus, conducted by Michael da Costa. It was not until the following year that the celebrated series of weekly orchestral concerts began to take shape through what Grove called 'the enlightened liberality of the Directors',[4] a development in which Russell played a conspicuous part. A full orchestra was formed under the baton of August Manns, a German bandmaster, who, like Da Costa, became a noted figure in British music-making, and the concert room was enclosed and roofed in. Musical history was made at these concerts, enhanced by the finest orchestral playing then to be heard in England. It was there that the London musical public was introduced to the orchestral works of Schubert and Schumann and to many standard favourites of the concert repertoire of recent times, all through the enlightened exertions of an engineer!

From about 1852 the Russells lived in a large villa called 'Westwood Lodge', surrounded by ample grounds, embowered in shrubs and trees merging into the as yet unspoiled undulating countryside around Sydenham. The family comprised three girls, Louise, Rachel and Alice, and one boy, Norman, who was being educated to follow in his father's footsteps.[5] At Peak Hill Lodge nearby lived their good friends the Von Glehns, a talented artistic family. Robert William Von Glehn, tall and distinguished-looking, was a native of Revel, the capital of Esthonia. He adopted British citizenship and conducted an export-import business with Russia from his premises in London, using his lodge at Peak Hill as a holiday home before he made it the permanent residence of his large family. He was an accomplished linguist and a master of the ballroom. His wife, Agnes Duncan, a Scotswoman, was much esteemed as a clever conversationalist,[6] and their daughter, Mimi, was a gifted pianist, whom that severest of critics, Hans von Bulow, regarded as the finest amateur exponent of Beethoven and Chopin he had heard and whom he arranged to study with him in Berlin without fee. George Grove, with whom she was a special favourite, in due course appointed her instructor of piano at the Crystal Palace.

Mrs Russell, a very cultivated Irish lady, as Cole remarked, was in her element in this society, interested in the arts and the social issues of the day, while John Scott Russell himself, though not, one suspects, as passionately devoted to music as his family, was nevertheless a man of eclectic tastes and exciting originality of thought and utterance. Here was a rich blend of superior human qualities through which George Grove wove a unifying thread. The national elements were an exciting mixture of Baltic, Scottish, Irish and English.

This harmonious interaction was at its height in the 1860s when the older Glehn and Russell children were growing up and contributing in increasing measure their own quota of vitality and talent. The Russell girls, Grove recorded, 'all inherited the talent and good looks of their parents; and compelled admiration by the irresistible union of beauty and intellect',[7] characteristics which doubtless caught the eye of James Sant, who was commissioned to make a painting of them. Sant, who became painter-in-ordinary to the Queen, was then only coming into prominence as a society painter.

The Russell's music room resounded perpetually to the piano which dominated it, often, likewise, the dining-room; books were read in French and German as well as English, and their writers quoted and discussed. All of the Russell children spent some time at school in France, Germany or Italy. It was not unusual that they should be largely oblivious to the financial difficulties which plagued their father during their adolescent years; Victorian parents excluded their children from such concerns. It tells us something, however, the the Russell girls had such a happy childhood, their attachment to each other finding expression in pet names— Alice, the youngest, was 'Dicky'; Rachel, 'Chennie'; and Louise, 'Lady'. Louise wrote that to have loving ways required training, she thought that the Coles could only be shocked at her and her sisters and wondered if they knew or could dream of what it was 'to be really fond of people', they were so 'immersed in propriety' that they would 'rather die than be the least demonstrative'.[8]

It is not surprising that the personality and tastes of these clever and romantic girls should appeal to the artistry, wit, and high spirits of Arthur Sullivan, Frederic Clay and Frank Burnand, especially, among the younger musicians, artists, and authors George Grove drew in his train after the Saturday evening concerts. John Everett Millais was often also one of the party. Sullivan in later years recalled their 'playing about the house and garden at Westwood like children',[9] and told Millais' brother and biographer that 'The girls of the family were brilliantly gifted and highly educated and we would discuss music, painting, poetry, literature, and even science until the clock told us that the last train back to London was nearly due ... Those evenings were amongst the happiest of my life.'[10] Grove, too, added an element of fun, invariably entering the room with a characteristic skip and beaming geniality all round. He had too great a sense of humour to be dignified and his friends loved him for it. He did his own share of entertaining and the Rev. A. T. Davidson wrote that when he became curate of St Bartholomews, Sydenham, in 1869, he participated in some of these occasions, and there met many distinguished people—'Arthur Sullivan, John Hullah, Henry Leslie, Joachim, L. Straus, Stockhausen (a noted tenor), Gounod, Ferdinand Hiller, W. H. Lecky (the historian), F. W. Myers, Holman Hunt, to speak of no others prominent in art, science and literature.'[11] In addition, Grove provided a link with Tennyson and Carlyle and other contemporary literary and musical giants with whom he was on friendly terms.

There seemed no end, too, to the steady stream of distinguished visitors who dined with the Russells—engineers, scientists and lawyers in particular.

The Russell girls had all the qualities and education that was calculated in Victorian times to ensure good—that is, economically advantageous—marriages; but their natural affinity was with musicians and artists and although they had many friends in the upper middle class to which they belonged, they were peculiarly exempt from snobbery. Thus Frederic Clay (b. 1838) and Arthur Sullivan (b. 1842) were drawn to the Russell household from the moment they entered George Grove's circle at the Crystal Palace. Clay had already embarked on a career of composing light music for the popular burlesque operettas of the period when Sullivan made his debut at the Crystal Palace concerts, with his Tempest music, in April 1862. Sullivan was then a slim dark-eyed youth of eighteen with a great head of curly black hair, and had just returned from a year of study at the Leipzig Conservatory whither he had gone on a scholarship. The son of an Irish bandmaster to Sandhurst Military College, he had been educated at a small boarding school and was admitted as a chorister to the Chapel Royal at St James's Palace when he was nine, so it is not surprising that he had no means and lived very much from day to day.

'It was part of [his] nature to ingratiate himself with everyone that crossed his path,' wrote one of his friends from this period, 'He always wanted to make an impression and, what is more, he always succeeded in doing it.'[12] He was received happily into the Russell household, the two older girls, Louise and Rachel, making much of him. By 1865, when he was twenty-one, Rachel and he had entered into their long, tortuous— but beautiful—love affair. Sullivan could never bring himself to destroy her letters—impassioned, poetic, loving, melodramatic and wise as they were by turns. He was no less loved by her retiring, less volatile and older sister Louise who devotedly accepted a subordinate rôle. He kept her letters too.

In comparison, Frederic Clay's courtship with Alice Russell was straightforward. He was a man of independent means whose compositions simply earned him pin money—as Rachel described it—but Sullivan's was a very different case. He had to maintain both his mother and himself from his earnings. Rachel tried strenuously to inspire Sullivan to a more purposeful fulfilment of his great promise, not only for himself, but also to make their marriage more feasible. It was not simply that she would have to overcome the objections of her parents, which were entirely based on economic, not social, considerations, but that she, herself, had no taste for penurious and insecure living. She was madly in love with Sullivan, but she did not want to start off their life together with a bank balance— as she expressed it—of £0,000, and debts! She had come through enough of this sort of thing. She pled, she cajoled, she challenged—'if I were a man I would show you how to win your pearl of great price!' She suggested Byron's translation of *Francesca da Rimini* as a libretto offering proper scope and substance, but Sullivan turned instead to Tennyson's *Guinevere*, and Rachel wrote:

> I care dreadfully that it should be a splendid work, and a success. Do it with your whole soul and your strength—work at it intensely and religiously, as the old masters worked—like dear old Bach—and it *must* be a great work, for you have the power in you. It is such a gorgeous book that it almost

makes me feel as if I could write the music myself. Ahem! The only thing I fear for are Guinevere's and Launcelot's love songs. They must not be too pure or they won't be in keeping with their characters.

Sullivan's temperament, however, was unsuited to the heroic mould Rachel—and others—would have him fill, and his serious aspirations were easily diverted by a suggestion of another of their circle, the witty librettist and contributor to *Punch*, Frank C. Burnand, that they convert Maddison Morton's farce *Box and Cox* into a short comic opera for private performance. Rachel felt close to this work, for she witnessed its creation at first hand and was consulted by Sullivan on the pros and cons of certain parts of the music, even helping him with the scoring which, as usual with Sullivan, was done in last minute haste.

The piquant fact was, of course, that if a composer were to make a fortune, he needed exactly Sullivan's particular limitations as well as genius. Millais rightly told Rachel that Sullivan would 'make a packet', but she saw no sign of it and was fearful of his taste for high living and idleness.

The summer of 1867 was a most unpropitious time to suggest to the Russells a poor marriage for one of their daughters in whom so much had been invested. So, it should be no surprise that when Mrs Russell got wind of the seriousness of Rachel's attachment she could scarcely contain herself and prohibited the house to Sullivan as long as he refused to abandon his intention. Thus began a long period of subterfuge and artifice for Rachel and Sullivan, aided by friends, to keep furtive trysts, sometimes at the garden shed, or by the 'field with the haystack' or in Grove's office or while in town on other business.

While Rachel recuperated with her father—and he must also have been glad of the break—at Zurich in the closing months of 1867, Sullivan joined George Grove in their famous expedition to Vienna to discover the lost *Rosamunde* music and other Schubert treasures. On their return Sullivan became again involved with Frank Burnand's irrepressible comic flair in another operetta, *The Contrabandista*. There is no doubt, too, that he would not have failed to notice the achievements of Offenbach and Johann Strauss in Europe. 'Mine own true love,' Rachel wrote after her return to Sydenham, 'I am so very happy and sweet today. So sweet that it is perhaps as well you cannot see me for you would be so hopelessly in love ... Freddie and I have been through the whole of *The Contrabandista* to-night, checking over all the passages, and more and more charmed with the whole.'

'Freddie', that is Frederic Clay, was soon to meet William Gilbert, a writer who had an even greater dramatic, if not comic, talent than Frank Burnand, for whom he composed the music for *Ages Ago*, one of Gilbert's early burlesque libretti. Not long afterwards Freddie introduced Sullivan to Gilbert and was thus the means of first drawing these great talents together. R. C. Lehmann described Clay as a 'bright and joyous spirit', an opinion which was endorsed by all who had dealings with him, and which corresponds with his facile and melodious music. He dressed accordingly, with 'fetching open-work shirt fronts, coloured silk beneath, one night pink, another night blue'.[13] His best remembered song is 'I'll sing thee songs of Araby', from his opera *Lalla Rookh* produced with great success at the Brighton Festival, February 1877. He practically lived with the Russells from about 1862 to 1868, and early in the latter year preparations were being made for his marriage to Alice, the youngest daughter, when there appears to have been second thoughts and finally, in August, the engagement was broken off. Alice was only twenty, ten years Clay's junior. She may be seen in Millais' picture, 'The Romans leaving Britain' (1865), in which as a British princess she 'looks steadfastly, with a passionate, eager, savage stare upon the melancholy waste of the grey and restless sea', her departing Roman legionary kneeling at her feet with his arms clasped about her body.

Several ardent suitors, including Frank Burnand, were competing for Alice's hand when there arrived at Sydenham a young Swiss gentleman, Franz Arthur Rausch, of Schaffhausen, who had become enamoured of Rachel during her recent sojourn in Zurich, and who soon transferred his attentions to Alice. They were married a little over a year later, with Cole proposing the health of the bride's parents. 'I was glad to see some tears in the Russell girls and Mother,'[14] he added. Alice thereby entered a circle of German noble families and her descendants survive in Germany.

Many famous musicians and singers gave recitals at the Crystal Palace in addition to the orchestral and choral concerts and there were all sorts of exhibitions and entertainments at a shilling a head as well as the ever popular firework displays which attracted trainloads of Londoners in late summer. The Russells enjoyed this bounty right on their doorstep; but there were also visits to the opera, to Royal Academy soirées and to concerts in London itself which the family made in the company of their friends.

In the summer of 1866, another gifted young musician, Charles

Villiers Stanford, then only sixteen years of age, was brought by his parents from Dublin to holiday in Sydenham, where they could partake of the musical fare offered at the Crystal Palace and in the city. Charles' uncle, Charles Stuart Stanford, was Rector of St Thomas' Church, Dublin, of which Mrs Scott Russell's family were members and in which she was married. Charles' mother, Mary Henn, was of an even more distinguished Irish legal family. One of her sisters was the wife of Robert Holmes, another lawyer, also Irish, who settled in London and resided in Sydenham. His family was destined to have various ties with the Russells in the course of time. It was probably through these connections that young Charles Stanford and his parents came to be invited to dine with the Russells and meet Sullivan, Grove and Clay.[15] This was the first of many visits over the years. Unlike Sullivan, Stanford embarked on an academic career as a professor of music at Cambridge and also at the Royal College of Music. It was Louise Russell, interestingly enough, who took 'Charlie' to his first performance of *Cox and Box*, but it was the singer Jenny Wetton he married in 1878 after a year of voluntary separation and silence imposed as a condition of his father's approval. The separation was eased somewhat by Charlie's cousin, Edmund Holmes, Norman Scott Russell's particular friend.[16]

Norman himself, however, was giving his father cause for concern. He had none of Rachel's mettle and clearly was unsuited for the career his father had planned for him. He was as interested in the arts as his sisters but had much more conventional friends. With the abandonment of the shipyard on the Taff, he was at a loose end and plans were made to send him to America where it was felt he would be 'sure to get on' with A. L. Holley to help him; Rachel had written to Holley to 'settle it all' and even considered accompanying him.[17] 'It is so bad' she remarked to Sullivan, 'for any one to live in that *fainéant* life with no object or work and it never was meant in this working world.' Norman's contributions to the Institution of Naval Architects and other writings show that he was well educated and not lacking in ability; but he appears to have had little initiative and been content to have his life run for him by his father. Whether Norman went to America or not is left to conjecture. If he did, it was for no more than two years, for in 1870 we find him in Russia serving as manager for Messrs Baird & Co the English shipbuilding and engineering firm long established in St Petersburg.

Russell rather doted on Rachel, she was clever, vital and strong willed above all his children and a great help to him, she even copied drawings for him. He was sensitive to the anguish and unhappiness of the situation and by the Spring of the year 1868, was at his wits end, as we gather from Rachel who wrote: 'Papa says we must either marry *now* or it must be broken off altogether, for it is quite impossible for us to go on living like this, or indeed for me to live with my mother for a long time to come.' But this was not really a solution, Rachel and Sullivan simply needed time. 'I could not—dare not marry now,' Rachel wrote to Sullivan,

> the very thought of it frightens me—and I want a time of quiet peace after all this dreadful business, to know my own mind truly, clearly. Mind, my heart, I do not doubt that I love you—you and no other—but marriage is either heaven or—the other thing—and if I were hurried into it like this I don't know what might happen ...

Some of Sullivan's earlier compositions were presented or dedicated to Rachel, her sisters, and her mother. His piano cycle *Twilight* was unassailable in Rachel's affections and his setting of a poem by Jean Ingelow 'O Fair Dove! O Fond Dove', also dedicated to Rachel, was being sung in drawing rooms and at concerts throughout England in 1868.

That Autumn, Rachel was again in Zurich and Sullivan in Paris. There was talk of his visiting her. 'I am afraid,' wrote Rachel, 'you could not come to us in Switzerland because it might create pain between Papa and Mama, and put him in a false position with regard to her—and we won't do anything to put more sorrow into his dear life will we Arthur?' Then, a week or so later, 'I do not like to ask Papa to-day, but I will to-morrow morning, and then oh darling how I hope the word will be "come".' Next day, probably while giving her father his customary evening row upon the lake, she asked permission to invite Sullivan to visit them, to which he generously assented and was

> so sweet about it and tender. But he says it must be done with a little *policy* for Mama's sake ... He says also you must not come for a fortnight ... I can scarcely rejoice for it, it seems so curious that anything good should come to us, and of course I wonder at once whether it can be *right*. The old story! You will make yourself very *nice* wont you darling, because Papa is as sensitive to all those things as I am.[18]

Professor Pole of the Chair of Civil Engineering at University College, London, also a Doctor of Music, was in Zurich at the time and gave Rachel daily lessons on the organ which she greatly enjoyed.

Sullivan's continued lack of purpose or devotion, as she conceived it, perplexed her, she was wracked by serious questionings. Sullivan's recent biographers have seen the end of his romance with Rachel signalized by a letter she wrote from Zurich in February 1869, but in the April of that year she is still beseeching Sullivan to help the situation: 'Why will you not write for my sake?' [i.e. write music, preferably music of substance] she asks, 'I do not understand it; do you not see that even if everything so befell that I could say to you tomorrow "take me"— you would have to answer "I cannot you must wait"'.[19]

The oratorio *The Prodigal Son* came and went in October 1869, and Rachel, who had devotedly copied it out for Sullivan, thought the 'divinity' of his 'gift from God' breathed through every note. She prepared to set out for St Petersburg where she was to join Norman and makes the revealing comment to Sullivan: 'We cannot be poorer you and I than we have been and *are*—here in our luxurious home—and ... it has not taken the poetry away.'[20] They had one more last tender meeting before she left early in January 1870—'spread your beautiful wings my eagle and show them where you can soar,' she wrote, 'I have just locked up my drawer full of your letters and all your music and all the relics of our beautiful past. Taking some of your sweetest letters with me, and the camellia you gave me on Christmas day.'[21] She called on the Mendelssohn family in Berlin, with a message from Sullivan. At the end of her six month stay in Russia, this star-crossed betrothal slips from our ken.

The glimpse of Scott Russell through his family corrects an unpleasant impression of fashionable snobbery which Sullivan's biographers have been all too ready to ascribe to him. It also shows that he had troubles at home no less than in his professional life, but also many compensations.

CHAPTER THIRTEEN

War and Peace

All my impressions of what is good and bad, wise and foolish, Christian and unchristian, in the lives and duties of men and nations, are materially different now from what they were before. I saw men making war, and men, women, and children suffering it.

J. SCOTT RUSSELL

Throughout 1868 and '69 Russell was barely maintaining himself through his contracts in Switzerland. Campaigning in the cause of technical education could only have been a drain on his pocket, and his new book would be doing well if its proceeds covered costs. In the same period, however, he was engaged by the French Government to collaborate with Dupuy de Lôme and the Ministry of Marine in the development of a French-sponsored Channel train-ferry. The original Russell–Fowler scheme had perished on account of conflicts between the railway companies and opposition—both French and English—to the requisite changes to the harbours at Calais and Dover. Fowler continued development of the plan without Russell—it is not known whether events at the Institution of Civil Engineers had anything to do with this, but certainly Fowler's new proposal involved the use of hydraulic docking gear provided by Sir William Armstrong. The Russell–French plan, in contrast, dispensed with docking machinery, and it is intriguing that Fowler and Ward Hunt, a former First Lord and Chancellor, had an interview with the French Emperor in 1869, and received encouragement from him, at the very time indeed that the plans for the French proposal were being carefully prepared by Russell and his French colleagues. Something of these plans was revealed by Russell in a paper to the Institution of Naval Architects shortly after his return to England early in the following year (April 6, 1870). Russell had not abandoned the plan to move permanently to the Continent and his family had been fully expecting to sell up and do so on his return from Paris as we gather from a letter received at this time by Arthur Sullivan from Louise: 'Dear Westwood to which we came 18 years ago, Rich prosperous full of life and joy. We leave it poor and in adversity leaving half our lives with much joy and sorrow buried there to begin a new life.'[1]

This move, however, was probably thwarted by the threat of war between France and Prussia. Russell had observed the machinations of the 'war party' in France with disquiet during his several visits to Paris in the period 1867–70. Indeed, he was actually in the company of high naval and military officials there in 1867 when a dispatch was received from the Emperor announcing that war preparations could now be abandoned as a communication from Bismarck was 'entirely satisfactory'.[2] This, however, was only a pause. There was a substantial force of opinion in the French Government favouring war with Prussia and it perplexed Russell to see the various sham pretexts invented to inflame public opinion to this end. One which he was able to help quash was the allegation that German and Italian financing of the St Gotthard Railway was evidence of a conspiracy against the security of France. Russell, who had been involved with the promoters of that railway, and indeed had surveyed and selected a considerable portion of the line, assured all his acquaintances in the French Chamber that the Swiss representative was telling no more than the truth when he said that it had been only with the greatest difficulty that the Italian and German Governments had been persuaded to contribute to a railway entirely running through Swiss territory, although the link offered economic advantages to both.[3] But the aggrandizement of Germany was shifting the balance of power against France and Russell witnessed, in his own words, 'one of those remarkable episodes in history which proves with how little wisdom the affairs of nations are governed'.[4]

The French opened hostilities against Prussia but were soon to regret it when the Prussians broke through into France. Russell, who had returned to Paris, left not long after this, fully convinced that the war had been unnecessary and avoidable. His work on the Channel ferry proposal seemed in ruins, but, even more depressing, he saw the war between the nations representing the highest modern civilization as a disturbing presage of the future. Surely in this he was ahead of the imagination of his time.

> We are bound to look upon it, not as an incident in the lives of these two nations only, but as a part of a great human revolution in which we ourselves form an inevitable and integral portion. It is the story of our own future which is being forecast on the stage of Europe.
>
> ... Are all our ideas of modern civilization and progress mere delusive dreams? Are refinement, invention, wealth, science, all worthless as an end

271

of human beings; and are war and conquest the only worthy direction and aim of manful human exertion? Are all machinery and engineering worthless, save the machinery and engineering of human slaughter? Is the great end and purpose of railways to transport armies, cannon, ammunition, and food for the devastation of continents? Are electric telegraphs applied to their highest destiny under the direction of Almighty Providence, when they serve but to point out to an invading enemy the time and place at which he may at least inconvenience to himself put to slaughter in the shortest possible time the greatest possible number of fellow-Christians? Is it possible that when the laws of motion and space and time and force were communicated to those inspired philosophers, Newton, Laplace, Bacon, Bernoulli, Kepler, and Galileo, and when men were encouraged to believe that this revelation of the ways of God to man in the starry heavens and in the fertile earth and in hidden depths was gradually to ennoble human nature and develop the divine part of man,—is it possible that all this knowledge and all this divine gift and this profusion of human genius had no other aim and end but a mighty Armageddon of Christian nations, and that the moral of human modern civilization is expressed in these words—'Behold with what skill modern Christians slay one another'?[5]

Hearing of the threatened siege and bombardment of Paris, Russell returned to France in November, hoping to rescue the wife and two children of Dupuy de Lôme, who was a prominent member of the Defence Committee of the city. From Le Havre, Russell travelled by train and coach to the headquarters of the Saxon army at Chantilly. Derailment of trains, 'a new element in warfare' disrupted traffic and after a wait of about twenty-four hours he hired a horse cart to convey him to Beaumont. He saw as one of the merits of Prussian organization the perfect equality and fraternity of its citizen army 'reconciled to a discipline, rigid, severe, and absolute beyond the measure of other armies, and a subordination in military ranks perfect, prompt, and unhesitating'.[6] This he attributed to their elaborate system of state education and to the compulsory education which accompanied the three years of forced military service.

Difficulty in obtaining food and shelter was eased by his being recognized as an 'Englishman'—through his speech and his umbrella. He joined a Jesuit missionary in another horse carriage and after many interruptions they arrived next day at Versailles where they separated. Russell was happy to find a vacant room in a small hotel which he could occupy until he could obtain authority to pass through the Prussian lines into Paris. This sanction could only be procured from the Prussian high command installed in several large mansions requisitioned to their use. Next day he set about determining how he could accomplish his objective, and had the good fortune to meet someone whom he described as 'a high ranking Prussian' who recognized him and invited him to call and relate the story of the recent tragic sinking of Cowper Coles' turret warship, the *Captain*. This officer would almost certainly be Prince Adelbert or one of his staff, and with such contacts Russell had good reason to expect his requests to receive a favourable reception, or, at least, consideration. By the third day he was ready to make his overtures through the most promising channels and soon Bismarck himself was studying Russell's careful but curious letter of explanation.

Russell saw himself in the position to play again the rôle of mediator between warring peoples with whose representatives he enjoyed the most friendly relations. He claimed that he had been encouraged in his laudable endeavour by some higher authority (would this be Pakington?) although he certainly did not have official credentials. 'It seemed to me far from improbable' explained Russell, 'that both the Prussians and the Parisians might be really desirous of peace.' He explained he had a friend actively engaged in the Committee of Defence of Paris from whom he expected 'to learn the aims, purposes, and views of the better class of the men still left to defend Paris', and, most important, the terms on which the defence of Paris ought to be continued or abandoned. On his return to Versailles, he went on, he should have been able to discover whether such terms were possible or impossible, and so he hoped that by acquainting himself with the views of both adversaries he might open the way to their resuming negotiations with better chances of success than before.[7]

The result was not what Russell expected. Bismarck had him placed under house arrest as a prisoner of war, asserting that he had broken the laws of war by passing through the Prussian lines without official sanction. The Prussian command clearly believed that Russell had observed too much to be allowed to proceed to Paris and, indeed, that he might in fact be an agent of the British Government—or even of the French!—a very reasonable suspicion.

> I said that I was at Versailles as an old friend of Prussia who had done her service when she wanted it, and that I therefore demanded the rights of friendship: thirdly, that although I was desirous of serving my French friends, I felt confident, and I thought Count Bismarck might also feel confident, that whatever I would do to benefit them would not and should not harm Prussia; that as to my own Government or any one connected with it, I had intentionally avoided giving it any knowledge of or allowing it to

have anything to do with my visit to Versailles, or be in any way responsible for its consequences.[8]

A day or two later, the Prussian commander reported to Russell that Bismarck had instructed him to express his high consideration for Russell as an individual, and his recognition of Russell's personal services to Prussia. He also was to assure Russell of their high consideration for his distinguished friend in Paris, but, in Russell's own words, 'in precise proportion to his [Bismarck's] high appreciation of both, was his reprobation of my communicating with Paris; it was the policy of Prussia to reduce Paris without resort to the extremes of war; they had therefore to starve her three ways—intellectually, morally, and physically. My entrance into Paris would interfere with this object.' Russell was released on the assurance that he would not attempt to reach Paris, and after three further days studying the situation and talking with the British military attachés and newspaper correspondents—including his celebrated namesake of *The Times*—he returned to Antwerp via Sedan through some further adventures and wrote a long account of his expedition for *Macmillan's Magazine*.

His book on his projected system of technical education published the year before was now being read and studied by many interested in this topical subject. One of these was A. J. Mundella who thought very highly of the plan and another was Henry Cole who pretended indifference. Now, after studying the conditions in France before and after the Franco-Prussian war, Russell was convinced that not only had something to be done about the education of the English working class but that something equally revolutionary had to be done towards ameliorating their deplorable social conditions. He explained it thus:

> I was led to make a comparative study of the condition and relations of the different classes in the two countries [England and France] and I thus came to the conviction that the social relations between the different classes of society in England are too intolerable to last long, they must either be speedily and timely cured, or they will suddenly cure themselves.
>
> Six months of [1870] I devoted to the purpose of studying the real evils which depress the condition of the working men. I conversed with the least educated and the most educated, the less skilled and the more skilled, with the object of learning not their imaginary grievances or their political fancies, but the real griefs of their daily life. I was soon able to reduce these by careful classification to the number of 12, and afterwards of seven; and it was thus that the seven points . . . were not the invention of any one, but grew naturally

out of the actual condition of English society. The seven evils which we thus discovered were:

1. The want of family homes, clean, wholesome and decent, out in pure air and sunshine.

2. The want of an organized supply of wholesome, nutritious, cheap food.

3. The want of leisure for the duties and recreations of family life, for instruction, and for social duties.

4. The want of organized local government to secure the well-being of the inhabitants of villages, towns, counties, and cities.

5. The want of systematic, organized teaching to every skilled workman of the scientific principles and most improved practice of his trade.

6. The want of public parks, buildings, and institutions for innocent, instructive, and improving recreation.

7. The want of the adequate organization of the public service for the common good.

It thus took six months to inquire into the disease, and next came the inquiry into the cure. To aid me in this work I sought advice from the ablest and most moderate of those who are considered representative working men. We found but two cures for these great social wrongs—revolution by force and revolution by goodwill. We chose the last, but we did not conceal from ourselves how difficult was the undertaking to secure to the community the benefits of a revolution without paying its terrible penalties.[9]

Russell wanted to avoid identification with any one party and thought more in terms of an alliance of socially enlightened peers and labour leaders crossing party lines. He took an opportunity to explore his ideas with a member of the Upper House who was 'of a distinguished Whig family' and whose associates were therefore primarily Liberals. In response to the request of this confidant, perhaps the third Duke of Sutherland (Russell's old friend the Marquis of Stafford), Russell expanded on his views in a letter (December 3, 1870):

The first great danger I see in England lies in the widespread growing poverty and demoralization of the poor.

The second lies in the growing deterioration of the breed of English men, women, and children, who are being reared in the lanes, alleys, and filth of our wealth-growing towns.

Next, in the higher class of our skilled workmen, I find a fixed antagonism to the wealthy, middle, and mercantile classes, of which they are the tools and the victims.

Lastly, I find the aristocracy of England, which has so long maintained its standard socially and intellectually higher than that of the aristocracy of other countries, I say I regret to find that aristocracy ceasing to occupy itself with the direction, government, and well-being of the people of England, who would be only too glad to be instructed, guided, and led by educated and well-bred men, instead of being ruled by the classes whose interests are directly antagonistic equally to the cultivators of the land and the skilled workmen.

I am satisfied that these feelings, little expressed, are widely and strongly felt. I am sure that the working men are gradually tending to some great social revolution, and I think it has been brought much nearer by the present war of irresponsible Sovereigns.

The practical question I now think is merely whether the great social changes which are necessary and inevitable shall now take place by means of a large and friendly organization of the educated, wise, and refined men who form the English aristocracy with the able, skilled, uneducated, but well-meaning working men who form the bone and sinew of the English nation.

In that case we may expect the revolution to be wise, gentle, rapid, and peaceful. If, on the contrary, it is let alone, it will be an explosion from below.

My personal opinion is that an intimate union of the working men of England with a self-denying, hard-working, patriotic aristocracy could successfully root out of England the terrible germs of political anarchy and social degradation which are now spreading social disease throughout the community ...[10]

This idealistic vision of a brotherhood of patriotic aristocracy and proletariat may appear a trifle naïve to modern eyes but it was not considered so by many people at the time and the subsequent history of Europe justified his diagnosis of the problem. Some notable politicians and trade unions treated it very seriously or, at any rate, saw political advantage in treating it seriously. There is no reason to doubt Russell's own idealism and sincerity in the matter.

The political life of the nation was assuming a new complexion. The British trade unions and associations of working men had become more united and coherent in their pursuit of political influence and social reform. The Tories and the Liberals, thanks to division in the ranks of the latter, were in precarious balance, and an uneasy Tory Government was led by Disraeli on a tortuous course to maintain power. This included the stealing of Liberal thunder by the passing of the Reform Act of 1867 which extended the franchise to a large number of wage-earners in the towns. Despite this, however, they lost to the Liberals in the election of the following year. The Conservatives then felt desperately in need of some scheme with sufficient popular appeal to woo the new working-class vote from the Liberals. Consequently, when Sir John Pakington carried Russell's visionary scheme to Disraeli, the latter and some Conservative peers evinced some interest and Russell was given encouragement.

One of the first trade union representatives Russell consulted on the subject was George Potter, founder of the London Working Man's Association and proprietor of *The Beehive*, a vigorous working-class periodical. He received Russell's ideas with enthusiasm and a meeting with influential trade union representatives was quickly arranged in January 1871. These representatives were informed that certain noblemen and members of Parliament, both Liberal and Conservative, were anxious to co-operate with them in a concerted effort to improve the lot of the skilled artisan.[11] This meeting was followed by others until, on February 4, 1871, under Scott Russell's presidency, the following seven objectives were formulated:

1. The families of our workmen shall be rescued from the dismal lanes, crowded alleys, and unwholesome dwellings of our towns, and placed 'out in the clear', where, in the middle of a garden, each family shall have its own detached homestead, and, where, in wholesome air and sunshine, they may grow up strong, healthy, and pure under the influence of well-ordered homes.

2. There shall be created a perfect organization for the self-government of counties, towns, and villages, with power for the acquisition and disposal of land for the common good.

3. A day's labour shall consist of eight hours of honest work.

4. In addition to schools for elementary education, there shall be established schools for technical education and practical knowledge.

5. Places of public recreation, knowledge, and refinement shall be established and maintained as parts of the public service.

6. Public markets shall be erected and maintained in every town for the sale of goods of the best quality in small quantities at wholesale prices.

7. There shall be provided a great extension and reorganization of the public service on the model of the Post Office.[12]

This apparently was too much for Russell's correspondent in the Upper House and we have Russell's word for it that he only then turned to his old Tory friend Sir John Pakington. Sir John gave the proposal a very ready ear and expressed agreement with the bipartisan approach, but one can understand how Disraeli and his colleagues in the Tory caucus, with whom Sir John discussed the matter, would regard it in a more pragmatic light. The Tories had just lost power to the Liberals, despite a desperate effort to steal Liberal thunder by introducing and passing the Reform Act of 1867, an act which extended the franchise to a large proportion of urban artisans who expressed their gratitude by rejecting their benefactors. Pakington, himself, had only narrowly retained his seat, contested for the first time since its creation in 1832 and now embracing a large body of enfranchised salt workers employed by his Liberal opponent. He would not need much to persuade him of the desirability of wooing the new working-class vote from the Liberals. Russell's scheme offered something to the Tories on this ground as long as it was expressed in generalities. Some of his points no doubt had the serious support of the more reform-minded, but the vision of a brotherhood of patriotic aristocracy and proletariat had something of the ridiculous about it. The associations of working men and the nascent T.U.C., on the other hand, could take the seven points of the manifesto very seriously. There is no reason to doubt Russell's own idealism and sincerity in the matter.

The negotiations were dramatically interrupted by a most welcome invitation from an old acquaintance, Baron Schwarz, of Vienna, to submit a bid for the construction of a grand covered arena for state ceremonies at the Vienna Exhibition planned for 1873. Baron Schwarz had been Chief Commissioner of Austria at the Great Exhibition of 1851, and recalled then discussing domed structures with Russell in connection with the latter's submission of a design of a building for that event. The baron arrived in London in May and entered into negotiations with Russell who proposed an immense dome of 800 feet diameter. But resources and space being inadequate for this, a maximum diameter of 400 feet was settled upon.

Russell had only a fortnight to prepare the drawings and estimates for presentation to the Technical Committee of the Imperial Commission at Vienna in August 1871.[13] There, after long and searching enquiry, the Committee recorded 'that Mr Scott Russell's idea was ingenious, excessively simple, and moreover, well suited to show how iron could be employed in a new and hitherto untried manner'.[14] He returned to London with the authority to proceed, and, with the assistance of George Holmes, son of the family with whom the Russell's had a close friendship in Sydenham, then just beginning his career as an engineer, completed the design and detail drawings by the second week of September. The two wasted no time in heading off to Vienna, preparing the specifications and inviting bids for the construction of the rotunda, the diameter of

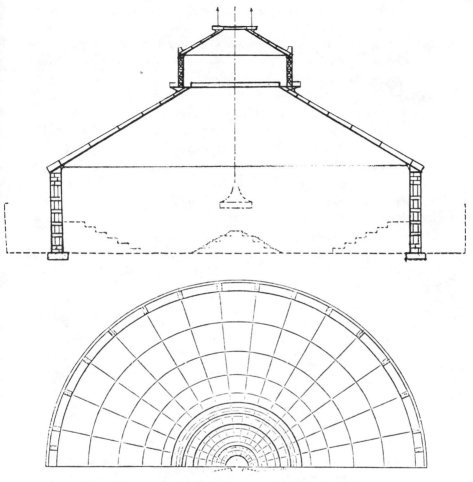

The Vienna Rotunda—riveted ironplate cone stiffened by
tapering radial ribs and concentric iron rings.

which was now set at 354 feet. The contract was placed on October 7
with Harkort of Duisburg.[15] This was remarkably quick work.

The dome was formed of a conical envelope of riveted iron plates,
sloping at 30° and tapering in thickness from $\frac{1}{2}$ inch for the outer strake
to $\frac{1}{4}$ inch for the inner. It was truncated at 100 feet diameter by a cylindrical 'lantern', 30 feet high, covered by a further conical roof truncated
at 30 feet diameter by another 'lantern' surmounted by an imitation
of the Austrian crown imperial. The whole was supported around the

279

periphery by fabricated wrought-iron columns, the colonial roof being stiffened by a radial framework of built-up girders tapering to the apex and held together transversely by a series of concentric rings or webs. The lower ring on which the cone rested was thus subjected to the maximum tensile stress, while the upper ring at the truncated end of the cone experienced the maximum compressive stress. The intermediate rings experienced lower stresses, ranging from a maximum of tension through zero at some neutral ring to compression. Consequently internal and radial ties were not required, it being only necessary to stiffen the surface of the cone so that it should remain undeformed even should there be settlement of one or more of the supporting columns.[16] Some would consider the Vienna rotunda Russell's greatest structural engineering achievement. It certainly was the largest dome built up to that time and a conception of great engineering originality.

The contractor was allowed free choice of any system of erection which he might consider safe and expeditious (Brunel would not have permitted this). In consequence a great many alterations in detail were imposed by the contractor. Once the work was under way, Russell entrusted the supervision to George Holmes.

Meantime, on August 10, Russell had secretly reported to the Working Men's Council that he had first attempted to 'unite Peers and Legislators chiefly with what is called the Liberal Party' and had failed, and that he had then directed his further efforts to the Conservative Party with some success.[17] A representative body called the Council of Legislation, he told the working men, had been drawn together, which body, he said, comprehended earls, lords, baronets and one commoner, to a number at present limited to ten, but which might if expedient, be extended to fifteen, the number comprising the Council of Working Men. 'So soon as desirable, with the consent of all the members of both Councils, a complete list of their names shall be exchanged, and it shall be a matter for the consideration of the two Councils when and how publicity should be given to the objects and the organizations now undertaken.'[18]

He withheld the names of this 'Council of Legislation' until he returned from Vienna to preside over a further confidential meeting on September 28 at which he revealed them to be: The Earl of Lichfield, the Earl of Carnarvon, the Marquis of Salisbury, the Marquis of Lorne, Lord Henry Lennox, Lord John Manners, Sir John Pakington, Sir Stafford Northcote and Mr Gathorne Hardy.

At the same meeting, the following were elected as a 'Council of

Skilled Artisans': Robert Applegarth (Gen. Secy. Carpenters), Daniel Guile (Secy. Ironfounders), George Howell (Secy. London Trades Council), T. W. Hughes (Leading Christian Socialist, author of *Tom Brown's Schooldays*), Lloyd Jones (writer on Trade Union matters), H. Broadhurst (Stonemasons, future Secy. of T.U.C.), F. Whetstone, John Deighton, Alfred Barker, J. Squires, R. M. Latham, Joseph Leicester, William Swindlehurst and George Potter.

The latter council agreed to study the accepted programme and to prepare to recommend means of implementing it at a future meeting with their lordly counterparts.[19]

These deliberations were conducted with all the secrecy and discretion the cause demanded; but a few days later, October 4, by which time Russell had returned to the Continent, Sir John Pakington alluded to one or two of the points of the manifesto in a long opening address to the Social Science Congress at Leeds. Sir John announced that his speech would be devoted to

> some of those questions which affect more or less directly the character and position, and thereby the happiness and contentment of the working classes of this country ... It involves not only our character as a civilized and Christian people, but it involves also the permanence of that manufacturing and commercial prosperity upon which our national greatness and power so much depends. I hope I shall not be misunderstood if I here express a wish founded upon my long experience as a member of the House of Commons, that the attention of successive Parliaments could be somewhat more devoted to these questions of domestic importance to which I am now referring, and somewhat less occupied by questions of mere party interest.

He then elaborated on the theme of national education. When he came to technical education he quoted freely from Scott Russell's 'able work', a work he wished were 'in the hands of all who feel interest in either the national manufactures or our national education'. The more intelligent English artisans, he claimed, had become conscious of their disadvantages in this respect.

> At a meeting of representative men of this class held in London early in the present year, their views as to their own most important requirements were drawn up under seven heads, of which the fourth was:
> 'In addition to schools for elementary education, there should be provided schools for practical knowledge and technical skill in the midst of their homesteads.'[20]

This was a tantalizing revelation of hitherto unsuspected deliberations which would have made little impact if Sir John had not followed it up with a paraphrase of some of the other items and presented a strong case for state intervention. It is perfectly clear that Sir John was well imbued with Russell's ideas and completely in agreement with them. Some called his speech socialistic, and it certainly lent substance to the unsympathetic remark that Sir John's 'babbling candour' made his colleagues fear to see him on his feet.

The hint of political deliberations among a representative group of workmen drew the attention of at least one newspaper, *The Observer*, which ferreted out the story, and published not only the seven points but the names of the people involved. This was picked up by other newspapers and quickly reproduced throughout the length and breadth of the country. The radical *Sheffield Independent* remarked: 'The novelty of the idea has electrified the old party managers, who are beginning to feel that the end of the world is at hand' (October 14). A. J. Mundella, a factory-owning supporter of the trade union movement and new Liberal M.P., was sceptical:

> The story about an alliance between Toryism and the leaders of the working men is all nonsense. I will answer for Applegarth [one of the Workers' Committee]. He is sound and true to the government and Liberal principles. I am quite sure from my conversations with Pakington that there is no danger of his side going in for reduced hours, but they are willing to take up social questions and ride them.[21]

There was no mistaking the alarm in the Liberal ranks. They were no more alarmed, however, than some of the Conservatives, including the editor of their principal newspaper, *The Times*, who scorned the whole idea. The peers and politicians associated with the New Social Alliance, as it was now called, were anxious to clarify their uncommitted position with respect to it and therefore arranged for the publication of the memorandum they had submitted to Russell on August 1. This revealed the reservations attached to their sympathetic interest:

> At the request of Mr Scott Russell, as chairman of a council of representative working men, we, the undersigned, have consented to consider in a friendly and impartial spirit whether and in what manner we can co-operate with this Council in measures calculated to remove the disadvantages which affect the well-being of the working class.
> We appreciate the confidence thus shown to be placed in us; we fully

recognize the national necessity of a hearty good feeling between the different classes of society; we believe that this good feeling can and ought to be secured where both parties are in earnest on the subject.

Awaiting communications from the Council, we readily engage to give an attentive consideration to the measures which may be hereafter submitted by them to our judgment.

At the same time, we do not conceal from ourselves that the task which we have been requested to undertake is not free from difficulty.

We cannot become parties to any legislation which we do not believe to be consistent with the real interests of all classes. We must reserve to ourselves the most unfettered discretion in the selection of objects and in the modification or rejection of measures proposed to us for consideration; and we must hold ourselves free, either collectively or individually, to retire from the task to which we have been invited whenever we may be of opinion that our assistance is not likely to be for the advantage of the public or satisfactory to ourselves.

Salisbury	John Manners
Carnarvon	John S. Pakington
Lichfield	Stafford Northcote
Sandon	Gathorne Hardy.[22]

At the other extreme, the London Patriotic Society convened a meeting of 'representative working men' to discuss the Social Alliance and concluded that it had all the appearance of a clandestine compact. It was suggested that the Council of Skilled Workmen were being paid by some party and asserted that it was not the first time that Potter and Howell had coquetted with the despised Tories.[23] This was refuted by Potter, who insisted on the non-political intention of the Social Alliance as far as the working men were concerned,[24] as also did Russell in his long explanatory letter which he wrote to *The Times* on his return from Vienna around the middle of November.[25] He closed this with the comment:

I trust this short statement has shown that this social movement was neither a revolutionary conspiracy nor a political manœuvre—that it was an endeavour to unite more closely in a band of brotherly kindness some separated, if not alienated, classes of Englishmen—that it was a work dictated by patriotism, directed by common sense, reconciled with common justice, and, in short, a work of plain practical Christianity.

Russell presided over the Workmen's Committee for three hours on Saturday evening, November 25, and the meeting resolved that in the absence of definite response from the Legislative Council they would defer further steps but they reiterated their willingness to co-operate with any members of the Legislature without reference to political party.[26]

Undaunted, Russell expanded on the Social Alliance in letters to various newspapers. It is intriguing that these visionary proposals were being discussed at a time when the engineering employees of Sir William Armstrong were striking for a nine-hour day!

As life began to return to normal in France, Russell did not allow the Channel ferry proposal to be forgotten, as is evidenced by his further paper on the subject published in 1872.[27] The contesting claims of 'the tunnel under the earth, the tunnel in the water and the bridge in the air', as he expressed it, continued to attract attention. Probably Russell sometimes broke his journeys to and from Vienna by calling upon his friends in Paris.

Meantime, towards the end of September 1871, he received a letter from an Italian politician, Giuseppe Dassi, inviting comments on a proposal to utilize the Colosseum as the central building in a complex of structures for an international exhibition at Rome. Dassi had been a member of the Committee of the Working Men's International Exhibition held in London in 1870, and it was he who had borne an invitation to Garibaldi to allow his name to be added to the list of Vice-Presidents of that event, the President, incidentally, being W. E. Gladstone.

Dassi requested Russell's advice on the feasibility of so using the Colosseum without damage to 'that great and splendid monument to antiquity', and on the requisite additional buildings, expectations of success and cost.

Russell, not unexpectedly, replied with great enthusiasm, and a little high-flying encouragement: 'What a sight it would be and how characteristic of modern civilization in contrast to ancient to witness a union of the representatives of science, art and industry, from all the world brought together in peaceful harmony within the vast area of the Colosseum at Rome.'[28]

He had hoped to see such a replica of the Colosseum erected in England (this appears to have been the basis of his design of a building for the 1851 Exhibition) covered by a single span iron roof supported by discreetly hidden columns round the periphery. He was therefore able to state at once 'that an iron roof can be constructed to replace the ancient velarium which shall span the entire area of the Colosseum so as to protect it both from sunshine and rain while perfectly admitting the necessary illumination'. He found the Colosseum thus roofed over to be as large as the whole of the International Exhibition building of 1851. He advised underwriting by the Government and subtly insinuated a further recommendation of himself as engineer by remarking that the quantity of iron required and the 'dimensions' were almost exactly those of the *Great Eastern* steamship![29]

Dassi's reply shows that Russell had struck exactly the right note of romantic enthusiasm. 'That you should have responded to my questions I might have expected' effused Dassi, 'but that you should enter as fully as you have done into my views, that you should have felt the artistic, the historic value of the proposition, the wonderful associations it is calculated to awaken was more than I looked for, and on which I can only congratulate myself.' Perhaps Mr Brodie, the Scottish friend of Russell's father who had conveyed Dassi's initial enquiry, had influenced the character of Russell's response.

Dassi, however, had been reading the news of the New Social Alliance:

> We of the liberal party in Italy, have been reading the accounts in the newspapers of your struggles for the amelioration of the lot of the working classes, and how we earnestly hope that endeavours to secure so glorious an object as to give to ia bour its just recompense, to put an end to the sad mistakes of past ages, to abolish the horrid scourge of war and to attain the great aim of all proper Government the greatest good to the greatest number, may be crowned with the success it merits. Myself founder of some of the operative Societies in this country and perpetual Honorary Vice-President of most of them, the question is to me one of paramount importance as I see in it the only hope for a solution of the difficulties which are now looming on our political horizon.[30]

Russell approved of the proposal to finance the undertaking with Government guaranteed debentures and thought he might be able to arrange that the constructors take part payment in these should capital be tight. 'What I will also guarantee,' he boldly asserted, 'is that the building shall not cost more than the sum I have named, as the contracts that have just been completed for the execution of the Vienna building are somewhat under the estimate I gave in.'[31]

Russell remained in London until the end of the year, and asked Dassi to consult his artists and architects regarding the degree of restoration of the Colosseum they would find acceptable, also—

> I wish that you and your friends would also consider for me whether you

would or would not permit that the roof should rise above the level of present highest wall so as to be visible from the outside, or whether you place great value on the roof being so nearly flat as to be from the outside, in the vicinity, invisible.

Will you also consider whether you would like the light to enter the building through one large central opening in the roof, or through a continuous ring of openings all round the outer iron ring? In both cases these openings being glazed.

Please give me your ideas as to the use to which you wish to appropriate the arena and how you mean to utilise the stone benches all round.

In discussing these matters with your friends pray give them to understand that their judgment on these points may be entirely disembarrassed of any consideration for me, or any supposed difficulties in my iron building. I wish you only to consider what is best, grandest, most useful and most wise to the preservation of this greatest monument of Roman genius. All the difficulties of execution I will cheerfully take upon myself and I will compel my iron work to do exactly what is best for you.

I have been studying here the exquisite model which was constructed for the Crystal Palace Committee of which I was a member. It is a complete restoration of the original Colosseum. That model shows how the Romans in using the amphitheatre covered it from the sun with a velarium, what I shall take care of (if you so decide) is that the iron roof shall occupy the place of the ancient velarium and so harmonise with the general character of the building.

Early in the new year, 1872, Russell returned to his great cause with a document entitled 'The New Social Movement—Programme of Legislation' which he sent to *The Times* and other papers and journals. *The Times* assailed it as 'a weak and ill-written exposition of the crudest Socialism', and interlarded selected quotations with disparaging comments. Those who thought that the seven-point manifesto could serve as a basis for negotiation and social reform or even as a means of wooing the trade union vote to the Conservatives must now have realized that they had greatly misjudged their prospects, and Russell was left to chalk up another well-intentioned failure in the field of public life. 'His essay in politics,' wrote the editor of one newspaper on the occasion of Russell's death some twelve years later, 'was more magnificent than Brunel's dream of the *Great Eastern*, grander than the Vienna dome, more striking than the spanning of the Thames. He attempted to turn the Conservative leaders into Socialists. . . . It was almost sublime. . . . Yet it bore fruit. To it we owe, there can be no manner of doubt, the finely conceived,

but rather unfortunate, Artizan's Dwellings Bill.'[32] Most of his programme, it will be noted, has since been implemented in one form or
another.

Dassi was as interested in Russell's 'seven points' as he was in the
proposed Rome Exhibition. Karl Marx had published the first volume
of *Das Kapital* in London less than five years before and European
socialist and liberal movements were growing in the wake of rapid
industrialization.

During April and May 1872, Russell visited Greece and Turkey and
had his 'conceptions very much enlarged of the beauty of the wonderful
world we live in'. He had found many artists and architects who opposed
the proposal to 'protect, restore and utilize' the Colosseum and he was
therefore hopeful that Dassi would 'continue to elicit the opinions of the
most eminent men' in Italy before he made 'a final decision on a controversial point of so much importance'.[33] A new building of equal size
would cost less, he added.

By January of the following year Russell had decided, and wrote to
Dassi from London: 'In regard to the general character of your proposed
buildings I have no longer any doubt. We must entirely detach and isolate
it from these great ancient monuments of Rome with which it could not
possibly harmonize.' Few will find fault with Russell's decision or his
care in not only consulting but accepting the best artistic and architectural
opinions available to him. He was not in favour of purely temporary
exhibition buildings but advocated substantial structures designed to
serve some permanent social purpose.

> We now know, that we can enclose under the roof of a single dome, a greater
> area of ground and a greater volume of space than was enclosed within the
> walls of the ancient Coliseum . . . The next point of great importance is the
> selection of a site for this building. Of this I can form no judgement until
> I know the wishes of the Municipality and the intentions of the Government
> regarding that new city of Rome which is to be the capital of Italy. The
> point to be kept in view at present is that all new buildings to be erected
> in Rome should form part of one great design.[34]

But the proposed International Exhibition of Rome seems no longer
to have been possible and with the grand opening of the exhibition at
Vienna in 1873, Russell was again out of a job. It would appear from
the fact that the Russell–Dassi correspondence was set up in print, the

proof sheets surviving in a collection in the British Museum, that Russell at one time intended to publish it, probably in support of the Social Alliance and most probably for the trade union members to whom he showed some of Dassi's comments.

CHAPTER FOURTEEN

The Last Decade

It will take some time before the intelligence and growing commerce of the world will call for much larger ships than the Great Eastern; it will be still longer before the growing skill of artillerymen, and the growing wish to dominate our neighbours, will require much larger ships than the Warrior, or than that class of vessel enlarged to the size of the Great Eastern.

J. SCOTT RUSSELL (1865)

How far Russell's career was damaged by the circumstances of his withdrawal—or as some would see it, his expulsion—from the Council of the Institution of Civil Engineers is not easy to determine. The whole matter seems to have been noticed only by the professional journals—*The Engineer* and *Engineering*—and does not seem to have reduced his standing with many distinguished contemporaries at home and abroad. He even had the honour of being written up in the 1878 edition of *Men of Mark*. The natural restlessness of his mind was not subdued and he was doubtless fortified in the knowledge that he had acquired sufficient stature to attract a hostility that could find its roots only in jealousy, or, in the case of Armstrong, in the spirit of the Border reiver. His pecuniary embarrassment, however, was a persistent impediment to the growth of his prestige and doubtless also to the honours to which his service to his country entitled him.

He withdrew from active participation in the affairs of the Institution of Civil Engineers and dropped his membership entirely from the Institution of Mechanical Engineers. A glance at the administration of the latter in 1870 could explain the reason in that instance—Sir William Armstrong was again President. But the Institution of Naval Architects was peculiarly his. There he was enjoyed and esteemed and, when necessary, tolerated, as a paternal and knowledgeable elder statesman of the profession. He was ready with a contribution to the discussion of every subject and set an admirable model in deportment and eloquence. His innovations in the structure of ships gained wider acceptance as larger ships were built and, of course, the longitudinal system was fully adopted by

289

the Admiralty. On the subject of the form of least resistance which had first drawn him into naval architecture he could take some satisfaction from the fact that his wave-line theory had stood alone for over twenty years and that he had been the first to attempt to explain the important part wave-making plays in resisting the motion of ships. Russell's elegant conceptions, however, were to be challenged and greatly superseded as the 1860s progressed. At the Institution, William Froude emerged as a new contributor to the field. Of about the same age as Russell, he took up engineering for a time after leaving Oxford with a first in mathematics, and entered the employ of I. K. Brunel. His interest in naval hydrodynamics began in 1856, when Brunel, with thought of the *Great Eastern* suggested that he investigate the rolling of ships, a subject to which Russell had also given some attention. Ample private means enabled Froude to devote all his time to the experiment and analysis for which he had genius, akin to Russell's but more orthodoxly mathematical. His attachment to Brunel perhaps prevented a closer relationship with Russell. Both were the sons of clergymen, the one high Anglican, the other Scottish seceder Presbyterian. This, however, was no greater barrier to their closer harmony than it was to that of Froude's brother, the historian, with Thomas Carlyle, the latter also a seceder Presbyterian. They were, however, potential rivals and Froude was now to take issue with Russell on some fundamental conceptions of ship hydrodynamics.

Their earliest disagreement occurred on the subject of the rolling of ships. While Froude admired the elegance of Russell's conceptions, particularly his idea of the stability of a ship as a combination in some degree of two extreme tendencies represented by a plank ballasted to float on edge ('vertical stability') and a plank floating flatwise ('surface stability'), he claimed that Russell erred in ignoring inertia and in some other respects. Although Russell knew Froude's views to be greatly at variance with his own on some crucial points, he gave Froude the proof of his paper on the subject (*Trans. I.N.A.*, 1863) to help Froude write an extensive rebuttal of it.[1] Russell lost some ground to Froude (and to Rankine) on this matter. Nevertheless, they debated and disagreed most courteously both professionally and socially, although Russell may have been a little patronizing to Froude in the early stages.[2]

Not the least attractive feature of Russell's discourse was his pawky humour. Even on the subject of stability he found an opportunity to sparkle—

If a vessel has great surface stability, whenever the highest breaking point of a great sea wave comes, the vessel absolutely ought to turn upside down, and sometimes does ... the moment you have an absolutely sharp wave it is the business of the ship, and the duty of the ship, and the ship cannot help it, to go up this side of the wave [referring to a sketch] till she gets near the top. Then encountering that portion of the wave which is coming forward, the sharp point of the wave on this side of the ship, is put over ... and the other side comes beautifully up on the second side of the wave, and if you are good enough to lash yourself fast and stay there till she comes to the next wave, then you are all right again, because at the next wave she turns upside down again, and as you know that two *minuses* make a *plus*, so immediately after this you are all right. That was one of my earliest experiences the first time I went to sea, and I have remembered it ever since, I quite understand that those who have not had the same experience will not take the same notice of it.[3]

A great controversy, in the press, the Admiralty, in Parliament, and in the Institution, during the late 1860s raged over the low freeboard demanded by Captain Cowper Coles for the first armoured warships fitted with his gun turrets. The low freeboard not only lowered the centre of gravity which the guns and armour tended to raise, but produced a steadier gun platform. The Chief Admiralty Constructor, F. J. Reed, opposed the reduction of freeboard on the grounds of safety and comfort, especially under canvas. In this he was supported by Russell who pointed out that once the vessel inclined beyond its 'point of greatest breadth', there was a 'rapid diminution of stability', and only one or two oscillations were required, aided by a 'good big wave' to make 'the dangers of a small freeboard very obvious'.[4] The Admiralty settled the matter by allowing Coles to have a ship built to his own specifications, the *Captain*, of very low freeboard (6·5 feet) and Reed to keep to a greater freeboard (13 feet) for his ship, the *Monarch*. The subsequent loss of the *Captain* on September 6, 1870, from the very cause described by Russell and Reed, enhanced the authority of the naval architect as opposed to that of the sailor on matters of ship design. It was an experiment, Russell observed, 'absolute, decided, and overwhelming ... it has settled all the questions it was to decide—one way.'[5]

This same period saw the extension of Russell's work on waves and its replacement by new conceptions. In the early 1860s the total resistance to the passage of a ship was conceived as comprising two components, the 'head' resistance, or ploughing of a channel related to the size of the mid-ship section of the ship, and the frictional resistance. The conception of the 'head' resistance was false, and was replaced by the idea of 'wave-making' resistance. Russell reasoned that the wave-line hull reduced the 'head' resistance to a minimum until the wave-making speed corresponding to the length of the hull was reached. Up to that stage, he correctly declared, the resistance was overwhelmingly due to dragging the ship away from the water which 'hung' to it—loosely called the frictional resistance.[6] The exact mechanism of the friction drag was a mystery to Russell, but he drew attention to the 'ribbon of water' sticking to the ship, a ribbon which he said 'was in the act of being torn to shreds', the innermost layer sticking to the ship and moving on with it. He was the first to draw attention to this phenomenon, later called the 'boundary-layer' and elucidated by Reynolds and Prandtl.

The power necessary for the propulsion of a ship at a given speed was rather uncertainly determined by empirical formulae based upon the mid-ship section and the known performance of previous ships. It was in pursuit of this that the first step to a fuller understanding of the flow of liquid around submerged and floating bodies was made by William Rankine. J. R. Napier started the chain of events by asking Lord Kelvin to derive a general formula for propulsive power, from a great body of data he had collected from his ships. Kelvin noted that existing theories ignored the viscosity of the fluid and he discussed the problem with his colleague Rankine, who soon offered a general formula which was of great use to Napier and which, incidentally, showed that the *Great Eastern* was under-powered. Extending this work, Rankine produced the streamline theory in the early 1860s, which, supplemented by the work of Kelvin and Stokes, provided the mathematical basis of modern ship hydrodynamics.

The universality of Russell's wave line criteria, however, was not contested until the next great step forward was taken by William Froude. This was stimulated by the report, in 1869, of a British Association committee on the state of existing knowledge on stability, propulsion and the seagoing qualities of ships.[7] The members of this committee were, Rankine, Merrifield, Captain Galton, Francis Galton, G. P. Bidder and Froude.

The inclusion of Bidder may be explained by his having dabbled in the subject of warship design at an earlier date, or by his being a member of a recently formed Admiralty committee 'on the design for ships of war', or by his assisting Froude in some experiments. He lent Froude his steam launch in the autumn of 1867 to be used as a tow in resistance experiments on a pair of contrasting models. The first pair were of 12-feet length, the next of 6-feet, then 3 feet. The results gave Froude confidence in the feasibility of using models to predict full-scale performance and enabled him to convince Edward Reed that this confidence was well founded. Froude's colleagues on the B.A. committee, however, had no confidence in model studies and requested the Admiralty to help in procuring full-scale data. In this they had the backing of Russell and the I.N.A. Froude, however, submitted a minority report which, with Reed's advocacy, in February 1870 gained a grant of £2000 to help build an experimental tank near Froude's house at Torquay and to finance experiments. It was an attractive suggestion, holding promise of great economy and utility.

At the next meeting of the I.N.A., Merrifield, chairman of the B.A. committee and principal of the School of Naval Architecture, presented a paper advocating experiments on full-scale ships and referred to the law of appropriate velocities, nowadays attributed to Froude, as having not yet been adequately substantiated.[8] The range of size of Froude's models could hardly be called adequate. The 'law of appropriate velocities' was understood to be that which asserted that the performances of a full size ship and its model were similar if their dimensions bore the same proportion to each other as the squares of their velocities. This arose even from the belief that 'head' and 'frictional' resistances were proportional to the square of the velocity. No one, however, had yet been able to demonstrate the law: there was either something unknown which frustrated it, or the experimental techniques were inadequate.

Russell, presiding, recalled that the Institution had concurred that full-scale experiments were wanted. But he was sure that all would be pleased that the Admiralty had shown its goodwill to the science of naval architecture by giving Mr Froude a sum of money to make an interesting series of experiments on small models. He warned the members not to expect too much, the reason being that the one valuable outcome of all his experiments upon small models was that the curious results led him to make

> quite other experiments on the large scale, and I arrived at the conclusion from the graduated series of models, that the results on a very small scale, and a very large scale were so far removed from each other, as to anything like practical ratio, that the result of the experiments on the small scale, and the only result which I considered of the smallest value, was to suggest

to me what experiments I should make on the large scale. Therefore you will have on the small scale a series of beautiful, interesting little experiments, which I am sure will afford Mr Froude infinite pleasure in the making of them, as they did to me, and will afford you infinite pleasure in the hearing of them; but which are quite remote from any practical results upon the large scale. Indeed the most interesting fact I ascertained was, that the results on a large scale, were precisely the contrary to the results on a small scale.

Nevertheless, he hoped the support given by the Admiralty to Mr Froude who was 'so capable of making beautiful scientific experiments with great accuracy, and with great ingenuity,' was a good augury for their getting the larger experiments.[9]

To all this, Froude declared that the reason model experiments had hitherto been a failure was that attention had not been paid to the

relation which must subsist between the speed at which the model is moved, and the speed at which the ship is moved ... No doubt, if you draw the model at some random velocity, and ascertain its resistance, and conclude you have thus measured the resistance of the ship for all velocities, you will be quite wrong; but if you follow the law of appropriate velocities, which to my mind is correctly ascertained to be the law of the square root of the dimensions, that is to say if to a vessel four times as long you give twice the velocity, you will find close correspondence between the resistances in the one case and in the other. So far as I can judge, the results of my own experiments, when compared with the results of known resistances of big ships, give a very fair scale of comparison indeed.[10]

But did they? It is now recognized that perfect dynamical similarity between a ship and its model is unattainable. Adherence to the law of appropriate velocities can achieve simulation of wave-making phenomena, but the other major sources of resistance, viscous drag or 'friction', cannot be simulated by the same model.

If the model were moved at the same speed as the full-scale ship, the waves would be seen to be proportionately higher than those of the ship. There is a suggestion that this was why models were distrusted. But the following abstract of a paper on ship resistance presented by Rankine to the B.A. in 1861 certainly suggests that both he and Russell understood the law of appropriate velocities at least seven years prior to Froude's pronouncements:

it follows that, in order that conclusions drawn from experiments on models may be applicable to actual ships, care should be taken not to move the model at a speed which raises a wave exceeding in proportionate height the wave raised by the large vessel; and that such may be the case, the velocities of the model and of the ship should be proportional to the square root of the linear dimensions. . . . This conclusion is common to the theory of the present paper, and to Mr Scott Russell's wave theory.[11]

In the face of all this, it is very difficult to accept that Russell and others had not tested the law of corresponding velocities. Thus Froude's confidence in this law must have seemed inexperienced to Russell, Merrifield and Rankine, and his dilating upon it as though it were new, a little naïve. As far as their experience went, the law did not give a fair scale of comparison between a small model and a full size ship.

It had certainly been one of Russell's early aims to 'show the law of relation between different scales'[12] and, in 1840, he criticized previous experiments in France and Britain for the lack of such a law.[13] Yet Frederic Reech had been propounding the law of appropriate velocities—commonly called Froude's Law today—at the *École d'application du Genie Maritime* at Lorient from as early as 1831, although he did not publish it until 1844. He referred to it again in his book *Cours de Mechanique*, in 1852.[14] Reech became head of the *École du Genie Maritime* in Paris and was referred to by Russell in 1863 as one whom he had known all his life 'through his works and heard of from his pupils',[15] and again, in 1870, as 'probably the man in the whole world the most profoundly conversant with the whole mathematics and mechanics of naval architecture'.[16] Yet, in 1860, Russell emphatically declared to the I.N.A. 'I believe the man does not yet live who can tell, from what he observes with a little model in a little trough, anything about what a ship of full size will do in open water or, upon the sea.'[17] His belief was well founded at that time because the full-scale data were difficult to obtain.

In summarizing the discussion, Russell stated: 'For the general interests of science, it is very agreeable to us to find that Mr. Froude has the intention of making an extremely exact series of experiments on little models, which cannot in his hands but produce us some scientific information . . .' He observed that unless Froude had at least three canals, he would 'not get out of the errors which any one canal would inflict on him'. He would find that 'everything which is true of one velocity in one canal, is utterly untrue of another [the same?] velocity in another canal, and that', concluded Russell, 'is among the reasons why experiments with small models are no good for large ships.'[18]

Froude, however, was not showing his hand. He was really bent on relating a full-scale experiment to tank results and he was enabled to do this by the Admiralty's placing H.M.S. *Greyhound* at his disposal. In the end the bare application of the law of appropriate velocities of course could not suffice. The data so derived had to be adjusted to take account of the frictional component of the total resistance and it was the artifice of doing this which really constituted Froude's break-through, apart from his experimental skill. Now models could be used intelligently to study the hydrodynamics of ships. It was a most important advance.

Russell applauded the achievement with enthusiasm and generosity; but he could not resist hitching himself a little to the success. He found it, he said,

> a matter of great personal gratification ... to find as one of the results of this series of experiments, that you can take a model and calculate the resistance of a model of a ship, and then by a little wisdom, a little judgement, and a little science take the model as the type of your ship, and from the model calculate the performance of your ship ... These results of Mr Froude merely show us that we should never despise any means of getting at approximate knowledge when we do not happen to have at hand the means of getting perfect knowledge.

Then he allowed himself to get a little carried away, elaborating on the theme in a way which, while not in some senses untrue, must have struck those with long memories as more than a little curious.

> I was often laughed at, because I believed in experiments on my small models. The laughing did not cease until I made experiments on the large scale, and until the models on the large scale worked upon the same laws as the models on the small scale. But referring to Froude's paper the diagram (in which the results given by the model are put down, and, by a little transformation, the results given by the ship), gives a curve so absolutely identical with the performance of the ship, that it is a complete proof that those who wisely took models as their guide up to a certain point, and then, by the best means that they had at their command, went a little further, and applied that information for what it was good for, and as far as it would go, to a large ship, were not so far astray as many people have thought they were.

Russell, of course, had himself become one of these people. Now he was having to eat his words and at the behest of his antagonists. It was too much for his ego and he indulged instead in a little double talk— to make his *volte face* as palatable as possible. After all, he had indeed predicted the full-scale performance of ships from a theory in the development of which model studies had played an important part. Allowance must be made, too, for the fact that he was speaking extemporaneously.

He could take some consolation from being able to criticize Bidder's speed recorder which Froude had used. The recorder was actuated by a length of twine payed out to a log-ship of large area. Russell thought this inferior to the pitot tube method he had used which gave instantaneous speed records. 'I dare say it was made by an ingenious man,' said Russell of Bidder's device, but, he added, 'it is a bad arrangement',[19] and so it was.

Some experiments on novel high-powered steam launches designed by Thornycroft had already revealed that at certain velocities in excess of the optimum predicted by Russell's criteria, the resistance actually fell below that which was proportional to the square of the velocity.[20] When Bramwell reported this to the Institution of Naval Architects in 1872, Russell declared it one of the most important papers the Institution had ever heard. 'When I was a very young man,' he said, 'I tried Mr Thorny-croft's experiment and failed ... for want of a boiler, or for want of courage, or for want of cleverness, all of which Mr. Thornycroft has had.' He explained the phenomenon as the result of a 'spurt' of speed which raised the boat into a surf-riding position on top of its own wave of transla-tion. In this position, he said, the boat drew far less water, particularly at the bow and hence the achievement of the 'victorious velocities'. He had already discussed this condition as early as 1865 in his great book (vol. 1, pp. 238–9). His plausible explanation is a good example of the habit of his mind. Russell thought far more in physical images than in mathematical terms. Another good example of this is his paper 'On the True Nature of the Resistance of Armour to Shot' (*Trans. I.N.A.*, 1880). Soon Froude's son was to show that at speeds in excess of the wave-mak-ing speed the curve of resistance versus speed passed through inflexions, which indicated that the resistance sometimes thereafter was proportional to the square, and at other stages to the cube and higher powers, of the speed.[21] At these speeds, the old-fashioned 'cod's head and mackerel tail' came into its own again, a fact which was suggested by Russell's canal experiments. He had noted that the wave-line vessel designed for the open sea did not perform as well in shallow water (the wave of translation being slower) as the corresponding vessel with convex lines.[22] The wave-form criteria still hold where the speed to length ratio ($v/\sqrt{L}$) is unity, as is frequently encountered in yachts. But even before such limitations were understood, the large racing yachts competing for the America's Cup in the late nineteenth century conformed in general to the wave-form cri-teria. When, in 1871, the *Livonia* (264 tons) was beaten by the American *Sappho* (310 tons), the fact that *Livonia* had not realized the high speed

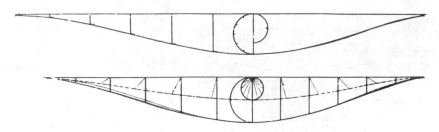

The America's Cup 1870. *Top: Sappho* the defender: pure wave-form; *below: Livonia* the challenger: modified wave-form

expected of her was attributed to an excessive departure from the wave form,[23] the *Sappho* on the contrary was of perfect wave form. Whatever else, it is a form of great beauty.

About this time the subject of the safe loading of ships arose with Plimsoll's bill introduced to Parliament. On his own suggestion, Russell led a delegation from the Institution of Naval Architects to police the proposed legislation. His ideas on this subject have been endorsed by history. 'I would legislate,' declared Russell,

> that every ship should have marked upon her side, not only so that technical men may see, but that passengers and everybody else may see, what I will not call the danger line—for that is an invidious phrase—but the 25 per cent line [a buoyancy term], and that will give offence to nobody. We paint nearly all ships—at least iron ones—red on the bottom to preserve them, and black above to please our fancy. Suppose we make a law that that margin between the red and black shall be put exactly at this 25 per cent line, and let us call that the arbitrary freeboard, or the legal freeboard, or anything you like.[24]

He was no less perspicacious on the subject of gun-cotton 'torpedoes':

> I am quite a believer in the extraordinary impossibilities (if I may call them so) which are accomplished by gun-cotton, and I am quite prepared to say, from my experience and knowledge of gun-cotton, that it will not take time to consider what a ship is made of, but will go straight through it without the least regard to the subject. That you may assume as an axiom; and, therefore, I would say the best mode of encountering gun-cotton torpedoes is to keep away from them—I know of no other. I think we had better give up that question, and study first how we are to carry and manage torpe-

298

does ourselves, and then how we are to keep out of the way of other people's torpedoes.[25]

Russell's comprehensive grasp, not only of the technicalities and science of shipbuilding, but of geopolitics and naval tactics drawn from his travels abroad and his communication with experts in the relevant fields, enabled him to present periodic appraisals of the future concerns of naval architects with acknowledged authority. In 1870 he reviewed the great events which had 'changed the surface of the world' in the past ten years—'the union of remote continents by submarine telegraphs', the 'Canal of Suez', the 'Pacific railway across America'. Ten more years, he said, would 'cover the bottom of every sea with lines of electric telegraph', the Isthmus of Panama would be cut through, and the 'Atlantic and Pacific oceans made one'. Railways were spreading out in a widening network the world over which would take the cream of local trade—the future of commerce by ships, he declared, 'lay in large ships, long voyages, commerce between continents, which would require larger and faster ships—3000 tons builders' measurements, 330 ft long, 44 ft beam, 22 ft load-draught of water and a speed of 10 knots with reserve power.' A well-worked steam trade from England to Bombay, through the Isthmus of Suez Canal, he declared, would pay at equal freights even better than sailing ships round the Cape. He believed implicitly the assurance M. Lesseps had personally given him that ships of this size would find easy and safe passage through the Canal. Ships of 4000 tons for the Calcutta voyage and 5000 tons for the China voyage were necessary and would be in use in ten years. These predictions were sound although the Panama Canal took longer to cut than he expected.

All of this demanded a 'new sort of war fleet' he declared and he was more original than we can appreciate in retrospect when he stated—

> In the next war the first aim of the enemy will not be to destroy fortresses, but to destroy our merchant steam fleet and its commerce. . . . The war ships must be longer, larger, fleeter than the merchant fleet—yet they must not draw more water. Where one goes the other must follow, or go before. . . . The value of speed is manifold—choice of time, choice of position, choice of action or inaction—speed gives that. . . . Speed at any price, that is the first point. . . . High speed and handiness . . . I place the value of armour only third in order.[26]

This was thirty years before Lord Fisher. The trend of the immediate successors to the *Warrior* was towards shorter, handier but slower ships,[27] of which E. J. Reed's *Belerophone* was the most innovative. When Russell referred to the matter five years later he could have been describing the British battleship and battle-cruiser fleet at the outbreak of World War I:

> *The Man-of War*—Large, fast, enduring, many and large guns, central battery perfectly shot proof, engines, boilers, and magazine perfectly protected; possessing also all the protecting precautions of the ´cruiser, but slower and heavier; enduring; a hard hitter, and hard to hit.
> *The Many-Large-Gunned Ocean Cruiser*—Long, wide, deepsided, fast, enduring, quick in her manœuvring, with destructive power, and small protection, able to do great harm and ready to run great risks.[28]

Russell's predictions, so fully endorsed in time, were thought highly fanciful by some of his fellow members. But he could stimulate the imagination with an unequalled felicity and charm of utterance and he was never better than at a festive board in honour of some person or event. Admiral R. Spencer Robinson spoke for many when he said—'There is nothing that Mr Scott Russell ever touches but what he ornaments. His facility for exposition is admirable, and the lucid manner in which he conveys an idea gives everything he ever thinks proper to handle the greatest possible charm in the ears of everybody who happens to listen to him.'[29] And listen to him they did, even though at times some must have recalled the feast of Darius—'and thrice he slew the slain and fought all his battles over again'. When, in 1879, he presented a final summary on his studies on the wave of translation, Merrifield paid tribute to Russell's contributions to the hydrodynamics of ship design as great discoveries—'great especially at the time when they were made, when harmonic motion was very little understood, and when the synchronism of waves was scarcely understood at all, except in the crudest form, and when there was no connection established between the motion of waves and the displacement of ships in motion.'[30]

In reporting on the last paper Russell presented to the Institution, *The Engineer* remarked with infectious enthusiasm: 'We regret that it is impossible to give an adequate idea of the spirit with which this lecture was delivered, the skill of the speaker in illustrating his meaning, or the ingenuity with which he enforced his arguments. Mr Scott Russell certainly performs a task of this kind better than any other engineer.'[31]

This was the note on which Russell ended his twenty years of devoted support of the Institution he virtually founded. The 1880 session was his last, and with his going went some of the glory of past history, a link with many of the great names of engineering, naval affairs, shipbuilding, government, and the arts, of the nineteenth century. Yet he long continued as a model of what Admiral Robinson called 'those eloquent periods, that magnificent declamation, and those very sound and sensible points which Mr John Scott Russell put before him'.[32]

At home, the best of the Crystal Palace days had passed. His daughter Rachel married George Holmes' older brother William, an Indian civil servant, in 1872, whom the wife of Edmund Holmes described as 'delicate'. George Holmes became Secretary of the Institution of Naval Architects in 1878, in succession to E. J. Reed, who entered politics. Russell's son Norman was still Director of Baird's Iron Works in St Petersburg, while Louise often attended concerts and exhibitions in the company of William von Glehn, the artistic brother of her friend Mimi. But she fell into a decline and died on Wednesday, March 6, 1878, a victim of tuberculosis. We are left to imagine what a loss this was to the Russell family, but strangely enough, Henry Cole who had so often noted the visits of Louise did not note her passing. Thirty years later, Charles Stanford, then Sir Charles, asked Alice Russell for Louise's photograph.[33]

There is a mention of Russell's being engaged on the design of a high level bridge to span the Thames below London Bridge and of his contracting a chill while on a visit to iron works in Newcastle and Scotland in connection with this.[34] Whatever the details, Russell was stricken by a protracted illness in 1881 and sold his house in Sydenham to retire with Mrs Russell to the Isle of Wight. Active in mind as ever, he applied his waning strength to the completion of a book he had begun to prepare comprising papers he had planned to present before the Royal Society, on the theory of waves.[35] This was published posthumously. Rachel came home on a visit, 'glowing with vigour and beauty'.[36] She had published some of her favourite recipes in a book entitled *Dainty Dishes for Indian Tables*, which enjoyed some celebrity among the pukka sahibs, and was now embarked on a translation of the recently published *Memoirs* of Hector Berlioz. On April 23, 1882, the South Kensington Museum was closed for the funeral of Henry Cole. There was a long and fulsome obituary in *The Times* with a list of many familiar names present in the cortege. A Victorian of Victorians was led off the scene midst black horses, black plumes, black coats and a forest of top hats, cut and dried. Six weeks later, on Thursday morning, June 8, John Scott Russell, too, breathed his last and was interred in the cemetery on the hill above Ventnor; the Queen's chaplain conducted the service. A brief obituary, a mere fraction of the proud space devoted to the great Cole appeared in *The Times*, cribbed from *Engineering*. Cole's public works could be comprehended by the multitude, Russell's were less conspicuous and had it not been for *The Great Eastern* and his New Social Movement, his passing might not have been publicly noticed at all, except by the technical press—and not least by the Institution of Civil Engineers—which, at home and abroad fulsomely and widely reviewed his achievements. It is an odd harmony of fate that Cole and Russell were born in the same year and died in the same year. Those who kept watch for the details of Russell's will would be disappointed—he lived rich and died poor. Indeed, there seems to be no will on record. No honours were bestowed on him as they were upon many who did very much less for their nation, but Harriet Russell was graciously assisted in her extremity in the year following his death by a civil list pension of £90. The Institution of Naval Architects generously acknowledged its debt to its devoted leader but there was something very characteristic of Russell's story that the vacancy he left in the vice-presidential ranks was filled by none other than Sir William Armstrong. It was Armstrong who profited most from Russell's strenuous advocacy of the use of private shipyards for the construction of the 'fleet of the future'. It was in large measure to be a fleet made from Armstrong steel and with Armstrong guns.[37]

The final testament of Russell's work on waves in air and water which he prepared for presentation to the Royal Society prior to his death was published in 1884,[38] falling stillborn from the press.

It is a frustrating and regrettable fact that Russell's manuscripts, letters, design sketches and possessions appear, like the 'good', to have been 'interred with his bones'. Nearly a century has passed and neglect and silence have been reinforced by the death of the generation which may have had something to tell, although Russell himself, it seems, must bear much of the responsibility; he had a large area of privacy which he preserved and protected.

In 1877, five years before Scott Russell's death, Isambard Brunel's biography of his father was published. This remains the definitive work on the great engineer. It makes no issue of controversial matters although it dwells on Brunel's difficulties. Brunel's second son, Henry, helped his brother in the preparation of the biography by elucidating engineering matters, and by assembling extracts from the correspondence. These extracts were carefully bound together to be preserved for posterity. Many of the original letters and memoranda came into the possession of Hollingworth, his resident engineer, who passed them to his son, John Hollingworth, F.I.C.E. The latter in turn, with the encouragement of Sir Alexander Gibb, another of Henry Brunel's former student engineers, had the papers copied and, desiring the Brunel material to be kept together, passed the originals into the custody of the late Lady Noble who later told Mr Hollingworth that they were destroyed during an air raid on London. Let us hope she was mistaken. The perverse fate which has dogged Russell was narrowly frustrated by the survival of copies of one or two letters from him and from Yates in the Hollingworth Collection. As far as the *Great Eastern* is concerned, an essential point of Henry Brunel's exercise seems to have been the justification of his father's plans for the launch and, not least, the desire to establish him as the supreme designer of every detail of the Great Ship.

We have noted the several solutions Russell adopted in the design of ships to meet novel and demanding requirements, from the smallest to the largest mercantile and naval applications. He eloquently advocated his methods among his colleagues in the profession. Abell tells us that the problems of erection 'put off the proper use of lengthwise structures until the early years of the present century'.[39] But E. J. Reed declared in 1872 that it was 'being every day adopted more and more in all parts of the country'.[40] Then in 1881 he declared 'I do not know of any circumstance of which any one need be more proud, as far as my judgement goes, than the part which Mr Scott Russell has taken in introducing the longitudinal system of construction into iron shipbuilding.'[41]

The structural design of a great ship is not so obvious to the layman as that of a bridge or a building, nor are its myriad problems appreciated half so well. Yet in so many ways a ship is the most complicated of these structures. As Russell expressed it:

> It is perhaps the most important thing, in designing a ship, to remember that, in regard to strength and strain, she has no top, no bottom, no sides; or to put it otherwise, it is equally true that, in a sea-way under storms, every part of a ship will be at some moment top, or bottom, or sides indifferently ... hence everything in a ship must be equally well supported in all ways, and should be able to hold its place unflinchingly not only upright, but across,—not only fore and aft, but even upside down.[42]

Many of the display models of Russell's ships have survived. These were given by Russell himself to the South Kensington Museum in 1867 and are now to be found in the London Science Museum with a few in the Hull Maritime Museum; but, with the exception of the H.M.S. *Warrior*, no other relics of him survive. Unlike the bridge-builder, his practical works were all impermanent. Ships quickly become obsolete and end in the breaker's yard, but it was fate that destroyed the Vienna rotunda by fire (September 1937). We are left with his books, articles, and the printed stenographic verbata of his addresses to the scholarly and professional bodies of which he was a member, valuable substance of his life nevertheless. Throughout the foregoing pages we have seen much of those qualities which captivated his friends and fostered envy in his rivals. His oracular and humorous style of address and writing, his clarity of exposition, the generosity warming his proud deportment, his high quality of living, his beautiful and gifted children, his energy, his civilized aspirations and, above all, his lack of political acumen and pecuniary caution. Such characteristics are acceptable in an artist or a poet, but in an engineer or a business man? In Russell's chosen profession and walk of life, material success was what mattered above all and, in these economic terms, it cannot be said that he ever recovered from a bad start. But, in his way, Scott Russell was an artist with that high concentration of originality of thought which cuts its own ingenious path and devises its own ingenious method. The brilliance of the talent is obvious to everyone who reads his works and was to whoever met him in person.

Russell's great love was applied science, and it was a perverse fate which channelled him into complicating it with the economic cares of a large and uncertain business. James Watt needed a Matthew Boulton, so also did John Scott Russell; but it would have been better for him to have remained a consulting engineer and naval architect—supplying the ideas and the practical science and leaving the financial speculation to others. This is what Brunel and Fowler did, along with every other practising engineer and naval architect of his time. He was a great patriot and he sought to serve great ends in the national interest and, indeed, in the affairs of mankind. He was not troubled by false modesty but his written works exhibit a generous spirit, a desire to acknowledge all scientific and intellectual debts and give honour where honour was due. He was not embittered by the shabby treatment he received from fate, from his fellows or from his country.

It is no small thing that E. J. Reed, one of the greatest of the Admiralty constructors of the century, who had known Russell for over twenty years, could, as he expressed it three or four years after Russell's death, 'cherish so many grateful and pleasant memories of this truly remarkable man'.[43] Or that the redoubtable Zerah Colburn, who knew life and men as well as he knew engineering, could express his belief that John Scott Russell, like his great book, would, 'notwithstanding some imperfections, become the more esteemed hereafter'.[44]

References

The abbreviations 'Bristol Coll.' and 'Holl. Coll.' refer to the following:

Bristol Coll.—The collection of Brunel letter books and papers at Bristol University.

Holl. Coll.—The Hollingworth Collection, Bath University.

1 THERE WAS A LAD

1 The caption to the engraving of another photograph, obviously taken on the same occasion, published in the *Illustrated Times*, Jan. 16, 1858, identifies this man as Treadwell and the mud on his shoes supports this. The Royal Photographic Society identifies him as Lord Derby; the resemblance is certainly striking, but there is no mention of the presence of Lord Derby in any of the press accounts and the *Illustrated Times* is unlikely to have made a mistake of this nature.

2 L. T. C. Rolt, *Isambard Kingdom Brunel*, London, 1957, pp. 233–313.

3 MacEwing, *Historic Church of Tollcross*, Glasgow, 1906.

4 I am indebted to Mr Arthur Garton for telling me of this teapot which was a proud possession of John Scott Russell's granddaughter, Beatrix Holmes.

5 Inducted 1811.

6 Inducted, Dec. 24, 1812.

7 Robert Small, *History of the Congregations of The United Presbyterian Church*, Edinburgh, 1904.

8 James Watt Anniversary Lecture, *Engineering*, Jan. 25, 1867, pp. 99–101.

9 J. Scott Russell, *The Modern System of Naval Architecture*, London, 1865.

10 Obituary, *Proc. I.C.E.*, lxxxvii, p. 431.

11 Vitae submitted to the University of Edinburgh in application for the Mathematics Chair, March 1838.

12 Lawrence Melville, *Errol*, Perth, 1935, p. 91.

A round hole in a flagstone of the kitchen floor which Russell was reputed to have used for experiments with explosives was still visible in 1935. *Ibid.*

13 Lawrence Melville, *op. cit.*, states that the Rev. David Russell had nine sons and one daughter. My own search of the birth records of Hawick and of Errol has disclosed only the following in addition to John: David, Nov. 1, 1813; George, March 11, 1817; James, March 11, 1822; Edward, March 12, 1824; Henry, May 31, 1826; Elizabeth, Sept. 14, 1830.

George Russell attended Glasgow University for a time and is reported to have entered the ministry in the Dumfries district. I have been unable to confirm this. James Eckles Russell was a merchant in London, living for a time at 4 Lansdowne Terrace, South Lambeth. He retired to his father's house in Errol, which he had purchased on the death of his father and in which his sister Elizabeth, who never married, lived until her death at a great old age in 1926. Eckles died in 1907, a kenspeckle character of Errol. His daughter, Anne Titterton Russell, lived with him in Errol until she married a John Anderson as his second wife and settled in Bristol. She possessed a red flag made by Eckles from J. Scott Russell's student gown, to celebrate the triumphs of Liberalism, a cause to which Eckles gave fanatical support.

14 J. Scott Russell, *op. cit.*, p. 480.

307

References

15 J. D. Forbes was the son of Sir William Forbes of Pitsligo and his wife, the daughter of Sir John Stuart of Fettercairn, who was Sir Walter Scott's first love. He was privately educated and originally destined for a legal career, but turned to science, for which he had some aptitude. Forbes made some important contributions to the early study of radiant heat.

16 *Cf.* MS. Correspondence in library of the Institution of Civil Engineers, London.

17 Quoted, Charles E. Lee, 'Centenary of the London Motor Omnibus', *Trans. Newcomen Society*, vol. xiii, 1932–33, London, 1934, p. 137.

18 John Head, 'Steam Locomotives on Common Roads', *Mins. Proc. I.C.E.*, vol. xxxvi, April 8, 1873, p. 50.

19 J. Scott Russell, *op. cit.*

20 J. Scott Russell, 'On the Late Mr. John Wood and Mr Charles Wood, Naval Architects of Port Glasgow', *Trans. I.N.A.*, 1861, p. 145.

21 *Ibid.*, pp. 145–6.

22 J. Scott Russell, *The Modern System*, vol. i, p. 208.

23 *Ibid.*, p. xxvi.

24 Reported in the *Liverpool Albion*.

25 *Memoirs of Mr Charles J. Yellowplush.*

26 *Cf.* 'Testimony to Steam Navigation to India', *Edinburgh Review*, 1835, pp. 246–7.

27 L. T. C. Rolt, *op. cit.*, p. 191.

28 Jan. 1, 1836, Bristol Coll.

29 *The Times*, Aug. 24, 1836.

30 *Ibid.*, Sat. Aug. 27, 1836.

31 L. T. C. Rolt, *op. cit.*, p. 85.

32 *Trans. I.N.A.*, 1882, p. 259.

33 J. Scott Russell, 'Elementary Considerations of some Principles in the Construction of Buildings', *Edinburgh New Philosophical Journal*, vol. xxvii, pp. 131–6. 'On the Application of our Knowledge of the Laws of Sound to the Construction of Buildings', B.A. *Report*, 1843, pp. 96–8.

34 Other referees were: Sir Thomas Macdougal Brisbane, Pres. R.S.Ed.; Sir John Robison; Robert Jameson, Professor of Natural History, Univ. of Edinburgh; Davies Gilbert, Vice-Pres., R. S. London; Rev. Thomas Chalmers, D.D., etc.; Rev. William Muir, D.D., F.R.S.Ed.; Students— J. W. Lubbock, John Campbell, M.D., F.R.C.S.E.; J. W. Semple and Sir W. A. Seton, Mem. Fac. Advocates; David Hunter, Deputy-Lieut., County of Forfar; John Scott, M.D.; James Hay, Secy. Mechanics Institute, Leith.

35 *Hutcheson's Greenock Register Directory*, 1841–2.

36 Robert M. Smith, *History of Greenock*, Greenock, 1921, p. 206.

37 James Napier, *Life of Robert Napier*, London 1912, p. 43, and J. Scott Russell, 'The Wave Line Principle of Ship Construction', *Trans. I.N.A.*, vol. i, 1860, p. 185.

38 J. E. Wilmot, *Thomas Assheton Smith, The Reminiscences of a Famous Fox Hunter*, London, 1859, pp. 155–8 and J. Scott Russell, *The Modern System*, vol. i, p. xxvi.

39 J. Scott Russell, *The Modern System*, vol. i, p. xxvi.

40 J. Scott Russell, *On Very Large Ships*, London, 1863, p. 17.

41 *Ibid.*, p. 18.

42 J. Scott Russell, 'On the Vibration of Suspension Bridges', *Edinburgh New Philosophical Journal*, vol. xxvi, pp. 386–95.

43 J. Scott Russell, *A Treatise on the Steam Engine*, Edinburgh, 1846.

44 Sir George Holmes, for many years secretary of the Institution of Naval Architects, remarked in the obituary he wrote for the *Proc. I.C.E.*, vol. lxxxvii (p. 431) that

References

the numerous plates which illustrated the report on waves, along with some of the results, were in the care of the Institution. These appear to have been lost or misplaced; but a copy of the 'Report on Waves, made to the meeting of the British Association, 1842–3', printed by Richard and John E. Taylor, 1845, is to be found in the Scott Collection (item 665) in the I.N.A. library, and in the Admiralty library.

45 J. Scott Russell, 'On an Indicator of Speed of Steam Vessels', *B.A. Reports*, 1842.
46 J. Scott Russell, 'Marine Salinometer for Indicating the Density of Brine in the Boilers of Marine Engines', *Royal Scot. Soc. Arts*, Feb. 28, 1842.

2. THE FLOWER OF CITIES ALL

1 Letter, Rachel Scott Russell to Arthur Sullivan, Jan. 1868.
2 Sir Henry Trueman Wood, *The History of the Royal Society of Arts*, London, 1913, p. 454, fn. 1 for details. W. F. Cooke, d. 1879, well known in connection with the electric telegraph. Thomas Webster, Q.C., d. 1875, eminent patent lawyer, father of Sir R. Webster, Attorney-General. Francis Fuller, d. 1887, a leading London property agent. Thomas Winkworth, d. 1865, partner in firm of Winkworth and Proctor, silk brokers.
3 Sir Henry Trueman Wood, *op. cit.*, p. 362.
4 Min. Comm. (Misc.), July 23, 1845, Royal Society of Arts.
5 Sir Henry Trueman Wood, *op. cit.*
6 Henry Cole, *Fifty Years of Public Work*, London, 1884, vol. i, p. 71.
7 Henry Cole, *Diary* (MS. Victoria and Albert Mus.).
8 *Ibid.*, Nov. 13, 1845.
9 *Ibid.*
10 *Ibid.*, March 6, 1846.
11 *Ibid.*, Dec. 10, 1845.
12 *Ibid.*, Feb. 13, 1846.
13 *Ibid.*, Aug. 3, 1846.
14 *Ibid.*, Aug. 5, 1846.
15 Henry Cole, *Fifty Years* ... vol. i, p. 106.
16 Robert Small, *History of the Congregations of The United Presbyterian Church*, Edinburgh, 1904.
    The Rev. David Russell was incapacitated from about 1846 and was admitted an annuitant on the fund for aged and infirm ministers from 1854, when he was 69.
17 Henry Cole, *Diary*, June 18, 1847.
18 *Cf.* Henry Cole, Diary for years 1846–1870s.
19 Henry Cole, *Diary*, Aug. 5, 1847.
20 Min. Council, July 5, 1848.
21 Henry Cole, *Diary*, Feb. 8, 1848.
22 B.A. Report, 1849.
23 Henry Cole, *Diary*, June 15, 1848.
24 Henry Cole, *Fifty Years* ..., vol. i, p. 93.
25 J. Scott Russell, *Statement of Proceedings Preliminary to the Exhibition of Industry of All Nations 1851*, p. 1. MS. papers relating to the Great Exhibition, Society of Arts.
26 Henry Cole, *Fifty Years* ..., vol. i, pp. 119–21.
27 The deputation comprised J. Scott Russell, Henry Cole, Sir J. P. Boileau, G. Bailey (Curator of the Soane Museum), P. Le Neve Foster, and J. S. Lefevre (Asst. Secy. B.O.T.).

28 *Jour. Royal Soc. Arts*, Nov. 6, 1896, p. 902, and Scott Russell Collection, Royal Society of Arts.
29 Henry Cole, *Fifty Years...*, vol. i, p. 126. Fuller's father-in-law, G. Drew, was a director of J. and G. Munday, building contractors.

In a report read to a general meeting of the Society of Arts, Feb. 8, 1850, Russell presented the early history of the Exhibition. Another primary source is the official illustrated catalogue of the 1862 Exhibition, mainly founded on Russell's report. A valuable collection of documents on the subject was purchased by the Society from Russell's family after his death.
30 Henry Cole, *Fifty Years...*, vol. i, p. 123.
31 Henry Cole, *Diary*, July 6, 1849.
32 George P. Mabon, 'John Scott Russell and Henry Cole: Aspects of a Personal Rivalry', *Jour. Royal Soc. Arts*, March 1967, p. 301.
33 Fuller's account, Scott Russell Collection, vol. ii, Royal Society of Arts.
34 J. Scott Russell, *op. cit.*, vol. i, p. 64. The italics are Russell's.
35 Henry Cole, *Diary*, July 14, 1849.
36 Letter, Phipps to Russell, Aug. 3, 1849, Royal Soc. Arts Coll.
37 There were several generations of C. W. Dilkes. The 'younger', referred to here, was the son of C. W. Dilke (born 1789), the editor of *The Athenaeum* and *Daily News*, and close friend of Keats, Lamb, etc., with whom Russell and Cole were associated. To differentiate between the two Dilkes, the son was called 'Wentworth'. His own eldest son, who continued the name, was born in 1843 and became an important politician whose career was checked by a successful conspiracy to frame him as the co-respondent in a notorious divorce case. Wentworth became a great man for exhibitions and served for a term as president of the Royal Society of Arts.
38 Letter, Phipps to Russell, Nov. 24, 1849, *loc. cit.*
39 Henry Cole, *Diary*, Dec. 12, 1849.
40 Fuller's account, Scott Russell Collection, *loc. cit.* vol. ii, p. 584.
41 Henry Cole, *Diary*, Jan. 1, 1850.
42 *Ibid.*
43 *Ibid.*
44 *Ibid.*
45 *Ibid.*, Jan. 2, 1850.
46 *Ibid.*, Nov. 19, 1846; Nov. 23, 1846; Nov. 24, 1846.
47 *Ibid.*, Mon. Dec. 7, 1846.
48 Henry Cole, *Fifty Years...*, vol. 1, p. 193.
49 Henry Cole, *Diary*, Jan. 7, 1850.
50 *Ibid. Crotchet Castle*, by Thomas Love Peacock, 1831. Cole knew Peacock and had rented Peacock's London house in 1823. He was later, 1874, to edit a collected edition of Peacock's novels.
51 Henry Cole, *Fifty Years....*, vol. 1, p. 155.
52 Webster's letter to the Council of the Society of Arts, March 29, 1850.
53 Min. Council, Jan. 23, 1850, and Trueman Wood, p. 359.
54 *Jour. Royal Soc. Arts*, Nov. 6, 1896, p. 902.
55 Henry Cole, *Diary*, Jan. 26, 1850.
56 *Ibid.*, Jan. 30, 1850.
57 *Ibid.*, March 7, 1850.
58 *Ibid.*, March 15, 1850.
59 *Ibid.*, April 15, 1850.
60 He makes no mention of it in his Memoirs.
61 Henry Cole, *Diary*, May 8, 1850.

References

62 Quentin Bell, *The Schools of Design*, London, 1963, p. 234.

63 Royal Commission for the Exhibition of 1851, manuscript letters, vol. ii, no. 96 (Victoria and Albert Museum).

64 Henry Cole, *Diary*, July 17, 1850.

65 *Ibid.*

66 *Ibid.*, May 15, 1850.

67 *Ibid.*, June 11, 1850.

68 *Ibid.*, June 25 and 26, 1850, and Wemyss Reid, *Memoirs of Lyon Playfair*, London, 1899, pp. 114–15.

69 Henry Cole, *Diary*, July 4, 1850.

70 Wemyss Reid, *op. cit.*, p. 114.

71 Chapter Two. See also K. J. Fielding, 'Charles Dickens and the Department of Practical Art', *Modern Language Review*, xlviii (1953), pp. 270–7.

72 Trueman Wood, *op. cit.*, p. 359.

73 Henry Cole, *Diary*, Oct. 16, 1851.

74 Henry Cole, *Fifty Years...*, vol. i, p. 199.

75 Lord Granville makes the remark: 'Mr Scott Russell has drawn his portion of the salary now due—and he is well paid considering that he only attends on *state* occasions.' Royal Commission for the Exhibition of 1851, manuscript letters, vol. v, n. 57 (Victoria and Albert Mus.).

76 Quoted by Nathaniel Barnaby, *Naval Development in the Century*, London, 1902, p. 279.

3. PRELUDE TO FAME

1 Letter to *The Times*, Aug. 28, 1851, p. 6.

2 J. Phipps, M.D., 'On the Sailing Power of two Yachts built on the Wave Principle', *B.A. Report*, 1846, p. 112.

The second of the wave-line yachts drafted by Dr Phipps was the *Enchantress*, a cutter of 45 tons, built by Peasley near Cork. So far, this was the largest sailing vessel of any importance to be constructed on the wave principle. Hitherto the applications had been chiefly to steam vessels. Fishbourne wrote that the seagoing qualities of the *Enchantress* were first tested in the English Channel in 1845 during rough weather and that her performance was such that 'all the unfavourable opinions to which the novelty of form gave rise, were speedily corrected; as it was found that she pitched, scended, and rolled far less, and was drier than others of her class.... She was also found to steer and work with remarkable ease and quickness, which, from her full after-body and fine fore-body, was not generally expected.... The superior speed of the *Enchantress* was first fully displayed in the great match at Kingstown, in July, 1846, where she had to compete with a large number of the best yachts of England, Scotland, and Ireland,—for the Hundred Guinea Cup.... Sixteen yachts entered for the race, nine of which started, and after a course of forty miles, she won the race by beating the *Sultana* of 100 tons, by 21 minutes.... The superior power of the *Enchantress* during the race was so manifest, that doubts were raised as to her real size, which was said to be much beyond her entered tonnage, but on a measurement by the arbiters, her tonnage was found to be only $44\frac{82}{94}$ tons; so that the prize was at once awarded.'

E. Gardiner Fishbourne, *Lectures on Naval Architecture*, London, 1846, fn. pp. xi–xii.

3 J. Scott Russell, *The Modern System*, vol. i, p. 613.

4 J. R. Napier, 'Sections of Least Resistance for ships of limited breadth and limited draft of water', *Glas. Philos. Soc.*, 1864.

References

5 *Cf.* Boyd Cable, 'The World's First Clipper', *The Mariner's Mirror*, vol. 29, n. 2, April 1943, pp. 66–91.
   John Lyman, 'The *Scottish Maid* as "The World's First Clipper"', *ibid.*, pp. 194–9.
6 John Lyman, *op. cit.*, p. 198.
7 *Scientific American*, May 15, 1852, p. 280.
8 J. Scott Russell, *The Modern System*, vol. i, p. xxvi.
9 To the B.A. in 1843, see *The Athenaeum*, Sept. 9, 1843, p. 830.
10 John W. Griffiths, *A Treatise on Marine and Naval Architecture* (new edition), London, 1857, pp. 74–5.
11 *Scientific American*, May 15, 1852, p. 280.
12 *B.A. Report*, 1849, p. 31.
13 *Ibid.*
14 David R. Gregor, *Fast Sailing Ships*, London, 1973, pp. 193, 256.
15 J. Scott Russell, *The Modern System*, vol. i, p. 63.
16 *Ibid.*
17 John Lyman, *op. cit.*, p. 196.
18 Boyd Cable, *op. cit.*
19 Colin Archer, 'On the Wave Principle applied to the Longitudinal Disposition of Immersed Volume', *Trans. I.N.A.*, 1878, pp. 218–29.
20 J. Scott Russell, 'On the True Nature of the Wave of Translation', *Trans. I.N.A.*, 1879, p. 86.
21 *Trans. I.N.A.*, 1880, p. 181.
22 J. S. Russell to I. K. Brunel, Feb. 16, 1852. Holl. Coll.
23 *Mechanics Magazine*, 1839, p. 432.
24 Ewan Corlett, *The Iron Ship*, Bradford-on-Avon, 1975, pp. 18–19.
25 *Ibid.*
26 *The Practical Mechanic and Engineer's Magazine*, vol. ii, Glasgow, 1843, p. 443.
27 *The Times*, Nov. 13, 1852, p. 5.
28 *Trans. I.N.A.*, vol. i, 1860, pp. 88–9.
29 Letters, Russell to Brunel, April 28 and May 11, 1852. Holl. Coll.
30 J. Scott Russell, *The Modern System*, vol. i, p. 622.
31 *The Times*, Nov. 22, 1852, p. 8.
32 The 'balanced' rudder, as it was called, was used by Brunel on the *Great Britain*, it may even have been invented by him. It ran into much criticism but was successfully re-introduced by E. J. Reed.
33 Letter to *The Times*, April 2, 1853, p. 8.
34 A curious letter in *The Times*, April 5, 1853, p. 7, tells of a mishap at the launch of the *Adelaide*'s sister ship...'Sir, In a leading article of *The Times* of this day, upon the Australian Screw Company, you say that the *Victoria* is not launched. Allow me to say that is an error, as I saw her last Monday lying off Scott, Russell, and Co.'s premises in the Thames, and a person in the steamer I was in said she was launched on Saturday, the 26th of March, and, having too much way on her, she ran into a Government vessel lying on the opposite side of the river; so that she does not begin her career very auspiciously. Not having seen any account of the launch in the papers, I suppose the builders or directors of the company wished to keep the event to themselves at present.'
35 J. Scott Russell, *The Modern System*, vol. i, p. 617.
36 L. T. C. Rolt, *op. cit.*, fn. p. 237.
37 *Pioneer, Vifredo, Lady Berriedale, Eagle* and *Nightingale*.

References

4. THE GREAT EASTERN

1 Bristol Coll., p. 16.
2
3 I.K.B. to Yates, June 16, 1852, Holl. Coll. and I. Brunel, *The Life of Isambard Kingdom Brunel*, London, 1870, p. 292.
4 Yates to I.K.B. (Brunel), June 16, 1852. Holl. Coll.
5 Bristol Coll., p. 16.
6 Reproduced, I. Brunel, *op. cit.*, pp. 296–7.
7 Letter to Russell, I. Brunel, *op. cit.*, p. 294.
8 Russell wrote: 'To support the great weight of machinery and boilers in the centre of the vessel, the American builders appear to have regarded their vessels as a sort of wooden bridge, resting on two liquid buttresses towards each extremity, and loaded with a great weight in the centre; and in this view they seem to have introduced into their vessels all the mechanical structures which the resources of terrene carpentry and civil engineering present in the construction of arches, wooden trusses, and iron suspension bridges, which extend along the vessel, transferring the proper proportion of the strain to those parts of it which are most distant from the load.' 'Steam Navigation', from *Encyclopaedia Britannica*, 1841, reprint of 1865.
9 Bristol Coll., p. 18.
10 'I. K. Brunel submitted tenders he had received from parties desirous of constructing the ships and engines for the Company.' Yates—E.S.N. Co., May 18, 1853. Holl. Coll.
11 Report on Tender, May 18, 1853, Isambard Brunel, *op. cit.*, pp. 302–3.
12 Bristol Coll., pp. 18–20, and Holl. Coll.
13 Account by I. K. Brunel, Bristol Coll., Feb. 25, 1854, p. 20.
14 J. Scott Russell, *Very Large Ships*, London, 1863, pp. 20–1.
15 *The Times*, Sept. 12 and 13, 1853.
16 *Ibid.*, Feb. 13, 1856, p. 10.
17 Andrew Henderson, 'On the Speed and other Properties of Ocean Steamers...', *Proc. I.C.E.*, Nov. 8, 1853.
18 *Ibid.*, p. 52.
19 I.K.B. to Manby, Nov. 21, 1853. Bristol Coll.
20 J.S.R. (Russell) to I.K.B., Feb. 24, 1854. Holl. Coll.
21 Bristol Coll., p. 242.
22 Holl. Coll.
23 Bristol Coll., p. 24.
24 *Ibid.*, p. 26.
25 *Trans. I.N.A.*, 1877, p. 343.
26 Charles H. Jordan, 'Some Historical Records...', *Lloyd's Register Staff Assoc. Trans.*, vol. v, 1924–5.
27 J. Scott Russell, *The Modern System*, vol. i, p. 632. Russell tells us that the friction clutch he describes for disconnecting the paddle shaft was invented by Humphreys, but the device by which the engine itself was used to tighten or loosen the clutch was due to Russell. It was not fitted to the *Great Eastern*'s paddle engines as intended, although it is to be seen on the model presented by Russell to the Science Museum, London. This clutch was first installed in the *Victoria* and *Adelaide*.
28 J. Scott Russell, *Modern System*, vol. i, pp. 516–17.
29 I. Brunel, *op. cit.*, pp. 313–14.
30 *Trans. B.A.*, 1854, Mech. Section, p. 161.

31 J.S.R. to E.S.N. Co., Dec. 28, 1854, Holl. Coll.
32 Jordan, *op. cit.*, p. 12.
33 Directors' Report, E.S.N. Co., Feb. 1855.
34 Letter, Phipps to Russell, March 24, 1855, Royal Soc. Arts.
35 J. Scott Russell, *Modern System*, vol. i, p. xxvii. See also Letter, Coles to *The Times*, April 5, 1862.
36 Yates to I.K.B. Holl. Coll.
37 I have taken Bauer's account from Fritz Scheffel, *Der Brandtaucher*, Wilhelm Bauer, Leipzig, 1941, pp. 94–133.

    Murray F. Sueter, *The Evolution of the Submarine Boat Mine and Torpedo*, 2nd edn. London, 1908, p. 39; also, Louis Hauf, *La Navigation Sous-maree*; *Les Bateaux Sous-marins*, Munich, 1859.
38 Dr Payerne designed and built about four submersibles in the period 1846–56, one of which bore some resemblance to Russell's and was used successfully in the harbour works at Cherbourg.
39 Derby Papers, Box 145/3, Victoria & Albert Museum.
40 Murray F. Sueter, *op. cit.*, p. 40.
41 Nathaniel Barnaby, *Naval Development in the Century*, London, 1902, p. 167.
42 Holl. Coll.
43 *Ibid.*
44 *Ibid.*
45 Holl. Coll., May 9, 1855.
46 I.K.B. to J.S.R., May 9, 1855, Holl. Coll.
47 J.S.R. to I.K.B., June 7, 1855, Holl. Coll.
48 *Ibid.*, May 29, 1855.
49 I. K. Brunel, *Report to Proprietors*, Feb. 5, 1855, Bristol Coll., p. 259.
50 Brunel Calculation Book, Bristol Coll., p. 1, Jan. 20, 1854.
51 Bristol Coll., p. 267.
52 L. T. C. Rolt writes: 'But it soon became evident that "Mr. R's" concurrence was so much lip service,' *op. cit.*, p. 253.
53 I.K.B. to Blake, Bristol Coll., p. 269.
54 E.S.N. Co. Directors' Report, Feb. 19, 1856.
55 I.K.B. to J.S.R., July 10, 1855, Bristol Coll., p. 268.
56 Bristol Coll., p. 270.
57 Quoted, L. T. C. Rolt, *op. cit.*, p. 253.
58 J.S.R. to I.K.B., Holl. Coll.

    The details were:

    By September 1—completion of the upper outside of the ship throughout seven of the eleven 60 ft compartments. By October 1—double bottom completed throughout some seven compartments, ready to receive both engines and their boilers. Upper deck completed to shelter the middle compartments and proceed with interior fittings and cabins. By November 1—top sides of ship and upper iron deck completed to extreme bulkheads. By December 1—entire upper works of ship completed and boilers and engines aboard. By January 1—double outer skin completed over seven middle compartments to allow launching ways to be prepared under that part of ship. On the remainder of the outer skin, 'work shall proceed at eight different places. Masting and rigging may commence on stocks.'

    The stern work included the screw bearings and 'the spare rudder'.
59 Holl. Coll.
60 J.S.R. to I.K.B., Sept. 29, 1865, Holl. Coll.
61 I.K.B. to J.S.R., Holl. Coll.

62 J.S.R. to I.K.B., Holl. Coll.
63 *Ibid.*, Oct. 13, 1855.
64 I.K.B. to J.S.R., Bristol Coll., p, 272.
65 Parl. Papers, vol. xl, 1856, p. 429.
66 J. Scott Russell, *Very Large Ships*, p. 26.
67 Letter, Phipps to Russell, Nov. 19, 1855, Royal Society of Arts. Russell's mother-in-law, then a widow, died on Nov. 17.
68 Bristol Coll., p. 284.
69 Memorandum as to launching for J. S. Russell, 30 Nov. 1855, Bristol Coll., pp. 276–7.
70 *Ibid*, p. 277.
71 Dec. 4, 1855, *ibid*, p. 254.
72 Edward J. Reed believed that J. R. Napier arrived at the same technique almost simultaneously.
   Shipbuilding in Iron and Steel, London, 1869, p. 183. See also Westcott Abel, *The Shipwright's Trade*, London, p. 119, 1948.
73 J.S.R. to I.K.B., Dec. 24, 1855, Holl. Coll.
74 I.K.B. to J.S.R., Jan. 9, 1856, Bristol Coll.
75 J.S.R. to I.K.B., Jan. 11, 1856, Holl. Coll.
76 'I lately let part of my premises at Millwall to Mr Scott Russell for the purpose of building a monster steamer, which I expect will turn out the most successful steam speculation that has yet been tried.'
   David Napier (1790–1869): An Autobiographical Sketch, Glasgow, 1912, p. 22. *Cf.* also p. 48.
77 I.K.B. to Yates, Jan. 10, 1856. Yates to I.K.B., Jan. 14, 1856 Bristol Coll.
78 Parl. Papers, vol. viii, 1860, and vol. xxxviii, 1861.
79 *Ibid.*, vol. viii, 1860, p. 5.
80 Edgar C. Smith, *A Short History of Naval and Marine Engineering*, Cambridge, 1937, p. 123.
81 See Philip Banbury, *Shipbuilders of the Thames and Medway*, Newton Abbot, 1971.
82 *Cf.* also Chas. H. Jordan, *op. cit.*, pp. 8 and 9.
83 Copy of Draft to E.S.N. Co., Jan. 16, 1856, Holl. Coll.
84 *Ibid.*
85 Bull to Brunel, Bristol Coll.
86 Letter from Yates to I. K. Brunel, Feb. 18, 1856, Holl. Coll.
87 *Ibid.*, and Directors' Report, *The Times*, Feb. 20, 1856.
88 Quoted, L. T. C. Rolt, *op. cit.*, p. 254.
89 *Ibid.*, p. 256.
90 *Ibid.*
91 Letter from C. H. Freshfield to I.K.B., Jan. 24, 1856, Holl. Coll.
92 L. T. C. Rolt, *op. cit.*, p. 257.
93 Report of Directors of E.S.N. Co., Feb. 19, 1856.

5. THE LEVIATHAN LANGUISHES

1 Yates to I.K.B., Feb. 18, 1856, Holl. Coll.
2 Report of Directors of E.S.N. Co., Feb. 19, 1856.
3 Yates to I.K.B., Feb. 18, 1856, Holl. Coll.
4 *The Times*, Feb. 13, 1856, p. 11.
5 *Ibid.*
6 Report to Shareholders, Feb. 1856.

References

7   Correspondence, Bristol Coll.
8   *The Times*, March 14, 1856, p. 8.
9   Holl. Coll.
10 Parl. Papers, vol. xxxviii, 1861, p. 162.
11 Yates to I.K.B., March 25, 1856, Holl. Coll.
12 J.S.R. to I.K.B., March 27, 1856, Holl. Coll.
13 Holl. Coll.
14 Quoted, L. T. C. Rolt, *op. cit.*, p. 260.
15 Holl. Coll.
16 *Ibid.*
17 J.S.R. to I.K.B., April 28, 1856, Holl. Coll.
18 *Ibid.*, May 2, 1856.
19 *The Great Eastern Steamship, The Past—Present*, pub. G. Vickers of Angel Court,
    Strand, 1858, quoted by L. T. C. Rolt, *op. cit.*, p. 262.
20 *The Times*, April 24, 1856, p. 6.
21 J.S.R. to I.K.B., July 25, 1856, Holl. Coll.
22 I.K.B. to J.S.R., Aug. 25, 1856, Holl. Coll.
23 J.S.R. to I.K.B., Aug. 21, 1856, Holl. Coll.
24 I.K.B. to J.S.R., Aug. 25, 1856, Holl. Coll.
25 J.S.R. to I.K.B., Aug. 30, 1856, Holl. Coll.
26 Holl. Coll.
27 I.K.B. to E.S.N. Co., Sept. 15, 1856, Holl. Coll.
28 Yates to I.K.B., Sept. 15, 1856, Holl. Coll.
29 J.S.R. to I.K.B., Sept. 16, 1856, Holl. Coll.
30 E.S.N. Co. to J.S.R., Sept. 24, 1856, Holl. Coll.
31 Draft Report, Oct. 7 (or Oct 2), 1856, Holl. Coll.
32 Yates to I.K.B., Oct. 3, 1856, Holl. Coll.
33 Yates to I. K. B., Oct. 14, 1856, Holl. Coll.
34 F. R. Conder, *Personal Recollections of English Engineers*, London, 1868, pp. 260–
    261.
35 Draft letter to Directors, Oct. 1856, Holl. Coll.
36 *The Times*, Feb. 19 & 20, 1857.
37 Pub. H. G. Clarke & Co., 252 Strand, London, (British Museum).
38 W. S. Lindsay, *History of Merchant Shipping and Ancient Commerce*, London, 1876.
39 Quoted L. T. C. Rolt, *op. cit.*, p. 264.
40 Robert Stephenson was no more generous to his colleagues than Brunel. He caused
    a furore among engineers and scientists, around the year 1850, by arrogating to him-
    self sole credit for the Britannia Bridge tube which owed its form and feasibility
    to the practical knowledge and investigations of William Fairbairn and Prof. Hodg-
    kinson.
        The issue was even the subject of discussion at the B.A. meeting of 1850. The
    facts were that Stephenson, faced with the need for a long rigid span to carry steam
    locomotives, had the idea of using a long oval iron tube but had no idea of its feasi-
    bility nor of the proper design of such a structure. He therefore referred it to Fair-
    bairn who, with Hodgkinson's analytical help, conducted the requisite experiments
    and developed the best form of tube for the purpose and application involved. It
    was in this task that Hodgkinson re-discovered the nature of the stress distribution
    over the cross-section of a beam in bending, including the conception and location
    of the neutral axis.
41 Russell made an offer to lease, or purchase, that portion of the land which was not
    already being used by the E.S.N. Co. David Napier, who was on very good terms

with Russell, had gone over the Great Ship during Russell's absence a short time before, and seems to have come to the conclusion that the land would be needed for the larger Great Eastern which he was convinced would be wanted before the first one had completed half-a-dozen voyages. Since he wished to give such an enterprise every facility, he accepted Russell's offer although he said he could have had more for the land. *David Napier...op. cit.*, p. 49.

42 Bristol Coll., Aug. 29, 1857.
43 Yates to I.K.B., *ibid.*
44 *The Times*, Oct. 24, 28, 29, 1857.
45 I.K.B. to S. Baker, Nov. 9, 1857, Bristol Coll., pp. 356–8.
46 This includes the weight of the engines, boilers, fittings, etc.
47 I. Brunel, *op, cit.*, p. 385.
48 I.K.B. to S. Baker, Nov. 9, 1857.
49 *Ibid.*
50 Jordan, *op. cit.*, p. 10.
51 Letter, Phipps to Russell, Nov. 6, 1857, Royal Soc. Arts.
52 I.K.B. to Yates, Nov. 22, 1858, Bristol Coll., p. 121.
53 Among them were Brunel, Hope, Yates, Lord Dufferin and Mr Bentinck, M.P.
54 J. Scott Russell, *Complete System*, vol. i, p. xxxii.

6. COMPLETION OF THE GREAT EASTERN

1 I.K.B. to Directors of the E.S.N. Co., March 23, 1858, Bristol Coll., p. 40.
2 I.K.B. to Fowler, March 23, 1858, Bristol Coll., pp. 37–8.
3 I.K.B. to E.L. Betts, March 18, 1858, Bristol Coll., p. 32.
4 *Ibid.*
5 Prospectus, May 22, 1958, British Transport Archives.
6 *The Times*, Aug. 11, 1858.
7 *Ibid.*, July 21, 1858.
8 *Ibid.*, July 22, 1858.
9 *Ibid.*, Nov. 25, 1858, p. 7.
10 *Ibid.*
11 *Ill. Times*, Jan. 29, 1859, p. 67.
12 *The Times*, April 26, 1861, p. 12.
13 I. Brunel, *op. cit.*, p. 393.
14 *New York Times*, Sept. 23, 1859, p. 1.
15 *Ibid.*, Oct. 26, 1859, p. 1.
16 *The Times*, Aug. 22, 1859, pp. 4–5.
17 *Ibid.*, Aug. 9, 1859, p. 4.
18 *Ibid.*
19 Rolt, *op. cit.*, gives an account of the speech which, he alleges, was widely published in the newspapers. It certainly was not published in *The Times*.
20 *The Times*, Aug. 22, 1859, pp. 4–5.
21 *Ibid.*, Aug. 22, 1859, p. 5.
22 *Ibid.*, Aug. 27, 1859, p. 10.
23 *Ibid.*, Sept. 8, 1859, p. 7.
24 *Ibid.*
25 *New York Times*, Sept. 23, 1859, p. 1.
26 *Illustrated London News*, Sept. 17, 1859.
27 *The Times*, Sept. 19, 1859, p. 9.
28 *Ibid.*

29 *Ill. Times*, Sept. 17, 1859, p. 198.
30 *The Engineer*, Sept. 23, 1859, p. 228.
31 *The Times*, Sept. 19, 1859, p. 9.
32 Patterson to Claxton, Bristol Coll.
33 *The Times*, Dec. 14, 1859.
34 *New York Times*, Oc. 26, 1859, p. 1.
35 *Ibid.*, Oct. 25, 1859, p. 1.
36 *Ibid.*, Oct. 26, 1859, p. 1.
37 *Ibid.*, Oct. 25, 1859, p. 1.
38 *Ibid.*
39 *New York Times*, Oct. 26, 1859, p. 1.
40 *Ibid.*
41 *Ibid.*
42 *The Times*, Nov. 28, 1859, p. 5.
43 *Ibid.*, Oct. 18, 1859, p. 7.
44 *Ibid.*, Nov. 3, 1859, p. 9.
45 *Ibid.*, Dec. 10, 1859.
46 *Ibid.*, Dec. 14, 1859.
47 *Ibid.*, Jan. 12, 1860, p. 9.
48 *New York Times*, Feb. 6, 1860, p. 2.
49 *Ibid.*
50 *The Times*, Jan. 3, 1860, p. 7.
51 *Ibid.*, Jan. 12, 1860, p. 7.
52 *New York Times*, Feb. 6, 1860, p. 2.
53 *Ibid.*, Jan. 31, 1860, p. 8.
54 *Ibid.*, Feb. 6, 1860, p. 2.
55 *The Times*, April 7, 1860, p. 9.
56 *Ibid.*, Feb. 8, 1860, p. 10.

7. THE IRON WARSHIP

1 J. Scott Russell, *Modern System*, plate XLIX.
2 Philip Banbury, *op. cit.* p. 249.
3 Admiral G. A. Ballard, 'British Battleships of 1870', *The Mariner's Mirror*, vol. 16, 1930, p. 170.
4 See Nathaniel Barnaby, *Naval Development in the Century*, p. 64, for details of these.
5 *Trans. I.N.A.*, 1869, p, 78.
6 *Ibid.*, 1870.
7 Letter Book, no. 20, June 17, 1859; Adm. 12/669, 59–I.
8 'I submitted designs of vessels with sharp bows for speed, with shot-proof coating amidships, with transverse backing, with all their guns on one deck, and with a deck overhead, forming the corvette class, or frigate of single deck, to which all the present designs belong; and I continued my designs through all the various sizes down to the present day.' J. Scott Russell, *Trans. I.N.A.*, 1861, p. 21.
9 *Trans. I.N.A.*, 1861, p. 21. Russell later declared: 'It is understood that the *Warrior* class was invented and created jointly between the Controller's Department and myself. We have agreed to say that we are joint and equal owners in the credit and discredit which may be attached to the *Warrior* class—I mean, as technical men.' *Trans. I.N.A.*, 1869, p. 77.
10 See 'Copy of correspondence between the Admiralty and the contractors who built

References

the *Warrior*, in reference to the non-fulfilment of their contract within the stipulated time', *Parliamentary Papers*, 1861, vol. xxxviii, no. 207.

11 'The Duke [Somerset] knew he was inviting and accepting impossible tenders, because I know that his technical officers were thoroughly aware of the fact.' Thus the Duke was enabled to reassure an impatient Parliament that a powerful iron fleet would be ready 'at such and such a required date . . . *because* the contractors had undertaken at those dates to deliver those ships.' Then, ready or not, the ships were launched to maintain the deception of forwardness, and were completed in the dockyards while blame was laid on the too facile contractor whose breach of contract left him in the Admiralty's power.' J. Scott Russell, *The Fleet of the Future*, pp. 50–1.

The *Warrior* was a year overdue, the *Black Prince*, 10 months. Penalty in each case was £50,000. *British Sessional Papers*, vol. xxxiii, p. 389.

12 *Proc. I.C.E.*, 1861, p. 417.

13 Charles H. Jordan, 'Some Historical Records . . .', *Lloyd's Staff Assoc. Trans.*, vol. 5, p. 13.

14 The smaller pair—*Snipe* and *Sparrow*, launched in May and June 1860; and the larger—*Eclipse* and *Lily*—September 1860 and February 1861.

15 J. Scott Russell, *Modern System*, vol. i, p. 629. Brunel submitted sketches of an armoured gunfloat together with a model of it constructed by Russell's model-maker, to the Admiralty in 1854. Brunel said it was inspired by Russell's drawings and models of his Prussian gunboats. I.K.B.–J.S.R., July 26, 1854, Bristol Coll.

16 Sir William White, *An Epitome of the History of the Institution of Naval Architects*, 1911.

17 *Cf.* Nathaniel Barnaby, *op. cit.*

18 *Modern System*, vol. 1, p. 638.

19 *Cf. Trans. I.N.A.*, 1862, p. 166.

20 *Trans. I.N.A.*, 1880, p. 180.

21 J. P. Baxter, *The Introduction of the Ironclad Warship*, Cambridge, Mass., 1933 and 1968, p. 191.

22 *Ibid.*, p. 188.

23 *Trans. I.N.A.*, 1868, p. 219; 1872, p. 34.

also: J. Scott Russell, *The Fleet of the Future* (ii), London, 1862, pp. 46–7; and *Modern System*, vol. i, p. 562.

24 Jordan, *op. cit.*, p. 14. Many rather interesting people served their apprenticeship in Russell's yard. Probably the most curious was Byron Noel King, Viscount Ockham, eldest son of the Earl of Lovelace and Ada, Byron's daughter. His mother was an amateur mathematician and friend of Babbage. He worked in the pattern and fitting shops under the name John Okey. The story goes that he led a dissolute life at Millwall and died there in disreputable circumstances; but there is more to it than that. His father, a self-taught architect and engineer, was a tyrant much hated by his three sons. He sent the eldest, a dreamy, silent child, into the Navy from which he deserted after many vicissitudes. He sought refuge with friends of his grandmother Lady Byron and found a job in Russell's employ. He died of tuberculosis in 1862 (Mary Lovelace [Countess], *Ralph, Earl of Lovelace*, London, 1920, pp. 6–7.).

Other apprentices were Ernest Benedict, the eldest son of Sir Julius Benedict the composer and teacher of piano at the Crystal Palace; William Walker, eldest son of the celebrated London engraver; Thomas Ridley Oswald, a noted shipbuilder in Sunderland and Southampton; and Charles H. Jordan, compiler of Lloyd's *Tabulated Weights of Iron and Steel* which ran to eight or so editions.

Russell named his personal assistants as Robert Pollock, Robert Wilson, John

References

Dickson, 'Mr Hepworth', Morgan Davies, 'Mr. Smith', B. Jensen, George Wright and A. W. Yates.

25 See *The Times*, Feb. 10, 11, 24; March 6, 7, 8, 10, 13, 1862.
26 The design of the *Annette* is discussed in *Trans. I.N.A.*, 1862, p. 160.
27 *Trans. I.N.A.*, 1861, p. 6.
28 *Ibid.*, 1863, p. 36.
29 *Cf.* S. W. Fullom, *Life of Gen. Sir Howard Douglas*, London, 1863 and *Annual Retrospect of Engineering & Architecture*, London, 1861, p. 321.
30 *The Times*, Oct. 11, 1860, p. 7.

8. THE MIDDLE YEARS

1 Letter to Russell, Trieste, Aug. 28, 1862 (Royal Society of Arts).
2 Letter, Grey to Russell, April 26, 1862 (Royal Society of Arts).
3 K. C. Barnaby, *The Institution of Naval Architects, 1860–1960*, London, 1960, p. 43.
4 *Ibid.*, p. 16.
5 Henry Cole, *Diary*, April 19, 1863.
6 J. Scott Russell, *Systematic Technical Education for the English People*, London, 1869, p. 337.
7 Henry Cole, *Diary*, Sept. 13, 1863.
8 Westcott Abel, *The Shipwright's Trade*.
9 See letter, Isambard Brunel to C. Manby (I.C.E.). May 24, 1867.
10 J. Scott Russell, *Very Large Ships, Their Advantages and Defects. A Lecture delivered at The Athenaeum Bristol, April 15, 1863*, London, 1863 (British Museum).
11 Ewan Corlett, *The Iron Ship*.
12 'Symonds cut away the bottoms of his ships . . . and made them all shoulder: it was not till they had jerked themselves over on the tops of the waves—had sent everything flying from starboard to port, and from port to starboard—had jerked their masts overboard, and swung from side to side of a wind-wave with intolerable speed, and to unheard-of angles, that it was found out, that a ship might have too much shoulder for stability, too much liveliness for safety, and too little bottom for use. The progress of his later experience was to diminish the extreme breadth of shoulder in which he had believed, and to add that capacity to bottom, which he had rejected.' J. Scott Russell, *Modern System* vol. i, p. 273.
13 Ewan Corlett, *op. cit.*, p. 19, writes that 'The peculiar and archaic midship section' adopted for the *Great Britain* 'was solely the result of a desire to accommmodate passenger capacity at the upper levels with a narrowed form at the level of the dock coping stones.'

It may be that Brunel—or Patterson—was reassurred in this matter by some knowledge of Symonds' form of mid-ship section. The *Great Britain* did have some excess of stability which Russell so vividly describes as characteristic of Symonds' hull.
14 J. Scott Russell, *Modern System*.

9. FATE AND FORTUNE

1 Letter, Mallory to North, *Official Records of the Union and Confederate Navies in the War of the Rebellion*, Series II, vol. ii, Washington, 1922, p. 71.
2 F. H. Morse to W. H. Seward, London, July 19, 1861, *ibid.*, Series III, vol. i, pp. 445–6.

References

3 Captain Blakeley before the Select Committee on Ordnance, 1863. A. L. Holley, *A Treatise on Ordnance and Armor*, New York, 1865, pp. 863–7.

4 *Ibid.*, pp. 868–71.

5 Quoted F. E. Comparato, *Age of Great Guns*, 1965, p. 317.

6 J. D. Scott, *Vickers, a History*, London, 1962, p. 32.

7 Stuart Rendel (F. E. Hamer, ed.), *The Personal Papers of Lord Rendel*, London, 1931, p. 277.

8 *Ibid.*

9 Holley was one of the most distinguished American engineers of his time; the co-founder, with Thurston, of the American Society of Mechanical Engineers, and Bessemer's leading advocate in America. He was a man in the Russell mould—erudite, cultivated and a journalist of distinction.

10 A. L. Holley, *Treatise, op. cit.*

11 Members of the Committee: J. H. Gladstone, W. A. Miller, E. Frankland, W. Fairbairn, W. Farban, J. Whitworth, J. Nasmyth, J. Scott Russell, J. Anderson, Sir W. G. Armstrong.

12 Letter 91 from A. Dudley Mann to Hon. J. P. Benjamin, Brussels, May 25, 1864, *Official Records of the Union and Confederate Navies in the War of the Rebellion*, Series II, vol. iii.

13 J.S.R. & Sir W.G.A. & Co, Minutes of Evidence, I.C.E. 1867, p. 71.

14 *Ibid.*, p. 149.

15 *Ibid.*, p. 155.

16 *Ibid.*, pp. 156–7, 164–5.

17 Stuart Rendel, *op. cit.*, p. 277.

The published Confederate Naval Records reveal that as early as April 1863, James H. North, the Confederate officer overseeing the construction of an ironclad at Clydebank, on the Clyde, was given to believe that he could obtain any number of Armstrong guns and ordered two 150-pdr muzzle loaders and two 12-pdrs on the assurance of three months delivery. In May, a further 150-pdr was ordered, but this was cancelled in July, and delivery was not taken of the two 150-pdrs until June of the following year; the ship for which they were intended having been impounded by the British Government in the preceding January. Letters: North to G. W. Rendel, April 22, 1863; to Noble, April 25, 1863; to G. W. Rendel, May 4, 1863; to Mallory, May 8, 1863; to G. B. Tennent, July 29, 1863; to G. W. Rendel, June 10, 1864. *Official Records of the Union and Confederate Navies in the War of the Rebellion*, Series II, vol. ii.

18 Evidence, p. 71.

19 C. F. Adams, *Diary*, MS., Massachusetts Historical Society, microfilm reel 77, Wed. Dec. 30, 1863.

20 Letter 31, Jan. 1, 1864, *Letters Official*, vol. 112, Archives of State of Massachusetts.

21 Letter 46, Ritchie to Forbes, Jan. 6, 1864, *ibid.*

22 Letter 62a, Ritchie to Forbes, Jan. 14, 1864, *ibid.*

23 Letter 46, Ritchie to Forbes, Jan. 6, 1864, *ibid.*

24 Letter 58, Ritchie to Messrs. Baring, Jan. 13, 1864, *Letters Official*, vol. 112.

In the previous year, when North was negotiating with Elswick for two 150-pdrs he expressed the opinion that their price was too high (Letter, North to Noble, April 25, 1863), but adjustments were made and he was charged £1200 per gun for two and £1160 each for three. Ritchie's order was much larger and he was charged £1100 for each of his 150-pdrs.

25 C. F. Adams, *Diary*, MS., Massachusetts Historical Society, microfilm reel 77.

26 Evidence, pp. 149 and 166.

References

27 Feb. 1, 1864, Letter 13, Evidence, p. 39.

28 Feb. 4, 1864, Letter 14, Evidence, p. 39.

29 Letter 72, Ritchie to Gov. Andrew, June 21, 1865, *Letters Official*, vol. 118.

30 *Ibid.*

31 Evidence, p. 121.

32 Letter 78, Ritchie to Gov. Andrew, July 24, 1865, *Letters Official*, vol. 118.

33 Letters, Bulloch to Mallory, Jan. 24, 1864, and May 13, 1864, *Official Records of the Union and Confederate Navies in the War of the Rebellion*, Series II, vol. ii. p. 577 and p. 655.

34 C. F. Adams, *Diary*, MS., Massachusetts Historical Society, microfilm reels 77–78, Tues. Jan. 12, 1864.

35 Letter, Adams to Seward, Jan. 14, 1864, *Adams Papers*, Film 170, Letter Books.

36 Letter, Jan. 14, 1864

38 C. F. Adams, *Diary*, Fri. Jan. 15, 1864.

38 *Ibid.*, March 25, 1864.

39 W. C. Ford, *A Cycle of Adams Letters*, vol. ii, p. 121.

40 *Ibid.*

41 C. F. Adams, *Diary*, April 4, 1864.

42 *Official Records of the Union and Confederate Armies in the War of the Rebellion*, Washington, 1900, Series IV, vol. i, p. 216.

43 C. F. Adams, *Diary*, Tues, May. 31, 1864.

44 *Ibid.*, May 18, 1864.

45 *Ibid.*, May 19, 1864.

46 Evidence, Letter 21.

47 *Ibid.*

48 Letter 78, Ritchie to Gov. Andrew, July 24, 1865, *Letters Official*.

49 C. F. Adams, *Diary*.

50 Letter 78, Ritchie to Gov. Andrew, July 24, 1865, *Letters Official*.

51 W. C. Ford, *op. cit.*, vol. ii, p. 200. Henry Adams to Charles F. Adams Jr., London, Sept. 30, 1864.

52 *Ibid.*, p. 231. Charles Francis Adams Jr. to his Father, Boston, Dec. 11, 1864.

53 C. F. Adams, *Diary*, Oct. 21, 1864.

54 *Ibid.*, Oct. 28, 1864.

55 *Ibid.*, Friday, Nov. 4, 1864.

56 S. W. Allan, *Reminiscences*, Cardiff, 1918, p. 92.

57 Letter, Mallory to Bulloch, March 21, 1864, *Official Records of the Union and Confederate Navies in the War of the Rebellion*, Series II, vol. ii, p. 613.

58 Letter, Bulloch to Mallory, Sept. 15, 1864, *ibid.*, p. 720.
    'The *Bat* and the *Owl*—and the two we expect to purchase on the Clyde are the four best steamers now being built in the kingdom and are greatly superior to most of the steamers heretofore engaged in the blockade business. They are built of steel...average speed 13 knots. Those to be built will be superior to these...'
    C. J. McRae to J. H. Seddon, July 4, 1864. *Ibid.*, Series II, vol. iii, pp. 525–6.

59 *Ibid.*

60 Letter 78, Ritchie to Gov. Andrew, July 24, 1865, *Letters Official*.

61 Letter 69, May 4, 1865, *Letters Official*, vol. 118.

62 *Ibid.*

63 *Ibid.*

64 Letter 71, *Letters Official*, vol. 118.

65 Evidence, Letter 61.

66 Letter, I. Brunel to Manby, May 10, 1867, I.C.E. MS.

References

67 Evidence, p. 57.
68 *Ibid.*, p. 61.

10 DEFENCE OF HONOUR

1 *The Personal Papers of Lord Rendel*, p. 277.
2 MS. correspondence, I. Brunel–C. Manby, I.C.E., London. It is a curious fact that while I. Brunel (Jr.) destroyed Manby's letters on request, Manby preserved Brunel's.
3 *The Engineer*, June 14, 1867, p. 542.
4 Brunel–Manby corres.
5 *Ibid.*
6 *Ibid.*, May 15, 1866.
7 *Ibid.*, May 19, 1866.
8 Evidence.
9 *Ibid.*
10 Brunel–Manby corres., Dec., 17, 1866.
11 Henry Brunel to William Froude, May 1, 1864, Letter Book, Bristol Coll.
12 'That a strong partisan feeling is, however, active was too well shown by the hostility exhibited on the occasion for the discussion of the price for a new house, and which ended in the loss to the institution of about £25,000 already subscribed for the purpose. It is well known that this faction is still as active, as jealous, as hostile as ever . . .', Editorial, *Engineering*, Dec. 7, 1866.
13 Editorials, April 3 and 10, *Engineering*, 1868. Colburn found it difficult to understand how Bidder and Co.'s evaluation of £7000 for a back yard could be reconciled with the £12,000 asked for the freehold of 25 George Street, a commanding site of more than 3300 square feet which was purchased at the same time.
14 *Engineering*, Dec. 1866, p. 488.
15 *Ibid.*, June 7, 1867, p. 594.
16 *Ibid.*, Dec. 21, 1866.
17 *Ibid.*
18 *Ibid.*
19 Editorial, *Engineering*, Dec. 21, 1866.
20 Anon., Letter to Editor, *ibid.*
21 Brunel–Manby correspondence, Jan. 7, 1867.
22 *Ibid.*, Jan. 19, 1867.
23 *Engineering*, June 7, 1867.
24 *The Engineer*, June 14, 1867, p. 531.
25 In the discussion of a paper by Bidder's son, 'The National Defences', presented to the I.C.E., April 1861, Bidder presiding, reprimanded Russell for casting aspersions on the political wing of the Admiralty. Russell had one or two digs at Bidder during the discussion (p. 423).
26 *Proc. I.C.E.*, 1856–7, pp. 331 and 368.
27 *Ibid.*, 1878, p. 299.
28 Memoir of G. P. Bidder, *Proc. I.C.E.*, 1876, p. 305.
29 At a meeting of the Institution in 1853, Charles Atherton, Chief Engineer in The Royal Dockyards, Woolwich, asserted that both the horse power and the coal consumption of the *Great Eastern* had been underestimated. In consequence of the expected savings in coal derived from this erroneous calculation, the prospectus predicted dividends of forty per cent per annum! Atherton maintained that it was 'disgraceful in the Institution to promote or countenance the public's being hooked with

such a gross bait', and he did his best 'as a Member of the Institution to expose such an imposition'. *Proc. I.C.E.*, Nov. 8, 1853, p. 46.

Atherton later alluded to this as his 'fracas'. (Letter to James R. Napier, July, 1856.)

30 *Cf. Proc. I.C.E.*, April 1861.

31 Charles Dickens asked Manby why he stuck to Hudson, and Manby said that it was because Hudson had so many people in his power, and had held his peace; and because he (Manby) 'saw so many Notabilities grand with him now, who were always grovelling for "shares" in the days of his grandeur'. Forster, *Life of Dickens*, London, 1872.

32 T. Mackay, *The Life of Sir John Fowler*, London, 1900, p. 96.

33 Henry Brunel to William Froude, Jan. 22, 1863. H. M. Brunel, Letter Books.

34 T. Mackay, *op. cit.*, p. 320.

35 *Ibid.*, p. 109.

36 *Ibid.*, p. 336.

37 *Ibid.*, p. 110.

38 J. D. Scott, *Vickers, a History*, p. 89.

39 *Ibid.*

40 Stuart Rendel continued to distort the Armstrong-Russell affair in his memoirs: 'Scott Russell had taken advantage, for purposes of his own, of the extraordinary secrecy required by Mr Adams. We had held back the execution of his order only because he did not produce the agreed-on instalments of price.' J. D. Scott, *op. cit.*, p. 278.

41 F. E. Comparato, *Age of Great Guns*, p. 317.

42 A. L. Holley, *A Treatise on Ordnance and Armor*, New York, 1865, p. 22, fn. 2.

43 J. D. Scott, *op. cit.*, p. 89.

44 Evidence, p. 108.

45 *Official Records . . . Navies in the War of the Rebellion*, Series II, vol. ii, p. 720.

46 Evidence, p. 193.

47 *Ibid.*, p. 201.

48 *Ibid.*, pp. 102–63.

49 Stuart Rendel, *op. cit.*, p. 277.

50 Letter 71, *Letters Official*, vol. 118, Gov. Andrew, Massachusetts Archives.

51 *The Engineer*, April 12, 1867, p. 323.

52 *Engineering*, July 5, 1867, p. 10.

53 *The Engineer*, April 12, 1867, p. 323.

54 *Engineering*, April 19, 1867, p. 384.

55 *Ibid.*

56 Brunel–Manby, May 24, 1867.

57 *The Engineer*, April 12, 1867.

58 In reporting the proceedings of the Mechanical Section of the B.A. meeting of August 1866, the editor of *The Engineer* thought that a remark made by Hawksley with reference to heavy guns, in the presence of Sir William Armstrong, was not in the best taste (*The Engineer*, Aug. 24, 1866, p. 130). The editor must have felt very defensive of Armstrong indeed that he could take exception to anything Hawksley was reported to have said.

59 *Engineering*, June 14, 1867, pp. 601–2.

60 *Ibid.*, April 19, 1867, p. 384.

61 Letter, Thomas Hawksley to James Forest, July 15, 1867, I.C.E.

62 *Mins. of Council*, I.C.E., July 15, 1867.

References

11. A NEW START

1 J. Scott Russell, *Systematic Technical Education for the English People*, p. 86.
2 *Engineering*, July 19, 1867, p. 48.
3 *Ibid.*, p. 49.
4 Letters, Rachel Scott Russell to Sullivan, May 24 and May 29, 1867.
5 Letter, Rachel to Sullivan, June 18, 1867.
6 *Ibid.*
7 *Trans. I.N.A.*, 1874, p. 141.
8 In 1863, the *Great Eastern* was laid up and the bondholders took possession. The ship was put up for auction, and, according to Gooch, he, Barber and Brassey 'being the largest bondholders (amounting to £100,000) determined to buy her if she went for £80,000 or less... Strange to state the ship was sold to us for £25,000'. *Diaries of Daniel Gooch*, p. 83.
9 Letter, Rachel to Sullivan, Sept. 1867.
10 The original members were; R. Bentley (K.C.L.), Grace Calvert, Edwin Chadwick, Harry Chester, Robert Hunt, T. H. Huxley, Fleeming Jenkin, G. D. Liveing, Thorold Rogers, and Bernhard Samuelson.
11 *Proc. I.C.E.*, Nov. 25, 1851.
12 *Engineering*, March 27, 1868.
13 Letter, Rachel to Sullivan, Oct. 1867.
14 Vol. xvii, pp. 447–58.
15 Henry Cole, *Diary*, March 19 and 23, 1869.
16 J. Scott Russell, *Systematic Technical Education...*, p. 342.
17 *Ibid.*, pp. 331–2.
18 Henry Cole. *Fifty Years of Public Work*, vol. ii, p. 373.
19 W. H. G. Armytage, *Civic Universities*, London, 1955.
20 Henry Cole, Diary, June 20, 1869.
21 *Ibid.*, June 25, 1869.

12. SYDENHAM SET

1 See Charles L. Graves, *The Life and Letters of Sir George Grove*, London, 1903.
2 Cole's diary entry reads: 'Crystal Pal. Met Fuller, Mr. Russell &c. Over the grounds with Paxton, Jones, Hudson, Cochrane, Russell etc. Paxton said Fuller had been nearly turned out—wd. not [look?] about his doing. Said I was the proper person to be manager.' (July 13, 1853.)
3 Charles L. Graves, *op. cit.*, p. 108.
4 George Grove, *Dictionary of Music*, vol. ii, p. 207.
5 Charles L. Graves, *op. cit.*, p. 42, and Russell's obituary in the *Proc. I.C.E.*, 1882, state that the Russells had five children. I have so far been able to account for only four. If indeed five children were born to the Russells, the greatest probability is that the child unaccounted for was born between 1837 and 1839, their first-born, in fact, and was not alive in 1845.
6 Charles L. Graves, *op. cit.*, p. 41.
7 *Ibid.*, p. 42.
8 Letter, Louise to Sullivan, Feb. 19, 1868.
9 Letter to Madame Rausch (Alice Scott Russell) (Private Collection).
10 J. G. Millais, *The Life and Letters of John Everett Millais*, London, 1899, vol. ii, p. 421.
11 Charles L. Graves, *op. cit.*, p. 171.
12 Clara Rogers, *Memories of a Musical Career*, Boston, 1919, p. 168.

13 Emily Soldene, *My Theatrical and Musical Recollections*, London, 1897, p. 191.
14 Henry Cole, *Diary*, Sept. 30, 1869.
15 Sir Charles Villiers Stanford, *Pages from an Unwritten Diary*, London, 1914, p. 82.
16 Harry Plunket Greene, *Charles Villiers Stanford*, London, 1935.
17 Letter from Rachel Russell to Sullivan, October, 1867.
18 Letter, Rachel to Sullivan, c. August 14, 1868.
19 *Ibid.*, April 8, 1869.
20 *Ibid.*, (no. 209b), n.d., 1869 from internal evidence.
21 *Ibid.*, Jan. 8, 1870.

13. WAR AND PEACE

1 Letter, Louise Russell to Arthur Sullivan, March 21, 1870.
2 J. Scott Russell, 'Into Versailles and Out', *Macmillan's Magazine*, vol. xxiii, 1871, p. 310.
3 *Ibid.*, p. 311.
4 *Ibid.*, p. 322.
5 *Ibid.*, p. 255.
6 *Ibid.*, p. 265.
7 *Ibid.*, p. 312.
8 *Ibid.*, p. 320.
9 Letter to *The Times*, Nov. 14, 1871, p. 6.
10 Quoted, *ibid.*
11 *The Times*, Oct. 26, 1871, p. 9.
12 *Ibid.*, Oct. 23, 1871.
13 *Engineering*, March 7, 1873, p. 159.
14 *Ibid.*
15 *Ibid.*
16 *Ibid.*, Jan.–June, 1873.
17 *The Times*, Oct. 23, 1871.
18 *Ibid.*
19 *Ibid.*, Nov. 14, 1871, p. 6, and Oct. 26, 1871, p. 9.
20 *Ibid.*, Oct. 5, 1871.
21 Letter from A. J. Mundella to Leader, editor of *Sheffield Independent*. W. H. G. Armytage, *A. J. Mundella*, London, 1951, p. 99.
22 *The Times*, Oct. 25, 1871, p. 9.
23 *Ibid.*, Nov. 7, 1871, p. 9.
24 *Ibid.*, Nov. 8, 1871, p. 3.
25 *Ibid.*, Nov. 14, 1871, p. 6.
26 *Ibid.*, Nov. 27, 1871.
27 J. Scott Russell, 'On International Communication between England and Europe by special Harbours and Train Steamers', *Trans. I.N.A.*, March 1872.
28 Letter, J. Scott Russell to Dassi, Oct. 12, 1871 (British Museum).
29 *Ibid.*
30 Letter, Dassi to J. S. Russell, Nov. 2, 1871 (British Museum).
31 Letter, J. S. Russell to Dassi, Nov. 13, 1871.
32 *Isle of Wight Express*, Sat. June 17, 1882.
33 Letter, J. S. Russell to Dassi, May 19, 1872.
34 *Ibid.*, July 25, 1873.

References

14. THE LAST DECADE

1 *Trans. I.N.A.*, 1863, p. 232.
2 Charles H. Jordan records witnessing Russell's patting Froude on the shoulder, during a visit to his yard, c. 1856, and saying 'There is nothing in it, I have tried it all'. *Lloyd's Register Staff Assn. Trans.*, vol. 5, p. 12.
3 *Trans. I.N.A.*, 1880, p. 151.
4 *Ibid.*, 1868, p. 210.
5 J. Scott Russell, 'The Loss of the Captain', *Macmillan's Magazine*, vol. xxii, Oct. 1870.
6 *Proc. I.C.E.*, 1862–3, vol. xxii, pp. 601–2.
7 *Trans. I.N.A.*, 1870, p. 80.
8 *Ibid.*, 1870, pp. 81–2.
9 *Ibid.*
10 *Ibid.*, 1870, pp. 87–8.
11 *The Annual Retrospect of Engineering and Architecture*, vol. i, London, 1862, pp. 358–9.
12 *The Athenaeum*, July 16, 1842, p. 644.
13 *Ibid.*
14 See N. W. Akimoff, *Resistance of Ships and Models*, 1930, p. 99, and P. A. Van Lammeren *et al.*, *Resistance, Propulsion and Steering of Ships*, Harlem, 1948, vol. 2, p. 22.
15 *Trans. I.N.A.*, 1863, p. 165.
16 *Ibid.*, 1870.
17 *Ibid.*, 1860, p. 210.
18 *Ibid.*, 1870, pp. 92–3.
19 *Ibid.*, 1874, pp. 61, 72.
20 Bramwell, 'On Quick Steam Launches', *Trans. I.N.A.*, 1872.
21 This is due to the interference of the bow wave with the stern wave. As these waves come into and out of phase, so is the wave-making resistance increased or diminished.
22 *Trans. I.N.A.*, 1870, p. 83.
23 Dixon Kemp, *Yacht Architecture*, London, 1897, p. 128.
24 *Trans. I.N.A.*, 1874, p. 142.
25 *Ibid.*, 1872, p. 14.
26 *Ibid.*, 1870, p. 330.
27 G. A. Ballard, 'British Battleships of 1870', *The Mariner's Mirror*, vol. xvi, 1930, p. 214.
28 J. Scott Russell, 'On the Duties, Qualities and Structure of the Modern Man of War', *Trans. I.N.A.*, 1875, p. 107.
29 *Ibid.*, 1875, p. 118.
30 *Ibid.*, 1879, p. 84.
31 *The Engineer*, March 26, 1880, p. 224.
32 *Trans. I.N.A.*, 1876, p. 54.
33 Letter to Alice, 1911 (private source).
34 Obituary notice of J. S. Russell, *Proc. I.C.E.*, lxxxvii, p. 431.
35 J. Scott Russell, *The Wave of Translation in the Oceans of Water, Air and Ether*, London, 1885.
36 Unpublished Diary of Mrs Edmund Holmes (private source).
37 J. D. Scott, *Vickers, A History*, p. 36.
38 J. Scott Russell, *The Wave of Translation* ...
39 Westcott Abel, *The Shipwright's Trade*.
40 *Trans. I.N.A.*, 1872, p. 191.

References

41 *Ibid.*, 1881, p. 1881, p. 134. For a full description of Russell's system see his *Modern System* and Abell, *op. cit.*, pp. 123–6.

42 J. Scott Russell, *Modern System*, p. 393.

43 Edward J. Reed, *The Stability of Ships*, London, 1885, p. 64.

44 *Engineering*, vol. i, Jan. 5, 1866, p. 2.

Index

With the exception of the *Great Eastern*
all ships are indexed separately (see p. 342)

CE = Civil Engineer
SR = Scott Russell
RSA = Royal Society of Arts

R = Brunel
ESN Co = Eastern Steam Navigation Co
Gt.E. = *Great Eastern*

329

Index

Index

Index

Index

'wave-line', 24; reports on tidal effects on Clyde, on sea walls, etc., 25; recommends ship to succeed *Great Western*, 25; on vibrations in slender structures, hull expts., report to B.A. on form of ships, 26; devises salinometer and Pitot tube, 26; ship as bridge, 67; explains shipyard payment and practices, 73; three cylinder engine, 77; experiments with mortars, 97; submits designs for iron fleet, 97; founds I.N.A., 165; testifies on behalf of proposed Irish mail, 166; turret ships, 167, 291; *Fleet of Future* published, equates himself to de Lôme, 169; satirizes the Admiralty, 174–177; criticizes Admiralty and latest warships, 172–173; attack on Lloyd's, on education of naval architects, 179; *Modern System* published, 181, 182; on *Very Large Ships* at Bristol, 183; paper on gun cotton, 189; trouble in I.C.E., 213–247; withdraws from I.C.E., drops I.Mech.E., esteemed in I.N.A. and honoured in *Men of Mark*, 289; contrasts with Froude, challenged on stability, 290; on low freeboard, 291; on frictional resistance, 292; on problems of models, 293, 295, 296; praises Bramwell's paper, 297; advocates loading marks, 298; larger and faster ships for long voyages, describes ideal men-of-war, 299–300; SR's discoveries great in their time, 300; writes final paper on waves, 301, 302; on design of ship, 303; display models preserved, 302; summing up, 304

Russell, Alice May (SR's youngest daughter), 261, 265, 266, 301

Russell, David, Rev. (SR's father), 3, 4, 32

Russell, David (Jr) (SR's half, brother), 3

Russell, George (SR's half-brother), 4

Russell, Harriette (SR's wife), 22, 28, 29; Cole enjoys her company, 31; with Coles, 33; asks her to vacate Adelphi house, 40; 254, 262, 266, 267, 301; civil list pension, 302

Russell, Lord, 253

Russell, Louise (SR's oldest daughter), 26, 33, 261, 264, 270, 301

Russell, Norman Scott, 29, 31, 146, 147, 155, 179, 251, 261, 267

Russell, Rachel Scott (SR's middle daughter), 31, 248, 252, 261, 266, 267, urges and inspires Sullivan, 264–5; *Cox and Box*, marriage with Sullivan prohibited, clandestine meetings, at Zurich,

Contrabandista, 265; concern for Norman, 267; won't rush into marriage, *Fair Dove—Fond Dove*, father permits Sullivan visit to Zurich, and Prof. Pole, 268; off to St Petersburg, last letters to Sullivan, 269; home from India, cookery book, translates Berlioz *Memoirs*, 301

Russia, 57, 267

St Andrews, 5

St Petersburg, 86, 301

Salinometer, 26

Salisbury, Marquis of, 281, 283

Saltash Bridge, 127

Samuda, J. A., 75

Sandon, 292

Sangen Schwalback, 252

Sant, James (painter), 263

Schools Inquiry Commission, 248

Schwarz, Baron, 278

Science Museum, London, 303

Scientific American, 187

Scotland, 49, 254, 301

Scott, Agnes Clark (SR's mother), 3

Scott, Sir Walter, 6, 7

Scottish Steam Carriage Co., 9

Sedan, 274

Seward (American Secretary of State), 198, 199, 201, 205

Sheridan, R. B., 246

Ship resistance—see 'Wave Line' and Naval Architecture, 33

Sibthorpe, Colonel, 66

Sinclair (Confederate agent), 190

Slidell, John (Confederate agent), 200

Smiles, Samuel, 2, 224

Smith, Adam, 6

Smith, Assheton, 24

Smith, F. P., 66, 113

Smith of Jordanhill, 14

Smith, Janius, 19

Solitary wave of translation, 16

Somerset, Duke of, 171–173, 177, 181

South Academy, 7

Southampton, 152

South Kensington Museum, 181, 257, 261, 301, 303

South Wales Railway, 72

Spanish Royal Mail, 197, 206

Squires, J. (labour leader), 281

Stafford, Marquis of (and Duke of Sutherland), 102, 137, 155, 275

Staffordshire, 248

Stanford, Chas. V., 267, 301

Steamboats, early, 6

339

Ship Index

342